THE RITUAL OF BATTLE

Krishna in the *Mahābhārata*

SYMBOL, MYTH, AND RITUAL SERIES
General Editor: Victor Turner

Shlomo Deshen and Moshe Shokeid, *The Predicament of Homecoming: Cultural and Social Life of North African Immigrants in Israel*

Mircea Eliade, *Australian Religions: An Introduction*

Frederick Karl Errington, *Karavar: Masks and Power in a Melanesian Ritual*

Raymond Firth, *Symbols: Public and Private**

Alf Hiltebeitel, *The Ritual of Battle: Krishna in the* Mahābhārata

Bennetta Jules-Rosette, *African Apostles: Ritual and Conversion in the Church of John Maranke*

Frank E. Manning, *Black Clubs in Bermuda: Ethnography of a Play World*

Sally Falk Moore and Barbara G. Myerhoff, eds., *Symbol and Politics in Communal Ideology: Cases and Questions**

Nancy D. Munn, *Walbiri Iconography: Graphic Representation and Cultural Symbolism in a Central Australian Society*

Barbara G. Myerhoff, *Peyote Hunt: The Sacred Journey of the Huichol Indians**

Victor Turner, *Dramas, Fields, and Metaphors: Symbolic Action in Human Society**

Victor Turner, *Revelation and Divination in Ndembu Ritual**

* Also available as a Cornell Paperback.

THE RITUAL OF BATTLE

Krishna in the *Mahābhārata*

Alf Hiltebeitel

Cornell University Press
ITHACA AND LONDON

First published 1976 by Cornell University Press.
Published in the United Kingdom by Cornell University Press Ltd.,
2-4 Brook Street, London W1Y 1AA.

International Standard Book Number 0-8014-0970-5
Library of Congress Catalog Card Number 75-18496
Printed in the United States of America by Vail-Ballou Press, Inc.

TO ADAM AND SIMON

Foreword

Recently both the research and theoretical concerns of many anthropologists have once again been directed toward the role of symbols—religious, mythic, aesthetic, political, and even economic—in social and cultural processes. Whether this revival is a belated response to developments in other disciplines (psychology, ethology, philosophy, linguistics, to name only a few), or whether it reflects a return to a central concern after a period of neglect, is difficult to say. In recent field studies, anthropologists have been collecting myths and rituals in the context of social action, and improvements in anthropological field technique have produced data that are richer and more refined than heretofore; these new data have probably challenged theoreticians to provide more adequate explanatory frames. Whatever may have been the causes, there is no denying a renewed curiosity about the nature of the connections between culture, cognition, and perception, as these connections are revealed in symbolic forms.

Although excellent individual monographs and articles in symbolic anthropology or comparative symbology have recently appeared, a common focus or forum that can be provided by a topically organized series of books has not been available. The present series is intended to fill this lacuna. It is designed to include not only field monographs and theoretical and comparative studies by anthropologists, but also work by scholars in other disciplines, both scientific and humanistic. The appearance of studies in such a forum encourages emulation, and emulation can produce fruitful new theories. It is therefore our hope that the series will serve as a house of many mansions, providing hospitality for the practitioners of any discipline that has a serious and creative concern with comparative symbology. Too often, disciplines are sealed off, in sterile pedantry, from significant intellectual influences. Nevertheless, our primary aim is to bring to public attention works on ritual and myth written by anthropologists, and our readers will find a variety of strictly anthropological approaches ranging from formal analyses of systems of symbols to empathetic accounts of divinatory and initiatory rituals.

Alf Hiltebeitel's explication of salient parts of the vast text of the *Mahābhārata* relates to several contexts, each endowed with a rich scholarly and exegetical literature. The result is a novel synthesis that advances our understanding of the nature and structure of the epic genre, elucidates its relationship to myth, history, and ritual, and contributes new perspectives for the study of Indo-European epics comparatively, the *Mahābhārata* specifically, and the role of Krishna as a "black" mediator in its successive crises, "epic" and "mythic." Hiltebeitel's method of "correlation" or "correspondence" offers a more satisfactory key to the nature of the relationship between myth and epic than does Dumézil's concept of "transposition." Dumézil (whose work on comparative Indo-European mythology and epic Hiltebeitel regards, with Wikander's, as absolutely fundamental) takes too rigid a view of the myth-epic relationship when he speaks of the heroes as inflexible "copies" of their mythic prototypes. Hiltebeitel sees, rather, the likelihood of a long process during which "an epic story of ancient contours," shared with other Indo-European cultural traditions, was "continually compared and integrated with mythic themes" by a succession of poets. The poets were visionary *bricoleurs*, "tinkers," who perceived connections, homologies, correspondences between "two levels of continually growing and changing tradition: myth and epic." To these strata Hiltebeitel adds ritual, notably Brahmanic sacrifice. The liminal figure of Krishna shuttles through the epic, appearing at major crises, and weaves its multicolored thematic strands together. Hiltebeitel views Krishna's role as that of a priest presiding over "the ritual of battle." The battle constitutes a crisis (and its resolution) of "eschatological proportions," and it remains paradigmatic for countless myths, rituals, theologies, folk tales, and even secular literatures and popular dramas of many scattered cultural and linguistic communities in India, Sri Lanka, and other regions of Asia. The epic narrative of the *Mahābhārata* is a dialectic of structure/antistructure, in which myths have been interpolated at key points to provide a reflexive metalanguage for assigning religious meaning to the flux of events. Scrupulously documenting his argument, Hiltebeitel stresses the dynamic unity of the epic, where "all the gods" are active in human form, and he establishes the "multivalent polarity" of Viṣṇu and Śiva, the "Pervader" and the "Outsider," as its underlying unifying principle.

VICTOR TURNER

University of Chicago

Contents

Preface

The *Mahābhārata* covers so much that one is tempted to say too much about it. I have tried to avoid the trap of diffuseness that has beset so many *Mahābhārata* scholars. Because no one argument about the epic can be developed without leading into others, I have not been wholly successful. Therefore I will try to identify the main threads—aims, assumptions, conclusions—that hold this book together.

First, I have looked at the *Mahābhārata* mainly as story—not, however, taking its narrative content as prior to its didactic, but as a story in which didactic intentions must always have been included. As its name indicates, the work is a "great" story, a claim justified by many criteria: its richness in levels of meaning, intricacy, and vigor, as well as its length and scope. It is too big to summarize in any adequate way, but it tells, in the main, of the intercession of Lord Krishna to help the five Pāṇḍava brothers regain the kingdom they have lost to their cousins the hundred Kauravas, and to restore the continuity of the Kuru, or Lunar, Dynasty (into which the two sets of cousins have been born) at the end of the yuga, or age, previous to ours. There are some inevitably inadequate abridgments of the *Mahābhārata*, the most useful being C. V. Narasimhan's,[1] but it is hoped that interested readers who cannot read the Sanskrit original will turn to one of the more available English translations: either the completed Kisari Mohan Ganguli text (sponsored by P. C. Roy, and thus with Roy's name on the title

[1] C. V. Narasimhan, trans., *The Mahābhārata* (New York: Columbia University Press, 1965).

page),[2] or the recent beginnings of full translations by J. A. B. van Buitenen and P. Lal.[3] Book-by-book summaries of the epic's contents can also be referred to with profit.[4] As I do not supply one of the latter myself, by way of compensation my chapters follow (except for a flashback in Chapter 7) the main order of the narrative and usually begin with a recapitulation of the story up to the point reached. I also supply a genealogy (see Appendix) which differs from others available in focusing on the continuity of the Kuru line, a main theme in my discussion.

This story has had great tenacity through different ages and cultural changes. Interior variation and modification can be seen in the main recensions of the text. It is a story that India has never ceased to rethink and retell. It has been one of the main carriers of Indian culture to Southeast Asia and Indonesia. And comparative studies by Stig Wikander and others have found strikingly similar stories and sequences of episodes in other Indo-European epic (not just mythic) traditions. I am convinced that *Mahābhārata* scholars would have little doubt of the epic's place in the Indo-European continuum if they would become familiar with Indo-European epic tales besides those of the Greeks, and then compare these Indo-European epics as a group with, say, the Gilgamesh, Gesar, or Mwindo epics. There is good reason to believe that the Indian story, at least in its basic contours and episodes, may have long and deep roots.

I thus prefer to view the *Mahābhārata* as a narrative continu-

[2] Kisari Mohan Ganguli, trans., and Pratap Chandra Roy, publisher, *The Mahabharata* (1884–1896; reprinted most recently in 12 vols., New Delhi: Munshiram Manoharlal, 1970).

[3] J. A. B. van Buitenen, trans. and ed., *The Mahābhārata*: I, *The Book of the Beginning* (Chicago: University of Chicago Press, 1973); P. Lal, *Mahābhārata* (Calcutta: Writers' Workshop, appearing in installments since 1967).

[4] See Barend A. van Nooten, *The Mahābhārata* (New York: Twayne, 1971), 5–42; Moriz Winternitz, *A History of Indian Literature*, S. Ketkar, trans. (2 vols., Calcutta: University of Calcutta, 1962), I, pp. 287–330; Georges Dumézil, *Mythe et épopée*, I: *L'Idéologie des trois fonctions dans les épopées des peuples indo-européens* (Paris: Editions Gallimard, 1968), pp. 32–42 (hereinafter referred to as *ME*, I).

um, as a "work in progress," rather than to choose one variant or portion of the epic as a fixed or original text. By the same token, it strains matters to regard all the variants as synchronically equal in value. Some features must be older than others, and although indisputable rules for determining textual priorities will probably never be established, historical development, through such processes as alteration, interpolation, and perhaps sometimes abridgment, must not be ignored. Thanks to the Poona Critical Edition of the *Mahābhārata*, one can begin to deal intelligently with these matters. If this edition cannot tell us what is old, it can at least give some indication of the principles behind the text's transmission and the changing and continuing bases for its appeal.

Assuming such a narrative continuum, I have thus been able to draw from both the Indo-Europeanist perspective on the epic opened by Stig Wikander and fostered by Georges Dumézil and the "Purāṇic" perspective opened by Madeleine Biardeau. In my view, each, in the main, is right; my research has continually showed new instances where their methods and results not only have borne up under close textual examination, but have generated new insights. In fact, the apparent irreconcilability of the two approaches is only superficial, for both draw on sources which can often be elucidated by a common frame of reference—the practical and conceptual milieu of the Brāhmaṇas. Within the same background that produced these sacrificial texts, the main contours of the epic's "narrative continuum" would seem to have been shaped as a "ritual of battle." Over a "sacrifice of weapons" (*śastrayajña*), says Karṇa, Krishna will preside as a witness (*vettṛ*) and as the main officiating priest, the *adhvaryu*.[5] The battle, with its preliminaries

[5] *Mbh.* CE 5:139,29. The commentator Nīlakaṇṭha glosses *vettṛ* by *upadrastṛ* ("onlooker, spectator, witness") and *adhvaryu* by *netṛ*—the latter interesting as it can mean both "leader, guide, conductor" and "charioteer." See Ramachandra Kinjawadekar, ed., *Shriman Mahābhāratam, with Bharata Bhawadeepa by Nīlakaṇṭha* (6 vols.; Poona: Chitrashala Press, 1929–1933), III, 231.

and aftermath, is Krishna's main theater of operation in the *Mahābhārata*.

My initial intent was to come to terms with the Krishna of the *Mahābhārata*, to fill the surprising gap left by the failure of epic and Krishna scholars to recognize a common subject. Early epic research either ignored Krishna (as Joseph Dahlmann virtually did), or rested the case against him with reductionistic summations of character (Christian Lassen saw him as a racial god; Adolf Holtzmann, as a deceitful adviser; Adolf Holtzmann, nephew, as a deified tribal hero of a frequently drunk and sensual nonbrahminical people, later linked with Viṣṇu through a "monstrous identification"; Alfred Ludwig, as the black spring sun; Edward Washburn Hopkins, as a demigod chieftain; Hermann Oldenberg and Walter Ruben, as not part of the original epic; G. J. Held, as a trickster). More recent epic studies, while offering important insights, have raised but not pursued the subject of Krishna (Sukthankar, Wikander, Dumézil, Biardeau; Held is transitional). On the other side, Krishna scholarship has focused on his "early career"—Bālakrishna's sports in the cow settlement of Vraja, Veṇugopāla Krishna's amours with the Gopīs and Rādhā, Krishna's conquests of incarnated demons culminating in the slaying of Kaṃsa. The "prince" of the *Mahābhārata* is barely treated.

This gap will be only partly filled by the present work, for, although I began my research in the hope of advancing the argument for seeing just one Krishna in the two "careers," my file of supporting evidence (or even evidence to the contrary) simply refused to grow. The *Mahābhārata* refers knowledgeably to the Vraja-Mathurā stories as background to main events, but it does not tell of Krishna's biography in any integrated way. I am not convinced, however, by efforts to split the biography into cycles of separate origins, in particular those that attribute the youthful stories to the pastoralist Abhiras or make a facile equation between Abhiras and Gopas (Krishna's cattle-folk companions).

As to the Krishna of the *Mahābhārata*, some new ground has hopefully been broken. Scholars have raised contradictory images of the epic Krishna which demand clarification. Certain issues are resolvable. Whatever fancies one might have about the origins of Krishna and Viṣṇu, their link with each other is not "monstrous" but, at least in respect to Krishna, fundamental, consistent, and significant. Second, I find no merit in the Oldenberg-Ruben view that Krishna was nonessential to the "original" epic poem. Indeed, regarding both of these points, one will learn most not from studying the epic Krishna and Viṣṇu alone (as did Ruben), but from examining their interrelations with various intersecting constellations of different figures, both human-heroic and divine. Examination of the structural relations between the epic narrative and Hindu and Indo-European mythology and ritual sheds surprising light on the epic Krishna.

On other points, I feel that most scholars have taken either/or positions that have led to one-sided distortions of an essentially complex figure. To say Krishna is either a divinized human or a euhemerized god is mere speculative nonsense. By the same token, to explain away his morally ambiguous counsels or to see him simply as a scoundrel is to constrain him, against everything that the text says, to only one level of operation. As to the Aryan/non-Aryan question (not to be confused with the two "careers" question), impressed as I am by the results of Wikander's and Dumézil's comparative studies, I am inclined to see, and to attempt to give supporting evidence for, an "Aryan" component. But it would be vain to speculate whether the evidence points to an Indo-European Krishna, or to Indo-European themes and concepts that have descended upon him. Far more obviously, Krishna is unintelligible from Indo-European comparisons alone. As we have him, he is all Indian.

Finally, certain matters seem to be beyond solution. Perhaps one is whether there are two "careers" or one. Another is whether the stories are "myth" or history. The purists on both sides probably will not find this problem solved by my insistence that epic, or legend, is a unique category that may draw from both myth and history, but ought not to be reduced to either. All I can say is that there seems to be much more to demonstrate in the way of a mythic background of the *Mahābhārata*, and of the epic Krishna, than a historical one. Although many scholars—especially Indian ones—are convinced that the *Mahābhārata* story preserves at least some kernel of historical fact, I would point out that this is not necessarily the only Indian attitude on the subject. As the *Viṣṇu Purāṇa* says of great heroes of the past, including Rāma Dāśaratha and Yudhiṣṭhira: "These existed. Is it true? Is it not the contrary? Where are they now? We know not" (*babhuvurete / satyaṃ na mithyā kva nu te na vidmaḥ*).[6] These words draw one almost to the end of the fourth book of this *Purāṇa*, the fifth of which begins with the request "to hear a more particular description . . . of the portion of Vishnu that came down on earth, and was born in the family of Yadu."[7] The reference is to Krishna. Skepticism is justifiable even where it touches on the "historicity" of the most sacred matters.

A few words are in order as to what this book does not contain or attempt, and why. The *Mahābhārata* has come off the shelves in recent years and new paths of study have been opened: on the relationship between the epic and traditional and contemporary Indian culture, on Śiva in the epic, on Nara and Nārāyaṇa, on different epic meters, on *Mahābhārata* and *Rāmāyaṇa*, and so on. It would be premature to respond to such investigations; some have not yet reached print. I would comment only that I think the spirit of the text requires that one be open to its many frames of reference, its many different levels of mean-

[6] *Viṣṇu Purāṇa* 4:24,146–49; slightly modified from H. H. Wilson, trans., *The Vishńu Puráńa* (1840; repr. Calcutta: Punthi Pustak, 1972), p. 393.

[7] Wilson, *Vishńu Puráńa*, pp. 394–95.

ing, and the many influences that would seem to have shaped it. No "theory" will ever do justice to the *Mahābhārata* that does not take its multivalence into account.

I do not supply a bibliography. A useful selected bibliography can be found in Barend A. van Nooten's *The Mahābhārata*,[8] but since my discussion enters into other than Indian literatures, a bibliography of works cited, no matter how selective, would be cumbersome and would duplicate the footnotes. An updated *Mahābhārata* bibliography is a desideratum, and fortunately one is being prepared by J. Bruce Long. I have not been rigid on matters of orthography. For Sanskrit, I generally use the standard transliterations, but where English usage is clear enough, diacritics are sometimes omitted. In the special case of Krishna, the Westernized form serves to distinguish him clearly from other figures—Kṛṣṇa Draipāyana, Kṛṣṇā Draupadī—who share his name. As to extra-Indian names and terms, I follow spellings commonly used in translations and scholarly works.

This book has been about ten years in the making, so there are many whom I wish to thank. First is Mircea Eliade: to him I owe my "initiation" into the history of religions, and my introduction to the epic via Indo-European studies. Second is Charles H. Long, whose lecture on the *Bhagavad Gītā* and the *Mahābhārata* crystallized in my mind several of the topics I would pursue. In the fall of 1967, Stig Wikander visited the University of Chicago to deliver the Haskell Lectures and conduct a seminar. His discussions of the concept of the "heroic age" and of epic—focusing especially on the *Shāh-nāma* and the *Mahābhārata*—were innovative and provocative. In 1968, I was invited to undertake the first of two translations of works by Georges Dumézil. My gratitude for his encouragement and warmth is immense and so too for some invaluable hints and a

[8] See above, n. 4.

gentle rejection of some early formulations. Translation of his study of Yayāti[9] gave me my first solid grip on what I was doing. Early in 1971, I became aware of the epic and Purāṇic studies of Madeleine Biardeau. She too has been a much-appreciated critic. In the summer of 1971 she raised many points concerning what now forms Chapters 12 to 14 of this book, and in the fall of 1973 she offered stimulating and often corrective views on an earlier version of the manuscript.

With the valuable translation of the *Mahābhārata* now begun by my former Sanskrit teacher J. A. B. van Buitenen, his interests and mine have converged and resulted in stimulating exchanges. Although I have used my own translations, I have benefited from checking his translation of the *Ādiparvan* and have used his rendering "marshal" for *senāpati*. His remarkable industry should gain the epic the wider public it deserves. I should also like to thank Victor Turner for discussions of epic and symbolism and for his help in turning this work into a book; Randy Kloetzli for discussions concerning Indian cosmology; Stephen Allee for conversations about the Norsemen; and James C. King for helpful suggestions on some problems of translation. I am also grateful to students of my courses on Hinduism and myth, epic, and novel at George Washington University, in particular Deborah Soifer and Alec Wood.

My parents, George and Lucille Hiltebeitel, have always given me inspiration and help, and I wish to thank them for, among so many intangibles, reading me the Norse myths when I was a child. Appreciation, too, of my son Adam, who, with amazing seriousness and enjoyment, has found a live place for both of the Indian epics in his imagination. My wife, Helen, has given much encouragement by her patience, humor, and complementary interests.

[9] Dumézil, *Mythe et épopée*, II: *Types épiques indo-européens: Un héros, un sorcier, un roi* (Paris: Editions Gallimard, 1971) (hereinafter *ME*, II), pt. 3 on Yayāti, translated as *The Destiny of a King* (Chicago: University of Chicago Press, 1973).

George Dumézil and Madeleine Biardeau kindly gave me permission to quote and cite letters they have written me, and Victor Turner graciously permitted me to quote from his unpublished essay "Comparative Epic and Saga." I am grateful, too, to the University of Chicago Press for permission to reprint, with some changes, my "*Mahābhārata* and Hindu Eschatology" (*History of Religions* 12 [1972], 95–135, © 1972 by The University of Chicago), reworked to appear here as the main portion of Chapters 12 to 14. And I thank The George Washington University for a research grant which provided payment for typing the manuscript.

Thanks to a grant from the American Institute of Indian Studies, I was able to spend a year in India from 1974 to 1975 to continue my work on the *Mahābhārata* and thus to amplify a number of points.

ALF HILTEBEITEL

Washington, D.C.

Abbreviations

AB	*Aitareya Brāhmaṇa*
ABORI	*Annals of the Bhandarkar Oriental Research Institute*
AJP	*American Journal of Philology*
AKGWG	*Annales der Kaiserl. Gesellschaft der Wissenschaften, Göttingen*
ANF	*Arkhiv för Nordisk Filologi*
AV	*Atharva Veda*
BAUp	*Bṛhad-Āraṇyaka Upaniṣad*
BEFEO	*Bulletin de l'Ecole Française d'Extrême-Orient*
Bhāg. P.	*Bhāgavata Purāṇa*
BR	Böhtlingk and Roth, *Sanskrit-Wörterbuch*
CE	Critical Edition of the *Mahābhārata*, Poona
Chānd. Up.	*Chāndogya Upaniṣad*
EMH	"Etudes de mythologie hindoue"
EPHE	*Ecole Pratique des Hautes Etudes, Annuaire de*
ERE	*Encyclopedia of Religion and Ethics, Hastings*
GB	*Gopatha Brāhmaṇa*
HRJ	*History of Religions Journal*
HV	*Harivaṃśa*
IAB	*Indian Antiquary* (Bombay)
IHQ	*Indian Historical Quarterly*
IIJ	*Indo-Iranian Journal*
Index	Sorensen's *Index to the Names of the Mahābhārata*
JA	*Journal Asiatique*
JAF	*Journal of American Folklore*
JAOS	*Journal of the American Oriental Society*
JAS	*Journal of Asian Studies*
JB	*Jaiminīya Brāhmaṇa*
JIES	*Journal of Indo-European Studies*
JRAS	*Journal of the Royal Asiatic Society* (London)
JS	*Journal des Savants*

KB	*Kauśitakī Brāhmaṇa*
Kauś. Up.	*Kauśitakī Upaniṣad*
Mārk. P.	*Mārkaṇḍeya Purāṇa*
Mbh.	*Mahābhārata*
ME	*Mythe et épopée*
MP	*Modern Philology*
MS	*Maitrāyaṇī Saṃhitā*
M-W	Monier-Williams, *A Sanskrit-English Dictionary*
NC	*La Nouvelle Clio*
NKGWG	*Nachrichten Königl. Gesellschaft der Wissenschaften, Göttingen*
OS	*Orientalia Suecana*
PAPS	*Proceedings of the American Philosophical Society*
PB	*Pañcaviṃśa Brāhmaṇa*
QII	*Quaestiunculae indo-italicae*
QJMS	*Quarterly Journal of the Mythic Society*
RB	*Religion och Bibel*
RC	*Revue Celtique*
ṚV	*Ṛg Veda*
ŚB	*Śatapatha Brāhmaṇa*
SBE	Sacred Books of the East
SKAWW	*Sitzungsberichte der Kaiserlich Akademie der Wissenschaften in Wien*
SKBGW	*Sitzungsberichte der Königl. Böhmischen Gesellschaft der Wissenschaften*
TB	*Taittirīya Brāhmaṇa*
TS	*Taittirīya Saṃhitā*
Vāj. S.	*Vājasaneyi Saṃhitā*
Vām. P.	*Vāmana Purāṇa*
VP	*Viṣṇu Purāṇa*
ZDMG	*Zeitschrift der Deutschen Morgenländischen Gesellschaft*

PART ONE

PRELIMINARIES

CHAPTER 1

Traditional Epics

Epic stories have never suffered from lack of attention, but all too often they have been viewed as extensions of something else: most commonly of myth, ritual, or history.[1] Granting that epic stories have almost always drawn something from these three areas, I hope to show that epic is best regarded as a unique category.

Nevertheless, the "myth and epic" approach has been fruitful in studying the *Mahābhārata*, since it has settled two points. First, the leading heroes of the epic, the five sons of Pāṇḍu and their wife Draupadī, "transpose" into human or heroic terms a mythic, apparently Indo-European, theologem. The oldest son representing sovereignty and moral virtue as they are connected with what Georges Dumézil has called the Indo-European first function, is Yudhiṣṭhira, the son of Dharma (the latter plausibly a substitute for the Vedic god Mitra). Representing the brutal and chivalric sides of the second, warrior, function are Bhīma and Arjuna, sons of Vāyu and Indra. Representing the third function are the twins, Nakula and

[1] On both myth and history as prior to epic, see Mircea Eliade, *Cosmos and History* (New York: Harper, 1959), pp. 34–48; *idem*, *Myth and Reality* (New York: Harper & Row, 1963), p. 190. For reflections on such assumptions in critical studies of Germanic legends, see Georges Dumézil, *From Myth to Fiction: The Saga of Hadingus*, Derek Coltman, trans. (Chicago: University of Chicago Press, 1973), pp. 15 and 26. On the evolutionary order ritual-myth-epic, see Gertrude Levy, *The Sword from the Rock: An Investigation into the Origins of Epic Literature and the Development of the Hero* (London: Faber and Faber, 1953).

Sahadeva, sons of the twin Aśvins, who show, like their divine parents, a capacity for service, beauty, healing, and a connection with cattle and horses. Complementing them all is their wife-in-common Draupadī, incarnation of Śrī. Following the seminal work of Stig Wikander,[2] Dumézil and Madeleine Biardeau have both continued to use this type of analysis and have filled the dossier of meaningful transpositions so as to include almost every major figure in the poem.[3] Second, with more controversy and with each of the three scholars pointing in a different direction, there is still agreement that the great *Mahābhārata* war, taking place at the end of the Dvāpara yuga and the beginning of the Kali yuga, is—at least in part—the epic reflection of a mythic eschatological crisis.[4]

The search for mythic foundations has also led Dumézil and Wikander to insights concerning the manner by which other Indo-European peoples have shaped their epic material. Not all is by "transposition": the euhemerized Scandinavian and Welsh stories, in which gods retain their names but are given human status; the Scandinavian, Roman, and Iranian "histories of origins" in which successions of kings are arranged to reflect the order of the functions; the Roman histories in which the trifunctional gods interact with various heroes, but without an expressed mythology. All of these cases present their own peculiar problems, but the prevailing assumption, the tool by which these discoveries have in fact been made, retains its value. Epic, legend, pseudohistory, and "roman" are all better

[2] See initially Stig Wikander, "Pāṇḍava-sagan och Mahābhāratas mytiska forutsattningar," *RB*, VI (1947), 27–39; trans. by Georges Dumézil, *Jupiter, Mars, Quirinus*, IV: *Explication de textes indiens et latins* (Paris: Presses Universitaires de France, 1948), pp. 37–53; discussed and amplified, pp. 55–85, hereinafter *JMQ*, IV.

[3] See Dumézil's summary work on the *Mahābhārata* in *ME*, I, pp. 33–257. On Biardeau, see the bibliography cited and discussed in later chapters, especially 2, 3, 6, and 13.

[4] See below, Chapter 13.

understood through an appreciation of their mythic backgrounds.[5]

I do not wish to take issue with the results, or even the methods, of such a successful, stimulating, and scrupulously carried-out enterprise. However, as a means of interpreting epic, the underlying assumption can lead to excesses and oversimplifications. Such I fear are what we find in two efforts to discover mythic foundations for the *Iliad*.[6] But this point is not crucial. One cannot fault a method because some have overextended its use or followed it uncritically, yet I think there is a lesson here. The assumption that myth has an inherent priority over epic has led scholars, discontent with epic tales as tales in themselves, to manufacture mythic patterns and prototypes for them. One result is that the epic story is ultimately robbed of autonomy. Taken to the extreme, epic becomes, in essence, a replica of myth.

In order to move beyond this impasse, it seems we must work toward a definition of the relationship between myth and epic. First I must admit—or better, insist—that my own usage is tailored to meet the requirements and the character, which are in some respects peculiar or exceptional, of the *Mahābhārata*. The generalizations that follow will thus proceed from this base, and there is no denying that the relationships between other epic and mythic traditions might suggest, and indeed

[5] For general reflections, see Dumézil, *Myth to Fiction*, pp. vi to xi, and *idem*, *The Destiny of the Warrior*, Alf Hiltebeitel, trans. (Chicago: University of Chicago Press, 1970), pp. 4–6.

[6] Jan de Vries, *Heroic Song and Heroic Legend* (London: Oxford University Press, 1963), pp. 227–33, viewing Achilles, Agamemnon, and Helen as heroized divinities; C. Scott Littleton, "Some Possible Indo-European Themes in the *Iliad*," *Myth and Law among the Indo-Europeans*, Jaan Puhvel, ed. (Berkeley: University of California Press, 1970), pp. 229–46, who wanders all over the Aegean to find heroes and themes to fit Dumézilian categories. Cf. Dumézil, *Destiny of the Warrior*, pp. 82–83, on the overapplication of the label "Odinic hero."

have inspired, other approaches. I do not, of course, suggest that the *Mahābhārata* is to be viewed as the norm of epic.

We must assume that the various Indo-European epic and mythic traditions survive, in their written form, as casualties: segmented, fragmented, or uprooted from the cultures which produced them. The final redactors of such epic traditions as are found in the *Shāh-nāma*, the *Mabinogion*, the *Táin Bó Cuailnge*, and in Saxo Grammaticus' account of the Battle of Brávellir conserve epic material that is no longer enriched in the authors' own minds by any contact with a living mythology. On the other hand, the various euhemerizers who conserve mythic traditions under the guise, or within the dimensions of, "history," are obviously prevented (even if the material in their hands retains a mythic structure[7]) from allowing their humanized gods any significant interplay with the mythic beings they once were. Only in a few cases is there a sustained interaction between the figures of myth and epic: for instance, in Rome, Greece, and India. In each of the first two cases, the mythology to which the heroic traditions allude has in one way or another been denatured. In Rome the primal kings of the "history of origins" interact frequently with the trifunctional divinities through prayers, omens, blessings, and punishments. But as Dumézil has emphasized, these gods are essentially without mythology, there being no divine adventures with which to compare those of the legendary kings. And in Greece, although Homer's Olympians interfere constantly in the affairs of the heroes, they appear essentially as "symbolic predicates of action, character, and circumstance"[8] whose adventures "are not myths in any strict sense, but literary inventions that have something in common with the ingenious mythological

[7] This is Kees Bolle's argument: "In Defense of Euhemerus," *Myth and Law among the Indo-Europeans*, pp. 25–32.

[8] Cedric H. Whitman, *Homer and the Heroic Tradition* (New York: Norton, 1965), p. 223.

elaborations of Euripides."[9] Only in India, then, are the epic poets not only fully aware of, but deeply involved in, a living mythology.

Such a continuum between myth and epic need not be regarded as totally peculiar, yet here terms have often been used loosely. Epic, whatever its stylistic features and its origins as a narrative and poetic genre, should be regarded, in terms of content, as falling under the heading of legend. And legend, with epic as a subcategory, should be distinguished from myth. All this is made problematic by authors who have treated myth as an imperialistic category.[10] William Bascom has shown that the distinction between myth and legend has a long scholarly history and is definitely applicable to the different types of narratives found in primitive societies.[11] In fact, one distinguishing feature, according to Bascom, is that while both myths and legends tell "true stories," they do so with different time referents: the former evoking the remote past, the latter a more recent past.[12] Moreover, as M. L. West has shown in the "Prolegomena" to his edition of Hesiod's *Theogony*, continuums between theogonic myth and heroic genealogies are also found in Hesiod, in Genesis, in the *Bundahishn*, the Purāṇas and

[9] G. S. Kirk, *Myth: Its Meaning and Functions in Ancient and Other Cultures*, Sather Memorial Lectures, vol. XL (Berkeley: University of California Press, 1970), p. 174.

[10] See *ibid.*, pp. 9–10, 19, 179 (but also 34, 40, and 173); Claude Lévi-Strauss, *The Raw and the Cooked*, John and Doreen Weightman, trans. (New York: Harper & Row, 1969), p. 4 (and then, defying his own refusal to make "preconceived classifications," p. 138).

[11] William Bascom, "The Forms of Folklore: Prose Narratives," *JAF*, LXXVIII (1965), 3–20; Kirk's argument (*Myth*, p. 32) that "the categories drawn by unsophisticated peoples can be confusing" is unworthy of refutation.

[12] Bascom, "Forms of Folklore," pp. 3–6; this double classification of "true stories," as distinct from the "false story" or "folktale," adds useful precision to the discussions by Raffaele Pettazzoni, *Essays on the History of Religions*, H. J. Rose, trans. (Leiden: Brill, 1967), pp. 11–12, and Eliade, *Myth and Reality*, pp. 8–9.

Mahābhārata, the *Kojiki* and *Nihongi*, in Polynesian oral literature, and in the *Kalevala*.[13] With such continuities in mind, let me thus propose the following definitions, solely in terms of the contents of the two genres.

Myths are stories which take place in the fullest expanses of time and space (they articulate a cosmology); they deal with the origin, nature, and destiny of the cosmos, and their most prominent characters are gods.

Legends are stories which take place at a specific time and on a specific terrain; they deal with the origin, nature, and destiny of man, and their most prominent characters are heroes.

Each item in this pair of definitions is capable of refinement, and there will certainly be some overlap.[14] But the main purpose is to provide definitions which, while maintaining distinctions, allow important rapports between the two genres to show through. With such distinctions in mind, and with epic seen under the larger heading of heroic legend, an epic morphology can be discerned. One should not confuse this subject with the "heroic morphology" of Angelo Brelich,[15] whose research points out a direction in which future *Mahābhārata* research might well evolve. Brelich tries to show the complex of associations, from both legend and cult, which the Greek heroes have with certain particular themes: death, combat, athletic contests, prophesy, healing, mysteries, oracles, founding cities, the initiation of young adults, and the founding of clan groups. While I shall often draw on Brelich's beautiful

[13] M. L. West, ed., *Hesiod. Theogony* (Oxford: Clarendon Press, 1966), pp. 1–16.

[14] Certainly these definitions allow "myths" about men (the Crucifixion of Jesus, the Buddha's Birth and Enlightenment), and hardly imply that gods do not make appearances in legends or epics. Also, I seek to avoid identifying myths solely with the past; obviously, eschatologies deal with the future.

[15] Brelich, *Gli Eroi Greci: Un probleme storico-religioso* (Rome: Edizioni dell 'Ateneo, 1958).

work, it is my intention to concentrate directly on a complex of various features within epics and heroic traditions themselves, rather than on the relations between such traditions and matters of cult. While the themes are not necessarily all unique to epic, together they constitute a complex whose outlines become easily intelligible once the place of epic is recognized in a continuum with myth. My hope here is to be suggestive rather than exhaustive, to set the exploration of the *Mahābhārata* in a comparative framework.

Fate

Brelich points to the way myth and legend, and the two dimensions of time which they present, are often related. Discussing the place of "la struttura eroica" with the larger "collettività mitiche" of Greece, Brelich says that whereas the activity on the mythic level concerns a past which involves the formation of the world and the childhood, or in any case, the not-yet-fulfilled life of the gods, "the heroes have an analogous position, only with respect to the formation of the human world."[16] This analogy, this coincidence of planes, between the formation and direction of the cosmos and the formation of the world of man, gives the lives of heroes their special gravity. Their activities are weighted with a burden of recompense. Whereas the gods and goddesses play out their intrigues in the fluid, formative, and free realm of myth, identical or similar intrigues, when acted out by heroes or heroines, take shape in a different mold which, in fact, hardens into their destiny. The cosmic order which the gods (whether polytheistic or monotheistic) create and sustain is nothing else for the hero than fate, sometimes happy, but usually cruel and harsh. Indeed, in epics where such themes are already articulated, the relation between these two forces—cosmic order and human destiny—is often a matter for great reflection. From

[16] *Ibid.*, p. 375 (my translation).

the heroes' standpoint, the forces may coincide, as with two of the *Mahābhārata's* words for fate: *vidhi*, "what is ordained," and *daivam*, "what pertains to the gods."[17] But fate is usually at least something with which the heroes must come to terms, as can be seen from Helmer Ringgren's study of epic fatalism in the *Shāh-nāma* and Cedric Whitman's essay on "Fate, Time, and the Gods" in the *Iliad*.[18]

What is important, however, is not so much that certain epics—the Greek, Persian, and Indian especially—have worked out clear formulations of fatalism, or that they reveal important correlations between the concepts of fate in the epics and those that have been worked out elsewhere in those cultures, in other types of texts.[19] What is significant is that epics present a context in which the heroes, coming to terms with the origin, nature, and destiny of the universe as it impinges upon them, inevitably make some type of response—submission, defiance, courage, faith, self-discovery, stoicism, humility, vacillation, doubt, cowardice—which takes on determinitive symbolic value in terms of an understanding of the origin, nature, and destiny of man.

I thus suggest that the concept of epic fatalism can be extended beyond those heroic traditions in which a specific philosophy of fate is worked out. In this respect, it would be more fruitful to compare the related themes in various epics directly, rather than try to interpret the fatalism of the *Shāh-nāma* and the *Mahābhārata*, for instance, as common derivatives from an

[17] On fate and destiny in the *Mahābhārata*, see Dumézil, *ME*, I, 162–70, and the bibliography on p. 163, n. 1.

[18] Helmer Ringgren, *Fatalism in the Persian Epics*, Uppsala Universitets Årsskrift, No. 13 (Uppsala and Weisbaden, 1952), especially Chapter V, "God and Destiny," pp. 111–23; Cedric H. Whitman, *Homer and the Heroic Tradition*, pp. 221–48 (Chapter X).

[19] This is essentially the focus of Ringgren, *Fatalism*, and also of R. C. Zaehner, *The Dawn and Twilight of Zoroastrianism* (New York: Putnam's, 1961), pp. 240–42, as if epic fatalism were a sort of phase—aberrant at that—in the religion.

anterior Indo-Iranian philosophy of fate.[20] In this sense, the term "fate" would, of course, have to be used open-endedly, implying that the heroes face the conditions that "determine" human existence, that "shape" human destiny. Examples are not necessary here, except to say that one highly visible type, the hero who faces up bravely to the conditions which will bring on his death, is responding to, or fulfilling, a personal fate, whether this be stated explicitly, as with Achilles, Karṇa, Siyāvosh, or Gilgamesh, or implicitly, as with Cúchulainn, the Christian martyrs, or the Australian heroes of the dreamtime. The lives and activities of heroes, then, imply a sort of crystallization of fate. Mythic meaning has impinged into human life, and the hero defines himself by his response to conditions which may never occur again, but are "true" for all time. For many heroes, their response of greatest import is in the case of their deaths. We thus move from the abstract to the concrete.

Births, Deaths, Fatalities

The devices which link the divine and the heroic are highly informative symbols of the relationship between myth and epic. Incarnations,[21] possessions,[22] and relations of favor or disfavor between particular divinities and individuals[23] all find their

[20] Ringgren, *Fatalism*, pp. 40–47, is unconvincing on a genetic connection between Indian Kāla- and Iranian Zurvan-speculation. He seems more credible when, noting the great number of terms for "time" in the *Shāh-nāma*, he says: "This must imply that the important thing is the conception of time, and that epic fatalism is no mere reproduction of ancient Zervanism" (p. 47).

[21] H. Munro Chadwick and Nora Kershaw Chadwick, *The Growth of Literature*, 3 vols. (Cambridge University Press, 1932, 1936, 1940), II, 525, see no parallel (I think correctly) to the *avatāra* theme in Western heroic literature, although several authors will speak of Cúchulainn as an "avatar" of Lug; cf. the incarnations in the Tibetan Gesar epic: Alexandra David-Neel and the Lama Yongden, *The Superhuman Life of Gesar of Ling* (rev. ed., London: Rider, 1959), pp. 30, 54–59.

[22] See, along with Śiva's possession of Aśvatthāman in the *Mahābhārata*, that of Hektor by Ares in the *Iliad* 17. 210–11.

[23] Out of countless examples, see the relationship between Odinn and Haraldus Hyldetan at the Battle of Brávellir, discussed below, Chapter 5.

places, in various epics, as indexes to a hero's "true" identity. The most common device is that which links heroes to gods by means of their births. As indicated at the beginning of this chapter, nowhere are the divine-human origins of heroes and heroines more significant than in the *Mahābhārata*, but, as is well known, pairings between mortal and godly parents also lie behind such illustrious names as Achilles, Aenias, Sarpedon, Helen, Heracles, Cúchulainn, the "two-thirds divine" Gilgamesh, and the Tibetan Gesar. But when Homer and Hesiod describe the heroes of Troy as "demigods" (*Iliad* 12. 23; *Works and Days* 160), they refer to a conception that extends beyond the immediate birth of every hero.[24] In addition, the heroes' closeness of contact with the gods, their life in a time when such contact was the norm rather than the near-impossible exception, a time when humans were greater than they are now, gives the heroes a special intermediary position between gods and men for which their births may serve as a primary symbol.

Such divine origins or affiliations, however, are never the "whole story." In and through the lives of the heroes, these conditions, these divine rapports, vanish, and in contrast to the conditions under which their lives are begun, their ends are marked by all-too-human themes.[25] As Brelich remarks,[26] very few of the Greek heroes die a natural death, while an incalculable number are slain. Most of the heroes, we are told

[24] See Chadwick and Chadwick, *Growth of Literature*, I, 13, who cite Jordanes' description of the "chiefs" of the Goths as *semideos*; also Dumézil, *Destiny of the Warrior*, p. 117, noting that in the *Ṛg Veda* the hero Trasadāsyu is called *ardhadevām*, "demigod."

[25] This generalization might be refined by pointing out that where the link with the gods is by means other than birth—such as by a possession or by initiation—this still constitutes a "new beginning" or "birth" in the hero's career. Heroes who die a "divine death"—like certain "Odinic heroes"—still do so as heroes and actually die, unlike Odinn (whose death at the Ragnarök is of a different order), in the corresponding conditions; see Dumézil, *Myth to Fiction*, pp. 129–53.

[26] Brelich, *Gli Eroi Greci*, pp. 88–89.

by Hesiod, died in war at Thebes or Troy, others in single combat; some were slain through treachery, some by near relatives; some were torn to pieces, some turned to animals, and some were destroyed by Zeus's thunderbolt; some fell victim to certain types of incidents, such as snake bites or mishaps during chariot races, hunts, or training exercises; and others committed suicide. One may certainly also recall here the two deaths most highlighted in the *Iliad*: those of Patroklus and Hektor. Before Achilles slays Hektor, he says to him: "I only wish that my spirit and fury would drive me to hack your meat away and eat it raw for the things that you have done to me" (22. 346–48). Then, when Hektor is slain and all the Achaeans stab his body (22. 371), there follows the "shameful treatment" (22. 395) by Achilles, who drags the corpse before the walls of Troy, then across the plain to the Achaeans' camp, and there three times around the body of Patroklus (24. 16). As to the latter's death (16. 784–867), three times (as Achilles' stand-in) Patroklus attacks the Trojans and kills nine each time, is then disabled by Apollo who strikes him on the back, is speared by the Dardanian Euphorbos between the shoulders, and then again in the belly by Hektor whom he tells, with his dying words: "You are only my third slayer" (16. 850). I do not know whether scholars more familiar with Greece have pondered the meaning of these various symbolisms. The invitation is to be found in some apt words of Victor Turner: "Since most epics are replete with combats, battles, wars and assassinations, the killing scene is often an epitome or multivocal symbol of the scheme of values underpinning the whole work."[27]

Although such matters will be taken up in subsequent chapters, let me mention here some general points. I will try to show that the *Mahābhārata* has taken special pains to lend coherence to thematic material of this type. Certain deaths follow

[27] Victor Turner, "Comparative Epic and Saga," p. 7 (unpublished essay).

directly on others, and I believe the symbolisms are related. Second, the heroes' deaths often involve mythic themes which, as the latter provide a background for "human" events, shape them into inevitable fatalities. The clearest case is the death of Karṇa: what is a mythologem on one level, a divine opposition between Indra and Sūrya which leads, in the mythology, to no more than the latter's loss of face and a gain for one of Indra's human protégés, is, on the heroic level, an intrigue shaped by a preceptor's curse which predestines the hero, Sūrya's son, to his death at the hands of Arjuna, Indra's son. But whereas the mythic drama involves an opposition between the gods of Storm and Sun—a drama which takes place at no particular time, or in a perennial seasonal time, and which demands no final resolution in terms of the relationship between the two gods—the heroic drama takes place once and for all and requires human motivation, a series of fatalities, to account for the hero's end.[28]

In later chapters I will discuss several cases where the causalities which bring on heroes' deaths have mythic dimensions. But even where no related myth is known, the deaths of the epic heroes are charged with symbolism. Almost always, and especially in the battle scenes, certain fatalities set up the conditions whereby a particular death becomes possible: not only curses and blessings, but oaths or vows (the deaths of Dhṛṣṭadyumna, Droṇa, Duḥśāsana, Jayadratha, Duryodhana, and others) and personal prohibitions, whether dishonored (as with Śiśupāla, who dies when he commits one more than the hundred offenses permitted him) or honored (as with Bhīṣma, who falls because he refuses to fight anyone who was formerly a woman). It is as if the hero were invulnerable to death—that his closeness to the gods, whether by birth or by his activities,

[28] For fuller exploration of this episode and the background myth, see Dumézil, "Karṇa et les Pāṇḍava," *OS*, III (1954), 60–66, and *ME*, I, 130–38. Added commentary can be found in my doctoral dissertation, Gods, Heroes, and Kṛṣṇa: A Study of the *Mahābhārata* in Relation to Indian and Indo-European Symbolisms, University of Chicago, 1973, pp. 5–8.

would make him immortal—were it not for some intruding and apparently arbitrary human factor, or series of factors, which, in his dealings and interactions with other heroes, has brought a nonetheless inevitable mortality upon him.

It would be instructive to examine the world's epics for the variety of forces which seal the fates of their heroes. No doubt the Indian stress on the power of curses, blessings, and vows owes something to Hindu asceticism (although parallels are easy to find elsewhere). But the device of the personal prohibition, which in Bhīṣma's case appears essentially as a negative vow, finds a close analogue in Ireland. There, a hero or heroine will have his or her destiny shaped by a *geis* (plural *gessa*), a personal prohibition, which may set the conditions for a woman's marriage (as with Medb of Cruachan, according to the *Táin Bó Cuailnge*[29]) or a man's death. Unlike Bhīṣma, who falls because he virtuously upholds his negative vow, Irish heroes often fall because their *gessa* are broken (as with Conaire) or, more particularly, where they have been broken because one *geis* has conflicted with another (as with Cúchulainn).[30] In any case, such epic devices are no doubt as ancient as the myths in which we find parallel dramas.[31]

Character and Psychology

The details of the hero's death and the fatalities that bring it on are telling strokes in the portrayal of his character. But throughout a hero's life, compelling motivations are produced

[29] See Dumézil, *ME* II, pp. 337–39; on Medb's *geis*, see below, Chapter 8.

[30] On Cúchulainn, see Whitley Stokes, trans., "The Tragical Death of Cuchullin," *The Cuchullin Saga in Irish Literature*, Eleanor Hull, comp. and ed. (London: David Nutt in the Strand, 1898), pp. 253–58, and the discussion (also covering Conaire) by Alwyn Rees and Brinley Rees, *Celtic Heritage: Ancient Tradition in Ireland and Wales* (New York: Grove Press, 1961), pp. 326–33. On *gessa*, see John Revell Reinhard, *The Survival of Geis in Medieval Romance* (Halle A. S: Max Niemeyer, 1933).

[31] Comparisons of fatalities will also reveal devices peculiar to specific epic and heroic traditions, such as prophesies, prayers, horoscopes, hecatombs, auguries, interpretations of omens, divinatory practices, games of skill and chance.

by desires, demands, and conflicts which, together, constitute the basic texture of epic drama. Aristotle appreciated long ago the importance of character in epic;[32] W. P. Ker, in contrasting the stress on character in epic and the emphasis on mood and sentiment in romance, picked up on Aristotle: "Without dramatic representation of the characters, epic is mere history or romance; the variety and life of epic are to be found in the drama that springs up at every encounter of the personages."[33] This conception very properly leads beyond the single figure to the more revealing depiction of the relations—conflicts and consolidarities—among characters.[34] Indeed, if one admits at least the general importance of character in epic, it should be possible to regard epic, and perhaps most heroic stories, as primary vehicles for the expression of psychological values. It is certainly no accident that the "Oedipus complex," the "Electra complex," and, as Brelich would have it, the "Iphiclus complex,"[35] all take their names from Greek heroes. Psychological disequilibrium seems to be a fundamental given of epic conflict and drama.

In this connection, certain problems arise with a point made by Dumézil, who seems to let the ease with which he finds

[32] *Poetics* 1460. a. 5: "Homer is the only poet who knows the right proportions of epic narrative; when to narrate, and when to let the characters speak for themselves. Other poets for the most part tell their story straight on, with scanty passages of drama and far between. Homer, with little prelude, leaves the stage to his personages, men and women, all with characters of their own."

[33] William Paton Ker, *Epic and Romance: Essays on Medieval Literature* (2d rev. ed., 1908; repr. New York: Dover, 1957), p. 17.

[34] This point is made partly to delimit the value which I attach, at least as regards epic research, to certain studies which deal with only one type of hero and his "monomyth," especially what I would call the composite "Oedipal Bodhisattva" of Joseph Campbell in his *The Hero with a Thousand Faces* (New York: Meridian, 1957).

[35] Brelich, *Gli Eroi Greci*, p. 243, n. 52, suggests that if Freud had known the Iphiclus legend, he would have used this term for the "castration complex"; see Apollodorus, *The Library* 1. ix. 12: as a child, Iphiclus ran away when his father laid beside him the bloody knife he had been using to geld rams; later, he had to be cured of impotence.

trifunctional and other mythical themes transposed into the *Mahābhārata* suggest a misleading contrast with the *Iliad*, where such patterns are harder to come by. According to him, in the *Mahābhārata* (and also in other non-Greek Indo-European epic and legendary traditions), "the personages, entirely defined by their function, present scarcely anything of psychological interest. Yudhiṣṭhira, Bhīma, Arjuna, Dhṛtarāṣṭra, Bhīṣma are all of one piece, and one can readily predict what each of them will do in each new circumstance." In contrast to the many-sided and open-ended character of Achilles, free of mythic prototypes, Dumézil sees Karṇa simply as the "son and copy of the Sun, of the enemy of Indra, . . . [who] can only confirm to his mother his inflexible resolution to kill Arjuna, Indra's son, or die by his hand." And he adds: "In brief, Greece has chosen, as always, the better part: to settled reflections, to the preestablished relations between men and things which she inherited from her ancestors of the North, she preferred the risks and chances of criticism and observation."[36]

This is a surprising paean to the West. Granting that Homer's psychological characterizations are largely free of preestablished mythological patterns (though hardly free of divine promptings) and have a critical and objective quality, this does not mean that other modes of epic characterization lack psychological interest. The depiction of Arjuna, the "warrior yogin,"[37] provides the basis for as complex a psychology as one could wish. But even where there are mythic models, the epic continuations (I avoid here the mechanical tone of terms like "copy" and "transposition") can be of the greatest psychological subtlety. Things occur differently on the two different planes, and that is the value—and for the *Mahābhārata* the purpose—of having both. It is perhaps presumptuous, and probably impossible, to analyze the psyches, the motivations,

[36] Dumézil, *ME*, I, 633 (my translation).

[37] See Madeleine Biardeau, *Clefs pour la pensée hindoue* (Paris: Editions Seghers, 1972), pp. 95–96, 160–66.

the inner struggles of the gods; from the human point of view, there is something whimsically pure about their actions. But when the themes of myth are viewed in terms of the lives, fates, and deaths of heroes, they can be examined with great psychological depth. Thus the motivations of almost every major figure in the *Mahābhārata*—except Krishna, who plays his hand mysteriously—are constantly under review. In the example already cited several times, Karṇa's inner struggles are actually of the highest interest: rich in loyalty, pride, courage, stubbornness, determination, and especially resentment, obvious but never overstated. Moreover, some of the *Mahābhārata's* most intriguing characterizations emerge directly from a juxtaposition of mythic and epic themes. One thinks of Arjuna, the son of Indra who is reluctant to fight, and of certain other mythic-epic correlations handled with restrained but unmistakable irony.[38] As for Krishna, although his mind can never be read, his involvement is often the foil by which the thoughts and true dispositions of others are bared. In the *Udyogaparvan* especially, his alleged peace mission is the catalyst by which all the various conflicting claims and desires are brought into the open, and thus into inevitable opposition.

One is thus compelled to think of different devices and different "epic psychologies" for different cultures. As to the *Mahābhārata*, one need only look to Irawati Karve's delightful and provocative *Yuganta* and to Vishnu S. Sukthankar's *On the Meaning of the Mahābhārata* to see how the epic has provided material for character studies and psychological delineations of considerable subtlety.[39] Sukthankar, in particular, interprets

[38] For example, Yudhiṣṭhira as incarnation of Dharma and Draupadī as incarnation of Śrī, topics discussed in several chapters below.

[39] Karve, *Yuganta: The End of an Epoch* (Poona: Desmukh Prakashan, 1969), and Sukthankar, *The Meaning of the Mahābhārata* (Bombay: Asiatic Society of Bombay, 1957). In Karve's work, one enjoys in particular her portrayal of Bhīṣma as a consistent woman hater (pp. 36–38) and her appreciation of the tender side of the relation between Bhīma and Draupadī (pp. 128–32). In Sukthankar, see the portrayals of Vidura and Dhṛtarāṣṭra

the epic in terms of a specifically Hindu psychology which, so long as he checks his impulse to fabricate new "complexes" à la Freud,[40] has much to teach us. Not unassimilable to my depiction of Krishna as a foil, Sukthankar's psychology is based on the recognition of Krishna as the "Inner Self" (*Paramātman*) and Arjuna, the warrior yogi, as the incarnate soul (*Jīvātman*). From this foundation, says Sukthankar: "If you pursue steadily the indications offered by the symbolism underlying the lineaments of Arjuna and Śrī Krishna and dive yet deeper into the plot of this great drama, you will discern as though in a dim twilight unmistakable traces of an exhaustive but carefully veiled allegory underlying the whole narrative, a very delicate tracery of thought reflected, as it were, in the subconscious of the poets and finding an elusive expression—now refined and subtle, now clumsy and, to us, grotesque—in the characterization of most of the *dramatis personae* as well as in the delineation of many of the scenes."[41] Preferring to see a mythic background for specific character traits rather than a subconscious allegorical patterning of various components of the psyche—like the empirical ego (=Dhṛtarāṣṭra), the *buddhi* (=Vidura), and various desires (=the Kauravas)[42]—I would nonetheless agree with Sukthankar's starting point, Krishna, and his conception of the sweep of an "epic psychology." After all, such a psychology becomes intelligible in a religious tradition which places such regular emphasis on the belief that the divine is found in every man, the center to which all else relates. One would hardly expect a psychology like this from Homer. It is one, nonetheless.

(pp. 54–57), and the concluding statement: "When we read the poem with attention we discover that from end to end the interest is held on character."

[40] See Sukthankar, *Mahābhārata*, p. 53, where he speaks of Karṇa's "frustration complex."

[41] *Ibid.*, p. 102 and, more generally, on the allegory of the psyche, pp. 102–10.

[42] Allegorical interpretations of the *Mahābhārata* by Indian authors go back at least to the thirteenth century *Tātparyanirṇayaprārambhaḥ* of Madhva.

Sins and Virtues

Contrary to popular assumptions, the epic hero is rarely a uniformly ideal figure. Peter Hagin says of eighteenth-century English efforts to create epics around idealized noble statesmen: "The numberless qualities of the neo-classical hero only conceal his narrative weakness."[43] Rāma, one of the few heroes to approach a standard of complete perfection, appears idealized.[44] When we find complex character and subtle psychology, however, we may expect characterization in depth. And in most cases, epic heroes—even the most honored and the most despised—are depicted ambivalently. Thus, when two of the *Iliad*'s most noble heroes, Aenias and Achilles, meet each other in combat, Aenias can say: "There are harsh things enough that could be spoken against us both, a ship of a hundred locks could not carry the burden" (20. 246–47). Similarly, Reuben Levy has remarked that the "lapses" of the heroes of the *Shāh-nāma* are no less evident than the nobler side of its villains.[45] Such ambiguity—wickedness among heroes, goodness among their foes—has misled some scholars, expecting heroic perfection, to propose the so-called "inversion theory" of the *Mahābhārata*: that the "bad" side must originally have been the good and the "good" side the bad.

One of the most stimulating treatments of this darker side of the hero is that of Brelich. The Greek heroes, he says, com-

[43] Peter Hagin, *The Epic Hero and the Decline of Epic Poetry: A Study of the Neoclassical English Epic with Special Reference to Milton's Paradise Lost* (Bern: Franke, 1964), p. 58.

[44] Rāma commits only one truly nefarious act, the treacherous and much-discussed slaying of the monkey king Vāli (*Rāmāyaṇa* 4:13–18); see most recently V. Raghavan, *Ramayana-Triveni* (Madras: Ramayana, 1970), pp. 1–12, giving it a dharmic interpretation; see also Benjamin Khan, *The Concept of Dharma in Valmiki Ramayana* (Delhi: Munshi Ram Manohar Lal, 1965), pp. 143–50; see pp. 140–41, for Rāma's less glaring offenses: two untruths.

[45] Reuben Levy, trans., *The Epic of Kings. Shāh-nāma* (Chicago: University of Chicago Press, 1966), pp. xx–xxi.

monly present two types of characteristics: "physical monstrosities" and "moral imperfections." The list of the former[46] is one which might be instructively compared with unusual physiological traits found elsewhere. Indian heroes of all sorts are described by their *lakṣaṇas* ("marks"),[47] one trait in particular having been compared to the famous *riastrad* ("distortion") or *delba* ("forms") that affect Cúchulainn; and one may also think of the *lus-ṅan* ("bad body") of Gesar.[48] Brelich, in fact, thinks that physical and moral abnormalities are intimately connected, sharing a "common denominator" of "monstrosity"; and he suggests that his proposed distinction may actually be culturally conditioned, imposed on the heroes through the more recent perspectives of Greek rationalism and Christianity.[49] Although I will not follow this lead, it is certainly true that physical and moral defects may complement each

[46] See Brelich, *Gli Eroi Greci*, pp. 233–48; giganticness and dwarfishness, theriomorphism, traces of androgyny, physical deformities of teeth (cf. Harald Hyldetan), of inner organs, humpbacks, headlessness, many-headedness, defects of legs and feet (wounds and lameness: see Claude Lévi-Strauss' treatment of this feature of the Oedipus cycle: *Structural Anthropology* [Garden City, N.Y.: Doubleday, 1967], pp. 210–13) and the eyes. One notes the apparent absence of the theme of arm loss which is so prominent in Roman, Irish, Scandinavian, and Indian (Bhuriśravas, Bhīma's son Sutasoma, Savitṛ) myths and legends.

[47] India's most famous case is the thirty-two major *lakṣaṇas* of the Buddha; see Eugène Burnouf, *Le Lotus de la bonne loi*, II: *Appendice (Mémoires Annexes)* (Paris: Maisonneuve Frères, Editeurs, 1925), 553–647; on Krishna's auspicious bodily features, see A. C. Bhaktivedanta, *The Nectar of Devotion: A Study of Śrīla Rūpa Gosvāmī's* Bhaktirasāmṛta-sindhu (Boston: Iskcon Press, 1970), pp. 158–60. *Mbh.* 12:102,6–20 gives an intriguing list of heroic marks (*śūra . . . lakṣaṇani*; 6). In this vein, Dumézil, *Destiny of the Warrior*, pp. 161–64, discusses the strange but similar grimaces—one eye raised, the other lowered, or, as with Arjuna, high cheekbones—of Cúchulainn, the Viking Egill (on these two, see also de Vries, *Heroic Song*, pp. 82–85), and Arjuna. Indeed, *Mbh.* 12:102,14 tells us that the brave are those of "crooked [or squinty] eyes, prominent foreheads, and fleshless jaws [or cheekbones]" (*jihmākṣāḥ pralalāṭaśca nirmāmsahanavo*)!

[48] See Rolf-A. Stein, *Recherches sur l'épopée et le barde au Tibet* (Paris: Imprimerie Nationale, 1959), pp. 544–45.

[49] Brelich, *Gli Eroi Greci*, p. 232.

other, as, for instance, with the doubly blind Dhṛtarāṣṭra and perhaps the pale and "impotent" Pāṇḍu.[50]

As this suggests, the sins of a hero, or of a group of heroes, may sometimes form a significant symbolic structure; but material of this kind is not always systematized into coherent patterns. For instance, I would not superimpose the scheme of the "three sins of the warrior"—which I shall discuss later—on the single episode in which Achilles, insulted, resolves not to fight.[51] Yet there is no doubt that his behavior in general—his wrath and hubris—is ambiguous and far less than "ideal." Such incidents, however, invariably provide important indexes to key cultural and religious values—whether they are systematized or not. Brelich has called attention to certain "moral imperfections" among the Greek heroes that find interesting analogues in the Indian heroic tradition: excessive violence and sexuality, incest, untruthfulness, deception, and insolence.[52] Equally important for comparative purposes, he observes faults that find few if any analogues in the Indian epos: hubris itself ("pride" is a common moral defect in the *Mahābhārata*, but it never has as much play, and certainly not the same connotations, as in Greece[53]), and also madness, patricide,

[50] On these traits, see, for both Pāṇḍu and Dhṛtarāṣṭra, Dumézil, *ME*, I, 151–52, 155–57, 162–74, and, for Pāṇḍu, *idem*, *JMQ*, IV, 76–80.

Regarding Brelich's thesis, it seems to me that the two types of "monstrositres" point in different directions: the physical defining the hero as *materia prima*, an emergence into human form of a mythic identity; the moral defining the hero not in relation to myth (or some inherent natural disposition) but to the structures of human society. Although such a formulation requires further thought, one may think of Śiśupāla, whose physical abnormalities at birth (three eyes, four arms) define him in relation to Śiva, but whose sins correspond to the three social functions; see Dumézil, *ME*, II, 59–68.

[51] See Littleton, "Indo-European Themes in the *Iliad*," p. 238, and see my article, "Dumézil and Indian Studies," *JAS*, XXXIV (1974), 133–34.

[52] Brelich, *Gli Eroi Greci*, pp. 248–65.

[53] For the most part, pride (*darpa*, *abhimāna*) seems in the *Mahābhārata* to be a fault confined to Duryodhana and to others whose pretensions to specifically *royal* prerogatives must occasionally be smashed: see, for example, Indra's pride, 1:189,17 (discussed in Chapter 7) and that of Yayāti (discussed in Dumézil, *ME*, II, 274).

and outright robbery.[54] However, as with its strange deaths, the *Mahābhārata* has correlated and systematized much of this ethical content into coherent frameworks, ones which I hope to make clear. In fact, the sins and deaths are in some instances intimately connected and form the nucleus of a complex and extensive fabric of symbols.

I would like once again to suggest that such material is more naturally "heroic" than "mythic." To be sure, there can be divine sins and follies, some of the same sorts as are committed by heroes: adulteries, incests, deceptions, sometimes even murders. And some sins are more clearly limited to heroes, such as sacrilege and impiety (only in India could Indra, a god, commit a sacrilege by killing a brahmin). But the main point is that only among heroes, as essentially human figures, can the full implications of violations and misdeeds be worked out and understood as sins. When Loki instigates the murder of Baldr, when Zeus indulges his sexual appetite, even when Indra commits his assorted crimes, these are pure deeds. They invite no moral investigation. The gods act out of their own essential natures, and that is that. But when a hero sins, whether the sin be implicit or explicit, one finds a dilemma, a matter of choice, which gives his act its special finality and tragedy and which leaves it open to investigation from every angle. It is perhaps from such considerations as these that the *Mahābhārata* supports our point with the following words: "Virtue and sin exist, O king, only among men; these do not exist among creatures other than men" (*mānuṣeṣu mahārāja dharmādharmau / na tathānyeṣu bhūteṣu manuṣyarahiteṣviha*; 12:238,28).

This quote makes my next point sufficiently obvious. Some correlation may be expected between epic sins and epic virtues, and the *Mahābhārata*, clearly systematizing once again, will not disappoint us, nor is it alone. The Chadwicks have said: "Statements of social standards are expressed in the *Mahābhārata* far

[54] Brelich, *Gli Eroi Greci*, pp. 248–65, 295–96. As far as I can see, Indian epic knows extremely erratic ascetics and stressful situations, but nothing like madness, whether feigned or real.

more frequently than in Western heroic poetry," a fact they attribute "in the main to the very large didactic accretions." But when they discuss the Western epics, they make it very clear that such material is there, too: sometimes explicitly, as in *Beowulf*, sometimes thematically important but not made the subject of discussion, as in the Norse, Irish, and Homeric stories. For the Chadwicks, of course, the cardinal virtues are those of the heroic age, and thus quite uniform: courage, loyalty, generosity. Moreover, the vices are these virtues' antitheses: cowardice, disloyalty, and meanness, plus others like avarice, arrogance, violence toward one's own household, and a disregard for oaths.[55] The virtues here are less interesting than the vices, for such "unheroic" qualities as wisdom and cleverness, which one finds in the *Iliad*, not to mention some of the stranger virtues which occur in the *Mahābhārata*, are left out of the Chadwicks' enumeration. Yet one step toward understanding the moral imperfections of epic heroes will be to investigate the ideals of moral perfection which they also embody, albeit inadequately, imperfectly, incompletely.

The Heroic Age

These various morphological features of epic come together in the heroic age. The idea of a "heroic age" was adopted by H. M. and N. K. Chadwick, and used before them by W. P. Ker and after them by Cecil Maurice Bowra and others, to refer to what they all regarded as the historic situation in which epic heroes lived and in which their peculiar life style was possible.[56] According especially to the Chadwicks and Bowra, the historical core of epic could invariably be uncovered by paring away the apparatus of nonhistorical and above all

[55] Chadwick and Chadwick, *Growth of Literature*, II, 490–91; I, 74–78.

[56] Ker, *Epic and Romance*, especially pp. 3–15; H. Munro Chadwick, *The Heroic Age* (Cambridge: Cambridge University Press, 1912); Cecil Maurice Bowra, *Heroic Poetry* (London: Macmillan), pp. 25–29, 535; *idem*, *The Meaning of a Heroic Age*, Earl Grey Memorial Lecture, No. 37 (King's College, Newcastle Upon Tyne, 1957).

"mythic elements," which would either reflect later accretions or "the beliefs of an uncritical age,"[57] that is, the heroic age itself. This procedure of taking epics primarily as repositories of historical events and social conditions has led to some interesting conclusions and comparisons, most notably those in the groundbreaking work of Ker, whose main contribution lies in the contrast he draws between epic and romance and the corresponding "heroic" and "chivalric" ages which they portray.[58] But though epic tales probably always reflect some actual past conditions in one way or another, even the Chadwicks realized that one must usually look outside the epics, wherever possible to concurrent sources, for criteria to determine what was historical and what was not. In many of the Germanic traditions they could, of course, demonstrate how historical personages had sometimes been worked into heroic poems, often anachronistically.[59] But since concurrent documents are usually wanting, and since epics, on their own, present no inner criteria for historicity, and in fact usually have distorted whatever history one might find in them, such efforts at reconstruction were, and still are, all too often guided by a pleasing but wholly unreliable combination of common sense and wishful thinking. Both the *Mahābhārata*[60] and the *Rāmāvana*[61] have been subjected to such an approach. Historical solutions to the peculiarities each epic presents are simply imagined, such as the hypothetical tribal practices and traits which

[57] Chadwick, *Heroic Age*, p. 130; cf. Chadwick and Chadwick, *Growth of Literature*, I, 198ff.; Bowra, *Meaning of a Heroic Age*, pp. 3–5, says that historicity may be assumed even where it is unknown and refers to mythic features like divine births as "incidental and almost irrelevant."

[58] Ker, *Epic and Romance*, pp. 19–20.

[59] See, for example, *Growth of Literature*, I, 199–204.

[60] N. K. Sidhanta, *The Heroic Age of India: A Comparative Study*. (New York: Knopf, 1930).

[61] Shantikumar N. Vyas, *India in the Rāmāyaṇa Age* (Delhi: Atma Ram, 1967); cf. P. C. Dharma, *The Rāmāyaṇa Polity* (Mylapore: Madras Law Journal Press, 1941), pp. 3–4.

are supposed to lie behind the polyandric marriage of Draupadī and the alliance of Rāma with the monkeys.[62]

Apparently it is impossible to view the "heroic milieu" of some epics as an historical record, for epics seem to play havoc with history[63]—if, indeed, they do not create it. The degree of distortions will have something to do with what Victor Turner has called the "epic relation," which he defines as a relation between two periods of time: "(1) the 'heroic time' of the narrated events, with its implicit background of 'heroic' society; (2) the 'narrative time' when the epic was first composed or believed to have been composed; (3) the 'documentary time' which covers the peiod for which we have manuscripts of the epic in their various recensions (revision)."[64] Turner has formulated this schema because he disagrees with Ker that epic poetry is a "direct reflection" (the term is Turner's) of the heroic age. As he says, "Much of the tension and mystery of epic derives from the ambivalence of the poet to the past." But even though Turner speaks of the past as "imagined," and as a combination of the "fanciful and factual," he is still inclined to see the poet's tension, however creative, as one which con-confronts two periods of history:

It may well be also that the derivation of epic's values, ethical imperatives and manners from several dissonant epochs may be the very cause of its well-known universal-human quality. The poet is forced by his materials away from the familiar paths of systematically connected customs and norms to make original assessments of character and individual worth. He is at a sufficient distance from the

[62] On the polyandry, see Chadwick and Chadwick, *Growth of Literature*, II, 519, 528; Sidhanta, *Heroic Age*, p. 120. On the monkeys, see Vyas, *India in the Rāmāyaṇa Age*, pp. 45–59.

[63] Most important in dispelling historicity as the necessary basis for an epic is the careful research of Stein, *Épopée et barde*, pp. 108, 142–45, 234, 249–50, 294–99, and *passim*.

[64] Turner, "Comparative Epic and Saga," p. 12; cf. Chadwick and Chadwick, *Growth of Literature*, III, 754–55.

standards of the heroic age to be objective about them and even daringly to judge those standards themselves by their good or bad effects on the fully human beings the multidimensional quality of his material has allowed to emerge.[65]

I have no argument with the idea that this attitude of the poet toward the past will involve a reflection on some facts of history, some ancient standards, combined with efforts of "creative imagination."[66] But in his allegiance to the view that the "heroic age" is primarily a category of history, perhaps Turner has not gone far enough.

It is perhaps best to begin with the classical source of this theme in Hesiod's *Works and Days*. After the hubris-ridden heroes of the bronze age had destroyed each other by their own hands and departed anonomously for Hades, Zeus "made yet another (generation), the fourth, upon the fruitful earth, which was nobler and more righteous, a godlike race of hero-men who are called demigods, the race before our own, throughout the boundless earth" (156–60).[67] Like their immediate predecessors, many of the heroes died in battle, but unlike them, many were given a place by Zeus "in the islands of the blessed along the shore of deep swirling Ocean, happy heroes" (171–72). It is widely argued that Hesiod's age of heroes is intercalated between the ages of bronze and iron,[68] and it is sometimes argued that the basic myth of the four ages is

[65] Turner, "Comparative Epic and Saga," pp. 15–17. Turner suggests additionally that frequently (Iran, India, Ethiopia's *Kebra Nagast*) "major religious changes have occurred between heroic and narrative times" (p. 14); cf. Bowra, *Meaning of a Heroic Age*, p. 19, speaking of intervening political changes.

[66] Bowra, *Meaning of a Heroic Age*, p. 21.

[67] Hugh G. Evelyn-White, trans., *Hesiod, The Homeric Hymns and Homerica* (London: William Heinemann; New York: Putnam's, 1914), pp. 13–15.

[68] See T. A. Sinclair, *Hesiod. Works and Days* (1932; repr. Hildesheim: Georg Olms Verlagsbuchhandlung, 1966), p. 15; Jean Pierre Vernant, *Mythe et pensée chez les Grecs: Études de psychologie historique* (2d ed.; Paris: François Maspero, 1966), p. 20; Kirk, *Myth*, p. 233.

originally oriental,[69] or perhaps even Indo-European.[70] We need not enter the discussions concerning source and diffusion, but it is easy to imagine how an Indian Hesiod might have fashioned a five-yuga system by intercalating a "heroic age" between the Dvāpara and Kali yugas, thus saving a special niche for the heroes of the *Mahābhārata*.[71] In such configurations, no matter how many ages are conceived—and one is reminded here of the Irish device of the five invasions of the island—the "age of heroes" stands out at a pivotal juncture between a past that is essentially mythic and one that is purportedly historical. One thus meets a continuum between two ages, or really three—the mythic, the heroic, and the "historical"—so it is highly significant that the interactions between the mythic and heroic realms are so basic to the fabric of epics.

Such connections establish the starting point for our discussion, for they determine the conditions which define the heroes as heroes and thus permit the heroic age to begin. In this respect, the heroic age must be defined primarily, in its inaugural conditions, as a category related to myth, not history; but it is more than roots and "beginnings," for other features of heroic ages exhibit a mythic structure. Here I am indebted to Stig Wikander, one of whose Haskell Lectures at the University of Chicago Divinity School in the fall of 1967 dealt with the question at hand. My notes on his lecture do not allow me to represent fairly the sequence of his thinking or the range of

[69] Richard Reitzenstein, *Studien zum antiken Synkretismus aus Iran und Greichenland* (Leipzig: Teubner, 1926), pp. 45–57; see the discussion between J. Gwyn Griffiths (pro) and H. G. Baldry (con), *Journal of the History of Ideas*, XVII (1956), 109–19 (Griffiths: "Archeology and Hesiod's Five Ages"), 533–54 (Baldry: "Hesiod's Five Ages"), and XIX (1958), 91–93 (Griffiths: "Did Hesiod Invent the 'Golden Age'?").

[70] See Georges Dumézil, *Jupiter, Mars, Quirinus*, I: *Essai sur la conception indo-européenne de la société et sur les origines de Rome* (Paris: Gallimard, 1941), p. 259; and, although noncommittal, Vernant, *Mythe et pensée*, pp. 42–43. Both see a trifunctional pattern in the concerns of the gold and silver ages with justice, of the bronze and heroic with war, and of the iron with labor.

[71] But the *Rāmāyaṇa* heroes would require a sixth age!

his documentation, but I can reconstruct three of his points.

1. The idea found in Ker, the Chadwicks, Bowra, and others, that a "heroic age" is an essentially "magnificent and aristocratic"[72] feudal stage through which a society may pass (and then recall), is seriously tested by certain features of such ages in different societies. First, no grounds, other than personal conviction, can be offered for regarding the primary material of the Indian or Iranian[73] (and also the Celtic) heroic ages as historical. Second, Iceland's heroic age had no antecedent heroic society; heroic tradition was developed in peasant conditions. Some societies recall two "heroic ages," like Ireland (with its Ossianic and Ulster cycles) and India (with its two epics). And last, it is, I believe, misleading to overemphasize the "aristocratic" and "warrior" aspects of the heroic age. Both the Chadwicks and Bowra speak of priests and magic as essentially alien to the heroic milieu.[74] This view ignores the close collaboration, or at least interaction, between warriors and such figures, in various epics, as brahmins, druids, seers, poets, and wizards. Interactions between "classes" would seem, after Dumézil's research, to be an archaic feature of Indo-European societies, which their epics reflect.

2. Within heroic ages there are almost always certain anomalies which either defy historical explanation or invite it only at considerable peril. A list culled from a variety of sources yields anachronisms and temporal incongruities, impossible time sequences (the fantastic life spans of such figures as the

[72] Ker, *Epic and Romance*, p. 7.

[73] That of the pre-Achaemenid kings, which Wikander discusses in his "Sur le fonds commun indo-iranien des épopées de la Perse et de l'Inde," *NC*, I (1950), 318–22.

[74] See H. M. Chadwick, *Heroic Age*, pp. 440 and 459: a heroic age need require no more than "Mars and the Muses." Bowra, *Meaning of a Heroic Age*, sees the heroic age as aristocratic and centered on war (p. 13), an age which has freed itself from the magic and superstition which preceded it (p. 9) and which must take opposition to the "priestcraft" of later times (pp. 9, 22–24) lest its story be "mangled" like the *Mahābhārata* (p. 23).

Mahābhārata's Bhīṣma and Vyāsa, the *Shāh-nāma*'s Zal, Rostam, and Afrāsiyāb, the Celtic Fintan, the Tibetan sPyi-dpon Khra-rgyan,[75] and certain Old Testament figures), initiations, journeys, combats, trials, unusual marriages (the case of Draupadī hardly stands alone), special relations or identifications with animals (Rāma's alliance with the monkeys is not unique), and then the various features already discussed: strange births and deaths, physical and moral "monstrosities," and so on. The list is not exhaustive, nor is it meant to imply that any one of these traits is to be found in every heroic age. Such features are hardly likely to record actual historic social conditions or practices. One must perforce look elsewhere for an interpretation.

3. Often a peculiar and very striking structure is apparent in the way that heroic ages come to an end. First, although Wikander did not mention this, the heroes usually receive some special reward: as Hesiod puts it, the Greek heroes were given a place by Zeus in the "islands of the blessed." This destiny usually holds out the high, and the sometimes impossible, hope for later mortals. But with their disappearance, there often come to an end the clearly shaped (if impossible) chronology, the well-rounded narrative, and the delineated characterizations that have attended their stories. In such cases we move from the heroic age to the "dark age," a time of flux and uncertainties out of which the outlines of factual history gradually emerge in the inevitably dry form of genealogies and chronicles, royal or otherwise. Victor Turner has nicely caught the tone of this transition as it is handled in the two Greek epics: the *Odyssey*, he says, "might be compared to a long cooling-off ritual in which the heroic age passes into the com-

[75] His name means "Universal-Chief Old-Falcon"; see Stein, *Épopée et barde*, pp. 464–65, and David-Neel, *Superhuman Life of Gesar*, pp. 105–6 (calling him Chipön). Like Zal, he is born with white hair!

monplace of mere history, through the tunnel, as it were, of a liminal legend, Odysseus' narrative of his wanderings."[76]

As Wikander pointed out, Denmark, Ireland, Greece, Persia, and India (and we might add Wales[77]) all have poor historical traditions, but rich lore concerning their heroic ages. One cannot maintain that these heroic ages, and the "dark ages" that follow them, are the result of diffusion. The datelines differ too markedly. Is one then to work backward, relying on these skeletal histories when they claim some form of descent for men of later ages from the heroes of old, as if the latter's "history" was preserved—in each and every case—while all else is vague and rudimentary? Or is one to work in the other direction, starting from the assumption of a legendary heroic past in which history, when and if it plays a role, conforms largely to mythic and heroic patterns, and to which later generations would have traced their ascent artificially? The second alternative usually recommends itself. In fact, the "dark age" must also be regarded as primarily a mythic construct, no less than the heroic age on which it relies. Although in some traditions, like the Roman, the link between "heroic ages" and actual history is made rather smoothly, usually it is not, even by some of the most "historically" oriented peoples in the world. There is chronological confusion, after the clear "history" from the patriarchs down to Moses, in the books of Joshua and Judges, out of which the dynastic history of Israel gradually emerges. Or one might think of H. G. Creel's statement on the most celebrated and "heroic" dynasty of Confucian China: "For the first centuries of the Chou dynasty we have no connected history. Even the orthodox Chinese histories give only scattered anecdotes and the names and order of the kings, not attempting

[76] Turner, "Comparative Epic and Saga," p. 8.

[77] See Chadwick and Chadwick, *Growth of Literature*, I, 531: after the heroic age, "a very long period which appears to be almost blank."

a continuous narrative."[78] The Christian age of martyrs and the Buddhist first age of the dharma both ended in "darker" periods, preceding our own, when sainthood or arhatship become more and more difficult. In primitive religions, where the question of historical documents does not come up, there is still an implicit temporal gulf between the knowable present and the formative ages peopled by such heroes as the Australian totemic ancestors,[79] the heroes of American Indian legends,[80] and the so-called Dema-Divinities of Ceram and New Guinea whom Wikander, most tellingly, referred to as comparable to the heroes of the *Mahābhārata*.[81] This is not to say that historical material may not in some of these cases find a place in a heroic age, or that a dark age may not correspond to an actual falling off from some earlier more "heroic" achievements. It does say that these temporal sequences exhibit a cosmological structure that is primarily mythic, not historical, and that such sequences are found not only in societies which have had heroic pasts of the type imagined by Ker and the Chadwicks, but in societies whose heroes are totally unheroic by these scholars' standards.

[78] Herlee Glessner Creel, *The Birth of China: A Study of the Formative Period of Chinese Civilization* (New York: Ungar, 1937), p. 237.

[79] Adolphus P. Elkin, *The Australian Aborigines* (Garden City, N.Y.: Doubleday, 1964), pp. 209–10, 217, even uses the term "heroic age" to describe the time of the heroic ancestors.

[80] See Paul Radin, *Winnebago Hero Cycles: A Study in Aboriginal Literature*, Supplement to *International Journal of American Linguistics*, IV, no. 3 (Baltimore: Waverly Press, 1948), 11, and George A. Dorsey, *The Pawnee*, pt. I: *Mythology* (Washington, D.C.: Carnegie Institute, 1906), pp. 13 and 141, both authors making distinctions between myth and legend which square with those discussed by William Bascom (see above, n. 11).

[81] See Adolf Jensen, *Myth and Cult among Primitive Peoples*, Marianna Tax Choldin and Wolfgang Weissleder, trans. (Chicago: University of Chicago Press, 1963), p. 91: the Demas' effectiveness "goes back to an ancient primal past or, better, to the end of the primal past." Jensen insists on using the term "divinities" for the Dema, as they have the primary religious mythic and cultic role among the paleocultivators; but he notes that they are of the type that has "often been called tribal or culture heroes." As to Wikander's comparison, my recollection is that he was referring to the Demas' "creative deaths."

Moreover, they occur in societies with strong historical traditions (China, Tibet, Israel), weak historical traditions (the Indo-European examples cited by Wikander), and "no" historical traditions (primitives, those without written records). In other words, heroic ages and dark ages occur irrespective of history.

One may thus reasonably ask whether the ancient Indo-Europeans, before and during their migrations, had a conception of a heroic age. Dumézil, in two of his most precise and illuminating studies, has shown that certain types of epic figures, both heroes and heroines, can be traced, with their legends intact, to an Indo-European source. Such is the legend of the monstrous birth, three sins, and final annihilation attached to the names of the Scandinavian Starkadr (or Starcatherus), the Greek Heracles, and the Indian Śiśupāla; and such is the case with the Indian and Irish legends of the homonyms Mādhavī and Medb: their quadruple marriages, their dealings with their royal fathers, and with other family matters of royal concern. Indeed, in both these cases Dumézil makes the point that the stories are primarily heroic. In the first, the gods provide a discrete background drama of their own; and in the second—even in the Indian story—they barely interfere.[82]

Such illustrations of the tenacity and durability of legend,[83] coupled with the insistence that myth and epic be maintained as distinct categories in a potential continuum, might give the appearance that I am poised, with Dumézil, to move beyond the comparison of individual legends to the larger question of a common Indo-European epos. But at least up to now, Dumézil's interests and his operating assumptions have led him elsewhere. He has been eager to reconstruct a comparative

[82] See Dumézil, *ME*, II, pt. 1; pt. 3, and above, n. 29; and pt. 3, pp. 21–22, 81–95, 118–21 (Śiśupāla and company), and 361 (Mādhavī and company).

[83] See Radin's remark, *Winnebago Hero Cycles*, p. 12, that "myths" (his term: "'sacred' folktales") are less durable than legends because of the fluctuating use made of them in rituals.

Indo-European mythology, but the possibility of reconstructing Indo-European epic has only lately commanded his attention. Referring to Stig Wikander as "pioneer once again,"[84] he cites with tentative approval the latter's explorations into this area: "*A priori*, the existence of Indo-European epic themes, or more generally of an Indo-European literature, is likely [vraisemblable] . . . . The study which Wikander begins is thus full of promise."[85]

At this point, a few comparative studies, by Wikander and others, have shown that the *Mahābhārata*'s story has close analogues in other Indo-European epic traditions. Its cousins include not only the main narrative segment of the Persian *Shāh-nāma*,[86] but the Norse Battle of Brávellir recounted in the seventh and eighth books of Saxo Grammaticus' *Gesta Danorum*.[87] One cannot yet be certain how to interpret the points of contact between these stories: common origin? similar story

[84] Dumézil, *ME*, I, 255.

[85] Dumézil has also pioneered in this area; see my review article, "Comparing Indo-European 'Epics,'" *HRJ*, XV (1975), 90–100. See also the loose but informed list of parallels in S. Srikantaiya, "Asvatthaman," *QJMS*, XXI (1931), 392–95, 401–2.

[86] Wikander, "Sur le fonds commun, pp. 310–29; James Darmesteter, "Points de contact entre le Mahābhārata et le Shāh-Nāmah," *JA*, X (1887), 38–75; Arthur George Warner and Edmond Warner, trans., *The Sháhnáma of Firdausi*, Trübners Oriental Series, 7 vols. (London: Kegan Paul, Trench, Trübner, 1905–1912), IV, 129. In both epics, one finds, in the same sequence, a leading "bad" hero (Duḥśāsana, Pirān) having his blood drunk (see only Wikander); the effort by the "bad" king (Duryodhana, Afrāsiyāb) to hide in a lake after his army's defeat (see Darmesteter and Wikander); and the ascent of the "good" king (Yudhiṣṭhira, Key Khosrow) to heaven, leaving his five loyal companions behind dead or about to die (see all three authors).

[87] Wikander, "Från Bråvalla till Kurukshetra," *ANF*, LXXV (1960), 183–93; *idem*, "Germanische und Indo-Iranische Eschatologie," *Kairos*, II (1960), 83–88. In both "epics," one finds a dynastic crisis shaped by similar incidents through four generations, culminating in a war between the forces of a blind old king (Dhṛtarāṣṭra, Haraldus Hyldetan) against his nephews which the latter cannot win until they eliminate a great champion (Bhīṣma, Ubbo Fresicus) by filling his body full of arrows. Some of these points, and others too, will be pursued and extended in Chapters 5, 11, and 13 below.

types from comparable heroic ages? parallel transpositions from a lost mythology? literary borrowings? My preference for the first of these options will become clear.[88] But one point is established: comparative research shows that the *Mahābhārata* does not stand alone in the Indo-European continuum; rather, one finds stories analogous to it in striking and cumulative details. Its story, at least in some of its basic contours and episodes, may thus be very old. Indeed, it may be our best preserved "record" of the Indo-Europeans' heroic age.

[88] So too Warner and Warner on the Indo-Iranian convergences and, seemingly, Dumézil on the Indo-Scandinavian, although Wikander does not commit himself, ruling out only the second possibility. Darmesteter, ruling out the third ("Points de contact," p. 49), takes the fourth option and argues that India borrowed from Iran (pp. 51–57, 72); but Wikander shows that if it is a case of borrowing, the reverse would be more likely ("Sur le fonds commun," pp. 311–12). An argument for borrowings has also claimed the *Mahābhārata* as a source for the *Aeneid*: Madeleine Lallemand, "Une source de l'Éneide: Le Mahābhārata," *Latomus*, XVIII (1959), 262–87. However, none of the features which may link these two epics are the same as those which link the *Mahābhārata* with the others, thus leaving the argument that the latter connections derive from a common epic heritage unaffected.

CHAPTER 2

Three Kṛṣṇas: Variations on a Theme

Nearly all the great theories about the *Mahābhārata* have turned upon their authors' images of Krishna.[1] Nevertheless, a curious set of facts has so far escaped mention in critical studies. The *Mahābhārata* knows not just one Krishna; it knows three Kṛṣṇas. The nomenclature is quite emphatic. First, there is the Krishna of our title, often called by the patronymic Vāsudeva, son of the Vṛṣṇi prince Vasudeva and his wife Devakī.[2] In this chapter, as elsewhere, I shall refer to him, and him alone, by the spelling Krishna. Second, there is King Drupada's daughter Draupadī, Kṛṣṇā (long "a" is the feminine ending) being her given name at birth because of her dark or black color or complexion (*kṛṣṇābhūtsā hi varṇataḥ*; 1:155,50). Third, there is Vyāsa, his proper name also being Kṛṣṇa, or more precisely Kṛṣṇa Dvaipāyana, "the Island-born Kṛṣṇa," since his mother Satyavatī (also called Kālī, "Black") gave birth to him the very

[1] I hope to write a separate article on the history of epic- and Krish-criticism. For the present, see Chapter 4 of my dissertation, Gods, Heroes, and Kṛṣṇa, pp. 133–90.

[2] A *Kṛṣṇa Devakīputra* appears in *Chānd. Up.* 3,17,6 in conditions that neither support an identification with nor a separation from the epic figure; for the most reasonable discussion, see S. K. De, "Vedic and Epic Kṛṣṇa," *IHQ*, XVIII (1942), 297–300. As to the patronymic Vāsudeva, many have assumed no "real" Vasudeva lies behind it; there is too little to go on one way or the other; Krishna's father Vasudeva does, however, appear in the epic and cannot be a Purāṇic invention.

day of his conception on an island in the Yamunā (1:54,2; 57,69–71).[3] A fourth Kṛṣṇa, Arjuna, receives this name only through his connection with Krishna Vāsudeva in instances where, recalling their mystical identity as Nara-Nārāyaṇa,[4] the dual case is used to refer to them as "the two Kṛṣṇas" (*kṛṣṇau*).[5]

As their roles in a number of incidents will show, the "three Kṛṣṇas" have things in common. For instance, they seem to cooperate in bringing about Draupadī's foreordained marriage. Beyond this, all are incarnations of main figures in the Vaiṣṇava "pantheon." Krishna and Vyāsa incarnate Viṣṇu-Nārāyaṇa (the latter more particularly Nārāyaṇa alone[6]), and

[3] Certain authors have discussed two of the three together: Christian Lassen, *Indische Altertumskunde* (1847–1862; repr. 4 vols; Osnabrück: Otto Zeller, 1968), I, 790, on Draupadī and Vāsudeva; Auguste Barth, review of Joseph Dahlmann's *Das Mahābhārata als Epos und Rechtsbuch*, pt. 2, *JS* (1897), p. 327; see also below, n. 6.

[4] For further discussion of Arjuna and Krishna in this identity, see below, Chapter 10, at n. 23.

[5] Concerning Arjuna, in two passages which describe the Pāṇḍavas' complexions, Yudhiṣṭhira and Bhīma are said to be *gaura* ("white, fair, shining, golden") while Arjuna is *śyāma* ("black, dark"); see 15:32,5–7 and a Northern passage, *Virāṭaparvan*, 1136*, ll. 1, 7, and 11. As to the "two Krishnas," S. Sörensen, *Index to the Names in the Mahābhārata* (1904; reprinted Delhi: Motilal Banarsidass, 1963), p. 425, gives over thirty citations.

[6] For Vyāsa as an incarnation of Nārāyaṇa, see 12:334,11: "Know Kṛṣṇa Dvaipāyana Vyāsa to be the lord Nārāyaṇa" (*kṛṣṇadvaipāyanaṃ vyāsaṃ viddhi nārāyaṇam prabhum*; var.: *nārāyaṇam bhuvi*, "Nārāyaṇa on earth"), and 12:337,4c: "born a portion of Nārāyaṇa" (*nārāyaṇāṃśajam*). Madeleine Biardeau, "Etudes de mythologie hindoue: Cosmogonies purāṇiques," pt. 1 (hereinafter EMH, 1–3), *BEFEO*, LIV (1968), 35, n. 1, remarks that Vyāsa is "a sort of doublet" of Vāsudeva in the epic, often repeating what the latter says. But she makes no further comment other than to reject a derivation of Dvaipāyana from *dvipad* or *dvipada*, which could make *dvipa* a synonym of Nara; see also EMH, 2, *BEFEO*, LV (1969), 82, n. 1, and Edward Washburn Hopkins, *Epic Mythology* (1915; repr. New York: Biblo and Tannen, 1969), p. 216, n. 1, for whom Vyāsa's link with Nārāyaṇa is "the last word of the Bhāgavatas and not early epic." Although true that the identifications of Vyāsa come in the presumably late *Nārāyaṇīya* section of the *Śāntiparvan*, they are probably based on the standard epic identification of Vyāsa as the "Island-born Krishna," an identity linking him with Krishna, Draupadī, and thus Viṣṇu-Nārāyaṇa as well.

Draupadī quite emphatically incarnates Viṣṇu's consort Śrī.[7]

One is tempted to seek some means by which to interpret this triple appearance of Kṛṣṇas, for although they are not explained by any single source or coinciding structure, their common designation is surely more than fortuitous. Rather than any one interpretive framework, the "three Kṛṣṇas" evoke several. Not surprisingly, the common denominator in most of these—and I will discuss four—involves connotations of the name Kṛṣṇa: "Black."

Signs of the Times

Black is the color of the Kali yuga, the yuga which is about to come into being as the *Mahābhārata* battle brings the preceding yuga to a close. According to Purāṇic traditions, the beginning of the Kali yuga is marked, among other things, by Krishna's death.[8] More important, this is the closest one comes to an epic articulation of our theme. One of the passages describing Vyāsa's relation to Nārāyaṇa seems to link two of the "three Kṛṣṇas" to the blackness of the Kali yuga. Asked about his emanation from Nārāyaṇa, Vyāsa tells that after Nārāyaṇa had completed the "seventh creation" by emitting Brahmā from his navel (12:337,17), and after he had determined to assume his various *avatāra* forms (337,32–36), he then, from a syllable of speech [*bhoḥ*! 37; the *śloka* identifies this sound with Sarasvatī], gave birth to the ṛṣi Sarasvat, also called Apāntaratamas,[9] and commanded him to divide and arrange the Vedas (39). At the fulfillment of this command, Nārāyaṇa delegated the ṛṣi to repeat this task at each Manvantara (41). Then, nar-

[7] There is some controversy here, on which see below, Chapter 7; but the CE makes it clear that Draupadī's connection with Śrī is authentic and that an effort to connect her with Śacī, and Kṛishna's wife, Rukmiṇī, with Śrī, is an interpolation (see 1:61,5 and 566*).

[8] See F. E. Pargiter, *The Purāṇa Text of the Dynasties of the Kali Age* (1913; repr. Benares: Chowkhamba Sanskrit Series Office, 1962), p. x.

[9] See Ganguli-Roy, *Mahabharata*, X, 616, n. 1: "The name 'Apantaratamas' implies one whose darkness or ignorance has been dispelled."

rowing the time focus still further to a single Mahāyuga, Nārāyaṇa predicted that at the beginning of the Kali yuga the ṛṣi would be the progenitor of "certain descendants of Bharata named Kurus, high-souled princes celebrated on earth," among whom would erupt "a dissension in the family [*kulabheda*] having its end in their mutual destruction, without you [*tvāmṛte*].[10] . . . And when that dark yuga arrives, you will be of dark complexion" (*kṛṣṇe yuge ca samprāpte kṛṣṇavarṇo bhaviṣyasi*; 337,42–44). Nārāyaṇa added: "And you shall see me in the world armed with a discus [that is as Krishna Vāsudeva]" (337,51).

From elsewhere, we know that black is Krishna's color for the Kali yuga alone, as he had assumed the colors white, red, and yellow in the preceding yugas (*śukla*, *rakta*, *pīta*, *kṛṣṇa;* 3:148,5–37; *HV* 2:71,31; but cf. *Mbh.* 3:187,31, reversing the middle pair). It is also reasonable to think of the blackness of the third Kṛṣṇa, Draupadī—given her identity as an incarnation of Śrī and thus her mythological consolidarity with the other two—as being similarly related to a periodic coloring. The *Vāmana Purāṇa* tells us that Śrī-Lakṣmī is created in four colors—white, red, yellow, and blue (*nīla*)—mainly showing her connection with the four varṇas, but also signaling a decline in dharma similar to that involved in the course of the yugas (*Vām. P.* 49,36–39). Thus, at the very least, the blackness of the three figures seems to be a sign of the times, that is, of the arrival or onset of the Kali yuga.

Glimpses of Popular Settings and Continuations

A second frame of reference is provided primarily by ethnological considerations and is based on the fragmentary evidence gathered from early texts outside the epic and from possible

[10] Presumably this means "without you taking part in the destruction." Ganguli-Roy translate "excepting yourself," which would imply that Vyāsa was the sole survivor of the war, something the epic story will not support. Ganguli-Roy then give alternate readings; *ibid.*, p. 618, n. 3.

cult survivals. I rely here heavily on the reconstructions of Walter Ruben and Suvira Jaiswal.[11]

First, Buddhist stories in the *Jātakas* refer to each of these figures as Kaṅha (-ā), that is Kṛṣṇa (-ā). In some instances, as Ruben observes, the stories seem to be slanderous distortions of the epic material. In others they seem to rely on ancient local and cult traditions which may have influenced not only the formation of the stories, but aspects of the epic as well. *Jātaka* 536 is a case of the first type. As Ruben says, Kaṅhā (Draupadī) is introduced as an example of vice. She marries the five Pāṇḍavas out of sexual greed, and, when they are absent, she lustfully seduces her attendant, a humpbacked cripple.[12] As the scene is summarized in verse, the cripple is in addition a dwarf:

In ancient story Kaṅhā, it is said,
A single maid to five princes was wed.
Insatiate still she lusted yet for more
And with a humpbacked dwarf she played the whore.[13]

Almost certainly this extramarital passion is a distortion or confusion of the relationship of Draupadī, as Śrī incarnate, with Viṣṇu in the latter's most easily derided form: the dwarf. If so, it provides testimony that the identification of Draupadī with Śrī was known, even if it was misrepresented, in Buddhist literature dating from a relatively early period of the epic's literary formation.

A less slanderous representation is found in the *Ghata Jātaka* (*Jātaka* 454), which presents the other "two Kṛṣṇas" together

[11] See Walter Ruben, *Krishna: Konkordanz und Kommentar der Motive Seines Heldenlebens*, Istanbuler Schriften, No. 17 (Istanbul: n. pub., 1944), pp. 60, 66–68, 249–51, 280; Suvira Jaiswal, *Origin and Development of Vaiṣṇavism* (Delhi: Munshiram Manoharlal, 1967), pp. 65–68.

[12] Ruben, *Krishna*, pp. 250–51; see Edward Byles Cowell, ed., *The Jātaka; or, Stories of the Buddha's Former Births* (6 vols.; Cambridge: Cambridge University Press, 1895–1907), V, 225–28.

[13] Cowell, *Jātaka*, p. 225.

in a drama that also involves a sister of Kaṅha Vāsudeva named Añjanadevī. Jaiswal refers to the latter as "the black goddess,"[14] *añjana* being a word for black pigment or collyrium. Here, although Ruben sees the story not as the kernel of Krishna Vāsudeva's biography but a work of "polemical, malicious origin,"[15] there is material of interest. The story concludes with the fulfillment of the prophecy of the destruction of Dvārakā, an episode found in the *Mausalaparvan* of the *Mahābhārata*. But the two accounts differ. After his advice has helped Kaṅha Vāsudeva capture Dvārakā, Kaṅhadīpāyana (Kṛṣṇa Dvaipāyana) takes a place held in the epic (see *Mbh.* 16:2,4–10) by three other ṛṣis: it is he who is taunted and insulted by the Vṛṣṇi youths (here the sons of the ten brothers), one of whom dresses up as a pregnant woman; they ask the sage what kind of fruit or offspring "she" will bring forth. Seeing that this is his moment to die, Kaṅhadīpāyana prophesies that the masquerade will result in the destruction of the family. The youths murder the visionary. His ashes are thrown into the river, but certain plants emerge from them and turn into clubs which at a festival slay everyone except Kaṅha Vāsudeva, Baladeva (Balarāma), Añjanadevī, and their chaplain.

Thus with no parallel in the *Mahābhārata* (where one never hears of Vyāsa's death), the death of Kaṅhadīpāyana is linked with that of Kaṅha Vāsudeva (who dies after the festival) and with the destruction of the latter's family. As to Añjanadevī, who is born to Devagabbhā (?Devakī), before her marriage to an adventuresome figure named Upasāgara,[16] she figures as

[14] Jaiswal, *Origin and Development*, p. 68.

[15] Ruben, *Krishna*, p. 250, with full summary, pp. 249–51.

[16] He replaces (?) Vasudeva; see above, n. 2. Having been expelled from his older brother's kingdom for intrigues in the latter's zenana, he comes to Kaṃsa's realm where he sees Devagabbhā (who is imprisoned to prevent her from bearing a son), bribes her maidservant Nandagopā to gain him entry to her tower, where the two conceive Añjanadevī. Ruben sees all this as a Buddhist denigration of Vāsudeva, whose parents will of course be these same two lovers.

the elder sister of her ten legitimate brothers. In place of one of the brothers, she takes charge of one-tenth of the earth over which the brothers have established sovereignty. She alone survives the final catastrophe.

Jaiswal views Añjanadevī as a variant name for a strange figure in the family of Krishna and Balarāma. This is Ekānaṃśā, another older "sister," the girl born to Nanda and Yaśodā in the cow settlement who is exchanged for Krishna to protect him from Kaṃsa at birth.[17] Once exchanged, her part in the usual story is brief: dashed against a stone by Kaṃsa, she rises into the sky to announce Krishna's birth and to predict Kaṃsa's destruction.[18] The name Ekānaṃśā, meaning "she alone who is without a portion," or "the single portionless one" (M-W), has been variously explained. Ruben suggests "she who was no portion (of Viṣṇu's)."[19] Another explanation stresses her "blackness" (Jaiswal refers to her as "the black goddess Ekānaṃśā"[20]): hers is a name for Kuhū (*Mbh.* 3:208,8), the dark invisible moon on the first day of the new moon; and this may be related to the *Harivaṃśa's* notion that Ekānaṃśā is an incarnation of Viṣṇu's *yoganidrā*, the yogic sleep which lasts for a "night of Brahmā."[21] In any case, Jaiswal shows that in popular and local traditions, Ekānaṃśā was identified, or at least grouped, with the dark heroine of the *Mahābhārata*. A variant name for Ekānaṃśā in certain Purāṇas is Ekādaśā (the "Eleventh," probably recalling the *Jātaka* tradition of her having ten brothers). According to the *Lalitavistara*, Ekādaśā is "a goddess living in the west, along with seven other goddesses, such as Alumbuśā, Kṛṣṇā, Draupadī, etc."[22] The association with

[17] See Jaiswal, *Origin and Development*, pp. 66–67, and Ruben, *Krishna*, pp. 66–67, citing *Harivaṃśa* 59, 8–49; see M. N. Dutt, trans., *A Prose English Translation of Harivaṃśa* (Calcutta: Elysium Press, 1897), pp. 255–57.

[18] *Harivaṃśa* 59,39–42; she is four-armed and clad in dark blue.

[19] Ruben, *Krishna*, p. 67.

[20] Jaiswal, *Origin and Development*, p. 67.

[21] *Ibid.*, p. 66; see *Harivaṃśa* 59,10.

[22] Jaiswal, *Origin and Development*, p. 66; see Ph. Ed. Foucaux, trans.,

the west may indicate Dvārakā. However, Ekānaṃśā's fate seems to have been an increasing absorption into the cults and identities of Durgā and Śrī.[23]

One thus has a means of glimpsing—often through Buddhist sources—the kinds of links that were sometimes forged or perceived between the epic figures and extraepic, often popular, traditions. In some respects the three Kṛṣṇas are more closely associated with each other in these sources than they are in the epic: just as Krishna's birth is marked by the birth, self-sacrifice, and prophesies of his black "sister," his death is marked by the self-sacrificing death and prophesies of Kaṅhadīpāyana.

This does not imply, however, that the nominal blackness of each of these figures would always have the same meaning. Here, our only good index is provided by the female member of the triad.[24] As Madeleine Biardeau has pointed out, the blackness of Draupadī and her link with Śrī call to mind the

---

Le Lalita Vistara, *Annales du Musée Guimet*, VI and XIX (Paris: Leroux, 1884–1892), Chapter 24, verse 137 (VI, 324), giving "Kṛṣṇā-Draupadī" as one of seven "daughters of the gods," all of whom are included in the lengthy charm by which the Buddha, having just accepted food from two merchants seven weeks after his enlightenment, calls for the protection of the merchants by the gods, goddesses, constellations, etc., of the four directions. Draupadī is today also a goddess in South India, called "Drowpathi-Amman" or "Panchali-Amman." At her temples, however, I was told either that she is not called Krishnai (Kṛṣṇā), or that the name is used because she was a devotee of Lord Krishna. On wooden festival idols her skin is painted pink, unlike Krishna's and Arjuna's.

[23] Jaiswal, *Origin and Development*, p. 68.

[24] Krishna's blackness is also pointed up in Tamil Śaṅgam literature where he is named Mayon or Mayavan, "the Black One"; see Bhagwansingh Suryavanshi, *The Abhiras: Their History and Culture* (Baroda: Maharaja Sayajirao University, 1962), p. 72. As to triads, the three Krishnas must not be confused with another triad, two brothers plus a woman, especially their sister or wife, such as is found with Vāsudeva, Balarāma, and Subhadrā or with Rāma, Lakṣmaṇa, and Sītā. As both Ruben (*Krishna*, pp. 59–61) and Jaiswal (*Origin and Development*, pp. 127–28) suggest, this type of triad may recall very early cultic and legendary traditions such as culminate (or survive?) in the cult of Jagannātha at Purī.

connection of both with the "prosperity" of the "black" earth.[25] But I insist that this is not the primary sense in which Draupadī and Śrī are related in the epic.[26] If earthy blackness and odor were the dominant features of Draupadī's divine antecedents, the epic poets would have done better to have made her an incarnation of Viṣṇu's other wife, the goddess Earth, Bhūdevī.

Red, White, and Black

A third approach to the "three Kṛṣṇas" may perhaps get us closer still to the symbolism of their common color, but the degree of speculation is higher than heretofore. It is suggested by G. J. Held's conception of a triadic circulatory marriage system in the epic, a system which he also sees reflected in the triads of the *trimūrti* and the three *guṇas*.[27] One may agree with Held that this latter pair of groupings is related,[28] and, moreover, that the triadic relationship that exists between the epic's dominant "families"—the "phratry"-like pair of the Pāṇḍavas and Kurus, and the "mediating" third group, the Yādavas—bears a similar structure.

[25] See Biardeau, "Brāhmaṇes et potiers," Article liminaire, *Annuaire de l'EPHE*, LXXXIX (1971–1972), 40–41; *idem*, *Clefs*, p. 187; in the former she notes that both Indian myths and Vaiśeṣika philosophy attribute blackness and odor to the earth—qualities shared by Kṛṣṇā-Draupadī and Vyāsa's mother Satyavatī or Kālī ("Black") and the latter's son Vyāsa (for whose smell, *gandha*, see *Mbh.* 1:99,42–43). Throughout India, of course, goddesses are frequently associated with blackness, not the least Kālī herself, but also South Indian goddesses (among whom one finds Draupadī; see above, n. 22) who, in some cases (Mundla Mudamme, Kulagollamma) are associated with black stones; see Wilber Theodore Elmore, *Dravidian Gods in Modern Hinduism*; *A Study of Local Village Deities in Southern India*, University Studies, X, no. 1 (Lincoln: University of Nebraska, 1915), 69 and 74.

[26] See above, n. 7, and below, Chapter 7: their connection through the theme of "royal prosperity."

[27] See Garrett Jan Held, *The Mahābhārata: An Ethnological Study* (London and Amsterdam, 1935), pp. 58–59, 70, 160, 170, 223–24.

[28] See Biardeau, EMH, 1, pp. 40–42; as is well known, Viṣṇu is linked with *sattva*, Brahmā with *rajas*, Śiva with *tamas*.

In the societal groupings, Held sees the basic triadic system as infinitely extendable.[29] Other families and their members may be involved, particularly in the "mediating" position. This would seem to apply to the Pāñcālas and in particular to Draupadī, for the latter, both in her Svayaṃvara (marriage rite by "Self-Choice") and in the dice game, is a figure who stands between the two sides, offering and presenting judgments on both. In the former case, she chooses the Pāṇḍava Arjuna over a host of suitors, including the Kaurava Duryodhana. In the other, she stands in the assembly hall amid her husbands and the Kauravas, provides the arguments by which it becomes moot whether Yudhiṣṭhira, the oldest Pāṇḍava, has truly gambled her away, and thus saves the day for her husbands.

Concerning this propensity to mediate, what is true of Kṛṣṇā Draupadī is true of the "three Kṛṣṇas." Where stress and opposition, as well as rituals and games, occur between the two "phratries," at least one of the "three Kṛṣṇas" is usually in a position to mediate between them. In fact, all three have their key moments. Along with Draupadī rescuing the Pāṇḍavas from the Kurus at the dice game, we find Krishna representing the Paṇḍavas' cause to the Kurus on his "peace mission,"[30] and Vyāsa (along with Nārada) "standing" between the missiles of Arjuna and Aśvatthāman (insofar as the latter represents the Kurus), saving the three worlds and ultimately, with additional help from Krishna, the Kuru-Pāṇḍava line.[31]

It is not, however, just a matter of three "black" mediators, but of a wider color symbolism, for, as I will insist again later,[32] the *Mahābhārata* has dressed a number of prominent themes in rich and suggestive hues. I have already mentioned color associations that pertain to the yugas and *varṇas*. Here, however, we are concerned with one of the "circulatory" triads men-

[29] See Held, *Ethnological Study*, p. 58: all that's needed is at least three clans.

[30] See Chapter 6 below.

[31] See Chapter 12 below.

[32] See below, Chapter 10, following n. 79.

tioned by Held in connection with the epic "families": the three *guṇas*. Well-known color associations belong to these three "strands" of matter (*prakṛti*), of which *sattva*, linked with lucidity, is white; *rajas*, dynamic energy, is red; and *tamas*, the tendency toward entropy, is black.

Now there is evidence, unfortunately somewhat tenuous on one point, that these same three colors are associated with the two phratries and their three mediators. As the latter are definitely black, the Pāṇḍavas are most readily connected with the color white and the Kauravas, perhaps distantly, with the color red. With the exception of Arjuna—who, despite his name ("White, Silver"), is described as dark[33]—the Pāṇḍavas' connection with whiteness seems to stem initially from their father Pāṇḍu, whose name means "Pale" or "White." In the text itself, however, I have located only one passage where a red-white contrast appears, and unfortunately it is somewhat ambiguous. With battle looming, Karṇa tells Krishna of a vision he has had in which he saw the Pāṇḍavas dressed in white turbans (*śvetoṣṇiṣaḥ*) and white garments (*śuklavāsasaḥ*; 5:141,28), and, on Duryodhana's side, either "all the kings" (*sarve . . . pārthivāḥ*; Northern recension) or "all the Kauravas" (*. . . kauravaḥ*; Southern recension) dressed in red turbans (*raktoṣṇiṣaḥ*; 141,39). In the passage itself, these colors seem to denote the survivors (white) and the slain (red) in the upcoming battle, as all the other survivors but Krishna—Sātyaki (36), Aśvatthāman, Kṛpa, Kṛtavarman (39)—are envisioned, along with the Pāṇḍavas, in white apparel. But the Southern recension's insistence that it is the Kauravas in particular, and their army only in general, whose headgear is red may rely on a long tradition. Alfred Ludwig first suggested a red-white opposition, backing up his association of the Kurus with red by showing that the name "*kuru*" itself sometimes carries the connotation "red."[34] Related symbolisms are

[33] See above, n. 5.

[34] Ludwig, "Über die mythische grundlage des Mahābhārata," *SKBGW*, Classe für Philosophie, Geschichte, und Philologie (1895), p. 4; cf. Held,

sometimes found in adaptations of the *Mahābhārata* story to drama: the South Indian Kathakali dances and the Indonesian shadow puppet theater, the Wayang Kulit or, as it concerns the epics, the Wayang Purva.[35]

Clearly, one cannot attribute such epic colorations simply to the model of the three *guṇas*. As Victor Turner has shown; the *guṇas* themselves seem to be an Indian philosophical utilization of a far more archaic and universal systematization of a basic color triad.[36] Turner's study of the symbolism of these colors in African and other cultures may help us to appreciate some of the connotations of blackness as a term in this triad, and, in turn, to interpret some of the meanings of the blackness of the "three Krishnas" in their roles as mediators between the representatives of the two other hues.

Ethnological Study, p. 297 and n. 1. Ludwig cites a Kuruvarṇaka people mentioned in some Northern manuscripts (see CE notes to 6:10,15), taking their name as "'kuru'-colored"; he also cites *kurupiśaṅgila* (a color mixed from "*kuru*" and yellow); *kuruvaka* (red amaranth); *kuruvinda*, *kuruvilva* (or *-bilva*; ruby); *kuruṅga* ("bloodshot eye"), and other compounds. See also the plate facing p. 121 of the CE *Bhīṣmaparvan* depicting the *Bhagavad Gītā* scene where the dark Arjuna and Krishna converse between white- and red-clad armies.

[35] On Kathakali colors, see Clifford R. Jones and Betty True Jones, *Kathakali: An Introduction to the Dance-Drama of Kerala* (San Francisco: American Society for Eastern Arts, 1970), pp. 23–35. According to them, the basic triad is white-red-black (p. 35), with other colors—especially green for good heroes—in permutations. On Wayang Purwa, see especially H. Ulbricht, *Wayang Purwa: Shadows of the Past* (Kuala Lumpur: Oxford University Press, 1970), p. 36: "Red, black, white and gold predominate. . . . Red symbolizes opposition to the cosmic order, black and white that the body is under the control of a mind which is reconciled with the universe, and gold stands for the splendour of youth. . . . The difference between black and white seems to be that black, the color of the ascetics, indicates harmony with the other world while white, the color of noble warriors, expresses righteousness on earth."

[36] Turner, *The Forest of Symbols* (Ithaca: Cornell University Press, 1967), pp. 85–86 (the *guṇas*) and 90: "Since the experiences the three colors represent are common to all mankind, we do not have to invoke diffusion to explain their wide distribution. We do have to invoke diffusion to explain why other colors . . . are ritually important in certain cultures."

Turner's main contention is that the three colors owe their universality to their ability to "epitomize the main kinds of universal human organic experience"[37]: white associated with milk, semen, life; red with blood and thus with both childbirth (life) and bloodshed (death); black with cessation of consciousness ("black out"), death, and sometimes (although rarely explicitly) feces and urine. These psychobiological experiences are then the basis for a wide fan of related social and cosmic referents which appear in rituals, myths, speculations, and so on.[38]

As regards the particular colors, Turner indicates that although a brief summary of the Ndembu material would identify whiteness as positive, redness as ambivalent, and blackness as negative, the latter color is highly multivalent. "Black is very often the neglected member of the triad" (p. 79), and, according to Turner, "its very absence may be significant since it is the true emblem of the hidden, the secret, the dark, the unknown—and perhaps also of potentiality as opposed to actuality" (pp. 81, 73). Along these lines, Turner shows that when the triad is reduced to dyads, white/black oppositions occur predominantly in abstract, conceptualized contexts while white/red oppositions occur most often in concrete, actual, ritual situations. Moreover, "Where a twofold classification of things as 'white' or 'red' develops, with black either absent or hidden, it sometimes happens that red acquires many of the negative and undesirable attributes of blackness, without retaining its better ones" (p. 80). And finally, in a specific instance, he mentions that blackness (alluvial mud as a symbol of love) "may repre-

[37] *Ibid.*, p. 88.

[38] Turner contends that life-crisis rituals provide the primary context in which these colors are applied, but one will note that the Ndembu root their ritual usage of the colors in the myth that the rivers of the three colors have their source in the High God Nzambi (*ibid.*, pp. 61–62,68). It thus does not seem necessary to take myth (or for that matter legend) as a secondary elaboration.

sent the cessation of hostilities between two intermarrying groups."[39]

When we turn to the *Mahābhārata*, all these remarks are highly suggestive. One thinks immediately of the hiddenness and mysteriousness of Vyāsa, who, setting his mind on asceticism, disappears into the forest at the moment of his birth, telling his mother Satyavatī-Kālī that he will appear when she needs him (1:57,70–71); he mysteriously reappears throughout the narrative in complicated and threatening situations. There are also two "significant absences" of Krishna, to be discussed in later chapters.[40] And all "three Krishnas" serve in various situations to "represent" (through marriage, counsel, consolation, embassies, and so on) the cessation of hostilities between the two groups.

Still more significant, however, is Turner's observation of a contrast between the "actual" and the "potential." The actual war between the Pāṇḍavas and the Kurus, between the white and the "red," confronts the two groups as a dyad in which the latter, the ambivalent Kurus,[41] "acquire many of the negative and undesirable attributes of blackness." But in the hidden, mysterious workings of the "three Kṛṣṇas" are the potential, the resources, to bring the conflict to cessation, whether through peace or, as happens, through war. More particularly, the "three Kṛṣṇas" have a common ability to turn moments of stress and conflict, where the Kurus and/or adharma appear to be on the verge of triumph, into scenes of victory for the Pāṇḍavas and "subtle dharma," *sūkṣmo dharmaḥ*.[42] Dharma in such

[39] *Ibid.*, pp. 71–81. Among ambiguities, black may represent sexual passion, p. 73 (a note worth pondering for Krishna scholars).

[40] See below, Chapters 4 and 12.

[41] The "inversionist" theories of the epic, associated with uncle-nephew team of the two Adolf Holtzmanns, sought to explain the ambiguous character of such "noble foes" as Duryodhana and Karṇa by supposing that the "original epic" favored their "party."

[42] For instance, most clearly in the actions of Draupadī in the dice game, of Vāsudeva in the battle, and of Vyāsa in justifying Draupadī's marriage.

instances is always "subtle," hidden, and ambiguous: the three Kṛṣṇas, by representing, using, and expressing this subtlety, thus represent the potential for restoring dharma out of adharma, even by the apparent use of the latter. It can thus be no coincidence that all three are incarnations of the "family of Viṣṇu," the god who appears, from yuga to yuga, to restore dharma (*Bhagavad Gītā* 4,8). Also significant is their triple appearance at a turning of the ages, between two yugas, in a sort of "liminal" time during which dharma and adharma are in a state of flux. In this context their blackness can signify a restoration of dharma, perhaps provisional, and, as the first section of this chapter suggested, an anticipation of the dark age to come.

Vaiṣṇava Triads

A final approach to the "three Kṛṣṇas" concerns their number. Dumézil has drawn attention to an analogous situation: India knows three Rāmas.[43] Dumézil has not gone out on any limbs to interpret this fact, as there is nothing to suggest that the three Rāmas form a coherent structure on their own. But his frame of reference, his hint at what such a structure might be, is roughly trifunctional: Paraśurāma, "Rāma with the Axe," is a brahmin; Rāma Dāśaratha, the Dharmarāja of the *Rāmāyaṇa*, is a kṣatriya; and Balarāma, Krishna Vāsudeva's brother, is the plow-bearing, wine-drinking hero widely recognized for his associations with agriculture.[44] This is also their order of appearance.

The "three Rāmas" share certain traits, at least in essentials, with the "three Kṛṣṇas." First, whereas the latter are all in-

[43] Dumézil, *Destiny of the Warrior*, p. 72; *ME*, I, 113. The first to call attention to this triad of Rāmas seems to have been Hermann Jacobi, *Das Rāmāyaṇa* (Bonn, 1893), p. 135; see S. N. Ghosal, trans., *The Rāmāyaṇa: Das Rāmāyaṇa of Dr. Hermann Jacobi* (Baroda: Oriental Institute, 1960), pp. 100–1. Jacobi argues unconvincingly that Rāma Dāśaratha and Balarāma are eastern and western variant forms of Indra.

[44] See Hopkins, *Epic Mythology*, pp. 12, 203, 212; Jaiswal, *Origin and Development*, pp. 51–60.

carnations of Viṣṇu's "household," the former are all more specifically *avatāras* of Viṣṇu himself. The major difference is that whereas the "three Kṛṣṇas" appear synchronically, all in the same time span, the three Rāmas appear separately, scheduling themselves diachronically, in different yugas, in accord with the *avatāra* doctrine. Second, and still more intriguing, as Jacobi points out: "The word Rāma means 'black,' 'dark colored' in the Veda, but in the classical Sanskrit—'delightful,' 'lovely.'[45] One can only wonder at this coincidence. As far as I know, the second connotation always predominates in the descriptions of Rāma Dāśaratha, but it is certainly possible that the older meaning, or a combination of the two meanings, may have provided the three Rāmas with their original names.

Admitting the danger of interpreting one mute or unstated structure by referring it to another, certain coincidences do occur, for possibly in both cases there is a residual trifunctional symbolism reflected in the disposition of Viṣṇu or his "household" to be apportioned in such threesomes. In fact, in the case of the "three Kṛṣṇas," a trifunctional interpretation suggests itself as easily as in that of the "three Rāmas": Vyāsa is a brahmin and a ṛṣi-poet (*sūta*), the highest exemplar of "Vedic" teaching; Vāsudeva is a kṣatriya; and Draupadī, in addition to being a woman, is Śrī, "Prosperity" incarnate, affiliated with the "black" earth.[46]

Each of these threesomes would thus seem to represent a totality. The central figures in whom Viṣṇu incarnates himself (Rāma Dāśaratha, Krishna—both kṣatriyas) are flanked by mysterious satellites who complement them, whether their tasks be performed simultaneously or at different times. The characterization by the functions is admittedly loose and provisional,[47]

[45] Jacobi, *The Rāmāyaṇa*, p. 100, n. 74.

[46] See above, n. 25.

[47] It is worth noting, however, that neither with the Rāmas nor the Kṛṣṇas can the three identifications be reduced to caste: neither Balarāma nor Draupadī is a *vaiśya*.

and I do not wish to go further on this limb than Dumézil. But it may possibly explain not only why the three Kṛṣṇas are black, but why they are three. It also presents an appropriate arrangement whereby Viṣṇu, the god associated with the restoration of dharma, can appear, along with his consort Śrī, in forms that are related to three traditional zones of dharmic activity.

PART TWO

BEFORE THE WAR

CHAPTER 3

The Marriage of Draupadī

The epic Krishna becomes more tangible as we move to some of the episodes in which he appears. Mine is not the first attempt to follow his involvement from scene to scene, but I believe the paths my few predecessors have taken have either covered unyielding terrain or gone off in thin air. First are those—led by Hopkins and Tadpatrikar—who have sought out only what they judged to be of historical plausibility.[1] Second are those—led by Walter Ruben—who have envisioned an epic originally without Krishna and sought to show Krishna's superfluousness to the "main story."[2] This second fancy must occasionally be dispelled, and nowhere is there a better starting point than Krishna's first *Mahābhārata* appearance: his presence—declared "unnecessary" by Ruben because he comes only to watch, not to participate[3]—at Draupadī's wedding ceremony, her Svayaṃvara or "Self-Choice."

This status as a spectator is not insignificant. First let us recount the events that set the background for the Svayaṃvara

[1] See Hopkins, *Epic Mythology*, pp. 215–16; Tadpatrikar, "The Krishna Problem," *ABORI*, X (1929), 269–343.

[2] See Ruben, *Krishna*, especially pp. 282–84, anticipated in his views by Hermann Jacobi, "Incarnation (Indian)," *ERE*, VII, 195, and Hermann Oldenberg, *Das Mahābhārata: Seine Entstehung, sein Inhalt, seine Form* (Göttingen: Bandenhoed & Ruprecht, 1922), p. 42. For an impassioned denunciation of such guttings of the epic, see Vishnu S. Sukthankar, *Mahābhārata*, pp. 94–95.

[3] Ruben, *Krishna*, p. 283.

scene. The childhood and adolescent conflicts between the Kurus and Pāṇḍavas have just come to a head in the lacquer house episode, in which Duryodhana's scheme to burn the Pāṇḍavas and Kuntī in this firetrap has been foiled. To prevent news of their escape and thus forestall further attempts on their lives, they travel disguised as brahmins, or more exactly as *brahmacārins*, and settle in a brahmin's house in the town of Ekacakrā. There, on two occasions (1:153 and 157), they hear—the second time from Vyāsa—about the upcoming wedding ceremony of Draupadī, the princess of Pāñcāla. Intrigued, they make their way to the capital of this kingdom and take up residence where their concealment may be maintained: in the "atelier" of a potter (*kumbhakārasya śālāyām*; 1:176,6) of the Bhārgava line (182,1; 183,2; 184,1).[4]

Draupadī's marriage to the Pāṇḍavas has provided one of the most important keys to the Wikander-Dumézil analysis of the epic, for Draupadī complements this trifunctional team of brothers in a way reminiscent of several Indo-European goddesses.[5] Some of the issues raised by these two authors will be discussed in Chapter 7, but here, where the focus is more directly on Krishna, let us note an observation by Biardeau: Draupadī's marriage to five husbands is "the result of an intervention by Śiva."[6] This is true of both of the stories known to the epic which account for her multiple marriage.[7] In one case, as Vyāsa tells it twice (1:157,6–14; 189,41–49), Draupadī, in a

[4] Biardeau's interpretation of this curious scene is most suggestive: in their present condition, the Pāṇḍavas embody the union of the *brahman* and the *kṣatra* powers, a condition also found in legends about members of the Bhārgava *gotra* and in the cult of the South Indian god AiyaNār-Śāstā who is served by potter-priests; see "Brāhmaṇes et potiers," pp. 31–37, 45–55.

[5] See Dumézil, *JMQ*, IV, 50–52 (translating Wikander's study) and 75–76; also *idem*, *ME*, I, 103–24.

[6] Biardeau, "Brāhmaṇes et potiers," p. 38 (my translation). Dumézil minimizes Śiva's importance here; see *ME*, I, 111, and below, Chapter 7.

[7] *Mārk. P.* knows another version which omits Śiva, which Dumézil thinks is older: *ME*, I, 113–16. But the *Mahābhārata* is consistent in relating her to Śiva; 18:4,10 speaks of her as *nirmitā śūlapāṇinā*, "fashioned by the holder of the trident" (that is, by Śiva); see also below, Chapter 7.

former life, was an anxious maiden whose repeated requests for a husband were granted by Śiva to the number (five) of her entreaties.[8] In the other (1:189,1–39), also recounted by Vyāsa, it was as Śrī herself that, in a most curious scene, she witnessed the subjugation by the dice-playing Śiva of five Indras, and, when the latter obtained Śiva's agreement to let them take birth as "five Indras among men" (the Pāṇḍavas), she (Śrī) was appointed by Śiva to be their human wife (Draupadī).

Biardeau draws these two scenes together. In both accounts, she points out, the adharmic side of Draupadī's irregular marriage is initiated by Śiva: "When Śiva intervenes and breaks the rules of the ideal society, it is always with an eye to destruction, but a destruction necessary to the renewal of the world."[9] In the legend of the overanxious maiden, it is Śiva's insistence on the polyandric marriage that introduces the adharmic note; and in the myth of the five Indras, it is his intoxication with dice that not only sets up the conditions for the marriage but links the marriage symbolically with (a) the dice game between the Kurus and Pāṇḍavas, and (b) the course of the yugas—the names for which are those of different dice throws—which in themselves comprise a steady waning of dharma.[10] Against this background, let us now follow Krishna through the Svayaṃvara episode. Śiva is not alone in working behind the scene.

Krishna first appears when Dhṛṣṭadyumna, Draupadī's brother, calls the roll of those present at the Svayaṃvara. Krishna is there with his kinsmen (177,16–17), and when Dhṛṣṭadyumna completes his announcements, he does not exclude Krishna when he says to Draupadī: "These and many others . . . have come for the purpose of obtaining you" (177, 21). As the scene develops, it is said that the limbs of all were

[8] The Southern recension has the story told a third time; see V. S. Sukthankar, "Prolegomena" to *Ādiparvan*, (Critical Edition), p. xxxix, and *Ādiparvan*, Appendix I, no. 100.

[9] Biardeau, "Brāhmaṇes et potiers," p. 38 (my translation).

[10] Summarizing *ibid.*, p. 38, n. 4.

overcome by the god of love (*saṃkalpajenāpi pariplutāṅgāḥ*; 178,3), making them rise up in unison with the words "Kṛṣṇā [Draupadī] shall be mine" (*ibid.*). But is Krishna really among those who are so affected, and is he really a suitor? The words of Walter Ruben are instructive: Krishna comes "without doing anything on his own, but as a spectator."[11] Indeed, in this status of "spectator" Krishna is "in action" for the first time.

In the first words to describe Krishna and Balarāma, it is said that, along with their kinsmen, they "made a viewing" (*prekṣāṃ sma cakrur*; 178,8) of the scene. In this posture, they are distinguished from the "other various sons and grandsons of kings with [their] inner natures, minds, and eyes set on Kṛṣṇā" (*anye tu nānānṛpaputrapautrāḥ kṛṣṇāgatairnetramanaḥsvabhāvaiḥ*; 178,11). But if Krishna and his kinsmen are the only ones not obsessed by the sight of her, their gaze wanders to something else that interests them greatly: it is their first sight of the Pāṇḍavas. Krishna is the first to see beneath their brahmin disguises. He meditates upon them (*pārthān pradadhyau*; 178,9) and then informs Rāma who, "having surveyed [*nirīkṣya*] them slowly and gradually, looked back at Janārdana pleased in mind" (178,10). These various emphases on "sight" (see also 180, 17–22) certainly support the view that Krishna is a spectator, not a participant, at the Svayaṃvara. Nor is he mentioned as one of those who attempts to string the bow that must be shot to win Draupadī's hand.

Krishna's spectator role does not, however, mark him as an extraneous figure. First one is reminded of Held's notion that there is a circulatory clan relationship in which Krishna and the Yādavas are mediators between the Pāṇḍavas and the Kurus.[12] Here, on the one side, Arjuna is successful in stringing the bow, on the other Duryodhana, although he is not mentioned as one of those to take a turn with it, is the first named by Dhṛṣṭadyumna in his roll call of those who have come to seek

[11] Ruben, *Krishna*, p. 283 (my translation).
[12] See above, Chapter 2 at nn. 27 and 28.

Draupadī's hand (177,1). This scene thus finds its place among others where Krishna appears betwixt and between the two sides and in inactive, nonparticipant roles.[13] Nonetheless, he is always able to maintain his favoritism for Arjuna and the Pāṇḍavas. The scene brings up a problem of myth and epic: if Viṣṇu's consort is Śrī-Lakṣmī, what is Krishna's relationship with Draupadī, Śrī incarnate, who is now about to marry Krishna's closest ally (or allies) and who maddens everyone with desire except Krishna himself—and his kinsmen? To untangle this second matter takes us back to the role of Śiva.

After Arjuna has succeeded with the bow where all others have failed, and after Arjuna and Bhīma—still disguised—have fought off all the assembled kṣatriyas who are outraged that Draupadī should be a brahmin's prize, Krishna intercedes: "He caused those lords of earth to be restrained, saying: 'She has been won righteously' [*dharmena labdheti*], thus conciliating them all" (181,32). Hearing his appeasing words, all the wonder-struck (*vismitāḥ*) kings stop their fighting and abruptly return to their respective realms (181,33). We are told that the wrath of the kings and princes against King Drupada for slighting them by bestowing his daughter on a brahmin was justified by a precept of *śruti*: "The Svayaṃvara is for kṣatriyas" (180,6). But Krishna, thanks to his secret recognition of the Pāṇḍavas (this is again stressed just before his statement; 181,32ab), is able to say: "She has been won in accordance with dharma." He is, of course, correct, and his authority, in this instance, goes unchallenged.

So far, however, Krishna sanctions only the first stage in Draupadī's marriage; it only concerns Draupadī and Arjuna. The crucial test of dharma is the "adharmic" situation instigated by Śiva: the polyandric marriage. And on this troublesome point, when it comes to those who justify and approve, we

[13] Krishna is "placed" between the two sides when he awakens from his sleep to find Duryodhana and Arjuna requesting his aid in battle (see below, Chapter 5), in his "peace mission" (see below, Chapter 6), in the *Bhagavad Gītā*'s setting, and, in general, in his noncombatant status during the war.

meet a most interesting group. First, as we have seen and as Biardeau has stressed, Vyāsa continually delivers the stories of Śiva's decree—first to the "dharmic" Pāṇḍavas and then to Drupada—as a "just" imposition. In this, says Biardeau, there is nothing illogical: "Vyāsa, one of the two epic incarnations of Nārāyaṇa, is justly indicated to transmit the message and answer for this act of shocking appearance: he represents the positive and reconstructive phase of this restoration of the social order, of which Śiva symbolizes the destructive phase."[14] But this is not all. In the richer and, in my view, most important of the stories justifying the marriage—the myth of the five Indras—it is not simply a matter of Śiva decreeing that Śrī will have the five "Indras among men" as her terrestrial husbands. As soon as he has so "ordained" [*vyadadhāt*]: "The god [Śiva] then, indeed together with them [presumably the five Indras *and* Śrī[15]] went to the immeasurable [*apramemayam*] Nārāyaṇa; and he [Viṣṇu-Nārāyaṇa] also ordained [*vyadadhāt*] all this. Then all took birth on earth" (189,30).

The verb *vi-dhā-*, used here in connection with both Śiva and Viṣṇu, has many connotations, and it seems likely that whereas Śiva's part is simply to "ordain," Viṣṇu's is more complex. Monier-Williams gives six basic, nonspecialized meanings for the verb, the first five of which are: (1) to distribute, apportion, grant; (2) furnish, supply; (3) put in order, arrange; (4) ordain, enjoin; (5) form, create. Do we then view Nārāyaṇa as "granting" that this may happen, even "bestowing" or "supplying" his own wife to the five Indras? Does he "apportion" the others' lots (excepting Śiva's)? Does he put in order, even "form" or "create,"[16] where Śiva has initiated disorder and destruction? I doubt that one can totally dismiss any of these possibilities,

[14] Biardeau, "Brāhmaṇes et potiers," p. 39 (my translation).

[15] Ganguli-Roy, *Mahābhārata*, I, *Adi Parva*, 418, takes *tair* as referring only to the Indras, but what follows implies that Śrī is present too, being among the *sarve* ("all") who take birth on earth.

[16] The related substantive, *vidhātṛ*, often means Creator.

but the verb's total range of meaning would in any case seem to imply a connection between Viṣṇu-Nārāyaṇa's "approval" and dharma. Thus it is not only Vyāsa, one of Nārāyaṇa's incarnations, who lends dharmic approval to the polyandric marriage, but Nārāyaṇa himself. And what about Viṣṇu-Nārāyaṇa's other incarnation, Krishna? Does he give approval to this second stage of Draupadī's marriage as well as the first? Yes, this time not by referring to it explicitly as meeting the precepts of dharma, but by an act which is itself an implicit sanctioning of its virtuousness: the bestowal of wedding gifts (191,13–18).

The marriage of Draupadī is thus part of a vaster theological drama that involves, at numerous levels, both Śiva and Viṣṇu-Nārāyaṇa. This was hinted at by Biardeau, but as we have seen, not only Vyāsa but Krishna and Nārāyaṇa deepen the Vaiṣṇava "restorative" contribution. The various collaborations between different figures are of interest. We see the three Kṛṣṇas—Vyāsa, Draupadī, and Vāsudeva—mysteriously working to a common end. But more than this, if it is Śiva's role to instigate or signal the disruption of dharma, it is the role of Krishna, Vyāsa, and Nārāyaṇa first to sanction that disruption and, moreover, to perceive the hidden structure of dharma even while it has been suspended and to preserve it through its suspension. Thus, even while dharma wanes, it is being preserved in kernel, in essence, in the actions of Arjuna, the Pāṇḍavas, and Draupadī which only Krishna and Vyāsa perceive in their true context—as dharma.

CHAPTER 4

Krishna's Absence from the Dice Game and the Disrobing of Draupadī

After his appearance at Draupadī's Svayaṃvara, Krishna is involved in several incidents. Staying with the Pāṇḍavas a while after the wedding, he is present when they accept half the Kuru kingdom and set up residence at Khāṇḍavaprastha; indeed, Krishna leads them (*pāṇḍavās . . . kṛṣṇapurogamāḥ*) to this "terrible forest" (*ghoraṃ vanam*; 1:199,26–27) and helps them, along with Vyāsa, to build the heavenlike city of Indraprastha (199,28–47). Back home at Dvārakā, he encourages Arjuna to abduct Subhadrā, Krishna's own sister, from a festival so as to assure her compliance in marriage (1:211–213). Then, coming to Indraprastha to celebrate Arjuna and Subhadrā's wedding, he stays for the birth of their son Abhimanyu and performs the birth ceremonies for this new and beloved nephew (1:213,55–64). This visit includes Krishna in one of the strangest scenes of the epic, the burning of the Khāṇḍava forest.[1] Before he leaves he asks the Asura Maya to build the Pāṇḍavas their magnificent hall, "a *sabhā*

[1] This scene has drawn recent and varied comment from Madeleine Biardeau, Compte-rendu of "Conferences de Mlle Madeleine Biardeau," *Annuaire de l'EPHE, Section des Sciences Religieuses* LXXIX (1971–1972), 140–41 (hereinafter these will be referred to as *EPHE*, LXXVII [1969–1970], LXXVIII [1970–1971], and LXXIX), and from van Buitenen, *The Mahābhārata*, I, 1,9–11,13. See also my "The Burning of the Forest," *New Essays in Hinduism*, Bardwell L. Smith, ed. (Leiden: Brill, 1976), 208–24.

where we may see arranged designs that are godly, asuric, and human" (2:1,11)—in fact, the very architecture that will make a fool of Duryodhana, leading him to covet the Pāṇḍavas' prosperity (*śrī*; 2:43,13 and 17) and to formulate his plan to divest them of it by inviting them to a dice game (43,13). Last, Krishna is invited to Indraprastha to advise Yudhiṣṭhira on the latter's wish to perform a Rājasūya, the "royal consecration" ceremony which confers the title of *saṃrāj*, "universal sovereign" (2:12,11–12). Encouraging Yudhiṣṭhira to perform this rite, Krishna helps Arjuna and Bhīma, before it begins, to dispose of Yudhiṣṭhira's single rival, King Jarāsaṃdha of Magadha; and then, during the rite, he prevents its disruption by slaying Jarāsaṃdha's obstreperous marshal Śiśupāla. These two episodes have received their most satisfactory treatment in a beautiful study by Dumézil,[2] some of whose conclusions I will draw from in later chapters. From the building of the Pāṇḍavas' *sabhā* through the performance of the Rājasūya, we have entered the *Mahābhārata*'s second book, the *Sabhāparvan*.

At the successful conclusion of the Rājasūya sacrifice, Krishna goes home (2:42,51–58). He is not involved in the climactic scenes which close the *Sabhāparvan*: the two dice games which result in the Pāṇḍavas' humiliation, loss of kingdom, and exile to the forest. I will not discuss the dice games here in any detail.[3] Rather, noting that Walter Ruben sees Krishna's absence from this "turning point" as worthy of an exclamation point in support of his thesis that the original story did without Krishna,[4] let us examine this matter of

[2] *ME*, I, pt. 1, 17–123; see also Biardeau, *EPHE*, LXXIX, 141–46, and my "Comparing Indo-European 'Epics,'" pp. 93–96.

[3] See Heinrich Luders, "Das Wurfelspiel im alten Indien," *AKGWG*, *Philolgisch-Historische Klasse*, N. F., IX, 2 (1907), 1–74; Held, *Ethnological Study*, pp. 253–77; K. de Vreese, "The Game of Dice in Ancient India," in *Orientalia Neerlandica: A Volume of Oriental Studies* (Leiden: Sijthoff, 1948), pp. 349–62; J. A. B. van Buitenen, "On the Structure of the Sabhāparvan of the Mahābhārata," *India Maior* (Gonda Festchrift) (Leiden: Brill, 1972), pp. 78–83.

[4] Ruben, *Krishna*, p. 283.

absence more closely.[5] It is taken up by Krishna himself on his first visit to the Pāṇḍavas at the beginning of their period of exile in the forest. We are now in the *Āraṇyakaparvan*, and the Pāṇḍavas have already received two of the many illustrious visitors—Vidura and Maitreya—who will come to console them, on their forest travels, with edifying discourses that bear only a tangential relationship to the course of the epic drama. Krishna will make another visit, and a third visit by him is interpolated. Here, however, there are no illuminating tales or exhortations, and the relationship of this visit to the preceding events of the *Sabhāparvan*, and to what ultimately follows, is direct and, in my view, of considerable importance.

The visit serves one clear purpose: it reaffirms Krishna's relationship with the Pāṇḍavas after his absence during their time of distress at the dice game. In particular, he reconsolidates this relationship by a series of exchanges with Yudhiṣṭhira, Arjuna, and Draupadī. To Yudhiṣṭhira, whom he had helped consecrate as *saṃrāj*, he promises consecration anew and, his wrath mounting, punishment of his enemies (3:13,5–6). To Arjuna, who must pacify Krishna's anger by recounting his past deeds,[6] he recalls their identity as Nara and Nārāyaṇa (13,37–40). Most significant is the exchange with Draupadī; their words point beyond the surface events to the mythological identities of the figures involved.

Draupadī speaks first. Recognizing each of her five husbands as an "equal of Indra" (*pañcānāmindrakalpānām*; 13,108); acknowledging Krishna as "Viṣṇu," as "the sacrifice, the

[5] Actually, a famous tradition does have Krishna appear at the dicing scene; in an episode recounted in numerous versions (see CE notes following 2:61,40), Draupadī, distressed over Duḥśāsana's efforts to disrobe her, calls on Krishna to rescue her. But Franklin Edgerton's work on the *Sabhāparvan* CE proves this an interpolation; see Edgerton, "Introduction," *Sabhāparvan*, CE, pp. xxvii–xxix.

[6] 3:13,10–36: a strange list, accenting past lives (?) as an ascetic (10–14) and sacrificer (16–17,21–22), plus triumphs over human and demonic foes. The one *avatāra* reference has Krishna traverse the three worlds as a child (*śiśu*) rather than a dwarf (24).

sacrificer, and he for whom the sacrifice is to be performed" (*tvaṃ yajño . . . yaṣṭā tvamasi yaṣṭavyo*; 13,44), as well as a number of related identities (43–52), she asks: "How then, being the wife of the Pārthas [=five Indras], your friend [*sakhī*], O Krishna [=Viṣṇu], and the sister of Dhṛṣṭadyumna [=Agni], could one like me be dragged into the *sabhā*?" (53.)[7] Her tale of woe continues at some length (to *śloka* 108), followed by tears, sighs, and the concluding "angry words" that she has truly neither husbands, sons, brothers, father, nor friends if all this could happen to her (112–13).

In response to this expression of tears, anger, and bereftness, Krishna replies:

Surely the wives of those at whom you are wrathful shall also weep, O angry [or radiant] one [*bhāmini*], [seeing their husbands] covered with the arrows of Arjuna, bathed in torrents of blood, slain, having abandoned life, lying on the earth's surface. Whatever is suitable for the Pāṇḍavas, that I will do. Do not grieve. I promise you truly: you shall be the queen of kings [*rājñāṃ rājñī bhaviṣyasi*]. The sky might fall, Himavat might split, the earth might be rent, the ocean might dry up, O Kṛṣṇā, but my word shall not be vain. [13, 114c–117]

Note the plural: Draupadī (Kṛṣṇā!) will be the queen of king*s*. This is nothing but Krishna's reply-in-kind to Draupadī's question. Like her, he penetrates to the mythological identities of the principal figures: Draupadī, the queen of kings, is Śrī, "Prosperity," whose marriage to every king, not to mention the "five Indras among men," is the sign of a virtuous reign. In symbolic terms, as Draupadī says herself, she is without husbands, for, since they have lost their kingdom, the relationship between them and herself *as Śrī*, "royal Prosperity," has

[7] An equal sign indicates a heroic-mythic consolidarity between the figures outside and inside the parentheses or brackets. On the five Indras, see above, Chapter 3 and below, Chapter 7, and cf. 5:80,20–26 where, just before Krishna departs on his "peace mission" to the Kuru court, Draupadī reminds him that even as his "dear friend" (*priyā sakhī*; 21) and the wife of five husbands "resembling five Indras in splendor" (*pañcendrasamavarcasām*; 22), she was dragged and insulted in the *sabhā*.

"dissolved." But although earth, sky, mountains, and ocean might be destroyed—imagery of the *pralaya* or universal "dissolution"—their relationship shall once again, at Krishna's true word, be reconstituted.

It is altogether fitting that the destructive dice game, which has dissolved the royal relationship and identities of Draupadī and the Pāṇḍavas, has occurred in Krishna's absence. As Biardeau has shown so well, in the symbolism of the *pralaya* that pervades the epic at many points, the destructive role of Śiva is counterbalanced by the reconstitutive role of Viṣṇu-Nārāyaṇa. And during the time that each of these two great gods performs his role—Śiva burning the three worlds, Viṣṇu lying on the cosmic ocean—each is alone; the other, if one may say so, is out of the picture. Such a pattern of presences and absences is discussed again in Chapter 12.

Krishna, having just reaffirmed his consolidarity with the Pāṇḍavas and Draupadī, also provides a most thorough and illuminating explanation of his absence and a response to the events which transpired without him. Had he been at Dvārakā when the game was announced, he would, he says, have come to Hāstinapura to prevent it. First, addressing the Kuru elders, he would have sought to impress upon them the many evils of dicing, the very worst vice of the "fourfold addiction" *(vyasanaṃ catuṣṭayam)*—women, dice, hunting, and drinking—by which "prosperity [*śrī*] vanishes" (3:14,7).[8] Then, should his advice, "healthy for dharma" (*anāmayam . . . dharmasya*; 11), go unheeded by Dhṛtarāṣṭra and Duryodhana, he would have stopped the game "by force" (*balena*; 12). "However," he concludes, "my nonpresence [*asāṃnidhyam*], being at that time among the Ānartas, has become [the cause] by which you have obtained this calamity brought about by dice" (14).

Krishna then turns at great length to the matter that detained him away from Dvārakā: his combat with King

[8] These same four occur at 2:61,20 and in *Manu* 7,50.

Śālva, lord of the city of Saubha. The story is placed as a sequel to the Jarāsaṃdha and Śiśupāla episodes, as Śiśupāla was Śālva's brother (3:15,13). Outraged at Śiśupāla's death, Śālva had attacked Dvārakā while Krishna was still at Indraprastha, attending and protecting Yudhiṣṭhira's Rājasūya (3:21,1). Śālva destroyed all the city gardens, slew many heroic Vṛṣṇi youths (3:15,7), and led his army to a standoff fight against some of Krishna's sons. In the featured match, however, Pradyumna—Krishna's son by Rukmiṇī[9]—was prevented from slaying Śālva by Indra, Kubera, and the entire divine host (*devagaṇāḥ sarve*), who sent the ṛṣi Nārada and the Wind (*śvasana*; 20,21) to tell Pradyumna: "It has been ordained by the Creator [*dhātrā*] that Krishna the son of Devakī shall be [the cause of] his death in battle" (20,24). This reminds one of the prophecy concerning Śālva's brother Śiśupāla,[10] and the interest of the entire divine host suggests that Śālva is a figure of no mean significance. One may even wonder at the gods' interference in this duel, for the postponement of Śālva's death results in Krishna's fateful absence from the dice game. But we know little of the gods' interest in Śālva's death, for his file is full of gaps. Although, like Jarāsaṃdha and Śiśupāla, he is an incarnate Asura,[11] his own pedigree is a matter of doubt. Krishna refers to him as "an innately sinful descendent of Diti" (*pāpaprakṛtirdaiteya*; 21,19), but it is only belatedly, in various Northern texts, that the epic connects him with a particular Asura, and this is the inconsequential Ajaka (see notes to 1:61,17). Moreover, a glance at Sörensen's *Index* reveals the deplorable situation of three,

[9] A long-standing family feud may lie behind this duel: Śiśupāla was once betrothed to Rukmiṇī; see Dumézil, *ME*, II, 109–13, and 2:42,15.

[10] See 2:40, 3–5 and 9–10: an "incorporeal voice" (*vāg . . . aśarīriṇī*; 3) reveals that the person who will eventually be Śiśupāla's slayer (Krishna) is the one on whose lap Śiśupāla will be placed so that his extra eye will vanish and his extra arms drop off.

[11] On the Asuric precedents of Jarāsaṃdha and Śiśupāla, see *ME*, II, 84–85,89.

and possibly four, Śālvas in the epic: one slain on each side in the great battle; one slain in the present episode by Krishna; and one the cautious fiancé who refuses to marry the princess Ambā—previously engaged to him—after she and her two sisters were abducted from their Svayaṃvara by Bhīṣma (5:170–93, the *Ambopākhyānaparvan*). There is certainly one good reason to suppose that this last figure is identical with Krishna's victim: both are referred to as Saubhapati, lord of Saubha (cf. 5:175,24; 176,2). But the two characterizations are markedly different. In the famous *Ambopākyhāna*, Śālva is the king of an apparently earthly realm who refuses to marry Ambā partially because of fear of Bhīṣma (5:172,22). In the other, with Śālva seemingly raised to the status of a foe of Krishna, Saubha becomes a remarkable sky-ranging city which goes wherever its lord wishes (3:15,6; cf. 20,27; 21,25), and which Krishna, with his discus, finally manages to split and dislodge from the sky, "like Tripura shaken by the shaft of Maheśvara" (32,24). After this, Krishna uses the *cakra* to divide Śālva himself in two and burn him with its energy.

This is not the only conquest of an aerial city in Indian mythology,[12] but the important point is that Śālva's miraculous capacity as Krishna's foe contrasts sharply with his characterization as a potential opponent of Bhīṣma. This would seem to indicate that the two stories reflect different milieus with contrasting literary and theological interests. Indeed, one may note further that Krishna's conquest of Śālva follows upon one of the few incidents where the epic dwells at length on the exploits of Krishna's children. Moreover, unlike the slayings of Jarāsaṃdha and Śiśupāla, Krishna's conquest of Śālva, like his victory over Kaṃsa—which is also told to the Pāṇḍavas only as background information to more pressing

[12] Ruben, *Krishna*, pp. 217–18, like the passage just cited, compares the conquest of Saubha with Śiva's conquest of Tripura; see also Hiraṇyapura (3:170,1), conquered by Arjuna, as mentioned in a note to me by van Buitenen.

events (2:13,30–33)—has direct concern only for Krishna's people, and not for the Pāṇḍavas. In short, it would seem that the Krishna-Śālva episode finds its closest analogues in stories, like the slaying of Kaṃsa, which come to their fullest expression in the Purāṇas. One suspects that the *Mahābhārata* has elaborated here upon a fragment of tradition about Krishna, a fragment similar to those in the list of sins against Dvārakā and its people with which Krishna charges Śiśupāla before he slays him (2:42,7–11).[13] Whether these and other fragments ever formed a continuous narrative is debatable, but only this one episode, the conquest of Śālva, is given full dramatic treatment in the *Mahābhārata*. This has probably been done to meet the structural requirements of the main epic narrative, for it is a requirement that Krishna be absent from the dice game. As he has said, had he been there, the result would have been different. And as he prepares to return to Dvārakā, his closing remarks make the same point: "For this reason, O king, I did not come to Hāstinapura; if I had come, surely Duryodhana would not be alive" (3:23,41).

Putting this more into the terms of the epic scenarists, Krishna's absence from the dice game does not hinge so much on this adventitious episode as on the fact that had he been present, the dice game could not have taken place, or, perhaps better, could not have taken place with the same results. But his distance from and dislike of dicing are consistent with his attitude elsewhere. It is not the only place where Krishna speaks out against gambling. When, at the end of the war, Yudhiṣṭhira stipulates that Duryodhana can still win back the kingdom should he defeat just one Pāṇḍava opponent of his own choosing in a mace duel, Krishna rebukes Yudhiṣṭhira, comparing this to the beginning of another *dyūta* (*dyūtam-ārambham*) that will be "dangerous and uneven" (*viṣamam*; 9:32,7).

[13] See Dumézil, *ME*, II, 66–68, and below, Chapter 9.

But Krishna is not the only divinity whom the epic characterizes by an attitude toward dicing. In fact, we are faced with an intriguing, and probably quite significant, opposition. If, to begin with, Krishna is opposed to dicing, his obvious counterpart is Śiva, whom the epic describes as "fond of dice" (*akṣapriya*).[14] Perhaps one may see an early trace of such an inclination where the *Śatarudriya* litany exclaims: "Homage to the cheater, the swindler, to the lord of burglars homage."[15] In any case, in the myth of the five former Indras, we find Śiva "exceedingly intoxicated with dice" (*akṣaiḥ subhṛśam pramattam*; 1:189,15) as he and Pārvatī absorb themselves in the game on the top of Mount Kailāsa. As we have already observed,[16] Biardeau has argued that Śiva's connection with dice in this scene has a symbolic link with the dice game in the *Dyūtaparvan* between the Kurus and the Pāṇḍavas:

> Śiva's dicing with Pārvatī atop Mount Kailāsa is rich in meaning if one recalls that it is at a throw of the dice that the fate of the Pāṇḍavas is played out, that the four yugas, or the four ages in which the course of dharma declines, bear respectively the names of the four dice throws, and that the epic narrative is situated at the juncture of the two last yugas, the game of dice being won by [Śakuni] the incarnation of the Asura Dvāpara (the next-to-last yuga) for the benefit of [Duryodhana] the incarnation of the Asura Kali (the final yuga).[17]

These remarks should be supplemented by those of Held. Comparing Śiva's dice play to a "heavenly potlatch ceremony," Held argued that dicing was a potlatchlike ritual game

[14] *Mbh.* Calcutta Edition 12:285,47, cited by Held, *Ethnological Study*, p. 278, n. 1. I do not have consistent access to this fascicule of the Critical Edition, where it appears only in an Appendix.

[15] *TS* 4,5,3d; Arthur Berriedale Keith, trans., *The Veda of the Black Yajus School, entitled Taittiriya Sanhita* (1914; repr. in 2 vols.; Delhi: Motilal Banarsidass, 1967), II, 326.

[16] See above, Chapter 3, n. 10.

[17] Biardeau, "Brāhmaṇes et potiers," p. 38, n. 4 (my translation).

played in a specially constructed *sabhā*, and then stated: "We are firmly convinced that the game of dice [the game in the *Dyūtaparvan* being the case in point] has something to do with Rudra-Śiva."[18] This conviction, apparently shared by Biardeau, leads to our basic problem.

Some of Held's evidence for a connection between Śiva and ritual dicing is intriguing, for instance the use—according to him—of wood from the house of the *akṣāvāpa*, "dice keeper," for Rudra's altar during the Rājasūya ceremony.[19] Indeed, this ceremony, as it is described in the Brāhmaṇa literature, shows other instances where Śiva is associated with dicing. In *Śatapatha Brāhmaṇa* 5, 3, 1, 10, during the Rājasūya, Gavedhukā seeds are brought to the sacrificing king's house from the houses of the Akṣāvāpa and the "Slaughterer" (Govikartana) —an interestingly "destructive" pair—and are made into a pap that is offered, as the last of the Ratnin offerings, to Rudra. And *Taittirīya Saṃhitā* 1, 8, 9 says of the same segment of the Rājasūya: "To Rudra [he offers] an oblation of Gavīdhukā in the house of the thrower of dice."[20] All this leads to an important point made by van Buitenen: just as in the ritual texts the Rājasūya is concluded by a dice game,[21] similarly, in the *Sabhāparvan*, Yudhiṣṭhira's Rājasūya, ostensibly complete,

[18] Held, *Ethnological Study*, pp. 274–278, 258.

[19] *Ibid.*, but given without citation. Held also says that Śakuni can be a name for Śiva: p. 318, n. 1. See also p. 193 and n. 1, noting that the last day of the Dīvalī festival "is usually held to be an exceptionally lucky day to gamble upon. . . . It is said that Śiva, playing at dice upon that day with his consort Pārvatī, forfeited to her all that he possessed."

[20] Keith, *Veda of the Black Yajus School*, I, 120. See J. C. Heestermann, *The Ancient Indian Royal Consecration* ('s-Gravenhage: Mouton, 1957), chart facing p. 49, n. 12. Böthlingk and Roth give the same tree—*coix barbata*—for Gavedhukā and Gavīdhukā.

[21] See Heestermann, *Ancient Indian Royal Consecration*, p. 153; the dice game in the Rājasūya "may be considered a cosmogonical rite intended to bring about the recreation of the universe and the birth of the king." If this interpretation of the Brāhmaṇic rite is correct, the inverse of this applies to Yudhiṣṭhira, who loses the game.

is technically incomplete without the dice game.[22] Thus, if Rudra is significantly connected with the dicing that concludes the Vedic ritual, there are additional reasons—beyond those proposed by Biardeau and Held—to link him, at least implicitly, with the dice game of the epic.

Biardeau and Held have thus led us to an impasse. They have shown the importance of Śiva's connection with dicing and have pointed to a symbolic continuity between the two dicing scenes: the game between Śiva and Pārvatī and the game at the end of the *Sabhāparvan*. But only by looking at the two dicing scenes in their full complexity, *with all the figures involved*, can we see that "the game of dice [in the *Dyūtaparvan*] has something to do with Śiva."

As Chapter 3 made clear, the dice game on Mount Kailāsa concerns not just Śiva and Pārvatī, but Śrī and the five Indras, and ultimately Viṣṇu-Nārāyaṇa. The world's present Indra has followed a trail of tears-turned-to-golden-lotuses to the source of the Ganges. There he meets the "ill-fortuned" (*mandabhāgya*) Śrī. The latter is weeping because while Śiva and his spouse intoxicate themselves with dice, her husbands—four former Indras whom the fifth, our Indra, is now carelessly imitating—have insulted Śiva by their folly and pride and have been forced to lie dormant in a cave. At Śiva's insistence, only by being reborn in human wombs (as the Pāṇḍavas) can they perform karman that will regain them the "world of Indra." As for Śrī, Śiva, with Nārāyaṇa's "approval," will allow her to rejoin them by taking birth as Draupadī, their wife-in-common.

By viewing this not only as a myth about Śiva dicing, but—as seen in Chapter 3—as a myth about the dissolution and restoration of the relationship between Śrī and the five Indras,

[22] Van Buitenen, "The Sabhāparvan," pp. 79–83; according to him, this *parvan* "borrowed its structure from the Vedic *rājasūya* . . . ; two events in this book are so basic that they must have been given from the beginning: the *unction* and the *dicing*" (p. 82). For an analogous continuity between royal legend and royal ritual (the Vajāpeya), see Dumézil, *ME*, II, 359–60.

Krishna's explanation of his absence from the *Dyūtaparvan* dice game, his words to Draupadī, and his denunciation of dicing make sense. Indeed, the two dice games and their aftermaths provide a number of instructive parallels, oppositions, and inversions, which I present graphically for the sake of the greatest simplicity and clarity:

Parallels

1. Śiva and Pārvatī play at dice, symbolizing the course of the yugas on a mythic or cosmic scale.	1. Śakuni (= Dvāpara) and Duryodhana (= Kali) play dice, symbolizing the course of the yugas in a transitional microcosmic moment "between the yugas," on an epic, linear, or "historical" scale.
2. This involves the fall of Indras one after another (diachronically) from the "world of Indra,"—from heavenly world sovereignty.	2. This involves the fall, all at once (synchronically) of "five equals of Indra" (3:13,108), and, in particular, of Yudhiṣṭhira from the position of *saṃrāj*, earthly universal sovereign.
3. In connection with the game of dice—here through the Indras' folly and pride—the relationships between them and Śrī are dissolved.	3. Through Yudhiṣṭhira's folly, the Pāṇḍavas' relationship with Draupadī is symbolically dissolved: as Krishna puts it, a result of playing dice is that "*śrī* vanishes" (*bhraśyate śriyaḥ*; 3:14,7); and as Draupadī puts it, she is now without husbands, and so on. (3:13,112).[23]
4. The "ill-fortuned" Śrī weeps tears that turn into golden lotuses.	4. Draupadī weeps continually when dragged into the *sabhā* (2:60,15; 62,3 and 22) and laments her condition when Krishna visits in the forest.

[23] This question of status is the turning point around which the first "invitation" of the dice game revolves. Draupadī was the last stake bet by Yudhiṣṭhira (2:58,32–43—see *śloka* 33, in which Yudhiṣṭhira compares her with Śrī and Lakṣmī). Thus Draupadī's first question (2:60,7) is whether Yudhiṣṭhira wagered her before or after himself, for if it were the latter, he was not her husband. This dangerous question is never answered by Yudhiṣṭhira and is evaded by Bhīṣma (60,40–42;62,14–21); its insolubility helps her win her husbands their freedom.

5. At Śiva's command, the first four Indras gestate in a cave; they will ultimately be reborn in "human wombs."

5. At Duryodhana's command (I draw here from a well-attested symbolism) the Pāṇḍavas must go through their forest exile stripped of their royal identities (wearing ascetic garb), after which, disguised in the royal court of Matsya, they will live "undiscovered like infants in the womb" (4:66,10).

6. Viṣṇu-Nārāyaṇa agrees that Śrī may be reunited with the five Indras by taking birth as Draupadī.

6. Krishna promises Draupadī that once again she will be "the queen of kings" (3:13,116).

Oppositions and Inversions

1. Śiva is present at the dice game as a player.

1. Krishna is absent from the dice game.

2. Śiva is intoxicated with dicing (1:189,15).

2. Krishna denounces dicing as the worst of addictions (3:14,7).

It is not a matter here of myth providing the model for epic, or, for that matter, vice versa. The course of the epic narrative strays too far from the story of the myth to suggest any significant structuring influence. For instance, the two stories diverge sharply at point 5, leading into very different thematic areas which only I, and not the epic poets, have contrived to put together. An important difference in direction and motivation is also indicated by the following: whereas the *Dyūtaparvan* dicing scene involves an opposition between the Pāṇḍavas and the Kurus—incarnating the Devas (in particular, the five Indras) and the Asuras (or Rākṣasas)—the dicing scene atop Mount Kailāsa involves no Asuras, but a direct conflict between the boastful Indras and the higher god Śiva. Rather, as Chapter 7 will seek to show, the myth of Śiva and the Indras has its analogue and prototype elsewhere. And last, the myth is not told at a point adjacent to the epic episode: the poets have connected it with Draupadī's marriage, not her humiliation.

Given all these hesitations, however, clearly the words which Krishna exchanges with Draupadī, and the words with which he denounces dicing, are heavy with mythological allusions. The references to the five "equals of Indra" (item 2), to Śrī vanishing and to Draupadī's loss of husbands (item 3), and to her once again becoming the "queen of kings" (item 6) are all clear in their mythic import. And it is not just the general theme of the loss and return of "Prosperity," but the specific myth of the former Indras, that makes this clarity apparent.

A lesson may be drawn here. There is more than one way in which myth and epic have been interrelated in the *Mahābhārata*. While in some cases whole episodes are correlated with myths, in others, where there are moments in the lives of the heroes and heroines that evoke mythical themes, the poets allow their personages to reveal glimpses of their mythical identities and to relive, as it were, scenes from their "prior" mythical adventures. In the present case, not just one allusion but a whole cluster of parallels makes the alignment of the two dicing scenes meaningful and coherent. But it is not just the parallels that are coherent—so too are the oppositions and inversions. The pattern of Śiva being present and Krishna or Viṣṇu being absent at moments when violence is done to dharma is one I will discuss at greater length in Chapter 12. In the present instances, however, the oppositions are not wholly complete. In the myth, Śiva is present and Viṣṇu-Nārāyaṇa is elsewhere, available for consultation and his required approval; but only the first fact is given any weight in the telling. And in the epic, no matter how "firmly convinced" one may be that "the game of dice has something to do with Rudra-Śiva," we are faced with a near opposite situation: the only matter given weight, this time the only matter given mention, is the fact of Krishna's absence. Our situation thus has the following look:

Myth:	ŚIVA PRESENT	Viṣṇu absent
Epic:	(Śiva present [?] symbolically or implicitly)	KRISHNA ABSENT

One might say, then, that the two episodes are constructed around different poles: in one case highlighting Śiva, in the other, at least in its aftermath, Krishna. But from these polar emphases, the two episodes once again reveal their complementarity. The opposite attitudes of the two "divinities" toward dicing can be appreciated as reflections upon each other. If in the hands of Śiva and Śakuni the dice reflect the course of the yugas, the increase of adharma, the loss of "prosperity," and, in the case of Śiva, an intoxicated aloofness to matters of gain and loss, there is a clear contrast with Krishna, who leaves nothing to chance. The arbitrary, addictive, and destructive character of dicing runs counter to his application of suitable "means" for every perilous situation, his patient, constructive efforts toward the "restoration of dharma."

Moreover, in terms of the construction of the epic story, the continuities demonstrated by van Buitenen between the *Dyūtaparvan* and the Rājasūya bring Krishna's absence from the former into a still sharper focus. According to the *Mahābhārata*, "the great armed Janārdana [Krishna] protected that sacrifice [the Rājasūya of Yudhiṣṭhira] until completion" (*taṃ tu yajñaṃ mahābāhurā samāpter janārdanaḥ / rarakṣa*; 2:42,34). But as the poets no doubt knew,[24] it was not really complete without a dice game, which, as Krishna says himself, the Pāṇḍavas could not have lost had he been present. The situation thus suggests two possibilities. Perhaps, out of dramatic necessity, the poets simply provided an interval (the *digvijaya*, the "conquest of the regions" by Yudhiṣṭhira's brothers) between the Rājasūya and the dice game in order to remove Krishna from the scene. Or, viewing the entire *parvan*, including the *digvijaya*,[25] as a coherent whole structured from

[24] Van Buitenen, "The Sabhāparvan," p. 78: "I do not pretend to propose that our present *Sabhā* 'grew' out of a baronial account of the *rājasūya*, but only that the composers of the *parvan* were aware of the sequence of events in the Vedic *rājasūya* and used it in building the narrative analogously."

[25] *Ibid.*, see pp. 73–75; van Buitenen points to the parallels between the *digvijaya* and the Rājasūya rite of the *digvyāsthāpana*.

beginning to end by the *entire* Rājasūya, we may suppose some rapport between Krishna-Viṣṇu and the sacrifice[26] through the completion of its chief purpose, the unction; and, second, a similar rapport—one certainly hinted at in the Brāhmaṇa passages cited above—between Rudra-Śiva and the concluding segment of the rite, the dicing. My leaning is toward the latter alternative. It seems to me that, whether or not we follow Biardeau and connect the dicing with Śiva through the waning course of dharma through the yugas, we are presented in the dicing segment, or sequel, of the Rājasūya—both in the epic and in the traditional rite—with an element of destructive chance, randomness, which the king must overcome for his sovereignty to be complete. Indeed, as Heestermann suggests,[27] it is this game—if he "wins"—which may symbolize the king's "recreation of the universe" and "new birth." It is not difficult to see how this potentially destructive and random element would, or could, have been associated with Rudra, or how Krishna, the exponent of dharma, would have taken exception to it.

[26] The relation between Krishna, Viṣṇu, and the sacrifice will be treated more fully in Chapters 11 and 12; for the moment, recall Draupadī's recognition of Krishna as "the sacrifice" (3:13,44) toward the beginning of this chapter.

[27] See above, n. 21.

CHAPTER 5

Krishna and Odinn: Interventions

The study of Krishna in the *Mahābhārata*, as the last three chapters show, cannot be a study of Krishna alone, but involves his relations to other heroes and heroines and his rapports, as *avatāra* of Viṣṇu-Nārāyaṇa, with many of the major divinities of the Hindu pantheon. But this is not all, for, as I will attempt to show, the Krishna of the *Mahābhārata* sometimes takes us beyond India to the mythic and epic traditions of other Indo-European peoples. I call attention now to two episodes from Germanic legends concerning Odinn which find close analogues in consecutive scenes in the *Mahābhārata*'s fifth book.

At the Waking Krishna's Bedside

After his first visit to the Pāṇḍavas in the forest, Krishna sees them there two more times (3:118,15–120; 3:180–224), or three counting a clear interpolation (*Āraṇyakaparvan*, Appendix I, No. 25). Then, after the Pāṇḍavas have successfully concluded their year of concealment at King Virāṭa's court, Krishna brings Subhadrā and Abhimanyu (who have stayed with him at Dvārakā) to join them and attends the latter's wedding to Uttarā, Virāṭa's daughter (4:67). This visit of the fourth book, the *Virāṭaparvan*, is extended to the beginning of the fifth, the *Udyogaparvan*, or book of "preparations" for war. Meeting with the Pāṇḍavas and their allies at Upaplavya, a town in Virāṭa's kingdom, Krishna advises the Pāṇḍavas to send a messenger to the Kurus to demand that Duryodhana comply with the terms of the dice game: Yudhiṣṭhira must be returned his half of the kingdom now that the Pāṇḍavas have completed their thirteenth year of exile unrecognized. Then Krishna leaves for Dvārakā with parting words that are soon invested with meaning. First, underlining his supposed impartiality, he says: "Our relationship [*sambandhakam*] to the Kurus and Pāṇḍavas is equal, wishing well to both . . . while they are occupied with each other" (5:5,3). And then, noting that Duryodhana might reject the messenger's entreaties, he urges that in such a case the Pāṇḍavas should summon him and the other kings as well.

The Pāṇḍavas do not wait for the failure of their first ambassador's mission to begin their search for allies. The reason is clear from certain words of Drupada's at the Upaplavya meeting: "Duryodhana will now also call everywhere [for allies]; and approached beforehand, the good partake of the earlier invitation" (*pūrvābhipannāḥ santaśca bhajante pūrvacodakam*; 5:4,9). The obligation to grant the initial request thus takes precedence over any personal preference for one side or the other.

Krishna himself must be courted, and each side sends its "best." Duryodhana comes to Dvārakā for the Kauravas, Arjuna for the Pāṇḍavas. There "they found Krishna sleeping, and approached him [as he was] lying down" (*suptaṃ dadarśatuḥ kṛṣṇaṃ śayānaṃ copajagmatuḥ*; 5:7,5). But they do not arrive at the same time or in the same manner: "As Govinda was sleeping, Suyodhana [a euphemism for Duryodhana] entered [his room] and sat down on a choice seat toward Krishna's head. And after him entered the highminded Kirīṭin [Arjuna]. And he stood, below Krishna, bowing and joining his hands. And when Vārṣṇeya awoke, first off he saw [*dadarśāgre*] Kirīṭin" (7,6–8ab). Duryodhana, however, is the first to speak, and his words remind us of those of Krishna at Upaplavya stressing his "equal relationship" to the Kurus and Pāṇḍavas. "As if with a smile" (*prahsanniva*), Duryodhana says to Krishna: "Surely your friendship [*sakhyam*] is equal for both myself and Arjuna, just as our relationship [*sambandhakam*] is equal with you, O Mādhava" (7,10). Letting Krishna know that he arrived first, Duryodhana also evokes the maxim previously cited by Drupada: the good (*santaḥ*), of whom Krishna is the best in the world (*śreṣṭhamo loke*), side with those who are the first to come to them for help (11–12).

Krishna acknowledges these claims, but, he says, although Duryodhana was the first to arrive, "Arjuna was the first seen by me." Thus assistance must be granted to both, and up to this point everything has reinforced the idea of parity in the relationship of the two heroes and their parties to Krishna. Here Krishna introduces a note that breaks the deadlock: "The first choice is to be made by whoever is younger, so it is heard [*pravāraṇaṃ tu bālānām pūrvaṃ kāryamiti śrutiḥ*]; therefore Pārtha Dhanaṃjaya [Arjuna] is worthy of the first choice" (15). With his supposed impartiality, Krishna then dictates the terms. The choice will be between a large *arbuda* of cowherds (*gopas*) known as the Nārāyaṇas, "equalling me in strength" (16), or Krishna himself, "alone, not fighting in battle, my weapons laid down" (*ayudhyamānaḥ saṃgrāme nyastaśastro 'hamekataḥ*; 17). With little fanfare,[1] Arjuna picks Krishna, and Duryodhana, with the "utmost delight" (*paramāṃ mudām*; 20), accepts the thousands upon thousands of troops. When Duryodhana has left, Krishna agrees to be Arjuna's charioteer (32–35), and the two set off to join Yudhiṣṭhira at Upaplavya to continue the "preparations" for war.

This brief but crucial episode presents some intriguing difficulties as well as some striking symbolism. Neither has captured much attention. Walter Ruben, however, touches upon one difficulty, noting that it is "illogical" that Duryodhana should try to win over Krishna, as the latter is ever on the Pāṇḍavas' side.[2] V. S. Sukthankar appreciates

[1] Except in certain Northern manuscripts, which interpolate a gratuitous glorification of Krishna (41*, after 5:7,19).

[2] Ruben, *Krishna*, pp. 220–21.

the symbolism in terms of his "ethical" and "metaphysical" planes, first seeing the two heroes as a "static representation" of the Deva-Asura, Pāṇḍava-Kaurava conflicts, and then the full scene as an allegory of the daivic and asuric elements before the central Self.[3] These are all points worthy of further examination.

Ruben is right that there is little "logic"—at least in human terms, whether emotional or social—in Duryodhana's appeal. Not only are Krishna's affections for Arjuna and the Pāṇḍavas common knowledge, even to Duryodhana. Genealogically, Krishna's relation to the Pāṇḍavas is far closer than his relation to the Kurus. His father Vasudeva is Kuntī's brother, and Arjuna is married to Krishna's sister Subhadrā, making their son Abhimanyu Krishna's cherished nephew. Yet Krishna mentions his equal disposition toward the two sides.

Excluding preferential and genealogical explanations, then, we should examine the mythological one suggested by Sukthankar. Here Arjuna, the third member of this threesome, not only agrees with the others about Krishna's intermediary position but supplies a key to the mythic background. Urging Krishna, before he sets out as the Pāṇḍavas' next emissary for Hāstinapura, to seek peace there, Arjuna says: "You are the foremost friend [*paramaka suhṛt*] of both the Pāṇḍavas and the Kurus, even, O hero, as Prajāpati is among the Devas and Asuras" (5:76,7). As several authors have shown, a coalescence of Prajāpati with Viṣṇu is well attested in the Brāhmaṇas,[4] and this identification is sometimes carried over to Krishna, especially where he is connected with the sacrifice.[5]

[3] Sukthankar, *Mahābhārata*, pp. 70, 110–11.

[4] See Sylvain Lévi, *La Doctrine du sacrifice dans les Brāhmaṇas* (Paris: Leroux, Editeur, 1898), p. 15, n. 3; Jan Gonda, *Aspects of Early Viṣṇuism*, pp. 78, 173; *idem.*, *Les Religions de l'Inde*, I: *Védisme et hindouisme ancien* (Paris: Payot, 1962); Sukumari Bhattacharji, *The Indian Theogony* (Cambridge: Cambridge University Press, 1970), pp. 291–92.

[5] See especially 14:70,21, cited below, Chapter 11; cf. 3:13,44–52, cited above, Chapter 4, n. 26 and preceding; and see Sörensen, *Index*, s.v. Prajāpati[4], p. 558.

Prajāpati is not only "impartial" toward the Devas and Asuras as their father;[6] his status is more generally one of kinship to both parties, that which allows Arjuna to imply that he is their mutual "friend" or "family member."[7] And just as Arjuna and Duryodhana are in rivalry here for Krishna, so the Devas and Asuras are ever in contention for the "indivisible" Prajāpati.[8]

Thus, as Arjuna indicates, the two sets of relationships—one divine, the other heroic—are homologous. But more than this, the comparison leads to the meaning of the terms by which Krishna determines that the first pick, in the choice between himself and the Nārāyaṇa *gopas*, goes to Arjuna. It goes to the younger. And it is not simply that Arjuna, in epic chronology, is a year younger than Duryodhana. This fact—at least as it shapes the present scene—is itself a reflection of a mythical paradigm. The Devas are usually the "younger brothers" of the Asuras.[9] The epic scene is thus more than "a static representation" of the Deva-Asura conflict. It is a dynamic one. Duryodhana comes first, Arjuna comes second, but—by a mythically identifiable turnabout, hinging on youth—Arjuna gets the first choice.

The passage is a rich one, however, and calls to mind other themes. In particular, the picture of Krishna asleep, "lying down" (*śayānam*) and then waking (the only such scene to

[6] See Lévi, *Doctrine du sacrifice*, pp. 27 (with citations in n. 5) and 36ff.

[7] Van Buitenen, "The Sabhāparvan," p. 81, n. 2, says "a *suhṛd* in the epic is most often a family member"; but *sambandhaka*, *sakhi*, and *suhṛd* all seem to evoke both friendship and family.

[8] Lévi, *Doctrine du sacrifice*, p. 36.

[9] On this theme in the Brāhmaṇas, see Lévi, *Doctrine du sacrifice*, p. 36 and n. 2, citing *MS* 4,2,1 and *TB* 2,3,8,1–3; p. 99 and n. 1, citing *MS* 4,1,2; and p. 43, where he speaks of the Asuras' "right of prior ownership" in certain matters concerning the sacrifice. Although Lévi says that "the right of seniority is undecided between the two groups," the majority of passages he cites favor the Asuras. The *KB* passage cited in opposition simply lists the beings Prajāpati created in the order Devas, Men, Asuras; they may not have been born in that order. On the Asuras as elders in the epic, see E. W. Hopkins, *Epic Mythology*, p. 47, and Held, *Ethnological Study*, p. 169.

be included in the Critical Edition) cannot help but remind us of Viṣṇu Anantaśāyin, Viṣṇu, asleep and reclining on the serpent Ananta or Śeśa, whose awakening signals the dawn of a new *kalpa*.[10] Krishna himself tells Arjuna at one point (7:28,25cd–26) that of his four forms (*mūrtis*), the fourth is that which, upon awakening at the end of a thousand years (*mahāyugas*?) of sleep, "grants excellent boons to those deserving of boons" (26cd). This symbolism is open-ended enough to support two epic myths: in one, the goddess Earth comes to Krishna to request boons for her son Naraka (7:28,27–35); and in the other, Viṣṇu sees the Dānavas Madhu and Kaiṭabha when he awakens and offers them the "choicest boon" (*varaṃ śreṣṭham*), which they foolishly reject (3:194,8–30). As both concern the offering of boons only to Asuras, and as neither concerns a request for the service of Krishna or Viṣṇu in person, they cannot be linked structurally with the epic scene. But the underlying theme is shared: Arjuna and Duryodhana come before the sleeping Krishna to obtain "boons" when he awakens. Moreover, Krishna is "awakening" to his longest act of service: assisting the Pāṇḍavas in preparing for, fighting, and then resolving the effects of the Kurukṣetra war. Indeed, noting the contrast with the comfortably seated Duryodhana, perhaps one may see in the devotional pose of Arjuna, who stands at the foot of Krishna's bed with hands joined (*kṛtāñjaliḥ*; 5:7,7), a recognition by Krishna's dearest *bhakta* of the cosmic meaning of his friend's position.

One crucial theme has so far gone unmentioned in these comparisons. What makes it possible for Krishna to maintain his stance of impartiality once he learns that Duryodhana had entered his room first, and what makes it possible for him to set up the choice which will allow him to side with the Pāṇḍavas, is the fact that, upon waking, "first off he saw Arjuna."

[10] On the waking-sleeping myth, especially its yogic patterns, see Biardeau, EMH, II, 73–74.

This theme finds a remarkable analogue from a Germanic tradition, the legendary history of the Langobards (Lombards). From Paulus Diaconus' *Historia Langobardorum* 1,7–8, which bases its account on an anonymous seventh-century work called the *Origo Gentis Langobardorum*, we have the following account.[11] First known as the Winnili, the Langobards settled in a region called Scoringia[12] where they were confronted by the Vandals. The latter, "coercing all the neighboring provinces by war" and "elated by many victories . . . sent messengers to the Winnili to tell them that they should either pay tribute to the Vandals or make ready for the struggles of war." With the approval of their mother Gambara, Ibor and Aio, the two leaders of the Winnili, determined that liberty was preferable to tribute and sent messengers back to the Vandals with the reply that they would "rather fight than be slaves." Here Paulus gives us a description of the men on the favored side that accords well with themes in the *Mahābhārata*: "The Winnili were then all in the flower of their youth, but they were very few in number."[13] Although the present story of youths in migration would seem to imply a *uer sacrum* ("sacred spring"), we are reminded of the youth of Arjuna. The matter of inferior numbers could also just as well characterize the Pāṇḍavas at Kurukṣetra (see, for example, 5:152,23).

Now, with the two sides set for battle, we meet the theme of the waking god:

At this point, the men of old tell a silly story that the Wandals coming to Godan (Wotan) besought him for victory over the Winnili

[11] See William Dudley Fourke, trans., *History of the Langobards by Paul the Deacon* (Philadelphia: University of Pennsylvania, Department of History, 1907), pp. 11–17; cf. H. Munro Chadwick, *Heroic Age*, p. 115, and E. O. G. Turville-Petre, *Myth and Religion of the North* (New York: Holt, Rinehart, and Winston, 1964), p. 72.

[12] Fourke, *History of the Langobards*, p. 11, n. 1, says this was probably in the region of the lower Elbe.

[13] *Ibid.*, pp. 13–15.

and that he answered that he would give the victory to those whom he saw first at sunrise; that then Gambara went to Frea (Freja) wife of Godan and asked for victory for the Winnili, and that Frea gave her counsel that the women of the Winnili should take down their hair and arrange it upon the face like a beard, and that in the early morning they should be present with their husbands and in like manner station themselves to be seen by Godan from the quarter in which he had been wont to look through his window toward the east. And so it was done. And when Godan saw them at sunrise he said: "Who are these long-beards?" And then Frea induced him to give the victory to those to whom he had given the name. And thus Godan gave the victory to the Winnili. These things are worthy of laughter and are to be held of no account. For victory is due, not to the power of men, but it is rather furnished from heaven.[14]

Such is the account of Paul the Deacon. Certainly the role of Frea and the theme of the false beards find no analogues in the story of the waking Krishna, but there is a basic similarity in outline. In both stories, before the battle, each of two opposed sides seeks the boon of ultimate victory from a god who favors the side which he sees, or will see, first upon waking. Moreover, one cannot help wondering whether, as mentioned above, the youth of the Langobards might not have something to do with Godan's (Odinn's) attraction for them. Possibly their youth is to be connected with another theme that, at least according to Paulus,[15] has to do with Godan's seeing them first: their place in the east, the direction of the "young" sun. And the false beards imply either shaving or juniority.

Shapers of Strife

The second confrontation of Krishna with Odinn, or more exactly with a figure whom Odinn impersonates was first

[14] *Ibid.*, pp. 16–17.

[15] In the *Origo Gentis Langobardorum*, Frea must trick Godan into looking eastward; contrary to Fourke, however (see *ibid.*, pp. 16–17, n. 1), it seems unlikely that this earlier account shows an original preference of Godan for "his Wandal worshippers."

presented by Stig Wikander in one of his two articles comparing the events surrounding the battles of Brávellir and Kurukṣetra.[16] His remarks on this momentous comparison are very cautious, as is certainly proper. But perhaps another look will uncover further evidence that the points in common concerning Krishna and Odinn are well integrated into these two stories, in which Wikander has discovered so many remarkable parallels.

In both stories, a blind old king leads his forces—whether actually (Haraldus Hyldetan) or nominally (Dhṛtarāṣṭra)—against those of his nephews in a great battle which the nephews finally win. In both cases, as Wikander observes, a god in human form intervenes in the strife and, "with an ambiguous and sly maneuver, secures the victory for the side he favors. So it is with Odinn at Brávellir and with Krishna at Kurukṣetra." He also says it is "striking that Harald has the servant Bruno, Odinn disguised, as his driver. This reminds us of Arjuna in the *Mahābhārata*, who did not know that his driver was the god Krishna before he revealed himself to him."[17]

To be sure, the dissimilarities strike one as soon as the similarities are mentioned. Krishna drives the chariot for the chief hero of the side he favors, serves only as a noncombatant, and, in revealing himself to Arjuna, bestows the highest divine blessing upon him; Odinn, as Bruno, drives the chariot of the chief figure of the side he opposes, and, when he reveals himself, clubs the blind old king to death.

[16] See above, Chapter 1, n. 87.

[17] Wikander, "Från Bråvalla," pp. 184, 189 (my translation, aided by David Goldfrank). The presence of Bruno and Haraldus on the chariot is, according to Wikander, un-Scandinavian, such vehicles being unused in warfare; but this, he says, is ambiguous evidence for the provenance of the Scandinavian story: it could at this point be a poorly understood retelling of the Indian story, or of a story ultimately from India, where Krishna appears on his chariot with Arjuna; or it could be a reminiscence of a genuine epic tradition from an older cultural stage.

No such fate befalls Dhṛtarāṣṭra. But a closer look at Bruno will keep us from easily dismissing the possibility of some connection with Krishna. Just after telling us that Haraldus has transferred one of his nephews, Olo (prince-regent of Norway), to the service of his other nephew and eventual chief rival Ringo (prince-regent of Sweden), Saxo describes the machinations of Bruno:

At this time one Bruno was the sole partner and confidant of all Haraldus' councils. To this man both Haraldus and Ringo, whenever they needed a secret messenger, used to entrust their commissions. This degree of intimacy he obtained because he had been reared and fostered with them. But Bruno, amid the toils of his constant journeys to and fro, was drowned in a certain river; and Odinn, disguised under his name and looks, shook the close union of the kings by his treacherous embassage; and he sowed strife so guilefully that he engendered in men, who were bound by friendship and blood, a bitter mutual hate, which seemed unappeasable except by war.[18]

Krishna, of course, does not have to kindle the strife between the Kurus and Pāṇḍavas, but as early as the Rājasūya sacrifice, and certainly after the dice game, we see him fanning it. The parallels are most striking, however, in the *Udyogaparvan*, where Krishna, like Bruno, is an ambassador between the two parties, the last to have the ear of both, and a figure of whom "treachery" and "guile" would hardly be unrealistic charges.[19] The position of intermediary is in both cases made possible by a special "intimacy": Bruno reared and fostered apparently with both Ringo and Haraldus, Krishna bearing an "equal relationship" to both parties. Different theologies may also account for the different modes of impersonation: Krishna the lifelong *avatāra*, Odinn, in what looks like either a much attenuated story or Saxo's monkish sleight-of-hand,

[18] Oliver Elton, trans., *The First Nine Books of the Danish History of Saxo Grammaticus* (London: Norrœna Society, 1905), II, 468–69.

[19] See below, Chapter 6.

the double of a figure who has drowned. Most curiously, while the name Krishna means "Black," Bruno would seem to mean "Brown."[20] One can only speculate on what if any connection these two dark colors might have; to be sure, there are no "three Brunos" to parallel the *Mahābhārata*'s "three Kṛṣṇas."

A final parallel is the apparent divine shaping of both crises and their resolution. It is, according to Saxo, Odinn "whose oracle was thought to have been the cause of his [Haraldus'] birth,"[21] and, after Odinn helps Haraldus to consolidate his kingdom and gains his confidence as the ambassador Bruno, it is by Odinn-Bruno's hand that he dies. In the *Marābhārata*, things are more complicated, but the underlying motivation is similar. Dhṛtarāṣṭra's father is not Krishna, but Vyāsa. Yet Vyāsa is in fact a second Kṛṣṇa, Kṛṣṇa Dvaipāyana, and, like Krishna Vāsudeva, an incarnation of Viṣṇu-Nārāyaṇa. Thus Odinn, only partly through Bruno, shapes the career of Haraldus from birth to death, and Viṣṇu-Nārāyaṇa, only partly through Krishna, shapes that of Dhṛtarāṣṭra from birth to defeat. In each case, the intrusive, deformed element which the god has helped to create and sustain is finally overcome, and the renewal of order is achieved by the triumph of the blind king's nephews.

[20] *The Oxford English Dictionary*, for "brown" gives the etymology OE brún, OFris brûn, ON brún-n (Sw brun, Da brunn), OTeut *brûn-o-z, *brûn-â; H. S. Falk and Alf Torp, *Norwegisch Dänisches Etymologisches Wörterbuch* (Oslo and Bergen: Universitetsforlaget, 1960), p. 107, shows that *brun* ("brown") has the root meaning of "bright, shining," as "of a color which looks like something burnt." Cf. Fr. *brunir*, Eng. burnish. It is thus possible that Bruno could mean "Shining"; but it seems unlikely the root meaning by itself would have supplied the hero with his name.

[21] Elton, *Danish History*, p. 456; on this oracle, see Wikander, "Från Bråvalla," p. 188: the "pilgrimage" of Haraldus' father to the oracle at Uppsala to cure his wife's sterility is uncharacteristic of Scandinavian religion but typical of Indian. But Wikander argues that this need not be taken as an indication that the story is borrowed from India, as Saxo could have placed a Christian pilgrim image anachronistically in heathen time.

These two confrontations of Krishna-Viṣṇu with Odinn—which will not be the only ones to engage us—are curious from several angles. Both concern interventions by these gods in human, that is, epic-heroic, affairs. More specifically, they involve interventions at the beginnings, and, at Kurukṣetra and Brávellir, also at the conclusions, of great, if not the greatest, heroic battles in their respective traditions. We thus find Krishna's activities before the war doubly elucidated by comparisons with Germanic legends. But his role as the Pāṇḍavas' ambassador must be investigated further by additional Indo-European comparisons, ones concerning not only legends but rituals.

CHAPTER 6

Two Theophanies, Three Steps

Nowhere is Krishna more conspicuous than in the *Udyogaparvan*, the "Book of Preparations," making speeches, representing the Pāṇḍavas on his embassage to Hāstinapura, and catalyzing the conditions that build up to the inevitable clash at Kurukṣetra. But the "preparations" for war actually culminate not in the *Udyogaparvan* but the *Bhīṣmaparvan*, where Krishna, Arjuna, and Yudhiṣṭhira[1] complete their readiness for battle. In the case of Arjuna and Krishna, this final "preparation" is, of course, the *Bhagavad Gītā*. Thus, in following this segment of the epic through its natural course, I will focus not only on dramatic themes that concern Krishna in the *Udyogaparvan*, but on ones that concern him in his famous dialogue with Arjuna.

Arjuna's Vision: Observer at the *Pralaya*

In her remarkable study of the Hindu myth of the *pralaya*,[2] Madeleine Biardeau has provided a new perspective on the eleventh chapter of the *Bhagavad Gītā*, in which Krishna reveals to Arjuna the *viśvarūpadarśana*, the sight of his universal form. The celebrated theophany, which most scholars, perhaps judiciously, have left to explain itself, is now appreciated within a ritual context. As Biardeau observes, the text—in particular verses 15–33, which concern Arjuna's description of the vision

[1] See below, Chapter 9.

[2] Biardeau, EMH, 3, *BEFEO*, LVIII (1971), 17–89.

(15–31) and Krishna's explanation of its meaning (32–33)—is one of two used in the ritual of entry into *saṃnyāsa*, the life of renunciation.[3] It must suffice here to summarize: one who performs this ceremony symbolically renounces the three sacrificial fires and the three saṃsāric worlds and enters into the enlarged universe in which there are four additional worlds[4] beyond those of the ordinary person, there to find himself in the company of the Devas and Pitṛs, "all of these, like himself, being admitted to deliverance at the moment of the cosmic *pralaya*."[5] The choice of *Gītā* 11,15–33 to be recited at this juncture is full of significance: "It recalls to the *saṃnyāsin* the cosmic—and terrible—dimension of the god of deliverance, as if henceforth the perspective of a purely individual deliverance was forbidden him and was bound to a cosmic catastrophe."[6] For, as Biardeau demonstrates, the *Gītā* theophany itself depicts such cataclysm: "The vision which Arjuna has is near to that which an observer of the *pralaya* would have were he situated beyond it."[7]

Others, of course, have noticed that several points of Arjuna's description call upon images of the end of the *kalpa*.[8] And

[3] Biardeau brushes aside the question of when the *Gītā* passage was put to this ritual use; as she points out, the *Gītā* does not seem to know the seven worlds (probably a later, Purāṇic formulation) upon which the ritual depends for its cosmology; EMH, 3, p. 54, n. 1; cf. Hopkins, *Epic Mythology*, p. 60.

[4] Maharloka, Janaloka, Tapoloka, and Brahmaloka (or Satyaloka).

[5] EMH, 3, p. 50 (my translation); the ritual, described in *Baudhāyana Dharma Śāstra* 2, 10, 11–30, and *Vaikhānasa Smārta Sūtra* 9,6–8, is summarized and discussed in EMH, 3, pp. 49–50,52–54, and in P. V. Kane, *History of Dharmaśāstra* (5 vols.; Poona: Bhandarkar Oriental Research Institute, 1941), II, pt. 2, 930–75, especially 953–62.

[6] EMH, 3, p. 53 (my translation).

[7] *Ibid.*, p. 54 (my translation).

[8] See Robert C. Zaehner, *The Bhagavad-Gītā* (Oxford: Clarendon Press, 1969), commenting on verses 19 and 25 on "Time's [devouring] fire"; W. Douglas P. Hill, trans., *The Bhagavadgītā* (Oxford: Oxford University Press, 1928), similarly on verse 25 and on verse 15, explaining Krishna's many bellies "as the storehouse of creatures at their dissolution"; Swami Nikhilananda, *The Bhagavad Gita* (New York: Ramakrishna-Vivekananda Center, 1944), on verses 18, 25, 32, and 33.

Walter Ruben has appreciated the mythic character of the theophany as a whole in his otherwise artificial comparison of Krishna, revealing himself as all-devouring Time (*Kāla*), with Chronos-Kronos, "Time" swallowing up his own children.[9] More precise points have led Biardeau to observe the correlations between the *pralaya* myth and the *Gītā* theophany. Purāṇic descriptions of the *pralaya* distinguish two classes of beings: those who have not escaped rebirth and the law of *karman*, and who are absorbed, after the great "fire of time," by the "one ocean" into which the three worlds dissolve; and those who have been delivered to oscillate between the four higher worlds on the way to final release.[10] Out of the "single ocean," through the awakening of Viṣṇu-Nārāyaṇa who lies upon it, the first group will re-emerge in the next *kalpa* as part of the substance of the new creation; but the delivered are free to witness and experience the transformations of the cosmos in the timeless and blessed company of the most sublime divine actors—Viṣṇu, Śiva, and Brahmā (or either of the first two, or the goddess, in their all-inclusive identities).

Now Arjuna, in witnessing Krishna's theophany,[11] is for a moment placed at this latter vantage point by Krishna's grace. I cite the most pertinent verses, dividing them according to the order in which Arjuna sees (1) the fate of the delivered, (2) the fate of the nondelivered, and (3) the fate of the (three)

[9] Ruben, *Krishna*, pp. 221–22.

[10] EMH, 3, pp. 19–37; *Vāyu Purāṇa* 1,7,18–19ab gives the most complete list of the delivered: Devas, Pitṛs, Munis, Manus, and Suras ("gods" as juxtaposed with Asuras); EMH, 3, pp. 19–20 (text and translation) and 34 (discussion).

[11] Experiencing the *pralaya* is a sort of absolute revelation: see the Mārkaṇḍeya myth (*Mbh.* 3:186,56–78, and Heinrich Zimmer, *Myths and Symbols in Indian Art and Civilization* [New York: Harper, 1962], pp. 35–53), and EMH, 3, p. 57, where Biardeau discusses the absolute experience of those who live through the *prākṛtapralaya*, the end of a life (not just a day) of Brahmā.

worlds:

(1) For into Thee are entering yonder throngs of gods [Suras];
Some, affrighted, praise Thee with reverent gestures;
Crying "Hail!" the throngs of great seers [Ṛṣis] and perfected ones [Siddhas]
Praise Thee with abundant laudations.

The Rudras, the Ādityas, the Vasus, and the Sādhyas,
All-gods, Aśvins, Maruts, and the Steam-drinkers [Pitṛs]
The hosts of heavenly musicians [Gandharvas], sprites [Yakṣas], demons [Asuras], and perfected ones [Siddhas]
Gaze on Thee, and all are quite amazed. [21–22]

(2) And Thee yonder sons of Dhṛtarāṣṭra,
All of them, together with the hosts of kings,
Bhīṣma, Droṇa, and yonder son of the charioteer (Karṇa) too,
Together with our chief warriors likewise,

Hastening enter Thy mouths,
Frightful with tusks and terrifying;
Some, stuck between the teeth,
Are seen with their heads crushed.

As the many water torrents of the rivers
Rush headlong toward the single sea (*samudram*),[12]
So yonder heroes of the world of men into Thy
Flaming mouths do enter. [26–28]

(3) As moths into a burning flame
Do enter unto their destruction with utmost impetuosity,
Just so unto their destruction enter the worlds [*lokās*]
Into Thy mouths also, with utmost impetuosity.

Devouring them Thou lickest up voraciously on all sides
All the worlds with Thy flaming jaws;

[12] The word "single" should be in brackets, as in Zaehner's translation, although it is implied.

> Filling with radiance the whole universe,
> Thy terrible splendours burn, O Viṣṇu![13] [29–30][14]

One could make further precisions and qualifications on the comparison: the enumeration of the delivered is much more generous (even including Asuras!) than in any Purāṇic list (see above, n. 9); Arjuna's vision is gained not from any ulterior worlds (see above, n. 2) but from a battlefield in this one; and Arjuna is not a *saṃnyāsin* but a prince, whom Krishna teaches that *karmayoga* is superior to *saṃnyāsa* (*Gītā* 5,2).[15] But the main fact stands: it is as lord of the *pralaya*—itself a theme which he weaves into many of the *Gītā*'s teachings[16]—that Krishna reveals himself to Arjuna.

One need not insist on the importance of this chapter in the structure of the *Gītā*. Here, as a final capping of Krishna's arguments, which have already dispelled Arjuna's delusion (11,1), Arjuna is turned back toward his kṣatriya dharma; and

[13] I assume that in identifying Krishna and Viṣṇu, the *Gītā* is revealing one if its essential "teachings" and not just some accident of history—Krishnaism incorporating Viṣṇuism, or vice versa. Too many scholars have allowed their search for separate origins to obscure the all-important significance of this relationship; on this verse and verse 24, where Arjuna also calls Krishna "Viṣṇu," see, for example, the labored efforts of Hill, *Bhagavadgītā*, p. 33, to keep them apart: "He [Krishna] is called Viṣṇu . . . in contexts where Arjuna may well have been reminded of the sun."

[14] Here and elsewhere (unless otherwise noted) I quote from Franklin Edgerton, trans., *The Bhagavad Gītā Translated and Interpreted*, Harvard Oriental Series, XXXVIII and XXXIX (2 vols.; Cambridge: Harvard University Press, 1956), XXXVIII. Again, one cannot insist on more than three worlds for the *Gītā* (see above, n. 3); the *pralaya* teaching would seem to have been able to develop around this core.

[15] But this question is much more complex, as *saṃnyāsa* and yoga form a unity in the *Gītā*; see EMH, 3, pp. 61–67.

[16] See *Gītā* 7,5–14 (in connection with the image of the universe "strung on me like heaps of pearls on a string"); 8,15–28 (in connection with the *devayāna* and *pitṛyāna*); 9,5–10 (on *prakṛti* at the *pralaya*); 14,2 (on devotees of Krishna being undisturbed by *sarga* or *pralaya*); 14,15–16 (in connection with the *guṇas*); cf. 16, 11, and see Etienne Lamotte, *Notes sur la Bhagavadgītā* (Paris: Guethner, 1929), p. 67, for brief discussion.

one may observe that once this chapter is over, Arjuna's questions no longer have dramatic value: he is "convinced" and is merely asking for clarification on points of doctrine.[17] Moreover, this is one of the two points in the *Gītā* where Krishna reveals to Arjuna something of his divine purpose and the significance of his part in the *Mahābhārata* war. The first is Krishna's famous identification of his activity with the *avatāra* doctrine and the yuga structure (4,8cd): "To make a firm footing for the right [dharma], I come into being in age after age [*yuge-yuge*]."[18] But now, seemingly going to a deeper level of his identity, he discloses that his activities are linked with the *kalpa* structure and the destructive side of Time.[19] With the vision still before him, Arjuna asks for an explanation; Krishna replies: "I am Time [Death], cause of the destruction of the worlds, matured / And set out to gather in the worlds here. / Even without thee (thy action) all shall cease to exist, / The warriors that are drawn up in the opposing ranks" (11,32).

It is against this second background, then, and immediately (11,32–33 and 51), that Arjuna comes to understand his duty to fight. Not only does he see himself as Krishna's friend and ally in the intrayuga struggle between dharma and adharma; at a deeper level,[20] as Krishna's *bhakta*—for it is only "by

[17] See *Gītā* 12,1; 14,21; 17,21; and 18,1; with his interest in dramatic continuity, Rudolf Otto, *The Original Gītā*, J. E. Turner, trans. (London: Allen and Unwin, 1939), regards everything from 11,51 to 18,58 as interpolation.

[18] It is a futile argument that because the term *avatāra* is not used here that the doctrine or the identification with Viṣṇu (see above, n. 13) is not implied.

[19] On the importance of recognizing the distinctness of yuga and *kalpa*, see EMH, 1, pp. 22–23, and EMH, 3, pp. 37 and 65, n. 1, 66, n. 2. In particular, Biardeau observes that while the yuga cycles have to do with the rise and fall of dharma, the *kalpa* cycle occurs irrespective of dharma.

[20] Note that Otto, *Original Gītā*, p. 136, regards 11,33 as "the principal verse of the *Gītā*, the *carama śloka* since it is solely from them that Kṛṣṇa's conversation with Arjuna receives its real meaning"; but he rejects 4,7–8 from the "original *Gītā*."

unswerving devotion" (11,54) that this vision is manifested—he now sees himself as a "mere instrument" (*nimittamātram*; 11,34) in the awesome process, totally without struggle and beyond dharma and adharma (see above, n. 19), by which Krishna-Viṣṇu, as Time, brings the worlds to ripeness and "gathers them in." Yet this double perspective completes Arjuna's instruction: he learns the secret that, with regard to the central teachings of the performance of duty and the desirelessness of man's activity, the end of the yuga and the end of the *kalpa* must be as one. To participate in Krishna's universe is to be his "friend and devotee" (4,3; see 11,44), that is, both to uphold dharma and to seek *mokṣa*.

The Theophany in the Kuru Court

Biardeau's insights allow us to appreciate that it is not just one chapter, but the whole *Gītā*, which presupposes such a significant cosmology. But more than this, we have been led to speak of the *Gītā*—theophany and all—as an integral part of the *Mahābharata*.[21] And it so happens that this is not Krishna's first theophany in the epic, but his second:[22] a fact which could hardly have been insignificant in the eyes of the *Mahābhārata*'s poets, but which has escaped the notice or mention of seeingly

[21] On the *Gītā*'s place in the epic, see, most recently, and rather inadequately, Georg von Simson, "Die Einschaltung der *Bhagavadgītā* im *Bhīṣmaparvan* des *Mahābhārata*," *IIJ*, XI (1969), 159, nn. 1 and 2, actually citing only those who more or less agree with him that it is an interpolation. For counteropinions, see S. Lévi, "Tato Jayam Udirayet," L. G. Khare, trans., *ABORI*, I (1918–1919), 13–20; V. S. Sukthankar, *Mahābhārata*, p. 119; Otto, *Original Gītā*, pp. 11–14; Dumézil, *ME*, I, 221, 93, 34; Zaehner, *Bhagavad-Gītā*, pp. 6–7; and Biardeau, EMH, 3, p. 61, n. 1. K. T. Telang, trans., *The Bhagavadgītā*, SBE, VIII (1882; repr. Delhi: Motilal Banarsidass, 1970), p. 5, registers "a feeling of painful diffidence regarding the soundness of any conclusion whatsoever."

[22] One other epic theophany (14:54,3–7), supposedly redisclosing the *Gītā* form (there called *rūpamaiśvaram*; 3) to the desert sage Uttaṅka, yields no *pralaya* imagery and holds no important narrative links with the other theophanies.

all the *Gītā*'s critics but one.[23] His name is famous: Rudolf Otto. Although I cannot share his views on an "original *Gītā*," we may note with admiration how two facets of his approach have borne fruit. First, not surprisingly, he has been guided by what we would call the *Gītā*'s theology rather than its philosophy; and second, surprising to me, he has insisted that the *Gītā* must be understood within its narrative context. He says that the *Gītā* theophany is "a quite obvious parallel to the Theophany in which Kṛṣṇa has already revealed himself to Duryodhana," and he insists that "these subtle parallels and contrasts of sublime epic construction cannot and must not be ignored."[24] I will return to his exposition of these relationships, but first let us familiarize ourselves with the new scene.

As Otto says, it is just "a short time before" the battlefield scene of the *Gitā* that the first theophany occurs.[25] Krishna has come to Hāstinapura as the last of a series of three emissaries who have gone between the two sides to perform acts of prewar diplomacy. He represents the Pāṇḍavas before the Kurus with a series of pro forma exhortations to peace and compromise, and these are backed up—since there is no real possibility that they will be accepted by Duryodhana—with lists of grievances, exchanges of insults, and threats of war. But Krishna's words are persuasive, so much so that Duḥśāsana, Duryodhana's foremost brother, is pressed to say that if Duryodhana does not accede, "assuredly, having bound you, the Kauravas will deliver you over to the son of Kuntī [Yudhiṣṭhira]" (5:126,22). Upon hearing these words, Duryodhana makes a memorable gesture: "sighing like a great snake" (126, 24), he rises from his seat in anger and quits the assembly, followed by his brothers and the assembled kings (whose silence earlier had shown deference to Duryodhana although "they

[23] Quite possibly someone has been overlooked, but generally *Gītā* criticism has been preoccupied with other problems.

[24] Otto, *Original Gītā*, pp. 14, 11, n. 4.

[25] *Ibid.*, p. 11.

applauded Krishna with their hearts" [5:93,62]). Krishna's persuasiveness, then, has no effect on Duryodhana other than to press him into an act of disrespect, for his defiant exit is an insult to Krishna and the various Kuru elders who remain behind.

Along with the exit, which Krishna will respond to in kind, the scene confronts us with another theme that builds now to a powerful climax. Earlier (5:86,12–15), Duryodhana had publicly expressed his intention to restrain and bind Krishna upon the latter's arrival at Hāstinapura; but Dhṛtarāṣṭra and Bhīṣma had denounced him. Now, with negotiations completely broken down, each side turns to this device as a last resort. First, with Duryodhana and his supporters absent from the court, Krishna urges the Kuru elders to do exactly what Duḥśāsana had feared (126,33–49): abandon Duryodhana, he says, as the Yādavas did Kaṃsa, and bind him—with his closest confederates—over to the Pāṇḍavas as Varuṇa, the lord of Waters, bound the Daityas and Dānavas in the ocean with his nooses and with those of Dharma (*tānbaddhvā dharmapāśaiśca svaiśca pāśairjaleśvaraḥ varuṇaḥ*; 46). These words provoke neither comment nor action. Rather, Duryodhana is summoned back to court to hear one more appeal from his mother Gāndhārī, and when he walks out again, disregarding her words, he meets secretly with Karṇa, Duḥśāsana, and Śakuni. Suspecting that Krishna and Bhīṣma will try to seize them, Duryodhana once again—but this time covertly—plans with his allies to seize Krishna and thus destroy the hopes of the Pāṇḍavas (128,4–8). Yet even as they state their resolution, one senses their apprehension of the difficulty of seizing the "quick-acting" (*kṣipra-kārin*; used twice: 128,4 and 8) Krishna.

At this point, rather strangely, it is not Krishna but his kinsman Sātyaki—"skilled in interpreting signs" (*iṅgitajña*; 128, 9)—who intuits the plan. He sees to it that Krishna's troops are alerted and then enters the court to warn him. There are some hurried deliberations in which Krishna says he would not object should Duryodhana try to seize him, as this censurable and futile act would only benefit the Pāṇḍavas (128,24–29). At this, Dhṛtarāṣṭra calls his son back one last time, together with his fellow conspirators and the kings (33). Amidst the final pleas for reconciliation, a restrained but charming expression of *bhakti* is evoked from Dhṛtarāṣṭra, once again taking us to a "deeper level" of insight into what is going on: "Like the wind, difficult to seize with the hand, like the moon (or the rabbit), hard to touch with the hand, like the earth, hard to bear on the head, Krishna is difficult to seize by force" (128,39).[26] But Duryodhana cannot be dissuaded. The impasse is complete, and the scene is set for Krishna's first theophany in the *Mahābhārata.*

Possessing energy [*vīryavan*], Krishna addressed Duryodhana: "Alone am I [*eko 'hamiti*]. That is how you regard me, O Suyodhana, from delusion [*mohāt*]. And surrounding me, O weak minded one, you wish to seize me. Yet here are all the Pāṇḍavas, as also the Andhakas and Vṛṣṇis. Here are the Ādityas, Rudras, and Vasus, together with the Maharṣis." Saying this Keśava, that slayer of hostile heroes, laughed loudly. And while the high-souled Śaurin was smiling, the thirty [the gods]—having forms of lighting, of the size of a thumb, flashing like fire [*vidyudrūpā . . . aṅguṣṭhamātrās . . . pāvakārciṣaḥ*]—were released [*mumucur* (Ganguli-Roy trans.:" from the body")]. Situated on his forehead was Brahmā, and Rudra was on his breast. The World Regents were on his [four] arms, and Agni [Fire] was produced from his mouth, as also the Ādityas, Sādhyas, Vasus, Aśvins, the Maruts together with Indra, and the Viśvedevas. And such also became the forms of the Yakṣas, Gandharvas, and Rākṣasas. So from his two forearms were manifested Saṃkarṣana and Dhanaṃjaya—Arjuna on the right with his bow, Rāma [Balarāma] on the left with his plow. Behind him were Bhīma, Yudhiṣṭhira, and the two sons of Mādrī, and the Andhakas, Vṛṣṇis, Pradyumna and others of prominence were in front of Krishna, their great weapons upraised.

[26] *durgrahaḥ pāṇinā vāyurduḥsparśaḥ pāṇinā śaśī*
durdharā pṛthivī mūrdhnā durgrahaḥ keśavo balāt.

And on Krishna's various arms were seen the conch, the discus, the mace, the dart [? *śakti*], the bow Śārṅga, the plow, and the sword, all upraised and ready for striking, blazing on all sides. And from his eyes, nose, ears, and from all sides were manifested highly terrible [*mahāraudrāḥ*] sparks of fire mixed with smoke, and also [sparks] like the sun's rays in the pores of his skin. And beholding this dreadful self [*ghoramātmanam*] of the high-souled Keśava, the kings shut their eyes, their hearts trembling, but not Droṇa, Bhīṣma, and the highly intelligent Vidura, and the highly favored Saṃjaya, and the Ṛṣis possessed of wealth of *tapas*, to whom the Lord [*bhagavān*] Janārdana gave divine sight. And beholding that very surprising [appearance] of Mādhava in the court, celestial drums sounded and a rain of flowers fell; the whole earth trembled and the ocean was agitated, and the inhabitants of the earth [or the kings (*pārthivāḥ*)] became deeply perplexed. [129,1c–15]

Krishna then withdraws this form (*vapus*), which is referred to as "variegated" (*citra-*) and "auspicious" (*ṛddhimat-*, literally: "possessing growth or increase"), and walks out—righteously where Duryodhana had just left unrighteously—with his kinsmen Sātyaki and Kṛtavarman (16–17).

Such is the theophany in which Rudolf Otto saw "subtle parallels and contrasts of sublime epic construction" with the theophany of the *Bhagavad Gītā*. But when we turn to his *The Original Gītā*, we find little indication of what he has in mind. Krishna "disarms the miscreant" in one instance and obtains obedience to his "supreme divine decree" in the other; both Duryodhana and Arjuna are "victims of anxiety": the former "about the issue of the contest," the latter "about the sacred laws of piety"; Duryodhana is "unmasked," Arjuna is "accepted as a tool for the exalted deeds of God, although he is at the same time humbled because of his 'wilfulness.'" These "parallels and contrasts" do not, of course, have much to do with the epic's narrative structure. Rather, the oppositions that preoccupy Otto concern the psychological states of the two heroes, what he several times refers to as their "specific situation." And it soon becomes apparent that in confining himself to parallels of this type, Otto is allowing his notion of an "original *Gītā*" to color his comparison of the theophanies. His "original" is pared of Sāṃkhya, Yoga, Vedānta, and Bhakti doctrines to reveal "Krishna's own voice and deed" by which he renders Arjuna "willing to undertake the special service of the Almighty will of God Who decides the fate of battles."[27] We need only point out that from the perspective opened up by Biardeau, the "fate of battles" is a trivial issue indeed.

There is, then, a sort of "Here I stand" quality to the manner in which the Lutheran scholar sees Arjuna and Duryodhana face to face with God, submitting to, or being submitted to, his will.[28] Not surprisingly, he sees the multiform aspects of the *Gītā* theophany as "expressions of the numinously terrible, not speculative symbols of Universal Unity." Even if we agree with this as it is phrased, we realize that Otto fails to see any importance in the symbols themselves and in what the principal figures represent. My earlier expression of admiration should now be qualified. Otto is guided by the *Gītā*'s theology, but it is a theology relieved of its cosmology (which Otto never discusses) and its symbols (which Otto is satisfied to explain by their numinousness). And although Otto insists on the significance of the narrative context of the two theophanies, Arjuna and Duryodhana are important to him only as recipients of revelations (presumably historical) by God. He is only barely interested in them as figures in a wider epic drama and not interested in—although apparently recognizing—the nature of this drama, at least on one level, as "myth."[29]

More commentary on the two theophanies may be added. First, with regard to narrative context, there is another incident, also forming part of the sequence of events leading up

[27] Otto, *Original Gītā*, p. 11 and n. 4; cf. pp. 153–54; other quotes at pp. 14, 136, 138, 146, 153.

[28] Presupposing a linear historical development of Indian "monotheism" behind these theophanies, Otto even suggests that the god to have originally inspired such an awesome vision as that in the *Gītā* was probably Rudra-Śiva; *ibid.*, pp. 156–57.

[29] *Ibid.*, pp. 149, n. 2, 137.

to the war, in which Arjuna and Duryodhana are juxtaposed to one another in their relationship to Krishna: the scene at the waking Krishna's bedside.[30] Krishna's "equal relationship" to the two invites a search for meaningful contrasts in the narrative implications of the two divine self-disclosures. On some points, it seems we are rewarded. In the court theophany, Krishna's ostensible purpose is to make peace, whereas in the battlefield theophany it is to make war. More than this, the first theophany takes place in a scene which has built up to the point where the deluded Duryodhana regards Krishna to be "alone," whereas the second occurs in the very midst of the battlefield, between the two drawn-up armies, where Arjuna has had Krishna take him so that he can view the assembled hosts which comprise in their ranks representatives of "all" the peoples of the world. And yet, when he appears to be alone, his manifestation is public (appreciated by all who do not close their eyes), whereas when he is in the midst of many, his revelation is private, reserved for his "friend and devotee."

These oppositions, however, begin to make sense only within the context of Hindu cosmology, with its symbols and structures. Here Biardeau's comments on the *Gītā* help us to extend Otto's rather narrow conception of the parallels and contrasts between the two theophanies. In brief, when Krishna appears alone, he produces or "releases" all classes of beings (except Asuras)[31] from his own person; and when he appears at the very center of all beings, he dissolves them into himself. If Arjuna is close to being "an observer of the *pralaya*," Duryodhana—or more accurately the elders and Ṛṣis to whom Krishna gives "divine sight"—is witness to a sort of creation. In the one case, Krishna shows his dissolving "dreadful form" (*ugrarūpam*: *Gītā* 11,31); in the other—even though the kings see it only as his

[30] See above, beginning of Chapter 5.

[31] Possibly the poets view the production of Asuras as a redundancy, since the Asuras are already present, incarnated in the assembled kings.

"dreadful self" (*ghoramātmanam*) and close their eyes—his form is "variegated and auspicious [or increasing]." In this connection, a comment by Zaehner takes on added significance: when Arjuna concludes his description in the *Gītā* and asks Krishna to explain this *ugrarūpam*, his words, in Zaehner's translation, are: "Fain would I know you as you are in the beginning" (*vijñātum icchāmi bhavantam ādyam*; 11,31). As Zaehner comments: "Arjuna does not yet understand the terrible side of his nature displayed by Krishna. . . . Nothing in Krishna's teaching had prepared him for this. He would sooner know Him 'as he is in the beginning', in his eternal rest, rather than his incomprehensible and seemingly savage activity."[32] The opposition thus seems to be implied within the *Gītā* itself, in Arjuna's uncertain response. What the epic poets have done, then, is give us two contrasting—or at least partially contrasting—visions of Krishna's form and modes of action. Or, to use an Indian terminology, the poets have used the device of presenting the divine nature from the standpoint of different *darśanas*, a device used with considerable frequency in connection with other subjects in the epic,[33] and one which has required in this case that we suspend the question of which theophany might be the older (certainly it is not a question of an "original") in order to examine them for the light they shed on each other.

However, although we can speak of meaningful contrasts on the levels of Indian theology and cosmology, we see that it is not simply a neat, sequential juxtaposition of cosmogony (*sarga*

[32] Zaehner, *Bhagavad-Gītā*, p. 311.

[33] See below, Chapter 12, discussing the two "views" of how Aśvatthāman could have succeeded in his night raid, and, in a similar vein, the many "views" on Droṇa's death expressed at the end of the *Droṇaparvan* (see below, Chapter 10); our general point should be set beside a memorable remark of van Buitenen's ("The Sabhāparvan," p. 79): "The epic is a series of precisely stated problems imprecisely and therefore inconclusively resolved, every inconclusive solution raising a new problem; until the very end, when the question remains: whose is heaven and whose is hell?"

or *pratisarga*) followed by *pralaya*. As we said, the court theophany is only a sort of creation. The narrative context, the modes of revelation, and the symbols involved in the description are in no way direct reminders of any Hindu creation myth, although in matters of mode and symbol it seems quite likely that the poets have kept the *Puruṣa Sūkta* in the backs of their minds.[34] Thus, although the two theophanies offer "perspectives" (*darśanas*) on Krishna's creative and destructive aspects, his all-out-of-one and his all-into-one dimensions, they do so without presenting them as a complete diptych. The court theophany seems to hint at something else, which would never have come to light were it not for a brief but important article by Dumézil.

Krishna and the "Three Steps"

Dumézil has explored the Indo-European myths and legends which show parallels with the ritual roles and practices of a college of Roman priests, the fetials, who were formally responsible for making peace and declaring war.[35] Their duties would take them as envoys or ambassadors in rituals of diplomacy into lands of "foreigners" and especially of enemies and could entail the making of treaties,[36] the presentation of demands

[34] For example, the general theme of the emergence of beings from the god's person, and more particularly the connection in both "theophanies" of Agni with the mouth. In an interpolation made in one Devanāgarī text, the description continues after *śloka* 11 (CE 5,495*) with mention of Krishna's thousand feet, arms, and eyes, and the sun and moon standing in his eyes; see Otto's trans., *Original Gītā*, p. 152). The text read along with the *Gītā* theophany in the *saṃnyāsa*-entry ritual (see above, n. 3) is the *Puruṣa Sūkta* (EMH, 3, 52–53)—the use in this ritual perhaps signifying a reflection on the two modes of divine action in creation and destruction.

[35] Dumézil, "Études et mémoires, I, Remarques sur le '*ius fetiale*'" (hereinafter "Remarques"), *Revue des Etudes Latines*, XXXIV (1956), 93–108; the study is reprinted with important additions in Dumézil, *Idées romaines*, pt 1, Chapter 3, "*Ius fetiale*" (Paris: Gallimard, 1969), pp. 61–78.

[36] At the conclusion of which they would invoke the trifunctional triad of gods: Jupiter, Mars, and Quirinus (Polybius 3. 25,6); see Dumézil, "Remarques," p. 108.

for reparation of wrongs and thus, if these were not met, preparation for a "just" war,[37] and also pseudonegotiations of considerable duplicity.[38] The key passage for our purposes is one from *Livy* concerning the procedure followed by the Pater Patratus, the fetial who would go to another city to demand justice on behalf of the Romans:

When the envoy [*legatus*] has arrived at the frontiers of the people from whom satisfaction is sought, he covers his head with a bonnet—the covering is of wool—and says: "Hear, Jupiter; hear, ye boundaries of"—naming whatever nation they belong to;—"let righteousness hear [*audiat fas*]! I am the public herald of the Roman people; I come duly and religiously commissioned [*iuste pieque legatus venio*]; let my words be credited." Then he recites his demands, after which he takes Jupiter to witness: "If I demand unduly and against religion that these men and these things be surrendered to me, let me never enjoy my native land." These words he rehearses when he crosses the boundary line, the same to what man soever first meets him, the same when he enters the city gates, the same when he has come into the market place [*forum*], with only a few changes in the form and wording of the oath. If those whom he demands are not surrendered, at the end of three and thirty days—for such is the conventional number—he declares war. [1,32,6–8 (B. O. Foster, trans., Loeb Classical Library, 1919); cf. *Dionysius of Halicarnassus* 2,72,6–9]

As Dumézil shows, in these four stops for invocations, the Pater Patratus marks out three zones in this "foreign world."[39]

There is ample documentation of Indo-European parallels to get us from Rome to India, and, as Dumézil says, it is not a matter of finding other examples of similarly specialized

[37] Dumézil, *Idées romaines*, p. 61; cf. Dionysius of Halicarnassus, *Roman Antiquities*, 72. 4.

[38] In a letter of January 5, 1969, which first alerted me to his study and to the possibility of this comparison, Dumézil refers to the negotiations after the episode of the Caudine Forks (*Livy* 9. 10, 7–10) as "the extreme case" of "the complicity of the *fetialis* and the Roman general." See also Dumézil, *Archaic Roman Religion*, Philip Krapp, trans. (Chicago: University of Chicago Press, 1970), p. 123.

[39] Dumézil, "Remarques," pp. 105–6.

priests ("the Indian priest is multivalent, omnivalent"), but of appreciating similar scenarios in myths and legends.[40] This does not mean making comparisons with other ambassador figures, although such an investigation might prove interesting.[41] Rather, the important common theme is that of stepping forth, usually with three strides, into or through uncharted or enemy territory so as to establish a just or religious base or foundation[42] there and to open up (one might say sacralize) the space necessary for conquest by war. Two other instances are the Iranian Rashnu who provides Mithra with the space necessary for his exploits and who takes part in opening the way for righteous souls to ascend through the three regions of Good Thoughts, Good Words, and Good Deeds;[43] and the strange Irish figure Amairgen, hero of the last race to occupy Ireland, whose first right-footed step on the island is given special textual emphasis and whose approach—on his initial prewar mission—to the island's capital is thrice arrested, each time by one of the queens of the land.[44] Both of the figures just cited have been compared with Viṣṇu,[45] for it is Viṣṇu

[40] *Ibid.*, p. 101.

[41] We have already noticed (Chapter 5 at n. 19) the embassy of Bruno in Saxo's account of the Battle of Brávellir. One should also look at Odysseus and Menelaos' embassy before the Trojan War (*Iliad* 3. 201–2,217–24, and 11. 138–40), and at Rostam's embassy to Mazandaran in the *Shāh-nāma* (Warner and Warner, trans., *Shāhnāma*, II, 63–70).

[42] See Dumézil, "Remarques," pp. 96–101, linking *fētiālis*, presumed from *fētis* ("fondement"), and Sanskrit *dhātu* ("fondation").

[43] *Ibid.*, p. 204; cf. Dumézil, "Viṣṇu et les Marut à travers la réforme zoroastrienne," *JA*, CCXLI (1953), 11–17.

[44] Dumézil, *Idées romaines*, pp. 75–78.

[45] On Rashnu, see above, n. 43. On Amairgen, Rees and Rees, *Celtic Heritage*, pp. 96–100, make two comparisons, the first the less plausible: (1) Amairgen on the sea before his first step on the isle (see R. A. Stewart Macalister, ed. and trans., *Lebor Gabála Érenn: The Book of the Taking of Ireland*, pt. 5, Irish Text Society, XLV [Dublin, 1956], 33) with Viṣṇu lying on the ocean, both empowered to "bring a new world into being"; and (2) Amairgen's theophany, which follows an "I am" formula ("I am Wind on Sea, / I am Ocean Wave, etc." (see Macalister, *Lebor Gabála*, pp. 110–13),

who has given the three strides their renown. First, in the *Ṛg Veda*, Viṣṇu's three steps create for Indra "the vast field which will be the theatre of their victory" over Vṛtra.[46] The cosmogonic overtones of this scenario have impressed F. B. J. Kuiper,[47] but from the comparative perspective, it looks as if this Vedic "opening of the cosmos" is but a variant of the wider and highly multivalent theme of the opening of alien or hostile space. Second, from the Brāhmaṇas to the Purāṇas, it is after entering the realm of the Asuras that Viṣṇu, in his Dwarf (Vāmana) form, enlarges himself so as to step through the three worlds and restore them to the gods.[48]

There are important structural differences between the two Indian myths. The Vāmana takes his three steps not *into* the enemy territory, as in other Indo-European scenarios, but, having already entered it, *from within it outward*. By the same token, the Dwarf, by his three steps, does not open the way for Indra to conquer the worlds, but conquers them himself.

---

with Krishna's description of his "supernal manifestations" (*vibhūtis*" in *Gītā* 10,20–42). However, whereas Amairgen describes his forms when he steps on land, at the start of his initial nonmartial compaign into the island, Krishna describes his after the nonmartial mission into Kuru-land, at the beginning of the war. In a wider framework another unsettling parallel emerges: in the series of five races that occupy Ireland, Amairgen's theophany occurs at the beginning of the last; in the series of four yugas, Krishna's also occurs at the start of the last, both coming at the juncture between "pre-history" and "modern times."

[46] Dumézil, "Remarques," p. 104, quoting from Hermann Oldenberg, *La Religion du Veda*, Victor Henry, trans. (Paris: Félix Alcan, Editeur, 1903), p. 193 (my translation).

[47] Kuiper, "The Three Strides of Viṣṇu," *Indological Studies in Honor of W. Norman Brown*, Ernest Bender, ed. (New Haven: American Oriental Society, 1962), pp. 137–51. Kuiper's article is of great importance in establishing the nonsolar character of the three steps (p. 141) and in insisting on the "central" character of the Vedic Viṣṇu (p. 144), a position analogous to that of the epic Krishna (pp. 145 and 150).

[48] On the many variations within this narrative framework, see Gaya Charan Tripathi, *Der Ursprung und die Entwicklung der Vāmana-Legende in der Indischen Literatur* (Weisbaden: Otto Harrassowitz, 1968), with English summary, pp. 237–43. My discussion of the Vāmana myth draws from this work.

Furthermore, the theme in the Vāmana myth concerning the *restoration* of territory to the gods differs from that of the *opening* of new territory which, as (still) seen in the Vedic "cosmogony," is most comparable to other Indo-European examples. It is worth keeping these contrasts in mind, for as we return to the epic Krishna, we find an intrigue that corresponds to the Vedic and Indo-European patterns in each instance but the last. First, however, let us note that Dumézil has invited the comparison: "In the *Mahābhārata*, Krishna is the incarnation and the epic transposition of Viṣṇu . . . ; his role as an ambassador, a veritable fetial, on the eve of the war, throughout the whole fifth book (*Udyogaparvan*), ought to be considered in the light of this present study."[49] No doubt Dumézil has precise points in mind, some of which, one hopes, will correspond with those offered here. In any case, let us now look more closely at Krishna's ambassadorship and the events surrounding his court theophany.

Krishna is the last of three emissaries to seek peace between the Kurus and the Pāṇḍavas, but he does not really expect peace. As he explains to Yudhiṣṭhira (5:71,25–34), he will go to the Kuru court to remove "the doubt of all men" (*sarvalokasya . . . saṃśayam*; 26) by praising Yudhiṣṭhira's virtues and denouncing Duryodhana's transgressions, thus persuading not only the assembled kings but also the people of town and country, the young and the old, and the four *varṇas* (29); although he sees no virtue (dharma) in suing for peace, he can represent Yudhiṣṭhira's desire for it while observing the inclinations and proceedings of the foes (32–33), all the while expecting war with them (*sarvathā yuddhamevāhamāśaṃsāmi paraiḥ saha*; 34). He departs after a morning ritual (81,9–10), taking Sātyaki (81,22) along with ten *mahārathas*, "great chariot warriors," and thousands of troops (82,1–2). Aside from the portents which accompany his movements—wherever he goes

[49] *Idées romaines*, p. 74, n. 2 (my translation)—a new note in the 1969 version of the original 1956 article (see above, n. 35).

there are gentle breezes and auspicious signs while everywhere else are disasters (82,4–12)—the poets are interested in a ritual concern, the matter of hospitality. Krishna first makes his way to Vṛkasthala (82,20), one of the five towns demanded by Yudhiṣṭhira (see below, note 54), and there spends the night. Hearing that he has set out, Dhṛtarāṣtra orders that sumptuous pavilions or halls (*sabhās*) be built to receive him there, and the task is carried out by Duryodhana (83,9–17). But Krishna sidesteps the entrapment that accepting these honors would bring, "not having even looked at [*asamīkṣyaiva*] all those diversely bejeweled pavilions" (83,18). Dhṛtarāṣṭra then plans a second time to honor Krishna upon his arrival at Hāstinapura by preparing a gala reception for him in the city and in his own palace and readying for him Duḥśāsana's mansion, the most splendid of all (85,19–21); instead, after a public welcome and a mere exchange of courtesies at Dhṛtarāṣṭra's home, Krishna takes up residence unostentatiously at the home of Vidura (87,22).[50] Then, after a visit to Duryodhana's mansion, Krishna refuses his hospitality: having been offered cows, honey, and then palaces and the kingship (88,9),[51] as well as food (11), he again accepts hospitality only from Vidura, pending the success of his mission.

Several things stand out among these three refusals to accept favors at three different stages in his journey. First, this is the only instance where the stages of one of Krishna's journeys are marked; elsewhere, as Ruben has noted, the poets allow him to cover vast distances without the blink of an eye.[52] Moreover, we see similarities to the approaches of some of the other

[50] Krishna's allegiance to virtue seems to be suggested here, as Vidura incarnates a portion of Dharma.

[51] *Nivedayāmāsa tadā gṛhānrājyaṃ ca kauravaḥ*; 5:89,9cd; on this mere formality cf. 1:117,18: Bhīṣma "offered kingship and kingdom" (*rājyaṃ ca rāṣṭram . . . nyavedayat*) to an arriving group of Maharṣis.

[52] Ruben, *Krishna*, p. 282; for Ruben, the failure to account for Krishna's manner of covering vast distances suggests that the epic has intermingled two originally independent story cycles.

figures we have discussed. First, noting what is similar in the three stops, just as Krishna must not be swayed by the offerings of palaces and other items of wealth, the Irish Amairgen must not be swayed by the three queens of the island. Quite possibly these are two variations—wealth and sex—of temptations by use of the third function. And noting what is different at each stage, we see similarities between Krishna's three stops and those of the Pater Patratus once the latter is past the boundaries of Rome: while Krishna stops at a town (the first?), the fetial stops to address the first man he meets; both then make their entrances into the foe's city; and while Krishna enters Duryodhana's court (where his dealings are with kings), the fetial comes to the forum or market place (where his dealings are with a people).

There is, however, more to link Krishna's gradual advance and successive refusals with the theme of the three steps. The text, by a strange recurrence at each of the last two stops, suggests as much itself. Having entered Dhṛtarāṣṭra's palace (just after arriving in the city), Krishna "stepped over [or crossed] three enclosures" (*tisraḥ kakṣyā vyatikramya*; 87,12a); and again, entering Duryodhana's palace, he "stepped over three enclosures unimpeded by gatemen" (*tasya kakṣyā vyatikramya tisro dvāḥsthairavāritaḥ*; 89,2cd). In all of Krishna's comings and goings, only on one other occasion does he follow this procedure of crossing three enclosures (*tvarītya . . . tisraḥ kakṣyā*; 2:19,28ab). Here too he is entering the residence of a rival of Yudhiṣṭhira for world sovereignty, King Jarāsaṃdha of Magadha, although in this case Krishna is accompanied by Arjuna and Bhīma, and their mission lacks even the pretense of peace making or diplomacy. *Kakṣya* can refer either to an enclosure inside a palace (a court or chamber) or outside (a wall); apparently the word has been used in the two *Udyogaparvan* instances first in the former sense and then in the latter. Most important, the passages in question seem to present, by their double employ of the words *tisro vyatikramya*, "having stepped over three," a clear double reminder of Viṣṇu Trivikrama, Viṣṇu of the Three Steps.[53]

The Third Step and the First Theophany

So far, then, Krishna's actions recall those of the Pater Patratus (and suggest those of Amairgen as well) both in terms of motive and procedure. With regard to Viṣṇu, in two of the three cases cited earlier where there are structural discontinuities between the Vedic three steps and his three steps as the Dwarf, Krishna's mission recalls the former. Krishna steps *into* the Kuru territory rather than *from within it outward*. He opens the space—of which Duryodhana will not yield so much as is covered by the point of a needle[54]—for the Pāṇḍavas to conquer in a just war rather than conquering it himself. One may thus suggest that the transposition has Vedic and para-Vedic roots traceable to Indo-European themes.

The third discontinuity between the two myths of the three steps points to parallels with the Vāmana myth: Krishna does not open up a new territory for the Pāṇḍavas; rather, as does Vāmana for the Devas, he helps restore to them what was formerly theirs. Here it is an Indian, and perhaps post-Vedic, mythic theme that provides the model for the epic struggle: the cyclical round of reversals and triumphs that marks the conflict between the Devas and Asuras. In a fashion similar to this, not only do the Pāṇḍavas and the Kurus reverse their

[53] Dumézil, "Les Pas de Kṛṣṇa et l'exploit d'Arjuna," *OS*, V (1956), 183–88, sees Viṣṇu's three steps transposed into the epic scenes where Krishna takes three "initiatives" (twice stepping forth from Arjuna's chariot) to inspire Arjuna against Bhīṣma. I think it is quite possible to have two transpositions of this multivalent theme. This other case, however, is the more fictionalized of the two and the further removed from a significant parallel context.

[54] Krishna demands half the kingdom back for the Pāṇḍavas, or at least five towns, but Duryodhana says that while he lives, the Pāṇḍavas shall not have so much of "our land" (*bhūmernaḥ*) as might be procured by the sharp point of a needle (5:125,26).

fortunes in the dice game and the great battle on earth, but—in the *Svargaparvan*—in heaven and hell as well.[55]

Correspondences also occur between the Vāmana myth and the mission of Krishna in certain matters of detail. First, there is the theme of the bound demon. From epic texts on, the Asuras in the Vāmana myth are championed by one figure, usually King Bali, and as early as the *Mahābhārata* there is reference to what in Purāṇic texts is clearly the result of Bali's encounter with Viṣṇu the Dwarf. Indra, on a tour of the domain which the Dwarf had presumably won for (or returned to) him—we are told that Bali was formerly a sovereign but is now divested of "prosperity"—finds Bali in a cave by the seashore (12:220,22) "bound with Varuṇa nooses" (*baddhaśca varuṇaiḥ paśair*; 220,18). This theme, which one finds in Scandinavia in connection with Loki, and which is well known elsewhere,[56] seems to appear in India only in connection with Bali. Thus Namuci (12:219,3) and Prahlāda (12:215,8) are bound in the set of scenes just cited where Indra encounters Bali and other past sovereigns; and, in a sort of inversion, it is Bali's son Bāṇa who has Krishna's grandson Aniruddha bound, thus precipitating a great war between the forces of Krishna and Śiva.[57] In the main narrative of the epic, the theme occurs only once, in the passage, or series of passages, that we have discussed: amidst plans and counterplans, Krishna urges that Duryodhana be bound over to the Pāṇḍavas as the demons had been bound with the nooses of Dharma and Varuṇa. The fact that neither Krishna nor Duryodhana is actually bound is a small matter. The epic restructures mythic themes in accord with

[55] Cf. above, n. 33.

[56] Stith Thompson, *Motif-Index of Folk Literature* (Bloomington: University of Indiana Press, 1955), I, 191–92, cites Scandinavian, Irish, Lettish and Lithuanian, Persian, Babylonian, and Christian parallels, but none from India. For a further comparison of Loki and Duryodhana (and Ahriman!) easily relatable to this one, see Dumézil, *Les Dieux des Germains, essai sur la formation de la religion scandinave*, Collection "Mythes et Religions," XXXVIII (Paris: Presses Universitaires de France, 1959), 99.

[57] See *VP* 5,32–33, especially 33,9.

its own pace and to suit its own ends. The allusion itself, especially from Krishna's own mouth, is transparent.

The second point, however, is the more crucial: the matter of the theophany itself. For if the wide strides of the Vedic god imply a great manifestation, it is only when he grows from the stature of a dwarf to that of a being who encompasses the three worlds that the nature of this manifestation as an expansion becomes explicit. Moreover, in what must be regarded as one of the earlier tellings of the myth even though it occurs only in the Northern recension of the *Mahābhārata* (*Āraṇyaka-parvan*, Appendix I, No. 27, lines 64–82), it is said that after the Dwarf reveals his "divine, marvelous form" (line 78),[58] "the gods thereby became manifest and the universe was called Vaiṣṇava" (*tena devāḥ prādurāsanvaiṣṇavaṃ cocyate jagat*; line 82). These are both prominent features in the court theophany of Krishna. Having entered seemingly alone, he "expands" so as to become "everything"—a procedure which now seems to be reflected in the description of his theophany as *ṛddhimat*, "possessing growth or increase." And out of his person not only do the gods "become manifest," but human heroes as well, his own kinsmen and the Pāṇḍavas—a theme which one may relate to the description of the theophany as *citra*, "variegated."

The Vāmana myth thus shows how closely, in the case of Krishna, the theme of binding is linked to the theophany. If Krishna cannot "expand" from the form of a dwarf, he can expand from a position where, as the foolish Duryodhana sees it, he appears alone and capable of being constricted. Indeed, the connection is implied in the words, cited earlier, of Dhṛtarāṣṭra: "Like the wind, difficult to seize with the hand, like the moon, hard to touch with the hand, like the earth, hard to bear on the head,[59] Krishna is difficult to seize by force."

[58] In some Purāṇic texts, it is called his *Viśvarūpa*; see Tripathi, *Vāmana-Legende*, pp. 80 and 239.

[59] It is tempting to compare this with the tradition that with his third step, Viṣṇu steps on Bali's head, but this does not appear earlier than in the *Bhāgavata Purāṇa*.

The Vāmana myth thus clarifies Krishna's court theophany by its combination of these themes, but there is a larger integration still possible if one takes up Dumézil's hint and looks at Krishna as a "veritable fetial." Let us recall the maneuvers that brought the Pater Patratus to the point where we left him: having approached the non-Roman territory in three stages and repeated his demands for satisfaction of wrongs, he waited thirty-three days and then declared war. Now Livy continues:

> . . . he declares war thus: "Hear Jupiter, and thou Janus Quirinus, and hear all ye heavenly gods, and ye, gods of earth, and ye, of the lower world; I call you to witness that this people"—naming whatever people it is—"is unjust [*iniustum*], does not make just reparation. But of these matters we will take counsel of the elders in our country, how we may obtain our right [*ius nostrum*]." Then the messenger returns to Rome.[60]

One could note further similarities in the Pater Patratus' deliberations, upon his return, with the *rex* and Senators, and in those of Krishna, upon his return, with Yudhiṣṭhira and his allies. Both concern the fact that war can now be waged which, in Livy's terms, is "just and righteous" (*puro pioque*).[61] In any case, the scenario is now complete: in Rome, a priest takes the "three steps" and represents all the gods[62] by invoking them. In India, the ambiguous, omnivalent, and in some respects not unpriestly[63] figure of Krishna takes the "three steps"

[60] *Livy* 1. 32, 9–10; Dionysius of Halicarnassus (2. 72, 8) shortens this but retains the essential: "He called both the celestial and infernal gods to witness and went away."

[61] *Livy* 1. 32, 12; cf. *Mbh.* 5:149,41, where Krishna, summarizing his efforts to Yudhiṣṭhira, says that by trying to make peace, his and the Pāṇḍavas' debt to dharma is gone, satisfied (*dharmasya gatamānṛṇyam*).

[62] From what I can tell, it is unusual that the Roman gods are all invoked like this, but this matter requires further study.

[63] Already we have seen in Chapter 4, where he protects the Rājasūya, that Krishna is connected with the sacrifice (see especially Chapter 4, n. 29); he is also preceded in his role of ambassador by Drupada's *purohita*, "chaplain" (5:20–21), and, in the upcoming "sacrifice of battle," it is said that he will be the *adhvaryu*, the main administrating priest (5:139,29).

and represents all the gods by being them. One need not search far for the differences in theology that would sustain such different modes of divine representation. In one case, it is the specialist priest who on the strength of invocation can channel the totality of divine power to the service of Rome; in the other, it is Viṣṇu immanent in human form as well as in the universe who, through his capacity to manifest his own divinity, can reveal how the totality of divine power is maintained at the service of the Pāṇḍavas, of dharma, and of the three worlds.

Krishna's two theophanies thus not only relate to each other, but to the theme of the three steps. The first theophany seems to be an Indian reinterpretation of an archaic gesture, Indo-Roman insofar as it concerns a mode of giving divine sanction to war at the moment when the ambassador realizes its inevitability, and probably, taking into account the one step, three stops, and theophany (see above, n. 45) of the Irish Amairgen, Indo-European. The second theophany, however, even though juxtaposed with the first in several significant ways, calls to mind not Indo-European or even Vedic themes, but rather what are usually thought of, despite their frequency in the epic, as Purānic ones. These considerations should allow us to reflect on a few matters concerning the *Mahābhārata* and two of its most prominent contemporary critics. First, even though the *Gītā* evokes the more recent mythology and cosmology, I have tried to suggest by examining the two theophanies together that the *Gītā* should be seen as a coherent part of the epic, not simply as one of its "didactic" portions. Second, by drawing from both ancient and recent myths, I have tried to show how the epic narrative itself has been structured in part to bridge the gap between Vedic and Purāṇic mythologies, conserving the former (and conserving pre-Vedic themes as well) and embracing it within the new "universe of *bhakti*"[64] of the great gods of epic and Purāṇic Hinduism.

[64] Biardeau, EMH, 3, p. 84.

Finally, one facet of what some have condescendingly called the "leisurely pace" of the *Mahābhārata* is its device of presenting countless *darśanas*, perspectives, on the drama that forms its core. I have tried to suggest here, although in Part Three I will steer a middle course between them, that the Indo-European perspective of Dumézil and the Purāṇic, one might say "Hindu," perspective of Biardeau are both valid, and that, to borrow from a Sāṃkhya similitude, they may at some points be as necessary to each other, in making a way through the *Mahābhārata* forest, as the blind man and the lame.

PART THREE

WORLD SOVEREIGNTY

CHAPTER 7

Śrī and the Source of Sovereignty

Having followed Krishna through his prewar appearances, we come now to the great battle between the Kurus and the Pāṇḍavas in which he helps the latter attain the "sovereignty of the world." Before we take up Krishna's involvement in the actual battle scenes, we must learn what is meant by "sovereignty." Indian mythology in general, and the *Mahābhārata* in particular, associate sovereignty with the goddess Śrī-Lakṣmī,[1] a figure whose importance for understanding Krishna is nicely summarized by the Pāṇḍavas, who at one point say to their cousin and counselor: "Surely you are not a leader of those on whom Lakṣmī has turned away her face" (2:18,10; *na hi tvamagratasteṣāṃ yeṣāṃ lakṣmīḥ parāñmukhī*).

Much has been written about Śrī,[2] but a number of issues deserve further attention. First is the question of origins. Both Gonda and Jaiswal agree that she is a "pre-Aryan fertility goddess";[3] in contrast, although some connection with fertility

[1] Although Jaiswal, *Origin and Development*, pp. 88–89, tries to show separate origins for their names and identities, I am not convinced this has much significance, at least for the *Mahābhārata*.

[2] Disagreement over the original meaning of the word *śrī* is found between Hermann Oldenberg, "Die vedischen Worte für 'schön' und 'Schönheit' und das vedische Schönheitsgefuhl," *NKGWG*, pp. 35ff. ("beauty"), and Jan Gonda, *Early Viṣṇuism*, pp. 178–81 and 204–7 ("prosperity"). Both Gonda, pp. 212–31, and Jaiswal, *Origin and Development*, pp. 89–109, provide useful accounts of the development of her iconography, mythology, and ritual. For further bibliography, see below.

[3] Gonda, *Early Viṣṇuism*, p. 213; cf. Jaiswal, *Origin and Development*, p. 109.

is never under dispute, her connection with kingship has prompted Alexander H. Krappe to include her among a number of Indo-European goddesses and heroines who bestow royal fortune.[4] Second, the question must be raised whether Śrī has a coherent mythology of her own, perhaps quite ancient, or whether her mythology is always to be reduced to patterns established by other goddesses, be they connected with fertility or some other "feminine" resource. And third, how do these matters bear on Śrī's epic incarnation as Kṛṣṇā-Draupadī?

Śrī's Transpositions

It has long been argued that Śrī's affiliations with Viṣṇu are not her earliest. According to Hopkins, "It is a late epic trait to make her exclusively Viṣṇu's (she is also Dharma's wife)."[5] Jaiswal insists that Śrī's position as Viṣṇu's consort "is the latest feature of her legends in the *Mahābhārata*,"[6] their union having been achieved at "the beginning of the Gupta period" (320 A.D.).[7] Gonda concurs: "This stage is not reached before the younger parts of the *Mahābhārata*."[8]

The Critical Edition of the *Mahābhārata* reveals that some of the recent redactors of the epic probably saw Śrī's different affiliations as something of an embarrassment. In one of the so-called "dictionaries of incarnations"[9] which enumerate the demonic and divine origins of long lists of epic characters, the closing verses tell about some of the women. First mentioned

[4] Alexander H. Krappe, "The Sovereignty of Erin," *AJP*, LXIII (1942), 444–54; on Śrī-Lakṣmī, see p. 450. Others have picked up on this comparison; see Ananda K. Coomaraswamy, "On the Loathly Bride," *Speculum*, XX (1945), 392–93; Rees and Rees, *Celtic Heritage*, pp. 73–76; Dumézil, *ME*, II, 342.

[5] Hopkins, *Epic Mythology*, p. 208; see also Isidore Scheftelowitz, "Śrīsūkta," *ZDMG*, LXXV (1921), 43.

[6] Jaiswal, *Origin and Development*, p. 100; see also pp. 16, 79.

[7] *Ibid.*, p. 79; see also pp. 16, 100–5; cf. A. K. Coomaraswamy, "Early Indian Iconography: No. 2, Śrī-Lakṣmī," *Eastern Art*, I (1928–1929), 177.

[8] Gonda, *Early Viṣṇuism*, p. 223.

[9] The term is Dumézil's: *ME*, I, 209.

are the sixteen thousand Apsarases who took birth as Krishna's harem (1:61,93–94). Then comes a *śloka* that at a certain point was altered.[10] Originally, as the reconstituted Critical text has it (61,95):

A portion [*bhāga*] of Śrī became incarnate, on the earth's surface,
in Drupada's family, a faultless maiden from the center of the sacrificial altar [*vedī*].

Between the two lines an amendment was inserted to read as follows:

A portion of Śrī became incarnate, on the earth's surface,
in the family of Bhīṣmaka, in the person of the chaste Rukmiṇī.
The faultless Draupadī, however, was born from a portion of Śacī
in Drupada's family. . . . [566*]

The interpolation thus makes Draupadī, "endowed with every mark [*lakṣaṇa*] . . . [and] a charmer of the hearts of five Indras among·men" (*puruṣendra-*; 61,97), a portion of Indra's wife Śacī, and thereby allows Viṣṇu's incarnation Krishna to find his partner in an incarnation of Śrī.

The identifications of Śrī with Rukmiṇī and of Draupadī with Śacī probably are recent, although this does not mean that the association of Śrī with Viṣṇu is equally late. What one finds on the mythic or theological level need not be duplicated exactly on the epic level. As I tried to show in Chapters 3 and 4, Draupadī's actions are often ambiguous; seemingly, they point to a double affiliation on the mythic level of Śrī with both Viṣṇu and Indra. But such ambiguities have gone unappreciated by those who see only a late connection of Śrī with Viṣṇu and, correspondingly, an early relation between Draupadī and Śacī.[11]

[10] The interpolation occurs in several scripts, including all but one in Devanāgarī.

[11] Biardeau seems to want it both ways: although the interpolated verse is "supplementary," it makes little difference whom Draupadī incarnates, "for, in her function as Indra's wife, Śacī also participates in the nature of Śrī" (my translation); "Brāhmaṇes et potiers," p. 40. This solves little.

In writing *Mythe et épopée*, I, Dumézil did not rely consistently on the Critical Edition; this helps to explain his acceptance of the authenticity of the interpolated passage along with its identifications.[12] The alternative, he says, would cause a "discordance which a western mind would easily turn into vaudeville, since Viṣṇu is actually incarnated in . . . Krishna, and the encounters between Krishna, Draupadī, and the latter's five husbands are very frequent."[13] The "oriental mind," except in interpolations like the one just mentioned, has handled this differently, as shown by a passage from the *Anuśāsanaparvan*. The speaker is Śrī, addressing Rukmiṇī herself:

In my embodied form [*śarīrabhutā*], single-heartedly [*ekamanā*], I dwell with my entire spirit [*sarveṇa bhāvena*] in Nārāyaṇa; surely in him is dharma penetrated to the fullest, piety [*brahmanyatā*], and also agreeableness [*priyatvam*]. Might I not explain here, O Lady [*devi*], that I do not dwell [elsewhere] in my embodied form [*nāhaṃ śarīreṇa vasāmi*]. But in that person [especially kings, for example, the Pāṇḍavas] in whom I dwell in spirit [*bhāvena*], he increases in dharma, fame [*yaśas*], *artha*, and *kāma*. [13:11,19–20]

The passage, from this inflated *parvan*, may be "late" by epic standards, and it does not explicitly link the "spiritual" form with Śrī's "portion" Draupadī. But it does indicate an attentiveness of the epic poets to different modes of activity on different levels, in particular what we might differentiate here as the theological or mythical and the heroic or "human."

For Dumézil, however, in the "original" transposition the overlap between the theological and epic levels must have been exact,[14] and he buttresses his view by an elaborate reconstruc-

[12] Dumézil, *ME*, I, 118 and n. 1; cf. Gonda, *Early Viṣṇuism*, p. 230, also accepting this version.

[13] *ME*, I, 118 (my translation).

[14] See my remarks in a review of *ME*, I, "Dumézil: Epic in the Balance," *HRJ*, IX (1969), 92, arguing that "epic need not be a carbon copy of myth"; see also above, Chapter 1 at n. 36.

tion of the transposition into three phases.[15] In brief, he argues that the original figure behind Draupadī was a variety of the Indo-Iranian goddess—Armaiti, Anāhitā, Sarasvatī, Vāc—who complements the male gods or Entities concerned with the three functions in a relation similar to that between Draupadī and her five husbands. Drawing from his interpretation of a myth from the *Mārkaṇḍeya Purāṇa* (which will be discussed below) and on the interpolated passage just cited, he proposes that the first goddess connected with Draupadī to have this trifunctional theology superimposed upon her was Indra's own wife, Śacī or Indrāṇī. Then, "intermediary" between the theological and epic "causalities," Dumézil sees a myth concerning Śrī (the myth of the five former Indras[16]) and a "romanesque" (fictionalized) legend as being more or less fabricated by the poets to justify the polyandric marriage in narrative form.[17]

My inclination is to take the epic as seriously as possible in its linking of Śrī with Draupadī. But Dumézil will only allow that, as a "choice" of a figure on whom to superimpose the theology of the Indo-Iranian trivalent goddess, the poets got by all right with Śrī, as she "is not badly adapted to the situation," being also the subject of old speculations connected with the three functions.[18] I believe, however, that from the moment of her literary debut in the Brāhmaṇas,[19] there are significant differences in the ways that Śrī and the Indo-Iranian trivalent goddesses interact with the functions. A closer examination of Śrī herself is needed: her theology, her myths, her symbols and settings.

[15] *ME*, I, 116.

[16] See above, Chapters 3 and 4.

[17] *ME*, I, 110.

[18] *Ibid.*, p. 118.

[19] Her first appearances as a personified figure, in addition to the Brāhmaṇa texts, occur in *VS* 31,22 (named with Lakṣmī as a wife of Puruṣa—probably Nārāyaṇa) and in the *Śrīsūkta*, the first fifteen verses of which constitute the earliest text eulogizing Śrī and date, according to Scheftelowitz, "Śrīsūkta," p. 41, from the Brāhmaṇa period.

Śrī and the Three Functions

A good starting point is a most interesting passage referred to by Dumézil: *Śatapatha Brāhmaṇa* 13,2,6,1–7.[20] The text, from the long thirteenth *kāṇḍa* on the performance of the royal horse sacrifice (Aśvamedha), finds the horse back from his eleven months of wandering and facing his last trip, the one to the sacrificial stake. At this point (following Dumézil's summary) three queens, in descending order of dignity, make three successive unctions on parts of the horse's body, which thus assure the king, in succession, of *tejas* ("spiritual force" or "majesty"), *indriyam* ("physical force"), and *paśu* (cattle)—the latter "having more social importance than 'beauty' in the third function."[21] But there is something more.[22] The Aśvamedha itself involves risks to the sacrificer. During his year-long *dīkṣa* in the horse's absence, the king has been abandoned by "the sacrifice," that is, by the horse (13,2,6,2). For the time of this absence, the three qualities just mentioned and one other also leave the king: "Indeed, fiery mettle [*tejas*] and energy [*indriyam*], cattle [*paśu*] and prosperity [*śrī*] depart from him who offers the Aśvamedha" (3).[23] When the three queens confer the three virtues on the horse (4–6), these qualities may return to the king. It would seem that the queens have acted as repositories for them during the absence of the horse, or of "the sacrifice." And the queens are themselves identified with the fourth quality mentioned in the stanza just cited: "It is the wives that anoint (the horse), for they—to wit, (many) wives—are a form

[20] Dumézil, *ME*, I, 118; *ME*, II, 352.

[21] Dumézil, *ME*, I, 118 (my translation). The English equivalents for these "qualities" or "virtues" are always problematic. *Tejas* in particular varies according to context. Fuller attention to these terms will be given in Chapter 8.

[22] Dumézil takes note of the added term himself in *Archaic Roman Religion*, p. 225.

[23] Here and elsewhere, I follow the translation of Julius Eggeling, trans. and ed., *Śatapatha Brāhmaṇa*, SBE, XII, XXVI, XLI, XLIII, and XLIV (1882–1900; repr. Delhi: Motilal Banarsidass, 1966).

of prosperity [or: a form (*rūpam*) of Śrī]: it is thus prosperity he [the horse] confers on him (the sacrificer), and neither *tejas*, nor *indriyam*, nor cattle, nor *śrī* pass away from him" (7).[24]

A debate over capital or lower-case letters for *śrī* should be discouraged: the two meanings would by this time have been interchangeable. The important point is that the trifunctional virtues are part of a wider drama. Briefly, (1) Śrī is connected with royalty; (2) she is specifically concerned with a formulation of royal virtues; (3) her "trivalence" does not lie so much in incorporating these virtues (her "forms" or representatives, the queens, are by no means saintly or strong) as in being able to confer them, actually transfer them (through the sacrificial horse to the king); and (4) *śrī* or Śrī may be said to "follow" the virtues, to be an additional and special member. Not only do the three "trifunctional" virtues abandon and return to the king, but so does Śrī: "Indeed, that glory (*śrī*), royal power, passes away from him who performs the Aśvamedha" (*ŚB* 13,2,9,1); and, just like the other virtues, returns—being "the top of royal power" (13,2,9,7).

Let us examine each of these points in turn to see if they hold up where the concept *śrī*, or figure of Śrī, appears elsewhere in the Brāhmaṇas.

(1) These early ritual texts include the claim that a sovereign is wedded to Śrī.[25] In a modification of the new and full moon sacrifices (the *dakṣayaṇa*; *ŚB* 2,4,4,1ff.), apparently worked out for a royal family called the Dākṣāyaṇas,[26] the sacrificer—like Prajāpati who, desiring *prajā* ("progeny"), sacrificed to obtain Prosperity (*śrī*; stanza 1)—obtains "generative power and prosperity" (*prajāti*, *śrī*; 4). In fact, having performed this sacrifice, "thereby Śrī is (wedded) to him without a rival and undisturbed" (6). This no doubt implies that either his wives (as in

[24] Parentheses are Eggeling's, brackets are mine.

[25] See Jan Gonda, *Ancient Indian Kingship from the Religious Point of View* (reprinted from *Numen*; Leiden: Brill, 1966 and 1969), p. 46.

[26] Eggeling, trans., *ŚB*, SBE, XII, 374.

the previous passage) or his kingdom (*rāṣṭram*) itself[27] is an embodiment of Śrī.

(2) As to her preoccupation, specifically, with royal virtues,[28] the Brāhmaṇas again present further information. The Mitravindā sacrifice (*ŚB* 11,4,3,1ff.), in which the sacrificer "finds Mitra" (stanza 20) who is here connected with *kṣatram* ("nobility," probably royal power), has its mythological setting in an account of the birth of Śrī. Born from the austerities of Prajāpati,[29] the gods "set their minds on her" (stanza 1). Then, in a strange moment—the gods are usually, as in the case of Uṣas or Vāc (see n. 29), more inclined to protect their sisters from their father's incestuous designs[30]—the gods desire to kill her and dispossess her of her qualities. Prajāpati stops them, however, by letting them know that one can take from a woman while leaving her alive! So the gods each claim an appropriate share: "Agni then took her food, Soma her royal power [*rājyam*], Varuṇa her universal sovereignty [*saṃrājyam*], Mitra her noble rank [*kṣatram*], Indra her power [*balam*], Bṛhaspati her holy lustre [*brahmavarcasam*], Savitṛ her kingdom [*rāṣṭram*], Pūṣan her fortune [bhaga], Sarasvatī her plentifulness [*puṣṭi*], and Tvaṣṭṛ her forms or manifestations [*rūpāṇi*]" (stanza 3). Thus despoiled, she complains to Prajāpati, who tells her: "Do thou ask it back from them by sacrifice" (4). She then makes a distinct offering to each god (5), and they all appear before her. Reciting their names forward and backward (6–7), and then

[27] Gonda, *Ancient Indian Kingship*, p. 136, citing *Aitareya Brāhmaṇa* passages identifying Śrī with *rāṣṭram*.

[28] Gonda, *Early Viṣṇuism*, pp. 182 and 186, refers to the "virtues" as "power substances"; see also his *Some Observations on the Relations between "Gods" and "Powers" in the Veda a propos of the Phrase Sunuḥ Sahasaḥ* ('s-Gravenhage: Mouton, 1957). His term is more "magical," mine—which I will stick to—more "ethical."

[29] Like other prominent goddesses in the Brāhmaṇas, Uṣas and Vāc; see Lévi, *Doctrine du sacrifice*, pp. 20–23.

[30] See *ibid.*, pp. 22–23.

invoking them one at a time (8–17), she implores them for the return of her qualities.

Clearly the virtues involved include those that are royal, even though the declared purpose of the sacrifice is to "find Mitra." The list of ten deities and ten qualities would appear resistant to trifunctional analysis, but when the ritual orientation of the Brāhmaṇa text is considered, several concordances with typical trifunctional lists suggest themselves.[31] Agni and Soma, connected with the sacrifice, fall easily into place as additions superimposed on the first level.[32] Bṛhaspati's position next to Indra probably reflects the ancient Vedic pairing of these two divinities[33] and the predictable priestly concern that Indra not stand alone.[34] In fact, a similar principle is found in certain trifunctional passages which place *brahmavarcasam*, "brahmic" or "holy luster," alongside second-function virtues. Thus, according to *Śatapatha Brāhmaṇa* 11,4,4,11: "If he [the sacrificer] think, 'There has been that which was disconnected in my sacrifice,' let him believe, 'That makes for my prosperity [*śrī*]; Prosperity, surrounded by splendor [*tejas*], fame [*yaśas*], and holy lustre [*brahmavarcasam*], will accrue to me." And, in a passage (*TS* 7,1,8,2) where the goddess Śraddhā, "Faith" or "Confidence," plays much the same role for a ṛṣi as Śrī does for a king: "Atri had Śraddhā for divinity [*śraddhādeva*]. When sacrificing, the four vigors [*catvāri vīryāṇi*] did not come to him: spiritual force [*tejas*], physical force [*indriyam*], holy lustre

[31] Cf. *ṚV* 10,125,1–3, where Vāc, referring to herself as the "queen" (*rāṣṭrī*), announces that she "sustains" (*bibharmi*) not only the "canonical" deities (see below, n. 34), but Agni, Soma, Tvaṣṭṛ, Pūṣan, and Bhaga.

[32] Cf. the place of Agni and Soma in *ŚB* 1,6,3,15, discussed below.

[33] See Hanns-Peter Schmidt, *Bṛhaspati und Indra: Untersuchungen zur vedischen Mythologie und Kulturgeschichte* (Weisbaden: Otto Harrassowitz, 1968); Charles Drekmeier, *Kingship and Community in Early India* (Stanford: Stanford University Press, 1962), pp. 26–43.

[34] Again, see *ṚV* 10,125,1, the famous verse where Vāc says: "I sustain Varuṇa and Mitra, Indra and Agni, and the pair of Aśvins."

[*brahmavarcasam*], and proper food [*annādyam*]." Then, presumably with the support of his "Confidence" in the sacrifice, Atri sings a four-part hymn to Soma and obtains the "vigors." Finally on the level of the third function, where the goddess Sarasvatī maintains a logical rapport with "plentifulness," the proliferation of additional deities—Savitṛ, Pūṣan, Tvaṣṭṛ—also finds a partial explanation in the Brāhmaṇa literature. *Śatapatha Brāhmaṇa* 7,2,2,12, citing *Vājasaneyi-Saṃhitā* 12,72, adds Pūṣan directly to the five "canonical" gods (see n. 34), just as Śrī's "forms," which Tvaṣṭṛ appropriates, usually range themselves in the province of the third function.[35] Savitṛ, for his part, bestows gifts. It is interesting that all the deities connected here with the third function are (excepting Sarasvatī) Ādityas, unlike the unincluded Aśvins. Śrī, it seems, will concern herself only with the most sovereign deities (the Ādityas) and with the deities connected with the sacrifice (Agni, Soma [who is also termed Rāja], and Bṛhaspati) in accord with the Brāhmaṇas' sacrificial orientation.

It is quite likely, then, that Śrī, in a different way from the "trivalent" goddesses Sarasvatī or Vāc, does bear a close relationship to deities who represent the three functions. One difference can be attributed to the ritualism of the Brāhmaṇa texts, but the second is directly connected to the specific gift which Śrī bestows: royalty. Ādityas replace the Aśvins.[36] So, too, the Aśvins' epic sons—Nakula and Sahadeva—will "actually" be Indras. Yet it is not so much the different divinities that hold the tripartite structure together in its relation to Śrī as the virtues with which these gods are connected. Here the trifunctional meanings are transparent enough on the third (forms, plentifulness, good fortune, kingdom [that is, subjects] and

[35] In the present passage, good "forms" in cattle are referred to (stanza 17); see above on royal wives as a "form" of Śrī.

[36] Cf. *Mbh.* 12:217,41: Bali tells Indra, referring to his former sovereignty and relation with Śrī: "Singly I bore the energies [*tejāṃsi*] of all twelve of the illustrious Ādityas."

second (power) levels. The first level contains surprises. But in relation to Śrī's concern with royalty, it is significant for the Brāhmaṇa literature that Mitra be associated with *kṣatram* rather than Indra and that Varuṇa represent the universal sovereignty (*saṃrājyam*), which Śrī may than bestow. On this level it appears most clearly, especially considering Soma's association with *rājyam*, that Śrī—in contrast to the trivalent goddesses—concerns herself specifically with virtues of royalty.

(3) The third point—that Śrī's trivalence does not so much lie in incorporating the virtues as in conferring or transferring them—would seem to be endangered by the myth just cited. To be sure, the gods take these qualities from Śrī (their first impulse is to do so by killing her, surely implying some notion that she "incorporates" them); and to Śrī they restore them. But there is never a question of her putting the virtues into effect on her own, whether to defend or to regain them. Rather, she wins everything back by sacrifice and formula. Śrī is then a repository for those virtues specifically connected with sovereignty which, in accord with the general outlook of the Brāhmaṇas, can be conferred or transferred, through the medium of the sacrifice, to others—here to "the gods," elsewhere, as we have seen, to a king, to Śrī's choice.[37] Thus, where she does incorporate an assortment of virtues, they are important not as a measure of her own stature but as a complement to the virtues of her royal counterpart(s). On this account, then, her relation to the three functions stands in marked contrast to the trivalence of the Indo-Iranian goddesses discussed by Dumézil, for instance Aredvi Sūrā Anāhitā ("The Humid, the Strong, the Immaculate") or Sarasvatī who, along with her third-function affiliations, is also called *vṛtraghnī* ("[female] Slayer of Vṛtra";

[37] A devotionalized form of this tendency occurs in *Śrīsūkta* 10, part of this text's "early" portion (see above, n. 19), where one prays that Śrī may *bestow* various virtues: "May we attain our heart's wish and intention and truth of speech [*vācas satyam*]; may Śrī allot me the form of cattle and of food [*paśūnaṃ rūpam annasya*] as well as fame [*yaśas*]."

ṚV 6:61,7) and *dhīnām avitrī* ("auxiliary of pious thoughts"; *ṚV* 6:61,4).[38]

(4) Finally comes the manner in which *śrī*, as a virtue or a goddess, follows after the other virtues. Actually, the Aśvamedha passage cited at the beginning of this section is the best Brāhmaṇa illustration, but there is an interesting passage (referred to in n. 32), in which *śrī* rounds out the other qualities. Let us also note the significant context. After Indra slew the divine artisan Tvaṣṭṛ's tricephalic son Viśvarūpa (*ŚB* 1,6,3,2), Tvaṣṭṛ sought revenge by creating Indra's arch foe Vṛtra. The latter was born from the combination of Soma poured into the fire (Agni) and "came to be possessed of Agni and Soma, of all sciences [*vidyās*], all glory [*yaśas*], all nourishment [*annādyam*], all prosperity [*śrī*; 8]." Indra then cajoled Agni and Soma into coming over to him (13), and "after them went forth all the gods (*devās*), all the sciences, all *yaśas*, all nourishment, all *śrī*: thus . . . Indra became what Indra now is" (15).

This myth bears certain resemblances to the much more clearly structured myth of *Mārkaṇḍeya Purāṇa* 5, which Dumézil finds so satisfying and which I will discuss below. There again Indra's virtues are bound up with his conquests of Viśvarūpa and Vṛtra and his accession to world sovereignty. The virtues in the Purāṇic myth are unmistakably trifunctional, and here too such an interpretation can be proposed—with prosperity and nourishment on the third level, *yaśas* (fame or glory) on the second, and *devās* and *vidyās* on the first. The two latter terms present the only stumbling blocks, but it seems that the authors have aligned *devās*, the Devas—in particular Agni and Soma (stanza 8)—with the sacrificial ordering of the cosmos and *vidyās* with the principles of the "scientific" ordering of the sacrifice itself. Whereas in the *Mārkaṇḍeya* myth, Indra, after the restoration of his virtues, is joined by his "great wife" (Śacī, Śrī? see below), here the last of the virtues to come to him is his

[38] Dumézil, *ME*, I, 103–7.

śrī. However, the pattern of Śrī, as a goddess, following the other virtues will have its clearest expressions in the *Mahābhārata*.

Thus, despite Śrī's connection with trifunctional groups of virtues and her importance to kings, the Brāhmaṇas give us no royal mythology to connect these two concerns. In the epic, the myth most frequently used to show Śrī's involvement with the virtues and with kings has Brāhmaṇa antecedents. But in the Brāhmaṇas, the myth is told about other goddesses than Śrī: Āpas, Bhūmi,[39] Dakṣiṇā,[40] Vedī (*TS* 6,2,7–8), and above all Vāc. The latter, whose capacity to make "choices" is already recognized in the *Ṛg Veda*,[41] is, in the Brāhmaṇas, a much sought-after figure who must frequently choose between two classes of beings. In their earliest form, the conflicts in these stories are probably most consistently represented in the Indo-Iranian opposition between the Devas and Asuras, an opposition which echoes through the Brāhmaṇas no less than the epics and Puraṇas. Vāc is one of a vast number of blessings (usually female) that the gods must win over from their adversaries, and several *Śatapatha Brāhmaṇa* passages tell how she comes over to the gods (whether by fair means or foul).[42] The common theme is that the goddess' chosen ones, inevitably the Devas, have triumphed on a winner-take-all basis.

To make matters as simple as possible, I will follow the hints of Gösta Johnsen and Dumézil[43] and refer to this scenario as the "Svayaṃvara mythologem," for just as in the Svayaṃvara,

[39] See Gösta Johnsen, "Varuṇa and Dhṛtarāṣṭra," *IIJ*, IX (1965–1966), 225, n. 47, mentioning the Bhūmi and Āpas passages.

[40] Lévi, *Doctrine du sacrifice*, p. 32, n. 1.

[41] See *ṚV* 10,71,4: "Many a one who sees [*paśyan*] has not perceived [*dadarśa*] Vāc, and many a one who hears has not heard her. But to another she has betaken herself [*tanvàṃ sasre*] like an amorous, finely dressed wife to her husband."

[42] See the fundamental discussion by Lévi, *Doctrine du sacrifice*, pp. 31–39.

[43] Johnsen, "Varuṇa and Dhṛtarāṣṭra," pp. 254–55, remarking on the seeming nonhistoricity of an actual Svayaṃvara marriage rite, and Dumézil, *ME*, I, 122.

at least in its name,[44] the emphasis is on a feminine figure, goddess rather than heroine, "choosing" her partner (or partners)[45] amidst a wooing contest. It is this mythologem that the epic poets found of the widest use in accounting for the relationship between the two concerns of the Brāhmaṇic Śrī: her interests in virtues and in kings.

Śrī and Her Choices

In the *Mahābhārata*, the most concentrated assemblage of myths connected with Śrī is found in the *Śāntiparvan*. A good deal of the material in this open-ended book is probably fairly late by epic standards, but there are reasons to suspect that the myths concerning Śrī contain old themes and material. As Dumézil says of one of them,[46] they were probably not invented by the epic poets.

The first account is structured according to the familiar theme of the virtues and the next (which actually comprises four accounts) is held together mainly by the theme of Śrī's inconstancy. This latter motif is not connected with Śrī in the Brāhmaṇas, but as it develops it is not unrelated to the theme of the virtues.

(1) Advised by the divine chaplain Bṛhaspati that the only way he can gain world sovereignty from the Daitya-Asura Prahlāda is to go to him disguised as a brahmin, become his

[44] Jean Przyluski, "Le Prologue-cadre des *Mille et une nuits* et le thème du *svayaṃvara*," *JA*, CCV (1924), 109–10, and Marie Delcourt, "The Legend of Sarpedon and the Saga of the Archer," *HRJ*, II (1962), 40, are of the opinion that the Svayaṃvara has nothing of "self-choice" but the name. There is, however, a tradition that Draupadī does "choose," at least negatively, when she refuses to accept Karṇa as a suitor. The CE has valid grounds for rejecting this passage (see 1:178,17 and 1827*), but it accords well with other passages concerning Draupadī and Karṇa.

[45] In the Brāhmaṇas, Vāc goes over to the Devas, not to Indra in particular; but probably he is the chief beneficiary. In the epic, Śrī, like Draupadī, chooses just one husband: Indra or Arjuna; but in each case, the beneficiaries are not only these two, but the gods in general or the Pāṇḍavas. As to her relations with the Asuras, see the following section.

[46] Dumézil, *ME*, I, 122.

disciple, and ask for his behavior (*śīla*; 12:124,42), Indra carries out these instructions to the letter. Honor bound to grant all wishes of brahmins, the virtuous Prahlāda reluctantly agrees to part with this most precious commodity. "And while he was thinking, . . . an embodied energy [*tejas*], having the form of a shadow, abandoned his body. Prahlāda asked that great form, 'Who are you?' It answered, 'Surely I am [your] behavior [*śīla*]; abandoned by you I am leaving. I will dwell blamelessly, O king, in that best of brahmins [Indra]" (12:124,45–47ab). "Behavior's" departure is followed by the exodus of other virtues, each one explaining to Prahlāda that it must go after its predecessor. Thus, coming after (1) *śīla* are: (2) dharma (also called a *tejas*), (3) *satya*, "truth" ("blazing up with *tejas*"), (4) *vṛttam*, "activity," and (5) *balam*, "strength." Last but not least:

A goddess made of effulgence [*prabhāmayī devī*] came out from his body. The chief [*indra*] of the Daityas asked her [who she was]. So she said, "Śrī. I dwelt happily, O hero, in you who are truly mighty [*tvayi satyaparākrame*].[47] Abandoned by you, I will leave. . . ."

Then the fear of the high-souled Prahlāda became visible, and he asked her besides: "Where are you going, O Lotus Dweller? Surely you are a goddess devoted to truth, the supreme goddess of the world. Who is that best of brahmins? I wish to know the truth."

Śrī said, "This *brahmacārin* who was instructed by you is Śakra. You are robbed by him, O splendid one, of that sovereignty [*aiśvaryam*] which was yours in the triple world. Surely it is by *śīla* that all the worlds were subdued by you, O virtuous one. Knowing this, your *śīla* was stolen by Mahendra. . . . Just like dharma and *satya*, *vṛttam* and *balam*, so do I have my root in *śīla*, O one of great wisdom. Never doubt it" [12:124,54–60]

[47] I follow Ganguli-Roy and Monier-Williams (s.v. *satya*) here, although if *satyaparākrama* could be taken as a *dvandva* used adjectivally (a rarity according to William Dwight Whitney, *Sanskrit Grammar* [Cambridge: Harvard University Press, 1889; repr. 1960], 2d ed., sec. 1293b), the passage would make more sense: "I dwelt happily in you [when you were] possessed of truth and might," that is, two of the virtues (*balam* = *parākrama*) he has just lost.

A few observations will indicate some of the significance of this passage, so reminiscent, in the exodus of virtues, of *Śatapatha Brāhmaṇa* 1,6,3,1–15.[48] First, it is striking that the initial three virtues to leave Prahlāda, and only these three, are characterized by their *tejas*, a virtue consistently represented in the Brāhmaṇas as one of the first function. Here, too, the virtues which *tejas* characterizes seemingly fall into the same range. *Śīla*, however, is clearly differentiated from the other two, being the root (*mūlā*) of all the virtues and a general requirement for association with Śrī.[49] *Satya* and dharma, a pair found frequently in the epic, present problems that I will reserve for the next chapter; but there is little doubt that even in their ordinary meaning—"truth" and "justice"—they are qualities connected with sovereignty. From this point on, the trifunctional list of virtues follows in descending order. *Vṛttam* has to do with activity, even "good deeds" as Ganguli-Roy translate it; and *balam* signifies sheer physical force. On the level of the second function, the latter constitute a pair that would seem to parallel the two warrior types analyzed by Dumézil: *vṛttam*-Arjuna-Achilles; *balam*-Bhīma-Heracles.[50] The third function's pattern appeared before in *Śatapatha* 11,4,4,11.[51] Śrī subsumes it. As a virtue she rounds out the list, and as a goddess—of all the virtues "she" is the only one who bears an epithet of divinity—she follows where the others have gone.

I might also mention two points where this myth runs parallel to prominent epic themes, showing how patterns from diverse portions of the epic reinforce each other. First, there is a strong

[48] See above (4) following n. 38.

[49] For a similar concept, cf. below, n. 57, where Vṛtti (Character, Conduct) is the *purogā* of all the goddesses associated with Śrī; cf. also *Mbh.* 17:3 where Yudhiṣṭhira, upon entering heaven, is joined with "prosperity" (*śrī*; 8–9) and covers the *lokas* with his *tejas*, *yaśas*, and perfection of conduct (*vṛttasaṃpadā*; 27).

[50] On the two warrior types, see Dumézil, *Destiny of the Warrior*, pp. 5, 59, 82–93. Arjuna is the epic's model for virtuous activity (*pravṛtti*), and Bhīma incarnates *balam* at birth (1:114,8, etc.).

[51] See above following n. 34.

hint that the most crucial of all these "virtues," even more crucial than *śīla*, is Śrī, the only one whose departure brings fear (*bhayam*) to Prahlāda's face. This final blow to Prahlāda's *aiśvaryam* is reminiscent of the hopelessness which overcomes the Pāṇḍavas at the loss of Draupadī, Yudhiṣṭhira's last stake, in the dice game.[52] Second, the brahmin disguise which Indra assumes to win Śrī is the same as that which the Pāṇḍavas assume when they win Draupadī. As Biardeau says, the latter disguise indicates the unification, in Arjuna (and his brothers), of both the *brahman* and *kṣatra* powers.[53] One might say, in addition, that both the myth and the epic point to a unification of these "two powers" with the third-function themes represented by Śrī and Draupadī.

This resonant but rather schematic narrative gives an account of Śrī's departure from Prahlāda's body, but tells little if anything about her coming to Indra. The gap is soon filled.

(2) *Śāntiparvan* 215 to 221 finds Bhīṣma telling Yudhiṣṭhira about further incidents in the career of Indra. On each of four occasions the chief of the gods encounters a former foe—Prahlāda, Bali, Namuci, and Bali again—who has been "abandoned by Śrī," but who, made wiser by defeat, confronts Indra with the most unsettling truths about the precariousness of his sovereignty. From Bali, Indra learns both times that dispassion comes from the insight that everything results from Time (*kāla*; 217,5–59; 220,21–87). In the first meeting with Bali, Śrī herself tells Indra: "Neither the Creator nor the Ordainer (*dhātṛ*, *vidhātṛ*] governs me; it is Time alone which causes my goings-about" (*paryāyān*; 218,10).

The second of the meetings with Bali informs us the most about Śrī's movements. The account opens by referring to the tradition that Bali sustained his defeat "when the [three] worlds were bestridden by Viṣṇu," thus making Indra king of the gods

[52] See Johnsen, "Varuṇa and Dhṛtarāṣṭra," p. 254 and, in agreement, Dumézil, *ME*, I, 118.

[53] See above, Chapter 3, n. 4.

(220,7). This reference to a "higher" divine entity than Indra is not the only one in this passage, and henceforth at least one of the two main gods—Viṣṇu and Śiva—will be present in most of the myths we discuss.

As king of the gods, then, but as yet (apparently) without Śrī, Indra sets out with all the classes of gods in train. Touring the worlds, he chances (?) on Bali in a seaside mountain cave (220,11), and the two hold their lengthy talk on the all-powerfulness of Time. But now, instead of Śrī coming directly to Bali's home, as she does in the first meeting, her appearance demands a new setting.

We are now introduced to Nārada, one of Viṣṇu's constant and most devoted *bhaktas*, with his ability to "rove at will through the three worlds" (221,5). "On a certain daybreak, rising up and wishing to perform pure ablutions, he went to the Ganges where it issued from the immovable pass [? *dhruvadvāra*], and plunged in" (221,6). The compound in question presents several possibilities. As the Ganguli-Roy translation says (with Dutt apparently following): "The commentator [Nīlakaṇṭha] is silent. Probably a Himalayan pass. The vernacular translators think it is the region of the Pole-star that is intended. Dhruva is a name of Brahman [Brahmā] the Creator. It may mean, therefore, the river as it issues out of Brahman's *loka* or region. The Puranic myth is that issuing from the foot of Viṣṇu, the stream enters the kamandalu of Brahman and thence [goes] to earth."[54] It could also be simply the same as Gaṅgādvāra, an epic name for the present Hardwar; but I think Ganguli is right in supposing that the context implies someplace more Himalayan. The term, however, seems to refer more to a mythological spot than to any of the venerable "sources" of the Ganges visited by pilgrims: Gomukh near Gangotri, Badrinath on the Bhāgīrathī tributary, or Kedarnath on the Mandākinī. But whether an "immovable Pass," a specific "Dhruva pass," a "gate of Brahmā," or an old name for a pilgrimage spot, one

[54] Ganguli-Roy, trans., *Mahabharata*, IX: *Santi Parva*, 156, n. 2.

is certain that the waters are pure, probably purer than anywhere else since Nārada—the literal translation of whose name is "Water-Giver"[55]—was free to go wherever he chose. In fact, this is the crucial point. Indra's encounter with Śrī will occur at a spot where the Gaṅgā's waters are purest, the river's earthly source. It is probably no accident that this is the spot at which other myths—one of which I will turn to shortly—locate their meetings.[56]

For what one might call no apparent reason, Indra too has come to this very same bank (*tīram*; 221,7). There the two of them, the god and the ṛṣi, perform their ablutions and recitations and listen to the meritorious narratives of the attendant *devarṣis*. Then, at sunrise, just as they are standing to sing the Sun god's praises, they see in the sky (*ākāśe*) a light to the west equal to that of the sun. This is Śrī, seated on Viṣṇu's chariot, looking like the solar disc, attended by numerous Apsarases, and illumining the three worlds with her unrivaled brightness (221,11–12). When Indra, as usual (cf. 12:218,1–8), fails to recognize her, she introduces herself by a total of sixteen names[57] and tells Indra that she has come over to him because

[55] See Gonda, *Early Viṣṇuism*, p. 221.

[56] Cf. *Vām. P.* 50,12–18: after Śrī goes over to Bali (49,15), Indra goes to Brahmā and asks: "In what place may I win great prosperity [*udaya*] in a short time?" The answer: "in the world of mortals" (*martye*). Indra then goes to a bank of the Mahānadī ("Great River"), a name frequently applied to the Ganges, although also to other rivers (see s.v., Böhtlink and Roth). Here the Ganges is almost certainly meant. For one thing, Mahānadī is referred to as "daughter of the divine sage" (*surarṣikanyā*; 18), probably Bhagīratha. Where Indra goes, the river flows "back to Himālaya in the guise of water" (18). And Mahānadī is where King Gaya performed many sacrifices (15 and 16): according to the *Mahābhārata*, Gaya's sacrifices were performed at Brahmasaras, a *tīrtha* were all rivers take their rise (*samudbheda*; 3:93,12), a spot further (according to Sörensen's *Index*) placed on the Ganges (13:25,1726 = CE 13:26,40?), but also on the Payoṣṇī (3:121,9–14).

[57] 12:221,20–22; cf. 218,7–8 where she has five names. Of the sixteen, four—Śraddhā (Faith), Dhṛti (Constancy), Vijiti (Victory), and Sannati (Humility)—are names found among the eight goddesses (the "foremost" [*purogā*] being Vṛtti [Conduct]) who, "distinguished from but dependent on her" (221,81), accompany Śrī to Indra (82).

of the declining morals of the Asuras. The account concludes with a sort of golden age that begins when Indra, Śrī, and Nārada return to heaven and rejoin the gods who have assembled to greet them "at a pure and reverenced spot" (*śucau cābhyarcite deśe*; 221,86).

Whatever the peculiarities of these two accounts, the first of which ends quite differently,[58] it is still true that Śrī is operating largely within the same self-choice mythologem that earlier pertained primarily to Vāc. One might object that Śrī's choices take her from one Asura (at a time) to the single figure of Indra while Vāc moves from class to class. But this difference is more apparent than real: as Śrī says in the second account, because the Asuras were initially highly virtuous, "I dwelt with them for many yugas, from [the time of] the creation of creatures" (*prajāsarga*; 221,48). We have, in fact, seen her associated with three successive generations of Asura chiefs: with Prahlāda, Virocana, and Bali. And, as the second version indicates, the gods all gather—as a class—to welcome her when she comes with Indra and Nārada to heaven.[59] Moreover, as regards the "free choice" element of the Svayaṃvara theme, she says in the first account that "Time alone causes [her] goings-about" (218,10), and, in the second, she tells Indra more pointedly: "I have come to you of my own accord" (*māṃ svayamanuprāptām*; 221,80).[60] Thus neither her affiliation in the second account with Viṣṇu nor in the first with the rhythm of Time—which *Bhagavad Gītā* 11,32 identifies with Viṣṇu but which here is

[58] Śrī tells Indra that she will dwell in him always if he divides her into four portions in accord with the Vedas (12:218,19)—one portion each to Earth, Ocean, Fire, and Brahmins.

[59] See also above, n. 45.

[60] Śrī's autonomy is instructively compared with the cautionary words of the Sun's daughter Tapatī; refusing the *gāndharva* mode of marriage which requires only mutual consent, she tells her suitor, King Saṃvaraṇa, to ask her father, explaining: "I am not my own mistress [*nāhamīśātmano*]; . . . I am not mistress of [my] body; . . . surely women are never independent" (*na svatantrā hi yoṣitaḥ*; 1:161,14–16).

regarded as more fundamental than "Creator or Ordainer"—does anything to undercut her freedom to bestow her favor as she will.

These epic passages thus present us with a far more elaborate royal mythology concerning Śrī than is found in the priestly books of the Brāhmaṇas. With it, there are certain new developments and certain basic continuities. On the one hand, Śrī's meanderings, in accord with nothing unless it be the rhythm of Time, give her a coloring unreported in the Brāhmaṇas: she is unfaithful to those she favors. Bali pointedly reminds Indra of this twice, once in each episode:

This Royal Prosperity [*rājaśrī*] which you have obtained and which you consider to be incomparable formerly dwelt in me. Contrary to that [?], she does not remain in one place [*naiṣā hyekatra tiṣṭhati*]. Indeed, she has dwelt in thousands of Indras who were superior to you. Fickle [*lolā*], having abandoned me, she has come to you. . . . Do not brag, O Śakra. You should become tranquil. [If you] go on in this way, having abandoned you she will quickly go to another. [217,57–59]

From delusion [*mohāt*], you long for this Royal Prosperity [*rājaśrī*]. Imagined to be stable [*sthira*], she is not so for you, nor for us [*na cāsmākam*], nor for others. Passing over many others, she now dwells in you. Having remained in you for a certain time, O Vāsava [she will prove to be] inconstant [*cañcala*]. Like a cow abandoning one drinking hole, she will go again to another. [220,44–46]

As Coomaraswamy points out, this theme of fickleness later reaches such a height that "she is described as so unstable that 'even in a picture she moves,' and if she clings to Nārāyaṇa, it is only that she may enjoy His constant changes of form (*vyūhas* and *avatāras*)!"[61]

[61] Coomaraswamy, "Early Indian Iconography: Śrī-Lakṣmī" (see above, n. 7), p. 178; cf. the *Anuśāsanaparvan* passage (11,19–20) cited at the beginning of this chapter.

On the other hand, there is one unbroken continuity in Śrī's behavior: her movements are related to lists of royal virtues. In the epic, a trifunctional order is often lost (as in the first passage below) or obscured (as in the second), especially when Śrī announces the virtues herself and declares them to be a requirement for association with her:

I dwell in truth, gift, vow, austerity, strength, and virtue. [218,12][62]

I dwell in the vans and on the banners of victorious kings [*rajñāṃ vijayamānānām*] of virtuous dispositions [*dharmaśīlānām*], as in their dominions and cities. I always dwell in an Indra among men, one appearing (2) like a conqueror [*jitakāsini*], a hero [*śūre*], unretreating in battles, O slayer of Bala. Ever do I dwell in one (1) constant in dharma [*dharmanitye*], of great intelligence [*mahābuddhau*], pious [*brahmanye*], humble [*praśrite*], and (3) liberally disposed [*dānaśīle*]. Formerly I dwelt with the Asuras, bound by *satya* and dharma, but having seen them assume adverse natures, I have left them to reside in you. [221,23–26; probable functional traits numbered in parentheses]

But there are instances where a trifunctional ordering is apparent, especially when Śrī is referred to in the third person. Indeed, this is most prominently the case in certain passages that show her to be independent of any requirements the three functions might be thought to impose upon her. In such cases the virtues are not positive requirements but qualities which in themselves—without Śrī—are negative, which put no hold on her freedom to choose, to be fickle, and to move on in accord with the rhythm of Time. So it is that Bali, persisting with his insight that Time is Śrī's only regulative principle, illustrates how the one, like the other, moves on irrespective of the virtues: "One who is possessed of great learning [*vidyā*] and one of little learning, one possessed of strength [*balam*] and one of little strength, one who is beautiful [*darśanīya*] and one who is misshapen [*virūpa*], one of good fortune [*bhaga*] and one of ill

[62] *satye sthitāsmi dāne ca vrate tapasi caiva hi / parākrame ca dharme ca.*

fortune—Time, which is profound [*gambhīra*], sweeps them all away by its own energy [*tejas*]" (217,18–19). The context leaves little doubt that Bali is referring to Śrī as well as to Time.

A parallel passage makes this even clearer. As Vidura tells Dhṛtarāṣṭra during the long, sleepless night that the latter spends dreading the prospects of war: "Surely Śrī does not approach [*upa-sṛp:* "for intercourse"; M-W] out of fear one who is exceedingly respectable [*ārya*, "of noble family"], one who is an excessive donor [*dātṛ*], one who is a superhero [*śūra*], one of superlative vows [*vrata*], or one claiming wisdom [*prajñā*]" (5:39,50).[63] One might say that the three functions are stable while Śrī is not. Indeed, the trifunctional character of both of these lists of virtues should be clear, the only problem being *ārya*, "respectable," "of noble family." This and other matters with respect to specific virtues will be discussed in the next chapter. It is curious that the most trifunctional arrangements of virtues are found in passages that treat Śrī as inconstant, perhaps indicating that if the trifunctional order is an archaic feature, then so is this inconstancy.[64] Or, since Śrī's fickleness coincides with a "pessimistic" view of Time not usually associated with the Brāhmaṇas, perhaps this "pessimism," preserving the archaic structure in short formulas, has reoriented the meaning of the virtues by pointing up the insufficiency of "merits" (to use the word which catches better than "virtues" the present turn of meaning) in the face of the fickle whims—better called the "grace"—of the goddess Śrī. That such pessimism was at least the message drawn from these passages, if not their preservative, is clear from an interpolation

[63] *atyāryamatidātāramatiśūramativratam / prajñābhimaninaṃ caiva śrīr bhayānnopasarpati.*

[64] This theme may surface first with Vāc who, swayed by the gods' playing of the *vīṇā*, is said in *ŚB* 3,2,4,3–6 to choose them "vainly" (*mogham*) over the hymn-singing Gandharvas. See also the figure of Apālā, "the Unprotected," a Ṛg Vedic goddess sometimes identified with Śrī (first by Coomaraswamy, "Loathly Bride," p. 393), who comes to Indra "having hatred for her husband" (*patidviṣ*: *ṚV* 8,91,4).

made in many Northern manuscripts immediately after the words of Vidura: "Nor [does Śrī dwell] in one of excessive virtues [*atiguṇavat*], nor one without virtues [*nirguṇa*]; she does not desire [a number of] virtues [*guṇān*], nor does she become attached to the absence of virtues [*nairguṇya*]. Mad like a blind cow, Śrī abides most anywhere" (*Udyogaparvan*, 257*). The cow simile had certainly caught on.

Śrī and Draupadī

Returning to a central problem: how seriously are we to take the epic's insistence that it is Śrī who is incarnate in Draupadī? Before I analyze the myths and legends that account for Draupadī's divine antecedents, let us recall what Dumézil regards as the second stage of this transposition. The trivalent theology of the Indo-Iranian goddess provides the first stage, which is grafted onto Indra's wife—originally not Śrī but Indrāṇī or Śacī—who, remaining unique, takes human form to rejoin her husband, who is essentially one but in appearance five. Does Śrī really need these figures to back her up?

Two prominent myths and one legend tell of Draupadī's divine identity. The legend and one of the myths were mentioned in Chapter 3, and the myth again in Chapter 4. There they were examined in connection with Śiva, Viṣṇu-Nārāyaṇa, Vyāsa, and Krishna, with comment stimulated chiefly by the insights of Biardeau. Now, keeping these earlier results in mind, we must face the questions raised by Dumézil.

(1) The popular legend[65] tells the story of the overanxious maiden—Draupadī in a former life—whose repeated prayers to Śiva for a husband result in her obtaining five husbands, one for each entreaty. The two versions in the Critical Edition, both told by Vyāsa, are much the same, differing only in a few matters of phraseology.

[65] See above, Chapter 3, n. 8.

According to Vyāsa, there once dwelt in a hermitage a certain unnamed ṛṣi with an equally unnamed "daughter [*kanyā*][66] of slender waist, fair lips, fair brows, and endowed with every virtue" (*sarvaguṇānvitā*; 157,6[67]). Though beautiful and chaste (*rūpavatī satī*; 7), she was unmarried, and to get a husband she prayed to Mahādeva "over and over again: 'I desire a husband endowed with every virtue'" (*patiṃ sarvaguṇopetamicchāmīti punaḥ punaḥ*; 10). These honorific descriptions will be discussed later.

(2) Fortunately, with the "first" myth, which Dumézil takes to be the oldest, I can be brief since Dumézil has twice produced translations of the text and commentaries upon it.[68] The passage, from the fifth section of the *Mārkaṇḍeya Purāṇa*, is structured by the theme of the three sins of the warrior.[69] First, guilty of brahminicide, Indra's *tejas* ("spiritual force") abandons him and goes over to the god Dharma; second, guilty of breaking a warrior's agreement, his *balam* ("physical force") leaves and goes to Vāyu; and third, having violated the brāhmaṇī Ahalyā, his *rūpam* ("beauty") leaves him for the Aśvins. At the request of the Earth, who is oppressed by incarnated demons, the same gods incarnate these portions *of Indra* in Yudhiṣṭhira, Bhīma, and the Pāṇḍava Twins respectively, while Indra donates a portion of his own, the remainder of his *vīryam* ("vigor, heroism"), to account for the "central" Pāṇḍava Arjuna. Dumézil has discussed these relocations of Indra's virtues admirably. Let us simply recall that this scene

[66] South Indian vernacular versions of the epic alter the story: Draupadī in a previous birth was named Nalayini; married to a ṛṣi-leper, she served him dutifully until, pleased, he assumed a comely form and they enjoyed sex. But when he renounced conjugal life she grew angry, and he cursed her to have five husbands. Here we have not an overanxious maiden but a sex-starved wife; see M. V. Subramanian, *Vyasa and Variations: The Mahabharata Story* (Madras: Higginbothams, 1967), p. 46.

[67] This description does not occur in the second version (1:189,41–49).

[68] Dumézil, *Destiny of the Warrior*, pp. 74–76; *ME*, I, 113–16.

[69] See below, Chapters 9 and 10.

bears a resemblance to *Śatapatha Brāhmaṇa* 1,6,3,1–16 (see above, after n. 38) and proceed to the crucial conclusion: "In these five ways did the divine performer of a hundred sacrifices [Indra] incarnate himself. His highly fortunate wife [*mahābhāgā patnī*] came out of the fire as Kṛṣṇā. Kṛṣṇā was the wife of Śakra and of none else" (*śakrasyaikasya sā patnī kṛṣṇā nānyasya kasyacit*; *Mark. P.* 5,24–25).[70]

Dumézil, of course, sees these verses as referring to Śacī, and as disclosing a stage of the tradition preceding that in which Draupadī is connected with Śrī.[71] Gonda, on the other hand, agrees with the identification, but reverses the order of precedence, saying that the passage "altered" the *Mahābhārata* version (which I will turn to next) "by declaring that it was Indra's own wife who became incarnate as Draupadī, without mentioning her name; . . . it is highly improbable that Śrī is meant here."[72] It seems to me that Gonda comes the closest to representing the tenor of the *Mārkaṇḍeya* passage, which is one in a series of four attempting to resolve difficult questions raised *by* the epic, and thus presumably raised *after* the epic. But if the *Mārkaṇḍeya Purāṇa* has sought to amend the epic tradition by substituting Śacī for Śrī, it has not made its intent clear. *Mahābhāgā* could easily describe Śrī. As the narrative progresses, one sees that it is not so much a matter—for the goddess in question—of following Indra in person as of following his virtues, one of Śrī's oldest traits. Perhaps, in placing first emphasis on clearing Draupadī of the charge of polyandry, the passage tones down the issue of which goddess figures behind her. Whether it be Śrī or Śacī, the passage is a postepic effort to smooth out one of the epic's trouble spots. There is no reason to suppose that Indrāṇī or Śacī plays any role in a second or "intermediate" stage in the construction of the transposition,

[70] From Manmatha Nath Dutt, trans., *A Prose English Translation of Mārkaṇḍeya Purāṇa* (Calcutta: Dass, 1897), p. 23.

[71] *ME*, I, 121–22.

[72] Gonda, *Early Viṣṇuism*, p. 225.

or even in connection with Draupadī's favoritism for Arjuna.[73] In Śrī's relation to Indra—and in particular to the virtues—both matters can be accounted for. As to the nonappearance of Śiva and for that matter of Viṣṇu, these can also be easily explained if the myth is viewed as a late effort to make a tight argument for the clearance of Draupadī's name. If Śrī is removed from the drama, this eliminates the need for any "approval" on the part of her consort Viṣṇu; and if the marriage is a throughly dharmic act, Śiva need not intervene as instigator of the adharmic activity.[74] Their nonappearance is not a sign that the *Mārkaṇḍeya Purāṇa* myth is the more ancient.

(3) Certainly the *Markaṇḍeya* myth, despite its admirably clear structure, gives no new specifics about either Śrī or Śacī. The myth of the five former Indras, from the *Mahābhārata*, is far more accommodating. I discussed in Chapter 4 the parallel lines between this myth and the epic dice game. Here, however, the question arises whether Śrī has a mythology of her own and whether the myth is an old one integrated into an Indian framework. Dumézil, for instance, speaks of a "Śaivite coloration of the account,"[75] and I have insisted in Chapter 3 that it is not just Śiva but Viṣṇu-Nārāyaṇa who is involved. Indeed, it would be more appropriate to reject any sectarian interpretation and speak of a "Hindu coloration."

When Drupada hears of the Pāṇḍavas' polyandric marriage plans with his daughter, he ventures his opinion that the union would be adharmic (1:188,7–9). Vyāsa then takes him aside to a private chamber. There the incarnation of Nārāyaṇa makes two revelations of the identities of the proposed partners. The second is a version of the overanxious maiden story. The first is close enough to the *Mārkaṇḍeya Purāṇa* account for Dumézil to assume a connection between them.

[73] Dumézil, *ME*, I, 121–22.
[74] See above, Chapter 3.
[75] *ME*, I, 111.

Once, when the gods had assembled to perform a great Soma sacrifice (*sattra*) in Naimiṣa forest, Yama became the officiant in charge of slaying the animals (the *śāmitra*; 1:189,1). With Yama thus preoccupied, there were no deaths in the world's human population. Disturbed at this loss of a distinction between the human and the divine, the gods complained to Prajāpati, who promised that as soon as Yama's work was finished the king of the dead would make up for lost time. Satisfied, the gods returned to their *sattra*.

"This strange assembly," as Dumézil puts it,[76] now serves as the starting point for the central narrative. The "high-powered" (*mahābalāḥ*) gods, with certain exceptions, find themselves beside the Gaṅgā. There they see a golden lotus which has floated downstream (189,9). Wonder-struck (*vismita*) at the sight, the heroic (*śūra*) Indra leaves the assembly and sets out alone to follow the river upstream. There "where the Gaṅgā is perennially brought forth" (*yatra gaṅgā satataṃ saṃprasūtā*; 189,10), that is, the same spot—at least symbolically—where we have seen Indra meet Śrī before,[77] he sees a weeping young woman (*yoṣā rudatī*) who has entered the "divine Gaṅgā" (*gaṅgāṃ devīm*) to bathe. Whenever her teardrops fall on the water, they turn into lotuses of gold (189,11). Beholding this marvel, Indra asks her who she is.

The answer is a promise: "You will know me here [*iha*], O Śakra; who I am and why, having little luck [*mandabhāgya*], I weep.[78] Follow me." (189,13). Śrī has gone unrecognized before, always on account of that awesome radiance which makes it impossible to distinguish one perfection of femininity from another: as Bali says to Indra, "I do not know whether she is an *asurī*, a *devī*, or a *manuṣī*" (12:218,4). But here Indra has

[76] *Ibid.*

[77] See above, at nn. 54–55.

[78] This promise (note the *iha*), and the mythological convergences discussed in the following, leave me unconvinced by J. A. B. van Buitenen's remark that "it does not become clear who she is"; van Buitenen, *The Mahābhārata*, I 465, note to 189, 10ff.

a better and more specific reason for failing to know her. Śrī is appearing as her own opposite, one might almost say in disguise: *mandabhāgya*, literally "having an impoverished share," and weeping, she is the very antithesis of what one would expect if he were looking for the goddess of Prosperity whose "share," one might say, is indicated by her name.

Led by the tearful girl, Indra soon sees a sight now familiar: a handsome youth and another young woman, Śiva (sometimes called the lord of tears) and his consort Pārvatī, seated not far off on a Himalayan mountain peak playing dice. Carelessly, Indra flings him a challenge, what may be no more than his standard, if boastful, form of address: "Know that this entire universe stands under my power. I am the lord" (*mamedaṃ tvaṃ viddhi viśvaṃ bhuvanaṃ vaśe sthitam / īśo 'hamasmīti*; 189,15). Undisturbed, Śiva continues his game, managing only a smile and a glance at the indignant Indra. The glance alone, however, is enough to leave Indra paralyzed, standing there "like a stake" (*sthaṇur-iva*; 189,16), apparently a pun on one of Śiva's names. And there Indra stands until the dice game is finished, at which point Śiva decides to quell Indra's pride (*darpa*; 189,17).

This segment of the myth points toward one of the features that has led Dumézil to speak of a "Saivite coloration." As he says: "Indra's sin . . . is a lack of respect, an involuntary one, toward a superior god. . . . That cannot be old. The mythology of the Brāhmaṇas certainly knows the sins of Indra. It has even drawn up inventories of them. No item is of this type."[79] This seems to suggest, in particular, that the theme of Indra's three sins has been submerged beneath a lesson in Śiva's superiority.

We saw in Chapters 3 and 4, however, that Śiva's part is well integrated with that of Śrī. Let us now observe their roles more closely. Śiva first tells the weeping girl to bring Indra to him. But "scarcely touched by her" (*spṛṣṭamātrastayā*), Indra's limbs are all loosened (*śrastairaṅgaiḥ*), and he falls to the ground.

[79] Dumézil, *ME*, I, 112.

This mysterious touch does not fulfill Śiva's command to bring Indra to him and seems strange in the text. In fact, Śiva seems to disregard its consequences when he tells the supposedly disabled Indra that "as your strength [*balam*] and heroism [*vīryam*] are unlimited," Indra should remove a huge stone that covers a cave in a mountain peak and enter therein. Inside Indra joins four others who, like himself, are "of the splendor of Sūrya" (189,19). Greatly distressed, he asks if he is to become like them, and Śiva—eyes widened in anger—answers: "Enter this cave, Śatakratu; from folly [*bālyāt*] you have insulted me" (189,21). Hearing these words, once again Indra's limbs are loosened, just as they were by the tearful Śrī (189,22), and he shakes like a fig leaf in the wind.

Śrī's touch is gratuitous, perhaps an anachronism in this myth; whatever its meaning, its effects are unrecorded. The theme of Indra's first contact (he does not recognize her) with Śrī and the kingship she represents has, it seems, been reinterpreted as a lesson in divine priorities. The king of the gods learns that he is not the lord of the universe. One might say that Indra, lured by golden lotuses, has gone to find Prosperity, or Sovereignty, and has instead learned about their limitations.

Hoping for a change of heart, Indra turns to flattery. But Śiva holds to his curse: "Here those of such behavior [*evaṃśīla*][80] as yours do not escape. Formerly even these were such as you. Therefore, having entered the cave all of you lie down [*śedhvam*]. Your escape shall no doubt be as follows: may you each enter a human womb. There, having performed irresistible [? unfeasible; *avisahya*] karman and having slain many other men, you shall again regain the much-valued world of Indra" (24–26).

Accepting these impositions, the four former Indras (*pūrvendrāḥ*) speak for themselves as well as for "our" Indra, the fifth, when they ask only that they may be fathered by the gods

[80] See above, following n. 46 (*śīla* in the Prahlāda episode).

Dharma, Vāyu, Maghavat (a name for Indra), and the Aśvins (27). "Our" Indra seems to solve the difficulty of how he could both be imprisoned and free, as Maghavat, to engender a human offspring, by adding: "By my heroism [*vīryam*] I shall create from myself a *puruṣa* to be the fifth of these for the sake of this task."[81]

Śiva then agrees to this set of proposals, "and he also appointed that young woman, desired by the world [*lokakāntā*], Śrī herself, to be their wife among men" (189,29). Furthermore, as we saw in Chapter 3, Viṣṇu-Nārāyaṇa gives his approval, and the way is thus prepared for the births of the Pāṇḍavas, of Draupadī, and—with Viṣṇu contributing his black and white hairs—of Krishna and Balarāma (31).

This is the end of the myth as presented by Vyāsa, but one must take into account the ensuing events fully to interpret it. Having concluded his exposition, Vyāsa grants Drupada a celestial eye (*divyaṃ caksuḥ*) with which to see the Pāṇḍavas and Draupadī in their "meritorious bodies of old" (189,35). Presumably this would be the way they saw each other, in particular the way that Indra saw Śrī, when, as she had promised him, he would come to know her. Yet when this was, we do not know; probably the marriage itself is the fulfillment of the promise. "Then he [Drupada] saw them [the Pāṇḍavas] as celestials, garlanded with golden diadems, each resembling Śakra, having the color of Pāvaka [Agni] or Āditya [the Sun], their chaplets tied, of delightful form, youthful, broadchested and tall as palmyra trees, exceedingly adorned with dustless celestial robes and the most excellent beautiful garlands, like so many Tri-akṣas [Rudras], Vasus, or celestial Ādityas endowed with every virtue" (*sarvaguṇopapannān*; 189,37–38). Wonder-struck, Drupada turns to his daughter, and, having admired her Śrīlike beauty, he regards her as "worthy to be

[81] Note that *vīryam* is the same virtue that stabilizes the *Mārk. P.* version, where it is also the last accounted for and the only one which Indra must contribute by choice.

their wife for her beauty [*rūpam*], majesty [*tejas*], and fame [*yaśas*]."[82]

This conclusion sharpens our focus on a theme observed in the story of the overanxious maiden, which I will pursue more thoroughly in the next chapter. Being like the Ādityas, Śrī-Draupadī's husbands are *sarvaguṇopapanna*, "endowed with every virtue." Most important, Śrī (or Draupadī seen as Śrī) is the Indras' (or the Pāṇḍavas seen as Indras) suitable partner because of her *rūpam* (why should it not be listed first in her case, especially as Drupada had just noticed it?), her *tejas*, and her *yaśas*. Each of these virtues has appeared on its appropriate functional level in the preceding discussion. In contrast to the trivalent goddesses, Śrī claims the second-function virtue of fame rather than one connected with strength. I have translated *tejas*, as "majesty" in this context, but it is the same term that has occupied the first rank in the Brāhmaṇas, in the downfall of Prahlāda, and in the birth of Yudhiṣṭhira from Dharma.

Dumézil thinks this myth has undergone a "clumsy Śaivite retouching."[83] But, as we have seen, it is not just a matter of Śiva, and Dumézil overlooks some of the more peculiar features of the myth. As to the roles of Śiva and Nārāyaṇa, although I have adopted the term "Hindu coloration," I do not mean to confine this to a late or even "postepic" period. As I began to stress in Chapters 3 and 4 and shall re-emphasize in Part 3, I believe that oppositions and relations between Viṣṇu and Śiva are too thoroughly ingrained into the epic to be automatically explained away as interpolations. The activities of these deities seem rather to have been worked into the epic in an early, formative period of the poem's construction. When an

[82] 189,39: *rūpatejoyaśobhiḥ patnīmṛddhām*; cf. the marriage of Abhimanyu and Uttarā, where Draupadī "surpassed all the beautiful women there by her form, fame, and beauty" (*sarvāścābhyabhavatkṛṣṇā rūpeṇa yaśasā śriyā*; 4:67,30).

[83] *ME*, I, 113. Although it is well integrated into the rest of the epic (see above, Chapter 4), Dumézil argues that the theme of "the multiple Indras" cannot be early and that the fundamental theme is that of the three sins; but on this, see Chapters 9 and 10 below.

Indian myth or legend is articulated through roles played by Viṣṇu and/or Śiva, it is sometimes possible to see that India has preserved ancient traditions and themes by linking them with these divinities. As Dumézil has shown, something along these lines seems to have happened, probably very early, with the Śiśupāla legend.[84] It is now time to see whether the same may be said of this myth concerning Śrī.

The Source of Sovereignty

With all its oddities and "colorations," the myth of Śrī and the five Indras is the *only* myth in which Śrī does something of her own, under her own name, not done by any other goddess. Comparing this myth with traditions about Śrī's analogue in Irish tradition, a figure with whom she has often been compared before[85]—the goddess Flaith or Flaith Érenn (Sovereignty [of Ireland])—results in some surprising parallels. Here follows a condensation of the two oldest versions of the Flaith legend.[86]

(1) When King Daire was told that a "son of Daire" named Lugaid would attain Ireland's Sovereignty, he gave each of his five sons this name. At the assembly of Telltown, where his sons had come to race horses, Daire learned from a Druid that "a fawn with a golden lustre" would enter the assembly and that whichever son caught it would rule. When the fawn came "into the assembly," Daire's sons pursued it until it was finally caught by Lugaid Laigde. Then snow fell, and one son went for shelter, finding a house occupied by "a huge old woman,

[84] See *ME*, II, 91.

[85] Coomaraswamy, "Loathly Bride," pp. 391–404; Krappe, "Sovereignty of Erin," pp. 448–52; Rees and Rees, *Celtic Heritage*, pp. 73–76; Dumézil, *ME*, II, 342.

[86] Both legends are from portions of the "Book of Ballymote," a manuscript from the fourteenth century, but containing much older material; Krappe has summarized them in "Sovereignty of Erin," pp. 444–45 and 448–49. I mainly follow his summaries, but also quote from the texts as translated by (for Lugaid Laigde) Whitley Stokes and Ernst Windisch, *Irische Texte*, III (Leipzig: Herzel, 1897), 316–23, sec. 70, and (for Niall) Whitley Stokes, "The Adventure of the Sons of Eochaid Muigmedón," *Revue Celtique*, XXIV (1903), 190–207; cf. Dumézil, *ME*, II, 335–36.

. . . her spears of teeth outside her head, and great, old, foul, faded things upon her." Refusing to lie with her on the bed she offered, he was told he had thus severed himself from "sovereignty." After three more brothers came and went with the same events, Lugaid Laigde went and said, "I will sleep alone with thee." Having followed her to the bed, to his astonishment "it seemed to him that the radiance of her face was the sun rising in the month of May. . . . Then he mingled in love with her. 'Auspicious is your journey,' said she, 'I am the sovranty, and the kingship of Erin will be obtained by thee.'" The other brothers then came and all feasted "on the freshest of food and the oldest of ale."

(2) Eochaid Muigmedón, king of Ireland, had four sons by the "witch-queen" Mongfind, and one, Niall, by a captive Saxon princess. In a test to see which of them was fittest to rule, they were told by a wizard to go on a hunt. When they stopped, they cooked what they had caught and became thirsty. Fergus, the first to volunteer, "went seeking for water, till he chanced on a well" guarded by a hideous hag who would let him drink only for a kiss. This he, and two more sons of Mongfind, refused to do and they got no water; then the fourth son, Fiachra, gave her only the barest brush of a kiss, and in return got a brief moment of kingship. Last of all Niall came for water and consented to kiss and "lie with" the hag, who then turned into a beautiful woman. Asked who she was, she answered "I am Sovereignty," and told him to establish "seniority" over his brothers.

Setting these two Irish variants beside the myth of Indra and Śrī, and recalling Indra's second meeting with Bali (B),[87] the parallels are obvious, especially if the myth's main narrative (1–6) and sequel ([7]–[8]) are differentiated from the problematic opening scene (A)[88] and the "Hindu colorations" (B-H).

[87] See above, n. 56 and preceding text.

[88] Cf. Dumézil, *ME*, I, 112–13, also detaching this scene.

Indra and Śrī	*Lugaid (L), Niall (N), and Flaith*
A. The gods undergo their initial difficulties with Yama in which the world order is undermined.	
1. The gods assemble at the grand sacrifice in the forest.	1. The brothers assemble for a test of who should be sovereign: quest for the fawn (L), hunt (N).
2. While assembled, the gods see a golden lotus drifting down the Ganges.	2. A fawn of golden luster passes through the assembly (L); all enter the forest (L and N) to chase it (L).
3. Indra, being a hero (*śūra*), sets out alone to find out where it came from.	3. Lugaid Laigde alone succeeds in capturing and eating the fawn (L).
4. The lotuses lead Indra to the source of the Ganges, where he has been before (with Nārada [B]), as, presumably, have the four other Indras before him.	4. Niall is the last of all his brothers to go after water, to a well (N); Lugaid Laigde is the last of his brothers to seek shelter in a house where, in special abundance, there is ale for the asking (L).
5. Presumably like the former Indras, "our" Indra sees a young woman who is not her "better self," weeping and "having little luck." He does not know who she is.	5. Like their brothers, Niall meets a horrible hag at the well (N), Lugaid at the house (L). She is not recognized.
B. She takes him before Śiva.	
C. Indra boasts to the higher god.	
D. Śiva paralyzes Indra with his glance.	
E. Śiva tells the weeper to bring Indra to him (which she never does).	
6. Scarcely touched by her, Indra's limbs are "loosened" and he falls to the ground.	6. Niall must kiss and lie with her (N); Lugaid must lie with her (L).
F. Ignoring this, Śiva tells Indra to remove a rock from a cave.	
G. Told to enter, Indra's limbs are loosened again by Śiva's words.	
H. Śiva, with Nārāyaṇa's collusion, determines the fate of the five Indras and of Śrī to be born in human wombs.	

[7] The Pāṇḍavas are revealed to Drupada as Indras, "kings."	7. The obligation for kingship is thus met (N and L).
[8] Draupadī is revealed to Drupada, either as she would have looked when, as Śrī, she fulfilled her promise to Indra that the latter would "know" her, or else as she looks now, fulfilling the promise through the marriage itself.	8. The former hag reveals herself as the Sovereignty of Ireland (N and L).
[9] Draupadī becomes the Pāṇḍavas' wife-in-common (no connection with Yudhiṣṭhira's seniority). Śrī comes with Indra and Nārada to heaven where the gods meet her in a "pure and reverenced spot," beginning a golden age under Indra's sovereignty (B).	9. The water (N), or the ale (L), is shared by all the brothers, but sovereignty has been given to only one.

Thus, beyond the roles of Śiva and Nārāyaṇa may be an archaic Indo-Irish, perhaps Indo-European,[89] myth or legend of sovereignty; but there are difficulties. First, the results of the "first contacts" with Śrī and Flaith (item 6) are entirely different, and if there is a connection, it must result from the Indian story's postponement of her self-disclosure until after things are straightened out with Śiva. Second, in the Irish stories the group that goes into the forest is identical with the one that benefits from the final disclosure, but the Indian story presents a disjunction. On the one hand, there are the gods who sacrifice in Naimiṣa forest, from among whom our Indra, *unlike* the

[89] Cf. Ferdowsi's "ancient legend" (Levy, *Epic of Kings*, pp. 81–83) in which three Pahlavāns and other knights hunt game and come upon a "ravishing maid." Though beautiful at the start, she has entered the forest "weeping tears of blood," her father having beaten her. In fact she is a Turanian princess, and her "coming over" to Iran reminds one of myths about Vāc and Śrī. The Pahlavāns argue over her and take her to Shah Kāvus for arbitration. The latter recognizes her for the prize she is with intriguing words: "This is a mountain doe, truly a heart ravishing gazelle; but game appropriate only to the highest," and marries her himself.

Irish brothers, is the only one to set out. On the other hand, there is the group of the five Indras, four of whom, *like* the four brothers who precede Niall and Lugaid on their searches, have preceded our Indra to the watery "source" of Sovereignty. The disjunction in the Indian story is difficult to explain. Perhaps the Indian authors would not imagine other gods to have preceded Indra and been turned back by failure. Or perhaps the four "former" Indras are the ones who did precede him. The fact of the disjunction, in any case, accords well with the general impressions, first, that the forest assembly is detachable and, second, that the theme of the previous Indras is anomalous.[90] Finally, Śrī herself is never described as loathsome. Moreover, within the context of the epic's myth, the reason she gives for her tears—the loss of her former husbands—is not unsatisfactory. As Coomaraswamy has pointed out, however, Śrī does have her unattractive opposite selves: Alakṣmī, Kālakaṇṇi.[91] Moreover, if he is right in seeing the Vedic and Brāhmanic Apālā as a precursor of Śrī, there is a precedent for Indra having a "loathly bride" who is transformed not at his touch, but by a series of operations in which the god removes her reptilian skin by drawing her through three different holes in his chariot and thus making her "sun-skinned."[92]

These differences and possible transformations are no less striking than the fundamental unity of outline. Moreover, the Indian and Irish accounts introduce a number of symbols that

[90] See above, n. 83; as argued there, the theme of the five Indras is not necessarily late. In fact, an effort to explain it along Purāṇic lines is an interpolation; see *Ādiparvan* 1916*, following 1:189,28, where at least two (Śānti, Śibi) and probably three (if Ṛtadhāmā = Ritudhāmā) of the four former Indras are given names which come to be those of the Indras of the fourteen Manvantaras (see *VP* 3,1).

[91] Coomaraswamy, "Loathly Bride," p. 395.

[92] *ṚV* 8,91; see Coomaraswamy, "Loathly Bride," and Hanns Oertel, "Contributions from the *Jāiminīya Brāhmaṇa* to the History of Brāhmaṇa Literature," pt. 2, "Indra Cures Apālā," *JAOS*, XVIII (1897), 26–31, giving Brāhmaṇic commentaries along with Sāyaṇa's.

are connected with sovereignty, some of which seem to be Indo-Irish and perhaps Indo-European. I have suggested that the golden lotus is an Indianization of the theme of the animal, usually wild and golden, that symbolizes and shows the way to Sovereignty.[93] Actually, the deer is not un-Indian. The royal deer hunt has altered many a royal destiny (Yayāti, Saṃvarana, Śaṃtanu, Pāṇḍu, Rāma Dāśaratha), although often adversely; and, as Jaiswal tells us, "the *Śrī-sūkta* calls her [Śrī] *hariṇī*, of the form of a deer, and on some Kuṇinda coins of the first century B.C. she appears with a deer by her side."[94] Again, in both the Irish and Indian traditions there are two liquids connected with sovereignty: water and beer, water and *soma*. In Ireland, Sovereignty, in addition to her place by the well, is depicted "wearing a golden crown and seated on a crystal throne, having before her a vat of red liquor, from which she pours a draught into a gold cup which she hands to each successive king of Ireland."[95] And in India, Śrī, with her affinity for the pure waters at the source of the Ganges, may have her prototype in Apālā who, as "a maiden coming down to the water" (*kanyā var avāyatī*), finds some *soma* (*ṚV* 8,91,1), masticates it in what Dumézil takes as an archaic fashion,[96] and transmits it to Indra by mouth—in fact, according to the Brāhmaṇa commentary (can this be the other side of Śrī's paralyzing touch?), by a kiss.[97]

These Indo-Irish themes and symbols would seem to allow extension of the number of traditions that stem from a common

[93] See above, n. 89; on this theme, Krappe, "Sovereignty of Erin," pp. 446–48, 450, assumes an Indo-European origin; Dumézil, *ME*, II, 336, rejects his Greek and Iranian examples.

[94] Jaiswal, *Origin and Development*, p. 91.

[95] T. F. O'Rahilly, "On the Origin of the Names *Érainn* and *Ériu*," *Ériu*, XIV (1943), 14.

[96] Dumézil, *ME*, II, 342.

[97] Oertel, "Indra Cures Apālā," p. 27 (Sāyaṇa's *itihāsa* commentary on *ṚV* 8,91) and p. 30 (quoting *JB* 1,220).

royal heritage[98] to include the myths of Śrī and Flaith. So far, however, our views of the epic passage and the Indo-Irish correspondence have been shaped by this comparison alone. Actually, there are traditions that would seem to be intermediary between the Śrī and Flaith stories, which will allow us to draw the correspondences more tightly together.

The first comes from a province that, to my knowledge, Indo-European comparativists have so far left untouched. This is Ceylon, an island whose major language, Singhalese, is Indo-European, but whose religious traditions, shaped by Buddhism, have seemed an unlikely preservative for Indo-European themes. My focus is on a royal legend related only loosely to Buddhism and connected much more revealingly with Hindu themes. It is the legend of Vijaya ("Victory," a frequent name for Arjuna), the island's first king.[99]

Vijaya's antecedents place his story in the category of "first king" legends.[100] His grandfather was a lion (the king of beasts; *Mahāvaṃsa* 6,3) and his mother a woman, and their children both bore the epithet "Lion" in their names: a son Sīhabāhu ("Lion-armed" as his "hands and feet were formed like a lion's"; 6,10) and Sīhasīvali, their daughter. These children marry and found a city called Sīhapura in a kingdom called Lāḷa; and they have sixteen sets of twin sons, Vijaya being the older of the eldest pair. He becomes prince regent, but he "was

[98] See Dumézil, *ME*, II, 316–77 (Mādhavī and Medb), especially p. 364, and on Indo-European **rēg-* as the prototype for Irish *rí*, Sanskrit *rāj*, and Latin *rex*, see *Archaic Roman Religion*, pp. 16–17, 577; see also D. A. Binchy, *Celtic and Anglo-Saxon Kingship*, O'Donnell Lectures, 1967–1968 (Oxford: Clarendon Press, 1970), p. 3.

[99] See Wilhelm Geiger, trans., assisted by Mabel Haynes Bode, *The Mahāvaṃsa or the Great Chronicle of Ceylon*, Pali Text Society (London: Henry Frowde, Oxford University Press, Amen Corner, E. C., 1912), pp. 53–58; and Geiger, ed., *The Mahāvaṃsa*, Pali Text Society (same publishing data as above, 1908), for the Pali text.

[100] See Dumézil, *ME*, II, pt. 3, and below, Chapter 8.

of evil conduct and his followers were even (like himself), and many intolerable deeds of violence were done by them." The people prevailed upon the king to rebuke them. "But all fell out again as before, the second and yet a third time; and the angered people said to the king: 'kill thy son' " (6,39–44). One would love to know what these "three sins" of Vijaya were.

Vijaya and his followers, seven hundred men, are then punished: the hair is shaved off half their heads,[101] and they are exiled to the sea, their children and wives also departing but in separate boats. The two groups land on separate islands, the men thus being without their women and children. Their final destiny is Lañkā (Ceylon). Here the story is linked with Buddhism: Vijaya "landed in Laṅkā . . . on the day that the Tathāgata lay down between the two twinlike sala-trees to pass into nibbāṇa" (6,46). But connections with figures of Hindu provenance are more immediately significant. As the Buddha lies in his final position, he tells Indra to protect Vijaya in Ceylon so that Buddhism may ultimately flourish there. Hearing this, "Indra handed over the guardianship of Laṅkā to the god who is in color like the lotus" (*devass' uppalavaṇṇassa Laṅkārakkam samappayi*; 7,5). Geiger identifies this guardian as Viṣṇu, the allusion being "to the color of the BLUE lotus (*uppala*)."[102] Just as Viṣṇu-Nārāyaṇa "approves" or even "arranges"[103] the union of Śrī and Indra (or Śrī and the five Indras), Viṣṇu now helps bring about the marriage of Vijaya. First, accepting Indra's directive, Viṣṇu comes to Lañkā, where he takes on the disguise of an ascetic. When Vijaya comes before him with his men, Viṣṇu promises them that "no dangers will arise," sprinkles water on them, and ties a protective thread about their hands. Then, disappearing into the air, he gives way to a Yakkhiṇī (Sanskrit Yakṣiṇī) who, in the form of a bitch, passes

[101] Geiger, trans., *Mahāvaṃsa*, p. 53, n. 1, says: "The shaving of the hair signifies loss of freedom."

[102] *Ibid.*, p. 55, n. 2.

[103] See above, Chapter 3.

before them (7,6-9). For men who have just set foot on an unknown terrain, it seems that a female dog is more alluring than a deer:

One [of Vijaya's men] went after her, although he was forbidden by the prince (for he thought), "Only where there is a village are dogs to be found." Her mistress, a yakkhiṇī named Kuvaṇṇā, sat there [where Vijaya's man followed the bitch] at the foot of a tree spinning, as a woman-hermit [*tapasī*] might.

When the man saw the pond [near the tree] and the woman hermit sitting there, he bathed there and drank and taking shoots of lotuses and water in lotus-leaves he came forth again. And she said to him: "Stay! thou art my prey!" Then the man stood there as if fast bound. But because of the power of the magic thread she could not devour him. . . . Then the yakkhiṇī seized him, and hurled him who cried aloud into a chasm [*tam gahetvā surungāyam ravantam yakkhiṇi khipi*]. And there in like manner she hurled (all) the seven hundred one by one after him.

And when they all did not return fear came on Vijaya; armed, . . . he set out, and when he beheld the beautiful pond [*pokkharaṇiṃ subham*; note its prominent lotuses cited above], where he saw no footstep of any man coming forth, but saw that woman-hermit [*tapasīm*] there, he thought: "Surely my men have been seized by this woman." And he said to her, "Lady, hast thou seen my men?" "What dost thou want with thy people, prince?" she answered. "Drink thou and bathe."

Then it was clear to him: "This is surely a yakkhiṇī, she knows my rank," and swiftly, uttering his name, he came at her drawing his bow. He caught the yakkhiṇī in the noose about the neck, and seizing her hair with his left hand he lifted his sword in the right and cried: "Slave! give me back my men, or I slay thee!" Then tormented with fear the yakkiṇi prayed him for her life. "Spare my life, sir, I will give thee a kingdom [*rajjam dassāmi te aham*] and do thee a woman's service and other service as thou wilt." [7,10–22]

Vijaya makes her return his men and provide food for them. The men prepare the food, and Kuvaṇṇā eats first, at which she was well pleased.

> . . . and assuming the lovely form of a sixteen-year-old maiden she approached the prince adorned with all the ornaments.[104] At the foot of a tree she made a beautiful bed, well-covered around with a tent, and adorned with a canopy. And seeing this, the king's son, looking forward to the time to come, took her to him as his spouse and lay (with her) blissfully on that bed; and all his men encamped around the tent. [7,26–29]

From here on the story veers sharply from anything in the other traditions we have discussed,[105] but the parallels that have emerged to this point are sufficient to guarantee some connection.

A number of themes here help us to draw the Indian and Irish stories of Śrī and Flaith much closer together. As in the myth of Śrī and the five Indras, Viṣṇu has a background role. In one case, the god "approves" the marriage and Vyāsa, an ascetic "portion" of the god on earth, is the medium by which the Pāṇḍavas are directed to Draupadī-Śrī; in the other, the god assumes the form of an ascetic to protect Vijaya and his men and prepare the way for their meeting with the Yakkhiṇī Kuvaṇṇā. Then too, just as Indra has his limbs loosened and his body paralyzed before he is told to enter a cave and join the four former Indras, so Vijaya's men "stood there as if fast bound" before being thrown into a "chasm." In fact, this parallel can solve an earlier quandary: unlike Śrī, whose limb-loosening touch is superfluous and who yields to Śiva when it comes to the paralyzing of Indra and the command that Indra join his predecessors in the cave, Kuvaṇṇā is able to do all these things by herself. The Irish stories offer no parallel to

[104] *solaṣavassikaṃ rūpaṃ māpayitvā manoharaṃ*
rājaputtam upāganchi sabbābharaṇabhusita (26–27).

[105] On the Vijaya story, see Coomaraswamy, *Yakṣas* (2 vols.; Washington, D.C.: Smithsonian Institution, 1928 and 1931), I, 13–14, and Nancy E. Falk, "Wilderness and Kingship in Ancient South Asia," *HRJ*, XIII (1973), 2–3; also 15 (failing to disclose her source for the parallel) on a scene, discussed below, from the *Mahābhārata*.

this dangerous side of the bestower of sovereignty, but the Ceylonese legend may be the most coherent version of an ancient Indian theme. In both the Ceylonese and Indian accounts, the contact with Sovereignty seems to hold inherent dangers for those who are rash or unequipped to deal with its burdens and benefits.

Seemingly, however, neither the Ceylonese nor the Indian account borrows directly from the other. In other respects, the Ceylonese and the Irish accounts are much closer to each other than either is to the myth of Śrī. For one thing, the theme of the "loathly bride," so famous in the Irish accounts, emerges far more clearly in the Ceylonese legend than in the Indian myth. Just as the Irish Flaith turns from hag to beauty, Kuvaṇṇā the Yakkhiṇī is transformed from a *tapasī*—an identity which no doubt connotes ragged clothes, unkempt appearance, emaciated physique—to the loveliest of young maidens. Second, the story linking the bitch and the Yakkhiṇī in some ways resembles Flaith and the fawn more than Śrī and the lotus, the latter two being connected principally by their golden color. In both the Irish and Ceylonese examples it is an unexpected animal—curious and alluring for different reasons—that leads the heroes (in this case, Niall and his brothers, not the five Lugaids) to the unpredictable maiden by the water. And finally, the Ceylonese and Irish legends are much more clearly concerned with the matter of the bestowal of kingship: *rajjam dassāmi te aham*, says Kuvaṇṇā, where Śrī only promises, for some time in the indefinite future, that Indra will come to "know" her.

Thus, as suggested earlier, the Ceylonese story seems to be an intermediary between the Flaith and Śrī myths, probably containing more archaic features than the latter but bearing many of the same themes. It is also close, especially on one point, to another legend which would seem to have a similar intermediary status. This one comes from the *Mahābhārata* and concerns none other than the Pāṇḍavas.

One might expect that if the myth of Śrī and the five Indras is an ancient parallel to the Irish and Ceylonese legends, the epic poets would have had the Pāṇḍavas—and King Yudhiṣṭhira in particular, not Arjuna—win Draupadī, Śrī's portion on earth, in a similar scene. Obviously they do not, as Draupadī is won in the Svayaṃvara. It seems fair to say that the poets have taken this "secondary" myth of Śrī—the "Svayaṃvara mythologem" which she shares with so many other goddesses—as their model rather than the older myth that finds her by the water, by the "source" of Sovereignty. Instead of using this latter myth as a model for Draupadī's marriage, the poets satisfied themselves by linking it to the marriage as a background myth. But if the Pāṇḍavas do not win their bride in such a scene, they do find themselves in an unmistakably similar situation. It occurs in the *Yakṣapraśna* section of the *Āraṇyakaparvan*.

Toward the end of their forest exile, the Pāṇḍavas and their wife enter the picturesque Dvaita forest (3:295,2–3). There, "for the sake of a brahmin, they underwent a great affliction whose consequence was happiness" (295,6). Their trial begins when the brahmin, "in great distress," rushes up to them with the news that the continuity of his Agnihotra has been threatened by a "great deer" (*mahāmṛga*) which, in butting about near his hermitage, has caught the brahmin's two rubbing sticks (*araṇī*) in its antlers and bounded off into the forest (295,8–9). "Quickly tracking down that great deer by its footprints, may you Pāṇḍavas bring them [the rubbing sticks] back" (295,10).

It is soon made clear that this is no ordinary deer: "Seeing the deer nearby, those great chariot warriors released barbs, javelins, and darts, but were unable to pierce it. And while they were so striving, the deer became invisible [*nādṛśyata*]. And not seeing it, fatigued and pained, those high-spirited ones approached a *nyagrodha* tree, deep in the forest, and sat down in its cool shade wearied by hunger and thirst" (*kṣutpipāsāparītāṅ-*

gāḥ; 295,13–15). Similarly, Niall and his brothers were "athirst and in great drouth" after eating the deer which Niall, unlike the Pāṇḍavas, managed to capture. Success of the hunt, however, may not be crucial. The central matter is that the animal (or flower) be mysterious and alluring, a device to draw the heroes into forested or uncertain terrain and, in the two cases just cited, to make them thirsty.

Choosing from among his wearied brothers, Yudhiṣṭhira tells Nakula to look around for water (196,6). Soon Nakula arrives at a lake of "pure water" (*vimalaṃ toyam*; 296,11). But a voice from the sky warns him against drinking: "Do not commit this rash act, O child; I have first claim to this lake. Having answered my questions, then may you drink and carry" (12). Nakula drinks, however, and falls dead, as do Sahadeva, Arjuna, and Bhīma, in turn, each after failing to heed the same warning from the disembodied voice (14–38).

Finally, when Yudhiṣṭhira arrives on the scene, he sees his brothers "fallen like the Lokapālas at the end of the yuga" (297,1). Realizing that there is something uncanny about their deaths (no weapon marks, no corpselike pallor), he asks who is responsible, and the voice from the sky introduces itself as a crane living off tiny fish (297,11). He too is warned not to drink the water before answering its questions. But when Yudhiṣṭhira ridicules the idea that a bird could have slain his brothers, the voice turns into that of a Yakṣa (297,18). Seeing his strangeness, Yudhiṣṭhira agrees to try to answer the Yakṣa's questions, and these—nineteen riddles (according to the Critical Edition), each with four parts—constitutes the long *Yakṣapraśna* section (297,23–24) of this episode and ostensibly its raison d'être.[106]

Yudhiṣṭhira is able to answer all the questions correctly, and the Yakṣa allows him to choose from among his brothers just

[106] On the riddles in this scene, see Durga Bhagwat, *The Riddle in Indian Life, Lore, and Literature* (Bombay: Popular Prakashan, 1965), pp. 10–11 and p. 74, n. 16.

one who can be restored to life. Yudhiṣṭhira selects Nakula (297,66), giving as his reason that both of his father's wives should have one living son (72–73). Thanks to this dharmic choice, the Yakṣa grants that all the brothers may be revived. In a moment they rise up, their thirst and hunger gone (298,1). Yudhiṣṭhira then asks the Yakṣa once again who he really is, and this time he reveals himself as Dharma, Yudhiṣṭhira's own father. Dharma gives two reasons for his behavior: he has "come here desiring to see you" (298,6) and "to examine you" (*jijñāsustvām*; 10). Satisfied, Dharma offers Yudhiṣṭhira a choice of boons, and Yudhiṣṭhira chooses three, each with its implications.

(1) First, Yudhiṣṭhira asks that the brahmin might have back his firesticks from the thieving deer to continue his Agnihotra. Dharma's answer solves a problem that appears elsewhere: "The firesticks of that brahmin that were borne away were carried off by me, having the antlers of a deer [several recensions: having the form of a deer], for the sake of examining you" (*hṛtam mayā mṛgaveṣeṇa* [*mṛgarūpeṇa*] *kaunteya jijñāsārthaṃ tava*; 298,13 and notes). And further on, Dharma repeats that the sticks were carried away "by me in deer form" (*mayā . . . mṛgarūpeṇa*; 20). Such double symbolism has intrigued Krappe and Dumézil; the alluring deer and the figure by the water are identical, in this case both being forms taken by Dharma.[107] We have seen similar solutions elsewhere: the bitch that takes Vijaya's man to Kuvaṇṇā is the latter's attendant; Śrī, who once appears in deer form and also with a deer beside her,[108] allures Indra by her own tears; and in a case which Dumézil handles beautifully, the Indian heroine Mādhavī, also a bestower of kingship, adopts the ascetic "deer-faring" mode of life (*mṛgacāriṇī*; *Mbh.* 5:118,7).[109] To this one may now add the

[107] For Krappe, see above, n. 93; for Dumézil, below, n. 109.

[108] See above, n. 94.

[109] Dumézil, *ME*, II, 324 and 342; for more on Mādhavī, see below, Chapter 8.

words of Shah Kāvus, cited above:[110] "This [girl] is a mountain doe, truly a heart-ravishing gazelle; but game appropriate only to the highest." What the convergence signifies in the present instance is quite clear: the epic poets have looked behind the cooperative interplay of the symbols of sovereignty for the underlying principle—dharma—that sustains it.

(2) Yudhiṣṭhira's second boon is Dharma's assurance that the Pāṇḍavas and Draupadī will pass their thirteenth year in exile unrecognized (298,15), thus fulfilling the terms of their wager with Duryodhana. If not world sovereignty, this boon confers a prize that is still tantamount to a share of kingship, for by completing the year incognito, Yudhiṣṭhira expects to fulfill the requirements for a return to his throne at Indraprastha.

(3) Urging Yudhiṣṭhira to choose again, Dharma says: "May you accept a third boon, O son, that is unequaled and great [*varamapratimaṃ mahat*]; surely you are sprung from me, O king, and Vidura shares a portion of me" (*mamāṃśabhāk*; 298,21). After briefly demurring, Yudhiṣṭhira asks: "May I always conquer covetousness, delusion, and greed, O lord, and may my mind be ever devoted to giving, austerity, and truth" (*dāne tapasi satye*; 298,23).

There is nothing trifunctional about these qualities, although, as I will argue in the next chapter, the ideal royal virtues often take on an increasing "yogic" or "Upaniṣadic" flavor. More important, for now, is Dharma's answer. Not only does Yudhiṣṭhira have these qualities; he has them in accordance with a particular formula—the one by which the overanxious maiden, Draupadī in a former life, requested a perfect husband and which describes the Ādityatlike Pāṇḍavas as her suitable partners when they are revealed to her father as the five former Indras. "You are by your own nature [*svabhāvenāsi*] endowed with every virtue [*upapanno guṇaiḥ sarvaiḥ*], O son of Pāṇḍu, and, moreover, you are the lord Dharma [*bhavāndharmaḥ*]; what you have asked for shall be yours" (298,24). As we

[110] See above, n. 89.

will see, this is a royal formula; once again, Yudhiṣṭhira receives a boon that is tantamount to "sovereignty."

There can be little doubt that this legend about the Pāṇḍavas is, like the Ceylonese Vijaya legend, a link between the stories about Śrī and Flaith. First, it shares with the Vijaya legend the substitution of a Yakṣa, male this time, for Śrī[111]—the choice of sex in the epic story no doubt being dictated by the identification of the deer and the figure by the lake with Dharma, a figure with whom Yudhiṣṭhira is identified rather than one he might marry. Then, on the Indian side, the Pāṇḍava story gives added evidence of themes that Ireland does not know. Contact with the figure by the lake, or the source of the Ganges, holds grave dangers for those unsuited to sovereignty: just as the five Indras are ordered into a cave and Vijaya's men hurled into a chasm, so Yudhiṣṭhira finds his brothers "fallen like the Lokapālas." But in its basic outlines, the Pāṇḍava story is, like the Vijaya legend, far more similar to the legends from Ireland: the "great deer," the figure by the "pure water," and especially the underlying theme of the test, this time by riddles, of Yudhiṣṭhira's worthiness, all find their analogues in the stories of Niall and Lugaid Laigde.

Finally, not only have we been able to show that Śrī has an ancient mythology of her own, but that this myth has survived, on the epic plane, without her. No doubt the "borrowed" myth of the Svayaṃvara has taken its place in Śrī's biography and has provided the model for Draupadī's union with the Pāṇḍavas, and in particular with Arjuna. For just as this "central" Pāṇḍava wins Draupadī for his brothers, Indra is the chief of the gods whom Śrī "chooses" in the epic's renditions

[111] See Coomaraswamy, *Yakṣas*, II, pp. 4 and 13, for connections between Śrī-Lakṣmī and Yakṣas; I, p. 11 for connections of both with prosperity; II, pp. 4,13–19, and 61 for connections of both with *soma* and waters. See also Falk, "Wilderness and Kingship," suggesting a number of symbolic links between Yakṣas and the attainment of kingship.

of the "Svayaṃvara mythologem." But insofar as the true sovereignty is Yudhiṣṭhira's, it is fittingly promised him in a variant of an ancient legend, one that has its closest analogues in Irish and Ceylonese traditions and in the very myth that is told when the Pāṇḍavas are about to take Draupadī, Śrī incarnate, as their common wife.

CHAPTER 8

The Royal Virtues

In the course of examining the myths and legends related to the figures of Śrī and Draupadī, repeated references have been made to the notion of "virtues": *guṇas* or *dharmas*. In many instances specific sets are singled out, often in what appear to be trifunctional arrangements. This unwieldy and diffuse problem nonetheless bears on many matters: on our understanding of Śrī and Draupadī, on the epic "sins"—opposite the virtues—which I will take up in the next chapters, and on the whole question of sovereignty.

The themes from such myths, legends, and rituals as those discussed in the last chapter must be drawn together with the extensive epic material concerning dharmic formulas. To do this, however, it must first be recognized that the *Mahābhārata* is open-ended as a source on ethical matters. Seeking some clarity, many scholars have separated the "narrative" from the "didactic" elements and viewed all moral pronouncements as one or another variety of Brahminical interpolation. I do not think it is that simple: questions of virtue and sin are part and parcel of the epic narrative. The problem is to understand how certain basic virtues and vices, often recognizable by their relations to other moral qualities and thus by their places in structures and formulas, enter into the fabric of the story. Determining such values will not, of course, rule out speaking of didactic intrusions and extensions. But it will not be simply a matter of explaining epic morality as a Brahminical veneer over a "heroic" core. The situation is too fluid: probably from its earliest Indian tellings, virtues of different types have found reflection in the story; and the story has probably continued to suggest different dharmic formulations to poets of different periods.

Inflations

One line along which epic morality has been rethought by the poets is that suggested by the Upaniṣads. Although scholars have commonly overlooked the ethical pronouncements of the Upaniṣadic sages and depicted their state as one beyond good and evil, the Upaniṣads do exalt certain types of behavior, certain virtues. The knower of the Self creates worlds of refuge for all other creatures (*BAUp.* 1,4,15(end)–16), worlds penetrated by the thunder-spoken qualities of *dama*, *dāna*, and *dayā*—control, giving, and compassion (*BAUp.* 5,2,1–3). There is also what Hajime Nakamura calls a "fondness for negative expression."[1] The central negative virtue is *ahiṃsā*, "nonharming" or "nonkilling." With these qualities, the Upaniṣads introduce the new idea of "universal virtues," *sādhārana dharmas*, virtues applying to all "worlds." Such trends may certainly be identified as post-Brāhmaṇic. As P. V. Kane says, "The reason for cultivating such virtues as *dayā*, *ahiṃsā* is based upon the philosophical doctrine of the Self."[2] Thus even knowledge and truth (*satya*) are virtues which come to have special Upaniṣadic significance.

These tendencies have their parallels and counterparts in Buddhism;[3] the influences of these two traditions have combined with a popular acceptance of yoga to produce what we could call a yogic expansion of epic virtues. This appears in certain passages of counsel, which range from the sententious and commonplace to the subtle and sublime. Vidura, for

[1] Hajime Nakamura, *Ways of Thinking of Eastern Peoples: India-China-Tibet-Japan*, Philip Wiener, trans. (Honolulu: East-West Center Press, 1964), pp. 52–57,85.

[2] Kane, *History of Dharmaśāstra*, II, 7.

[3] On Buddhist virtues in the epic enumerations, see P. V. Kane, "The Two Epics," *ABORI*, XLVII (1966), 23.

instance, tells Dhṛtarāṣṭra: "Truly, these six *guṇas* should not be forsaken by any man: truth, giving, nonidleness [*anālasyam*], nonenvy [*anasūya*], forbearance, and firmness" (5:33,69). In what is probably the most inflated passage in the epic, Bhīṣma tells Yudhiṣṭhira that proper royal conduct involves "thirty-six virtues [*guṇas*] related to thirty-six other virtues; accomplishing those virtues [*guṇān*], one possessed of virtues [*guṇopeta*] should obtain merit [*guṇam*]" (12:71,2). The list is an incoherent mélange.

Also showing a yogic influence is a process of infinitization of virtues. Certain figures—Arjuna (5:94,41) and Karṇa (1:126,5), Krishṇa (5:94,36–41; 7:10,39) and Aśvatthāman (5:164,10)—are said to have "uncountable virtues" (*asaṃkhyeyaguṇa* or the equivalent). This tendency seems to imply a yogic definition of these heroes' theological identities. In the cases of Krishna and Aśvatthāman, such terminology describes the figures who incarnate Viṣṇu-Nārāyaṇa and Śiva. Similarly, Arjuna benefits from such an assessment where he is identified as the incarnation of Nara. Thus when Paraśurāma tells how Nara and Nārāyaṇa humiliated the tyrant Dambhodbhava (5:94,29–41), he comments: "Very great was that feat achieved of old by Nara; [but] Nārāyaṇa then became superior in consequence of his many more virtues [or qualities]" (*guṇaiḥ subahubhiḥ śreṣtha*; 36). And, with transparent but also transcendental logic, he adds: "Countless are the virtues of Pārtha [Arjuna-Nara], [but] superior to him is Janārdana" (*asaṃkhyeyā guṇāḥ parthe tadviśiṣto janārdanaḥ*; 41). Elsewhere it is said that in Krishna "there exists an abundance of virtues forever" (*guṇa-sampat-sadā-eva*; 5:47,81), and it seems likely that these descriptions refer not only to ascetic merits but to the doctrine of Saguṇa Brahman, "*brahman* with qualities."[4]

[4] This does not mean that all theological formulations run to infinity. One can think of the "six powers" or "shares" (*bhaga*) of Viṣṇu-Krishna as represented in *VP* 6,5,74–76: lordship (*aiśvaryam*), dharma, *yaśas*, *śrī*, knowledge (*jñāna*), and nonattachment (*vairāgyam*); see Alain Danielou, *Hindu Polytheism* (London: Routledge & Kegan Paul, 1964), p. 36.

These inflationary processes in the epic are particularly apparent in descriptions of the Pāṇḍavas, whose basic trifunctional character, as a group, need not be doubted. In recalling her sons, for instance, Kuntī, along with evoking such functional traits as Yudhiṣṭhira's truth and virtue, Bhīma's strength and speed, Arjuna's prowess, Sahadeva's obedience and youth, and Nakula's beauty and taste for comfort, also praises the Pāṇḍavas for such Upaniṣadic qualities as restraint (Yudhiṣṭhira and Arjuna), compassion (Yudhiṣṭhira and Sahadeva), patience (Arjuna), and modesty (Sahadeva; 5:88,18–41).

The Pāṇḍavas, however, bring us closer to the epic's central dharmic concepts: a phrase which will bear some explanation. As the *Mahābhārata* tells of a struggle for sovereignty (the Pāṇḍavas being former Indras), it is natural that the virtues of royalty are a central dharmic issue. So it is on many planes: in exhortatory enumerations of virtues, in discursive teachings like the *Rājadharma* section of the *Śāntiparvan*, and in various narrative ramifications. I do not mean that other ethical concepts found in the epic are necessarily peripheral or that they are unrelated to the royal virtues; but they must not be confused with them. One will think especially of the four Puruṣārthas, "aims of human life," and the various virtues or duties ascribed to the four *varṇas*. In both cases the Pāṇḍavas are bound up with these classifications, and there is no question of regarding them as noncentral to the epic's ethical content. However, none of these sets of "virtues" can be reduced to any other. Dumézil has shown how the themes of dharma, *artha*, and *kāma* are articulated through the structure of the Pāṇḍavas;[5] but this is not because these Puruṣārthas serve to define the Pāṇḍavas in relationship to the three functions or to kingship.

As to caste, it is a special duty of the king—which Krishna says Yudhiṣṭhira will fulfill (5:29,20–24)—to protect the four orders and stimulate them to fulfill their "duties." But royal

[5] Dumézil, *ME*, I, 94–98.

virtues and caste duties are not interchangeable. In fact, the systematization of particular virtues for each caste seems to have been a gradual process. When Bhīṣma defends Krishna's right to the highest honors in the Śiśupāla episode, he cites Krishna's many *guṇas* (2:35,12), and in particular his knowledge and immeasurable strength (18). In contrast, he says, others deserve honor only for single virtues: brahmins for knowledge (*jñāna*) and kṣatriyas for strength (*balam*; 17). As an indication that the *varṇas* supply only a loose model for classifying virtues, numerous manuscripts interpolate an honor due to *vaiśyas* for being "rich in wealth" (*dhānyadhanavat*) and to *śūdras* according to their age (*janmatas*; 2,357*). Similarly, a relatively broad rearrangement of traditional ethical material seems to lie behind *Bhagavad Gītā* 18,42–44, where Krishna describes the "natural-born actions" (*karma svabhavajam*) that are "distinguished according to the Strands [*guṇas*] that spring from the innate nature" of the four *varṇas* (18,41–42). In this passage, it is only the last two classes that have actual "actions" attributed to them: agriculture, cattle tending, commerce (*vaiśyas*), and service (*śūdras*; 18,44). In contrast, the first two classes have virtues. In fact, several of the qualities attributed to kṣatriyas—*tejas*, *śauryam* ("heroism"), *dānam* ("generosity"; 18,43)—are ones which are elsewhere used in trifunctional lists to emphasize royalty. And the various Upaniṣadic and yogic qualities—calm, (self-)control (*dama*), austerities (*tapas*), patience—are for the most part attributed to brahmins (41). Such considerations make it extremely unlikely that the caste system, at least in its Indian form, could have served as the model for the classification of the royal virtues. This is not to say that the variety of formulas expressing royal qualities has not been continually reinforced by the caste system. But the conceptual or ideological structure cannot be reduced to the social structure.[6]

[6] This crucial methodological point is also made by Dumézil in *ME*, I, 15.

In relation to this last passage, by central dharmic teachings, I also do not exclude the emphasis on action, karman, which finds its fullest expression in the *Gītā*. This doctrine, which has a long prehistory, has also been transformed in the epic by yoga; and it finds its most fitting disciple and exemplar in the person not of the king, but of the warrior-yogi Arjuna.[7] Thus, whereas it is Yudhiṣṭhira's royal duty to balance every virtue and weigh every action, his kṣatriya mother and wife, and Krishna and Arjuna as well, can rebuke him for his often exasperating indecision. The warrior Arjuna can say to the king: "Even abandoned by every virtue [*sarvairapi guṇairhīno*], one possessed of heroism [*vīryam*] may overcome his foes; even united with every virtue, without heroism [*nirvīryaḥ*], what will one do? Surely, in prowess [*parākrame*] all the virtues exist in an elemental state" (2:15,9–10ab). Action, or heroism (*vīryam*, *śauryam*—cf. *Gītā* 18,43), springs essentially from the warrior's nature. But for the king it must be integrated among qualities of other dimensions.

"All the Virtues"

In speaking of the epic's central ethical or dharmic focus, I am thus addressing a concern which relates to, and extends into, all the areas just discussed, but which carries along the main thrust of the narrative: the "just" claim to sovereignty of Yudhiṣṭhira, the Dharmarāja, son and "King of Dharma."[8] In this and the next three chapters, I will try to show that to appreciate Yudhiṣṭhira's dramatic role, one must look beyond the passages that describe his virtues in basically yogic or Upaniṣadic terms.

[7] See above, Chapter 6 at n. 2, and Biardeau, *Clefs*, p. 95, using the term "*guerrier yogin*."

[8] Biardeau, *Clefs*, p. 96, prefers the translation "*roi-dharma*" to "*roi du dharma*," as also, apparently, does van Buitenen, who refers to "King Dharma" in "The Sabhāparvan," p. 70.

Foregoing discussions have made it clear that one of the key formulas connected with royal virtues is the one that describes a person as "endowed with all the virtues" (such as *sarvaguṇopeta*, *sarvaguṇasaṃpanna*, *sarvadharmopapanna*). It is a phrase used frequently with reference to Yudhiṣṭhira, especially in contexts which have to do with his fitness to be king. Thus we have seen it when Dharma, having shed his Yakṣa disguise, promises Yudhiṣṭhira he shall have more than just the specific qualities he requests.[9] And most important, it occurs when Krishna, invited to Indraprastha to advise Yudhiṣṭhira on whether to perform the Rājasūya, declares his support of Yudhiṣṭhira for the title of *saṃrāj*, "universal monarch," because he is endowed with "every virtue" (*sarvairguṇair*; 2:13,1; cf. 30,23).

It is curious that these epithets, which concern moral wholeness, are sometimes interchangeable with another mode of distinguishing excellence. Note the following parallelism. In the passage discussed in the last section in which Kuntī describes the Pāṇḍavas, she refers to Yudhiṣṭhira as a king "endowed with every virtue, who should even be the king of the triple world" (*rājā sarvaguṇopetastrailokyasyāpi yo bhavet*; 5:88,21). Similarly, Vidura says he is a king "endowed with lakṣaṇas, who should even be the king of the triple world" (*rājā lakṣaṇasaṃpannastrailokyasyāpi yo bhavet*; 5:34,81). By the substitution of one formula for the other, virtues are interchangeable with "physical marks." The *Mahābhārata* does not tell a great deal about Yudhiṣṭhira's physical features, other than that he is light-complexioned,[10] of "prominent" or "formidable nose" (*pracaṇḍaghoṇa*; 3:254,7: cf. 1:180,20; 15:32,5), and large-armed (*pīnabāhu*; 3:118,10). At least in the latter case, the mark is probably royal.[11] In other cases,

[9] See Chapter 7, following n. 110.

[10] See above, Chapter 2, n. 5.

[11] See Gonda, *Ancient Indian Kingship*, pp. 5,108–9, citing instances describing Nala.

however, physical marks and moral excellences clearly seem to complement each other. Krishna, for instance, is described as *sarvaguṇasaṃpannaṃ śrīvatsakṛtalakṣaṇam*, "endowed with every virtue and having the mark made by the Śrīvatsa" on his breast (5:81,36). And Karṇa is a "tiger of the splendor of the Sun, marked by every divine mark [*divyalakṣaṇalakṣita*], with earrings and armor" (1:127,15), whose death Yudhiṣṭhira mourns by saying, "born of Sūrya, endowed with every virtue (*sarvaguṇopeta*), formerly cast in the water" (12:1,22). Such a duplicate way of distinguishing a "great man," especially a "king of dharma," is—with little stretching of the term—also found in Buddhism, where the Buddha is recognized both by his thirty-two major and eighty subsidiary *lakṣaṇas* and by his perfection in the six *pāramitās*.[12] No doubt such double characterizations are very ancient. One is reminded of Angelo Brelich's discussion of the "moral and physical monstrosities" of the Greek heroes.[13] It would seem, at least from Indian examples, that the two types of disfigurations are balanced by combinations of "moral and physical perfections."

There is, then, a notion of wholeness, soundness, or perfection which includes both the physical and moral dimensions of certain epic characters. Moreover, at least with regard to the moral dimension, the epic clearly uses the phrase "endowed with all the virtues" almost exclusively with reference to royalty. First, regarding dynasties, Krishna can tell Dhṛtarāṣṭra that the Kuru family line (*kulam*) is "today the best among all royal dynasties, furnished with knowledge and [good] behavior [*vṛttam*] and endowed with all the virtues" (*sarvaiḥ samuditaṃ guṇaiḥ*; 5:93,5). Similarly, according to the opening of the *Ādiparvan*, royal races are endowed with virtues (*mahatsu rājavaṃśeṣu guṇaiḥ samuditeṣu*; 1:1,164), while the virtues of their kings are celebrated in *purāṇas* (legends "of old") by the most venerable *kavis* or bards (1:1,181–2). Nearly all the main

[12] See above, n. 3.
[13] See above, Chapter 1.

figures through whom the Kuru line is perpetuated are at one point or another given this accolade. Among the line's ancestors are Yayāti (5:120,18) and his sons (thus including his successor Pūru; 1:70,31), and probably Bharata (*guṇopeta*; 1:68,2). Within the context of the epic's dynastic crises are Bhīṣma (12:50,28–29; cf. 1:93,44–45) and Karṇa (12:1,22), both of whom are potential Kuru kings; Yudhiṣṭhira, the Pāṇḍavas as a group (all "Indras among men"; 5:35,67; 89,26[14]), Abhimanyu (7:33,8–10), and Parikṣit (1:45,14). In this second cluster, the only "royal" omissions seem (barring oversights) to be Pāṇḍu and Dhṛtarāṣṭra; and this may be significant, as these two are the only ones marked by physical defects: their paleness and blindness.

Outside of royal usages, the phrase seems rare. The only instances I have observed in the epic concern Janamejaya's snake sacrifice (1:49,26), various species of birds (1:60,57), Kubera's horses (3:158,24), and Brahmā (8:24,105). As to those who are not kings or potential heirs, but whose virtues are praised, it is notable that the terms usually differ. Vidura, for instance, is frequently *sarvadharmavid*, "knowledgeable about every virtue" (see 1:126,28; 133,18), in his role as an expositor of dharma. But the virtues are his to recognize rather than to possess.

The link with royalty obviously does not pertain solely to the males. As we saw in the last chapter and shall stress again, the notion of "all the virtues" is connected with Draupadī. Kuntī too is omnivirtuous in a way that bears upon her royal status. As Krishna says, consoling her in her knowledge that her sons—Karṇa and the Pāṇḍavas—will engage in mortal combat:

What hair-parter [woman] is there like you in the *lokas*, O aunt, daughter of an heroic king, admitted [by marriage] to the race of

[14] Also, see above, Chapter 7, at n. 67, citing 1:157,10 and 189,43 (Pāṇḍavas in overanxious maiden story) and 189,38 (myth of the five Indras).

Ājamīḍha, high-born, highly married, transplated [like a lotus] from lake to lake, all-auspicious mistress [*īśvarī sarvakalyāṇī*], adored by your husband, hero-bearing and wife of a hero [*vīrasūr-vīrapatnī*], endowed with every virtue [*sarvaiḥ samuditā guṇaiḥ*], endowed with great wisdom, it behoves you to bear both joy and sorrow. [5:88,90–92]

Similarly, one finds "all the virtues" in Śākuntalā (1:68,10), and again, within the context of the dynastic crisis, not only in Draupadī and Kuntī, but in Satyavatī (1:57,54), and in Ambā, Ambikā, and Ambālikā (1:96,45). Thus from Satyavatī on, nearly all the women brought into the dynastic line—the only exceptions appear to be Mādrī and Uttarā—come with a full complement of virtues. Finally, outside the dynasty, the story of Nala and Damayantī provides a close parallel. Just as Nala is "possessed of the desirable virtues" (*upapanno guṇairiṣṭaiḥ*; 3:50,1), Damayantī "became celebrated throughout the world for her beauty [*rūpam*], majesty [*tejas*], fame [*yaśas*], prosperity [*śrī*], and good fortune" (*saubhagyam*; 3:50,10). In fact, "repeatedly hearing of each other's virtues [*guṇān*], they conceived for each other an attachment not born of sight" (*adṛṣṭakāmo*; 50,16).[15] The virtues, then, are at the core of the narrative and remain there as a theme throughout.

It is thus apparent that the royal virtues must be found *in full* in both sexes. Only where the virtues of a lineage are found in its brides can there be a guarantee of omnivirtuous heirs. When disruptions and crises occur, the epic seems to suggest two possible solutions. One is to call upon gods, or incarnations of gods, to sire suitable sons. The other, which will occupy us now, is to find some sort of intermediary, some special figure whose function it is to provide a mechanism whereby the difficulties, whatever they are, can be overcome.

[15] On the "love of the unseen one" theme, see the interesting but rather tenuous comparisons of Myles Dillon, "The Archaism of the Irish Tradition," Reprints from the American Committee for Irish Studies (1947; University of Chicago reprint, 1969), pp. 11–12.

The Royal Virtues and the Three Functions

Although the phrase "endowed with every virtue" is primarily a royal epithet, the epic never explains this term—not even in the *Rājadharma* section of the *Śāntiparvan*—by any list, long or short, of particular virtues. One is thus left to the task of reconstruction.

The material will not allow one to insist that any single set of individual virtues forms the original "endowment." There are too many combinations. First, the various processes of "inflation" have created many new virtues and changed the meanings of others. Second, if one assumes a basic structure rather than an original combination, variations within and upon that structure would naturally be expected.

Although a number of authors have dealt with particular virtues,[16] only Dumézil has examined the tendency to group them in significant combinations. Gonda in particular has shown a reluctance to deal with any more than one "power substance" at a time.[17] Let us now attempt an overview of such combinations as they occur in the epic in connection with royalty. Thanks to Dumézil's study,[18] King Yayāti

[16] For Gonda's discussion of "power substances," see above, Chapter 7, n. 28, and his *"Gods" and "Powers,"* pp. 43–44,58–62; also *idem, Ancient-Indian* ojas, *Latin* *augos *and the Indo-European Nouns* -es/-os (Utrecht: A. Oosthoek's Uitgevers Mij., 1952). On *satya*, "truth," see most recently W. Norman Brown, "Duty as Truth in Ancient India," *PAPS*, CXVI (1972), 252–68, with bibliography, p. 252, n. 1; also Lévi, *Doctrine du sacrifice*, pp. 114,163–67, and Dumézil, *ME*, II, 289–91. On *tejas*, see Biardeau, *EPHE*, LXXIX, 145. For other terms and further discussion, see below.

[17] Gonda attributes the instances of "triads relevant to one of the three functions" to no more than a "stylistic tendency" ("Some Observations on Dumézil's View of Indo-European Mythology," *Mnemosyne*, IV [1960], 7–8). Thus he overlooks possible trifunctional features of some of the passages he cites, such as: "If a man's sacrificial post sprouts leaves his *tejas*, *indriyam*, *vīryam*, food, children, and cattle recede from him" (*PB* 9,10,7; see *"Gods" and "Powers,"* p. 60).

[18] Dumézil, *ME*, II, pt. 3, 243–377.

emerges, along with the other characters in his legend, as the figure most indispensable to the discussion.

Although Yayāti is only the fifth or sixth member of the Lunar Dynasty (of which Kuru will be a later member), Dumézil shows that he is an example, perhaps India's earliest, of what Arthur Christensen was the first to designate as a "first king."[19] Kings of this "type" are involved with the origins of institutions, in particular with the partition of the earth (which in one episode of his story Yayāti distributes among his five sons), with the establishment of the central line of succession (which Yayāti, in the same episode, allots to his loyal son Pūru), and with the foundation of the social classes. In Yayāti's case, in the second part of his legend, his rapport is not so much with the classes, or with their origin (the *Puruṣa Sūkta* accounts for this), as with the royal virtues that a king must have to epitomize the qualities needed for the proper working of all the classes and of society as a whole.

Let us now summarize some features of Dumézil's study. The second part of Yayāti's story concerns his daughter Mādhavī (who figures in a most compelling comparison) and, through her, his four grandsons. Mādhavī's name is equivalent to that of the Irish heroine (or heroines, there being two of them) called Medb, meaning, in both cases, "the Intoxicating."[20] Both princesses are daughters of the "central" or "high" king of their lands. Moreover, there is a sequence in the stories of Mādhavī and Medb of Connacht where each marries four kings in turn and thereby assures that a certain set of virtues is perpetuated. Not unlike Śrī,[21] Medb of Connacht sets up a requirement that each suitor, and thus rival for the

[19] See above, Chapter 7, n. 98, and Arthur Christensen, *Le premier homme et le premier roi dans l'histoire légendaire des Iraniens*, Archives d'Etudes Orientales, XIV, pt. 1 (Stockholm: Norstedt, 1917); pt. 2 (Leiden: E. J. Brill, 1934).

[20] Dumézil, *ME*, II, 329–30.

[21] See above, Chapter 7, following n. 63.

central sovereignty which she bestows, must be "without jealousy, without fear, and without niggardliness,"[22] or, in other words, he must be just,[23] brave, and generous. Medb displays these qualities herself[24] and apparently finds them—though not for long—in each of her successive husbands. With Mādhavī, the tale of the virtues concerns not her husbands so much as the sons she has by them, ultimately for her father. But the Indo-Irish comparisons do not end here. Medb of Connacht has a sister, perhaps a double, named Clothru, and she has a son who, like Mādhavī's four, is born apparently for her royal father's sake. His name is Lugaid-Red-Stripes, his body divided by stripes into three zones, suggesting the possibility that he was in origin a representative of the synthesis of the three functions.[25]

However one takes this last point, the main substance of Dumézil's comparison shows at least that the story of Yayāti, Mādhavī, and the latter's four sons is an Indian version of an extremely old legend. It is important enough to summarize it as it bears upon the question of the royal virtues.[26] Reputed to have fabulous wealth (*dhanam*; 5:112,2), Yayāti is approached by a brahmin named Gālava who has incurred an imposing debt to his guru Viśvāmitra. He must bring his

[22] See Dumézil, *ME*, II, 337–38; Rees and Rees, *Celtic Heritage*, pp. 130–31; and Thomas Kinsella, trans., *The Tain* (London: Oxford University Press, 1970), p. 53; see also above, Chapter 1, nn. 29 and 30.

[23] For the trifunctional interpretation, approvingly quoted by Dumézil (*ME*, II, 337–38), see Rees and Rees, *Celtic Heritage*, pp. 130–31: jealousy, the only problem, is interpreted as the vice opposed to the administration of royal justice. In support of this interpretation, see also *ME*, II, 339, on Medb's ability to maintain order—"without jealousy!"—among the fifteen hundred princes who form her entourage.

[24] Dumézil, *ME*, II, 339.

[25] *Ibid.*, pp. 350–53.

[26] The text of this portion of the Yayāti legend is found at *Mbh.* 5:104–21. The story of Yayāti and his sons, plus another version of the rescue by his grandsons, is found at 1:71–88; in this latter text, Mādhavī is not mentioned.

master eight hundred horses, all lunar white and each with one black ear. Yayāti doesn't have the horses and his wealth has diminished; but he cannot refuse to give alms.

"Therefore," he says, "take this daughter of mine, one who causes four lineages to stand, this one resembling a child of the gods, a promptress of every virtue, always sought after by Gods, men, and Asuras."

tasmāccaturṇāṃ vaṃśānāṃ sthāpayitrī sutā mama
iyaṃ surasutaprakhyā sarvadharmopacāyinī
sadā devamanuṣyāṇāmasurāṇām . . . / kāṅkṣitā. [5:113,11–12]

These words present a curiosity which I will return to. For the moment, Gālava is assured that the princess is worth far more than what he needs and sets off with her to obtain the horses.

Gālava first takes Mādhavī to King Haryaśva of Ayodhyā and offers her to him for the bride price of the eight hundred horses. This king, however, has only two hundred, which he will gladly exchange for the opportunity of having Mādhavī bear him a single son. Ever compliant but rarely assertive, Mādhavī for once interrupts: in her youth, a brahmin had granted her the boon of retaining her virginity after childbirths; she can thus make up the sum of eight hundred horses by bearing sons to four kings in succession (5:114,10–13). Her offer is accepted, and although it turns out that only six hundred of the horses are still in existence, Gālava's guru, none other than the royal kṣatriya-turned-brahmin Viśvāmitra, agrees to accept Mādhavī in lieu of the full payment so that he can father the fourth child himself. Gālava finally receives her back, a virgin for the fourth time, and as he returns her to Yayāti, his words to her yield what Dumézil has called the "trifunctional key" to the story:[27] "To you is born a son who is a lord of gifts [*dānapati*], another who is a hero [*śūra*],

[27] Dumézil, *ME*, II, 323.

another devoted to truth and virtue [*satyadharmarata*], and yet another who is a great sacrificer [*yajvan*]. Now go, O excellent woman, by these sons your father is saved [*tāritas*], as also four kings, and myself" (117,21–22).

Mādhavī passes from the scene for a while, choosing the Forest (*vana*, masc.; 118,5) as her final husband and adopting, as was mentioned in the last chapter, the peculiar ascetic mode of life of the "deer-farer" (*mṛgacāriṇī*; 118,7). The stage is again Yayāti's, and from here on, the *Ādiparvan* and *Udyogaparvan* present parallel, but varying accounts. Yayāti has ascended to heaven, where he dwells as a *rājarṣi*. There he is sustained, according to the *Ādiparvan*, because for thousands of years he had amassed virtues in areas that correspond to the three functions: truth, conquests, and gifts (1:88,21–24).[28] One day, due to an outburst of pride, he is expelled. By good fortune, however, he is able to guide his fall toward the spot where his four grandsons are performing a Vājapeya sacrifice. Withholding his identity, Yayāti tells them that he has fallen from heaven because of the loss of his merits (*puṇya*; 5:119,7), and, together, the four grandsons—each now a king in his own right—make the following offer: "From all of us [*sarveṣāṃ naḥ*] . . . [take] the fruit of our sacrifices and our virtue" (*kratuphalaṃ dharmaśca*; 5:119,18). Yayāti at first demurs but is soon persuaded, in the *Ādiparvan* by the sudden appearance of five celestial chariots which arrive to take him and his grandsons to heaven,[29] in the *Udyogaparvan* by the reappearance of Mādhavī and Gālava who offer, in addition to the merits of the grandsons, one-half and one-eighth of their own. Yayāti is thus refurnished. In the *Udyogaparvan*, "adorned with virtues" (*guṇopeta*; 120,2), his course is turned around. He reascends to heaven, propelled by the transparently trifunctional words of his grandsons.

[28] *Ibid.*, p. 281.

[29] See Dumézil's remarks, *ibid.*, pp. 359–60, and above, Chapter 4, n. 22.

First to speak is the youngest, Vasumanas, the "lord of gifts" (*dānapati*; 120,3),[30] who offers Yayāti "whatever fruit comes from the conduct of giving" (*dānaśīla*) and the fruit also of his "patience" and "depositing" (*ādhāna*; 120,4–5). Second, Pratardana, "that bull among kṣatriyas," "devoted to battle" (*yuddhaparāyaṇaḥ*), says Yayāti may have whatever "fame" (*yaśas*) has attached to his "virtue of power" (*kṣatra-dharma*) and whatever fruit attaches to the word "hero" (*vīra*; 6–7). Third, the "intelligent" (*dhīmān*) Śibi, citing his own infallible truth, his own allegiance to truth, and the truth that the gods Dharma, Agni, and Indra are near to him, intones three times (one for each of the "verifications"), with a "sweet invocation" (*madhurāṃ giram*): "by that truth ascend to heaven" (*tena satyena khaṃ vraja*; 8–11). And finally Aṣṭaka, knowledgable about dharma (*dharmavid*), offers the fruit of his thousands of sacrifices (*kratavaḥ*) and adds, citing the truth that nothing has been spared in these ceremonies: "by that truth [*tena satyena*] ascend to heaven" (13–14). Then speaking jointly to consolidate their gifts into a synthesis, the four utter a formula now familiar, showing that together the virtues they have offered constitute a totality:

Endowed with the attributes of royal virtue, possessed of every virtue and attribute,
We are your daughter's sons, O king. Ascend to heaven, O lord of earth.
rājadharmaguṇopetāḥ sarvadharmaguṇānvitāḥ
dauhitrāste vayaṃ rājandivamāroha pārthiva. [120,18]

[30] Dumézil, *ME*, II, 273, argues, I think convincingly, that while in the epic "giving" denotes generosity with alms, it probably has its "essence" in the more basic notion of "wealth" which he connects with the third function. Given such a transformation, the epic meaning would seem to reflect an Upaniṣadic (or perhaps Buddhist) re-evaluation; *dāna* is also praised in the *Ṛg Veda*: see Nakamura, *Ways of Thinking*, p. 84. On the element *vasu-* in the name connoting "material goods," see *ME*, II, 273.

The grandsons' offerings are in close accord with the virtues mentioned in the "trifunctional key." Certain difficulties pertain to the virtues of the first function, which is represented doubly, but in a combination different from pairings found elsewhere in Indian divisions of the first function. Second, Dumézil has remarked that Aṣṭaka's closing words—"by that truth ascend to heaven"—are borrowed "against our expectation" from the "truthful" Śibi. Dumézil attempts to resolve this problem by detaching *satya* ("truth") from the other virtues: "We have before us the merits of the three functions and, above them, the more important merits of veracity, the absence of lying." He sees the importance of this dominant virtue as deriving from an Indo-Iranian concept, one with its roots well displayed in the Yayāti legend and its partial Iranian counterpart, the lgend of Yima. This is the opposition *ṛta/drúh*, *asha* (*arta*)/*druj*, that is, between the "arranged" and "ordered" truth and the lie.[31]

This ancient notion of "truth" is no doubt at play in the Yayāti story, but insofar as *satya* is used in this present scene, it has a more immediate, although perhaps even more ancient, significance. *Satya* operates on two levels. In terms of identifying Śibi, it is his special virtue and thus a first-function virtue in its own right. But in the phrase *tena satyena*, "by that truth," it operates as what W. Norman Brown and others have called an "Act of Truth."[32] In brief, an "act of truth" can reverse the law of karman and reverse natural processes. But it can be performed only by that rare being,

> whether deity or man, who does his duty perfectly, that is, fulfills his obligations under the Ṛta. . . . Such a being may be said to be

[31] Dumézil, *ME*, II, 274–92; quotes at pp. 279 and 290. From this standpoint, pride (Yayāti's sin) is a form of lying (Yima's sin), of denying the true order of things.

[32] See above, n. 16; there are also Irish parallels; see Myles Dillon, "Archaism of the Irish Tradition," pp. 3–7; *idem*, "The Hindu Act of Truth in Celtic Tradition," *MP*, XLIV (1947), 137–40.

satyá (adjective) "true" or to have *satyám* (neuter noun) "Truth." He is *ánuvrata* "true to duty" and is *ṛtāvan* ["observing or conserving the Ṛta"] or *satyádharman* "having Truth as his principle." . . . When a person fulfills his duty perfectly, he gains this power; for he has observed the Ṛta, has met his obligations under it. He is one with the Sat; he is *satya*, that is, true in a complete sense and can "control" the Sat, for he and the Sat are one.[33]

On the point under question, Brown remarks that "this phrase (*tena satyena*) is a common formulaic item in the Act of Truth." And, as an indication of its antiquity and diffusion, he is able to cite examples from the *Ṛg Veda* (1:21,5), from the story of Nala and Damayantī, and from Buddhist literature.[34] In fact, as we shall see shortly, the *Mahābhārata* supplies another instance, a far more pivotal one, of the use of this formula, again relating an "act of truth" to an assortment of significant virtues and acts. So it seems that *satya*, in its epic contexts, must be viewed as both a virtue and a quality which can put other virtues or "duties" into effect. Thus, whereas Aṣṭaka cites the truth of his perseverence in sacrifices, Śibi can cite the truth of his truthfulness.

The Yayāti legend thus provides the clearest, and probably the oldest, narrative on the composition of a full assemblage of royal virtues. Representing "all the virtues," the identities and the donations of the four grandsons are structured according to the three functions. Once again, let us reiterate that the structure is more basic than any one set of royal qualities, as can be seen in other texts which describe Yayāti. His legend has given him wide recognition as an exemplar of royal qualities. In one case, Somadatta (a brother of the Pāṇḍavas' great grandfather Śaṃtanu) is described as an "old man thriving with every virtue [*vṛddhamṛddhaṃ guṇaiḥ sarvair*], like Yayāti, son of Nahuṣa" (7:132,6). More specifically, a

[33] Brown, "Duty as Truth," pp. 261–62; brackets are mine, quoting Brown's definition, p. 261.

[34] *Ibid.*, p. 264 and n. 30, pp. 255–56.

trifunctional structure may sometimes be discerned in references to Yayāti. In a passage from Aśvaghoṣa's *Buddhacarita* (2,11) mentioned by Dumézil,[35] the virtues that flourished in the realm of King Suddhodana at the time of his son Siddhārtha's birth are identified with those that thrived in the model kingdom of Yayāti: "At that time in his realm, as in that of King Yayāti son of Nahuṣa, no one was disrespectful toward kinsmen [*nāgauravo bandhuṣu*], nor ungenerous [*na . . . adātā*], nor unobservant of religious obligations [*na . . . avrato*], nor untruthful [*na . . . anṛtiko*], nor given to hurt [*na hiṃsraḥ*]."[36] Although these are society's virtues rather than the king's, and although they are not given consecutively, one may still propose that a trifunctional complement of royal virtues provided the model: (first function) observance of obligations and truthfulness (cf. Aṣṭaka and Śibi); (second) noncruelty, feasibly a Buddhist reformulation of the warrior function; and (third) generosity (cf. Vasumanas) and perhaps respect for kinsmen.[37] Finally, again from the *Mahābhārata*, one finds Saṃjaya trying to instill in Dhṛtarāṣṭra the fortitude to bear the bad news of battle by recalling the ancient *rājarṣi*'s example:

In prosperity, lineage, fame, asceticism, and learning,
the good now regard you to be like Yayāti, son of Nahuṣa.
śriyā kulena yaśasā tapasā ca śrutena ca
tvāmadya santo manyante yayātimiva nāhuṣam. [8:5,27]

Here, in ascendant order, is the third-function quality "prosperity" along with "family, lineage," the latter being a virtue (cf. "respect for kinsmen" in the *Buddhacarita*) that will demand further discussion; then "fame, glory," the kṣatriya's great

[35] Dumézil, *ME*, II, 360; he does not suggest a trifunctional interpretation here.

[36] Cf. Edward Hamilton Johnston, ed. and trans., *The Buddhacarita, or, Acts of the Buddha*, I, Sanskrit text, II, Translation and notes (Calcutta: Baptist Mission Press, 1935 and 1936), II, 22.

[37] "Respectfulness" is a Vaiśya trait sometimes identified with Nakula and/or Sahadeva (for example, 7:33,6); see Wikander, "Nakula et Sahadeva," *OS*, VI (1957), 70.

aspiration; and finally two matters of spirit and mind, *tapas* and learning.

Yayāti's legend and renown thus give an excellent base from which to seek a wider sample of royal virtue inventories. In addition to those which, in the last chapter, we found connected with Śrī and Draupadī, there are the following. First is a passage which requires treatment at some length and then a number of passages which can be summarized.

The culminating scene in Krishna's participation in the affairs of the Pāṇḍavas and Kurus is his revival of the royal baby Parikṣit, son of Abhimanyu. Krishna's role involves an activation of certain virtues. Should Parikṣit remain stillborn, the Kuru line will have ended. But Krishna has promised to revive the child (10:16,15) and is reminded of this by his sister Subhadrā, the dead child's grandmother. Her words are almost as significant a "key" as those of Gālava to Mādhavī: "Surely, O Keśava, you have a soul of dharma [*dharmātma*], are truthful [*satyavān*], and have true valor [*satyavikramaḥ*]. It [behoves] you to make this word [his promise] conform to *ṛta*" (*tāṃ vācamṛtām*; 14:66,16). The virtues which Subhadrā attributes to her brother thus range themselves within the first and second functions: (1) dharma and *satya*; and (2) true or real valor, *vikrama*. And we soon see that she knows him well, for it is these qualities, and actions related to them, that Krishna makes operative in the miracle that follows. He "withdraws" (*sam-hṛ*; 14:68,16) the weapon that afflicts the child, and then, "causing the entire universe to hear" (*sarvaṃ viśravayañjagat*; 17), he says:

18. I do not speak falsely [*na bravīmy . . . mithyā*], O Uttarā; it shall be true [*satyametadbhaviṣyati*]: I shall cause this one to live in the sight of all embodied creatures [*paśyatāṃ sarvadehinām*].

19. Never before has anything been spoken falsely [*mithyā*] by me, even in indifferent matters; and I have never turned back in battle [*na ca yuddhe paravṛttas*]; accordingly, may this one live [*tathā saṃjīvatāmayam*].

20. As dharma and brahmins above all [*brāhmaṇāśca viśeṣataḥ*] are dear to me, may this son of Abhimanyu, born dead, live accordingly [*tathā*].

21. As I have never brought about hostility [*virodha*] with Vijaya [Arjuna], by that truth [*tena satyena*] may this child live.

22. As *satya* and dharma are forever established in me, accordingly [*tathā*] let this dead child born of Abhimanyu live.

23. Kaṃsa and Keśin were righteously [*dharmena*] slain by me, by that truth [*tena satyena*] let this child return to life. [14:68,18–23]

Through these words the child comes to life (24).

There is, as one can see, a cadence here. After summoning his truthfulness (*śloka* 18), Krishna alternates between calling upon his second-function and first-function qualities. In *ślokas* 19, 21, and 23, he mentions virtues relative to his career as a kṣatriya prince: he has "never turned back in battle," he has "never brought about hostility" with his inseparable friend Arjuna, and he has "righteously" slain his foes Kaṃsa and Keśin. On the other hand, in *ślokas* 20 and 22, Krishna mentions his affinities with dharma and brahmins and then with dharma and *satya*. *Satya* operates on the same double level as in the story of Yayāti. It is one of Krishna's virtues, yet it also serves as the basis for an "act of truth."[38] Moreover, the "act of truth" itself involves not the first-function qualities but the second. In *śloka* 19, Krishna's never having "turned back in battle" is substantiated, activated, by his never having spoken falsely. And then, all the more pointedly, in the last two "second-function *ślokas*" Krishna activates his relation with Arjuna and his "righteous" conquests by the "common formulaic item" *tena satyena* (*ślokas* 21 and 23). Let us now recall the words of Subhadrā, according to whom Krishna has *satya*, dharma, and true valor as the virtues relevant to his promise.

[38] Dhairyabala P. Vora, *Evolution of Morals in the Epics* (Bombay: Bhatkal, 1959), p. 219, observes correctly that "Kṛṣṇa revives the still born child . . . by the power of his truthful character." I would only add that "truth," though basic, is not the only quality involved.

By "valor" especially, or more precisely by the related second-function achievements, Krishna is able to put his "truth" into "action." His word thus "conforms to *ṛta*."

It will not do, however, to say that Krishna uses only his second-function traits in this act of truth. Perhaps the formula *tena satyena* occurs on this level because his second-function achievements, some of them rather ambiguous, must be "verified" (*tena satyena*) and "justified" (*dharmena*) by the virtues of the first function. Actually, the whole speech constitutes the act of truth. Rather than drawing from one dimension, Krishna draws on at least two, more or less in the same fashion as the grandsons of Yayāti draw on all three functional areas. From these two cases, it would seem that an act of truth involving the destiny of a king requires the activation of virtues from each of the three functions. Yet it must be admitted that Krishna makes no mention of any virtue or activity that has reference to the third function. For the present, this problem must be left unsolved.

More briefly, other enumerations of royal virtues include the following:

(1) In Chapter 10, I will attempt to show that Śalya, king of Madra, is a special symbolic representative of kingship. When he is nominated to lead the Kuru army, it is with this royal character clearly in mind: "This one, with [his] lineage [*kulam*], heroism [*vīryam*], energy [*tejas*], fame [*yaśas*], and prosperity [*śrī*], is endowed with every virtue" (*sarvaguṇair samuditaḥ*; 9:5,18).[39]

(2) Opposite this, when Śalya is slain by Yudhiṣṭhira, the latter's troops acclaim him "firm in truth [*satyadhṛti*], one whose foes are conquered [*jitāmitra*]; today [with Śalya's death] King Duryodhana has been divested of blazing royal prosperity" (*hino dīptayā nṛpatiśriyā*; 9:18,14).

[39] The ordering of these virtues is apparently pyramidical, with *tejas*, first function, at top center (head?), *vīryam* and *yaśas* at the sides (arms?), and *kulam* and *śrī* suggestively at the base.

(3) Bhīṣma, having fallen in battle and lying on his bed of arrows, urges Karṇa, whom he had till then always degraded, to unite with the Pāṇḍavas and end hostilities: "I know your vigor [*vīryam*] in battle, so hard for foes to bear, your regard for brahmins [or piety; *brahmanyatā*], your heroism [*śauryam*], and your superior conduct in giving" (*dāne ca paramāṃ gatim*; 6:117,12). The last three qualities remind us that Karṇa, like Bhīṣma himself, is a potential king.

(4) When Bhīṣma introduces Yudhiṣṭhira to the subject of *rājadharma*, the "duty of kings," he begins by breaking the subject down into four topics: attendance on gods and brahmins, truth (*satya*), exertion (*utthāna*), and the maintenance of prosperity (*śrī*; 12:56,12–20).

(5) At a point where Arjuna's identity, as father of Abhimanyu and grandfather of Parikṣit, is defined by his role in continuing the Kuru line with its virtues intact, he is prised trifunctionally: for his "learning [*śrutam*], prowess [*vikrama*], and prosperity" (*śrī*; 7:33,10).

(6) Parikṣit is himself celebrated as "prosperous, truth-speaking, and of firm fortitude" (*śrīmān-satyavāg-dṛdhavikramaḥ*; 1:45,11).

(7) Then there is a formulaic *śloka* describing the ideal king, occurring twice with only the slightest variation: "Having obtained kingship, a virtuous [monarch] should win over some by gift, some by might, and others by sweet speech" (*dānenānyaṃ balenānyaṃ tathā sūnṛtayāparam* [or *anyaṃ sūnṛtayā girā*]; 5:130,27 and, variant in brackets, 12:76,31).[40]

(8) Paralleling this royal program in a more active form, we are told that "Three sounds never ceased in the abode of [King] Dilīpa: the sound of [Vedic] recitation, the sound of the bowstring, and the words 'let it be given'" (*dīyatām*; 12:29,72).

[40] *Sūnṛtā* as a substantive, or *sūnṛtā gir*, where it is used adjectivally, may evoke a derivation from *su-ṛta*, "good and true" (Monier-Williams). As the next citation (no. 8) shows, it probably evokes the sound of Vedic recitation.

(9) To these descriptions of kings should now be added one concerning a queen. Having notices in Chapter 7 that a trifunctional characterization of Draupadī placed her third-function trait, *rūpam* ("beauty"), first, before *tejas* and *yaśas*,[41] we may now recall a description of Damayantī: "celebrated throughout the world for her beauty [*rūpam*], majesty [*tejas*], fame [*yaśas*], prosperity [*śrī*], and good fortune" (*saubhagyam*; 3:50,10).[42] The introduction by beauty is followed by the same first- and second-function qualities as Draupadī's and then the indication of still further amplitude in the third.

(10) Finally, in a passage that is not royal on the human level but which nonetheless concerns *aiśvaryam*, "lordship" or "sovereignty," on the divine, Umā tells Śiva he deserves a share in Dakṣa's sacrifice because of his *tejas*, *yaśas*, and *śrī* (12:274,27).

The Virtues of the Functions

It seems beyond dispute that these passages, along with those cited in the previous chapter, demonstrate a predilection for trifunctional groupings of royal virtues, whether these be in triads, tetrads, or pentads. The examples have, of course, been selected with their trifunctional design in mind, and no doubt more could be found. To discuss the composition of these groupings in more detail, however, it will be helpful to have all the variants before us. The following table presents them in the order they have been discussed in the last two chapters.

Chapter 7	*1st function*	*2d function*	*3d function*
1. *ŚB* 13,2,6,1–7	*tejas*	*indriyam*	*paśu (śrī)*
2. 2,4,4,4	—	—	*prajāti śrī*
3. 11,4,3,3*	*saṃrājyam*	*yaśas*	*rūpāṇi rāṣṭram*
	kṣatram		*bhaga puṣṭi*
4. 11,4,4,1*	*tejas*	*yaśas*	*śrī*

[41] See above, Chapter 7, at n. 82, citing 1:189,39.
[42] See above, before n. 15.

Chapter 7	*1st function*	*2d function*	*3d function*
5. *TS* 7,1,8,2*	*tejas*	*indriyam*	*annādyam*
6. *ŚB* 1,6,3,8–15	*devās vidyās*	*yaśas*	*annādyam śrī*
7. *Mbh.* 12:124, 45–60	*dharma satya* (= *tejas*)	*vṛttam balam*	*śrī*
8. 12:217,18–19	*vidyā*	*balam*	*darśanīya bhaga*
9. 5:39,50	*prajñā vrata*	*śūra*	*dātṛ ārya*
10. *Mārk. P.* 5	*tejas*	*balam vīryam*	*rūpam*
11. *Mbh.* 1:189,39	*tejas*	*yaśas*	*rūpam*

Chapter 8	*1st function*	*2d function*	*3d function*
12. *Mbh.* 5:117, 21–22	*satya* (-dharma) *yajvan*	*śūra*	*dāna*(*pati*)
13. 1:88,21–24	*satya*	conquests	*dānam*
14. 5:120,3–14	*satya kratu* + dharma	*yaśas kṣatra-dharma vīra*	*dānam kṣamā*
15. *Buddhacar.* 2,11	*vrata na anṛtika*	*na hiṃsraḥ*	*dānam* (? *gauravo bandhuṣu*)
16. *Mbh.* 8:5,27	*śrutam tapas*	*yaśas*	*kulam śrī*
17. 14:66,16	dharma *satya*	*vikrama*	—
18. 14:68,17–24	truthfulness	no turning back in battle	
	fondness for dharma and brahmins	no *virodha* with Arjuna	—
	satya dharma	slew foes righteously	—
19. 9:5,18	*tejas*	*vīryam yaśas*	*śrī kulam*
20. 9:18,14	*satya*(*dhṛti*)	*jitāmitra*	foe's *śrī* lost
21. 6:117,12	*brahmanyatā*	*śauryam*	*dānam*
22. 12:56,12–20	serves gods and brahmins *satya*	*utthānam*	*śrī*
23. 7:33,10	*śrutam*	*vikrama*	*śrī*
24. 1:45,10	*satya*(*vāg*)	(*dṛdha*)*vikrama*	*śrī*
25. 5:130,27 etc.	*sūnṛtā (gir)*	*balam*	*dānam*
26. 12:29,72	*svādhyāyaghoṣa*	*jyāghoṣa*	*dīyatām*
27. 3:50,10	*tejas*	*yaśas*	*rūpam śrī saubhagyam*
28. 12:274,27	*tejas*	*yaśas*	*śrī*

* In these instances I omit *brahmavarcasa*, which consistently follows the second-function virtue as its "priestly" complement.

It is, of course, to be understood that related classifications of virtues or "power substances" could be found in other texts. I have stuck, however, primarily to the *Mahābhārata* and called upon other texts only where they provide variants on figures who have an epic career: Draupadī-Śrī, the Pāṇḍavas, and Yayāti. We may now look at these variants more closely, proceeding function by function. One suggestive line of investigation will be to observe how certain virtues occur primarily in combinations while others occur, within their "function," primarily alone.

(1) *First function.* The table shows that *tejas* appears most often (eight times) without any other virtue as its counterpart. The parenthetic case (no. 7) where Prahlāda's *satya*, dharma, and *śīla* go over to Indra refers to each of these virtues as a *tejas* and thus makes them not separate virtues but "forms" or "manifestations" of *tejas*. Gonda has protested Dumézil's designation of *tejas* as a first-function virtue, calling it "an oft-mentioned quality not only of representatives of the first function, but also of kings and warriors"[43]—but these terms can easily be met in the context of our present discussion, where we encounter *tejas* as a first-function *royal* virtue.[44]

The other virtues mostly occur in pairs. At first sight there seem to be four main classes of these "coupling" virtues: (a) those concerning truthfulness (*satya*, *na anṛtika*, occurring eleven times, seven in pairs); (b) righteousness (dharma; seven times, all in pairs); (c) knowledge (*vidyā*, *prajñā*, *śrutam*; five times, three in pairs); and (d) sacrificial activity and piety (*devās*, *yajvan*, *kratu*, *brahmanyatā*, fondness for brahmins, service of gods and brahmins, *sūnṛtā gir*, *svādhyāyaghoṣa*; eight times, five in pairs). Only one other virtue appears more than once. This is *vrata*, and the two times it does occur, it appears in combinations. Not, however, a virtue that stands completely

[43] Gonda, "Some Observations on Dumézil's Views," p. 11 (see above, n. 31); for Dumézil, see *ME*, I, 118, and *Destiny of the Warrior*, p. 76.

[44] Thus the kṣatriya of *Gītā* 18,43 (see above, before n. 6) possesses *tejas*, but alongside such other virtues as *śauryam* and *dānam*.

alone, *vrata* refers not only to vowkeeping but to the observance of religious obligations, and it is thus most closely related to the fourth and second of the classes just mentioned, that is, to sacrificial duties and especially to dharma. In this second case, a parallel has been demonstrated between *vratá* and *dhárman* in Ṛg Vedic texts, and the term *vratá* has been found most closely connected in the *Veda* with deities of the "first function": with Varuṇa especially, but also with Mitra and, secondarily, with the Ādityas and with kingship.[45]

With these remarks in mind, let us turn to the only pattern of pairing that occurs with any obvious frequency, that of *satya* and dharma (occurring three or four [no. 14] times). Clearly dharma is an elastic and imperialistic term in the epic, but as denoting righteousness in attitude and behavior, it is thoroughly bound up—especially in the ideology of kingship—with piety and the performance of sacrifices. Thus if dharma can be correlated with the sacrificial virtues, as well as with the ancient meaning of *vrata*, a pattern begins to emerge. For, just as truthfulness, *satya*, occurs with dharma in three or four of its seven pairings, so it occurs two or three times (no. 14 aligns *satya* with both dharma and sacrificial dedication) with the sacrificial virtues and once with *vrata*. Thus in all seven of its pairings, *satya* stands opposite a virtue identifiable with dharma.

Meanwhile, if there is a dependable correlation between the sacrificial virtues and dharma in their juxtaposition with *satya*, so there is a complementary pattern in the case of the remaining class of virtues, those concerned with knowledge. For where these are paired with other virtues, they are usually—like *satya*—set alongside the sacrificial virtues. Here the evidence is more limited and uncertain, but in two of the

[45] See Hanns-Peter Schmidt, *Vedisch* vratá *und awestich* urvăta (Hamburg: Cram, De Gruyter, 1958), pp. 90–91, 14–16, 52–54, 143–44; see also Brown, "Duty as Truth," p. 61; and Gonda, *The Vedic God Mitra* (Leiden: Brill, 1972), pp. 8–10 and 100, n. 3.

three instances mentioned, "knowledge" is set beside *devās* (no. 6), that is, probably sacrificial divine worship, and beside *vrata* (no. 9)—the remaining instance being a combination with the irreducible *tapas* (no. 16).

It thus seems that there is a fundamental dichotomy where the first-function virtues are mentioned in pairs. On one side *satya* is the basic term, occasionally giving way to a form of sacred knowledge. Possibly this is to be seen as an Upaniṣadic extension of the fundamental notion of truth: that is, that truth and the "knowledge" of it are one. And on the other is dharma, recalling and reflected in the virtues of sacrificial action, piety, and vows. It is this dichotomy, with the several terms indicating it, that is found in the characterizations of Śibi and Aṣṭaka in the Yayāti legend (nos. 12 and 14), in the *Buddhacarita*'s description of Yayāti (no. 15), and also in the "act of truth" by which Krishna revives Parikṣit (nos. 17 and 18 [conclusion]). Here I would point out, first, that although Dumézil has said that the qualities ascribed to Śibi and Aṣṭaka are not found elsewhere in Indian divisions within the first function, there are cases where the two Vedic gods of this function—Mitra and Varuṇa—are defined by them. For instance, the Rājasūya, one of the great royal rituals, provides a list of eight "divine instigators" or "quickeners" (*devasū*) of kingship in which the two gods are referred to as *Mitra Satya* and *Varuṇa Dharmapati*.[46] Thus, although these associations do not seem to point to a consistent set of correlations between the two gods and these particular virtues,[47] one can at least say that the latter are not irreconcilable with the theology of the "dual sovereigns." Second, if, despite the small

[46] See Heestermann, *Ancient Indian Royal Consecration*, p. 70, and *ŚB* 5,3,3,8–9; for parallel passages and discussion, see Gonda, *Vedic God Mitra*, pp. 62–66.

[47] For example, see Lévi, *Doctrine du sacrifice*, pp. 156–67, on Varuṇa and *satya* in the Brāhmaṇas. See also Wikander's and Dumézil's position that Dharma substitutes for Mitra as the divinity incarnate in Yudhiṣṭhira.

number of references, one can regard *vrata* as related primarily to dharma, or "vows" as related to "duty," we have a fact of capital importance for our forthcoming discussion of the epic's sins.

(2) *Second function.* On the warrior level there are fewer difficulties. *Yaśas* appears, like *tejas*, primarily alone (six times out of eight). Pairings of the second-function virtues, unlike those of the first function, are infrequent. But in most of the cases where they do occur, they juxtapose *balam* (raw "strength") with some more chivalric or domesticated virtue like *vīryam* ("heroism, energy") or *vṛttam* ("activity, occupation"). Although the evidence here is limited (two cases, one concerning the Pāṇḍavas [no. 10; cf. no. 7]), one is still inclined to suppose that these bipartitions are modeled after the same second-function division that distinguishes the Herakles-Vāyu-Bhīma type from the Achilles-Indra-Arjuna type.[48] Otherwise, the second function has been prone to characterization by single virtues which fall into several clusters. Thus, after *yaśas*, virtues of strength (*indriyam* [?], *balam*, *vikrama*) occur nine times, seven singly; of heroism (*śūra-śauryam*, *vīra-vīryam*) six times, three singly plus "no turning back in battle"; of conquest or victory two times, both singly; virtues involving honorable relations with other kṣatriyas (no *virodha* with Arjuna) occur one or two (? "slew foes righteously") times; virtues connected with the duty to act (*vṛttam*, *utthānam*) occur twice; and the virtue of not harming (*na hiṃsraḥ*) occurs once. Perhaps no one second-function virtue was able to keep pace with the changing ideologies of kingship and warfare. Nonetheless, several of these types of virtues will, like *vrata*, bear further watching in our discussion of the epic sins.

(3) *Third function.* On this level, by far the most frequent entry is *śrī*, occurring thirteen times, seven singly. In fact, one is struck by the frequency of *śrī*'s associations with *tejas* and *yaśas* (nos. 4,19,27,28; see also Chapter 7, n. 49). Perhaps

[48] See above, Chapter 7, n. 50.

this is a fundamental triad or a set any one or all of which may define its function in royal terms.[49] Next to *śrī* is *dānam* and its etymological affiliates (nos. 9 and 26), occurring eight times, four singly. Then come virtues having to do with beauty or "form" (*rūpam*, *darśanīya*), occurring five times, three of these in pairs or sets. One striking fact is that *śrī* rarely occurs with virtues of either of these other types, perhaps because *śrī*, in its two meanings, can well account for both: as "prosperity" partially covering *dānam* and as "beauty" fully covering *rūpam* (here no. 27 provides the one exception, in the description of the overample endowments of Damayantī). In terms of mythology, we are thus brought back to a point made in the last chapter. The goddess of Sovereignty and Prosperity, Śrī herself, "rounds out" and completes the royal virtues on the level of the third function, being represented in the virtue which she herself incarnates.

Nonetheless, while this mythology relates to much in the area of the third function, there are other virtues that seem to reflect this function's open-endedness toward what Dumézil calls "le nombre,"[50] toward multiplicity. Thus there are the early Brāhmaṇic references to material goods such as food (*annādyam*) and cattle (*paśu*), to nourishment (*puṣṭi*), and to the populace of a kingdom (*rāṣṭram*); and in addition there are references to good fortune (*bhaga*, *saubhagyam*), to creative or generative power (*prajāti*), and to continuity or purity of race, family, or lineage (*kulam*, *ārya*)—all of which, in this latter case, converge when it comes to kingship. The list, in other words, is heterogeneous. It does not seem to reflect any third-function mythology other than that of Śrī. There is, however, one other possibility connected with the virtues stressing

[49] On *śrī* as a "symbol and insignia of royalty," see M-W, s.v. See Coomaraswamy, *Yakṣas*, II, 28, on *tejas* and *yaśas* as similar to the Iranian *xvarenah*, "royal glory" (also connected with the three functions; see Dumézil, *ME*, II, 282–89).

[50] See Dumézil, *Les Dieux des Indo-Européens* (Paris: Presses Universitaires de France, 1952), p. 7.

continuity and purity of race and lineage. As Wikander has noted, Sahadeva, the youngest Pāṇḍava, is a sort of "stay-at-home" (*casanier*), ever close to Yudhiṣṭhira, and the true representative among his brothers of the Aryan domestic family and its purity, being twice the carrier and handler of Fire (Agni) for his brothers.[51]

These convergences of legend and formula may now lead us to some reflections. In the discussion of the Yayāti legend, when Yayāti offers his daughter Mādhavī to Gālava to help him obtain the eight hundred peculiar horses, he refers to her as "a promptress of every virtue" (*sarvadharmopacāyinī*; 5:113,11). This epithet, which defines Mādhavī at the very beginning of her story, is complemented by a similar description at the end. When she appears from the forest to offer half of her own merits to Yayāti, and thus to seal the bargain between her father and her sons, she says: "I am your daughter Mādhavī, O king, faring as a deer [*mṛgacāriṇī*]; by me too is virtue prompted [*mayāpyupacito dharmas*]; accept then half of mine" (5:119,24).

I have used the word "prompt" here for *upa-ci-*, retaining it from the Ganguli-Roy translation of the passage introducing Mādhavī.[52] For *upacāyin*, Monier-Williams gives the meanings "causing to increase" or "succeed"; and for *upa-ci-*, the meanings "gather together," "heap together," "increase," and "strengthen." The whole range of meanings is suggestive for Mādhavī's role with respect to the "virtues." The Critical Edition shows that if the verb and its derivatives, used consistently for Mādhavī, are representative of the text at its oldest, an inordinate number of emendations are made in the introductory description (on the contrary, no variants are

[51] See Wikander, "Nakula et Sahadeva," p. 87 on Sahadeva as "*casanier*," and pp. 73 and 89 on Sahadeva and Fire; on the latter, see 3:143,14 (protecting the Pāṇḍavas' Agnihotra) and 2:61,6.

[52] Ganguli-Roy, trans., *Mahabharata*, IV: *Udyoga Parva*, 234.

cited for the second usage). Thus, for *-upacāyinī* ("a promptress"; 5:113,11), other manuscripts introduce *-upacāriṇī* ("one who attends upon"), *-pādinī* (? "one footed in"), *-pravādinī* ("one who declares"), and several commentators cite *-apacāyinī* ("gatherer"). For *-dharmopacāyinī* ("promptress of virtues"), one text introduces the bland *-dharmārthadāyinī* ("producer of dharma and *artha*"). And finally, several manuscripts insert a whole extra line (455*) including the added description, or "correction," making Mādhavī *sarvadharmapradāyinī* ("a bestower of every virtue") or *sarvadharmapravādinī* ("a declarer of every virtue"). From so many variants, it would seem that the original term has been obscured or forgotten, with varying degrees of misrepresentation. Mādhavī certainly does not "gather" or "declare" the virtues (she says very little), nor does she produce dharma and *artha*. We thus seem to have here an old way of referring to a peculiar rapport with the royal virtues that would seem especially suited for a royal heroine. At least in the case of Mādhavī, it is clearly her sex, and moreover her repeated virginity, that makes it possible for her to be "one who causes four lineages to stand, . . . a promptress of every virtue."

In the main story of the *Mahābhārata*, just one heroine, Draupadī, shares a number of the characteristics of Mādhavī: an identification with Śrī, multiple husbands, and a return to virginity after each childbirth. But in each of these areas, the differences are as great and as obvious as the similarities.[53] They identify the two heroines only as broadly similar figures and indicate no common legend or mythological prototype. But within the similarities lies one general point at which their legends converge. Both are rescuers of royal lineages. Mādhavī saves four royal lines when she "prompts" the virtues that appear in her sons, and again, she rescues her father's heritage of royal virtues when she "prompts" the restoration that sends

[53] See *ME*, II, 363: unlike Draupadī, Mādhavī remains perpetually a virgin, wedded not to humans but to the Forest.

him back to heaven. Draupadī, on the other hand, rescues the Pāṇḍavas, and thus the "true" descent of the Kuru line, when they have lost everything at the game of dice in the *Sabhāparvan*.[54] This very scene, the dice game, provides the frame of reference for a message concerning Draupadī which Kuntī sends, through Krishna, to the twins. Urging these two more gentle of the Pāṇḍavas to avenge the humiliation of Draupadī in the *sabhā* by the use of force and the practice of *kṣatradharma*, Kuntī says: "While you were looking on, Pāñcālī, a promptress of every virtue [*sarvadharmopacāyinī*] was addressed with harsh words. Who can endure this?" (5:135,15).

Draupadī, then, shares this epithet with Mādhavī and, to my knowledge—after considerable checking—with no one else. Here, too, there is evidence of misunderstanding or tampering: thus we have *-dharmāpacāyinī* ("gathering every virtue"), *-karmopacāyinī* ("prompting every action"), and in some versions (followed by Ganguli-Roy), the original term is kept, but applied to the twins (*sarvadharmopacāyinām*) rather than Draupadī![55]

It thus seems likely that the epithet records an early conception of the virtues connected with a feminine incarnation of "sovereignty," whether Mādhavī-Medb[56] or Śrī-Draupadī. Perhaps the use of dharmas for "virtues" is earlier than its rival, *guṇas*, although this does not seem provable. The important point is that the virtues "prompted" by these heroines—whether *dharmas* or *guṇas*—are trifunctional and are "prompted" at junctures that are critical for the continuity of royal lineages and destinies. Indeed, they are most critical for figures who represent the kingship of the "central" Kuru dynasty, insofar as, in one case, they ultimately concern the salvation of Yayāti and, in the other, the origin and rescue of the Pāṇḍavas.

[54] See above, Chapter 4 and n. 23.

[55] Ganguli-Roy, *Mahabharata*, IV: *Udyoga Parva*, 275.

[56] On Medb, see above, n. 22: she may certainly be said to "prompt" the virtues of nonjealousy (?justice), bravery, and generosity.

Finally, it is quite possible that these "promptings" are the epic counterparts of themes and mechanisms that were at one point also found in rituals. One cannot, of course, reconstruct rituals from myths and legends. As Dumézil says, special royal rituals may lie behind the name Medb (with its connotation of "intoxicating drink"), but they are ones which "it would be as easy as it would be vain to imagine."[57] In the case of India, however, we have already noticed that the Aśvamedha involves a transfer of royal virtues from the horse to the king by three queens, all "forms of Śrī."[58] So it is not a question of trying to reconstruct an ancient royal ritual, but of observing a number of mythic and epic themes which may, at some point, have held ritual implications.

In several stories, special figures, of sacred or priestly status, facilitate the liaisons between the female personifications of sovereignty and their royal male partners. In the Yayāti legend, it is the brahmin Gālava who leads Mādhavī from one royal bed to the next. And in a myth from the *Śāntiparvan*,[59] the brahmin-ṛṣi Nārada ("Water-Giver") is present to perform ablutions with Indra at the purest spot (probably the source) of the Ganges just before Indra is united with Śrī. In the main narrative of the *Mahābhārata*—in one of its strangest passages—is a similar episode.

When Krishna is on his "peace" embassy to Hāstinapura, having found Duryodhana intractable, he visits the latter's greatest ally, Karṇa, to sound him out on some last-ditch proposals. Disclosing to Karṇa that he is "legally" (*dharmatas*) a "Pāṇḍava" (son of Pāṇḍu),[60] Krishna urges him to make his identity known and declare his seniority over his "brothers." The latter, Krishna promises, will then embrace his feet, as

[57] Dumézil, *ME*, II, 340.

[58] See above, Chapter 7, at n. 23.

[59] See above, Chapter 7, after n. 53.

[60] Karṇa is a son of either the *kānīna* ("born of a young woman") or *sahoḍha* ("brought with" a woman at marriage) type (5:138,8–9), having been born to Kuntī in her youth, before her marriage to Pāṇḍu. Thus, as said earlier, Karṇa is a potential king.

will Abhimanyu, the sons of Draupadī, and the Pāṇḍavas' allies (5:138,12–13). But in addition, Krishna makes a second promise that is psychologically fantastic, defying what we know from several other incidents, especially the Svayaṃvara and the dice game.[61] If Karṇa reveals his identity, says Krishna, he can prepare to be installed as king; "and, during the sixth period, Draupadī will come to you" (*ṣaṣṭhe ca tvaṃ tathā kāle draupadyupagamiṣyati*; 138,15). The Ganguli-Roy translation is surely right in following this with a parenthetic "as a wife."[62] There are but two real differences between this and the other passages cited: first, one has difficulty imagining Draupadī complying;[63] and second, Karṇa, unlike the partners of Mādhavī and the "chosen ones" of Śrī, is uninterested. The mysterious transferal is only proposed, and the proposal is kept secret.

There are, to be sure, mythological overtones to this passage. Some of these are echoed in a follow-up speech made to Karṇa

[61] On Draupadī and Karṇa at the Svayaṃvara, see above, Chapter 7, n. 44; in the dice game Karṇa insults her, calling her multiple marriage adharmic (2:61,34–6) and herself a slave (*dāsī*; 61,81).

[62] Ganguli-Roy, trans., *Mahabharata*, IV: *Udyoga Parva*, 279; Krishna explicitly promises Karṇa union with Draupadī in the *Andhra Mahabharatam*; see Subramanian, *Vyasa and Variations*, p. 201; but it would have to be implied even if one takes *ṣaṣṭhe kāle* as "meal-time": see M-W, pp. 278 and 1110. The commentator Nīlakaṇṭha is silent. See also Georg Buhler and Johann Kirste, "Indian Studies, No. II: Contributions to the History of the *Mahābhārata*," *SKAWW*, *Philosophisch-Historische Classe*, vol. CXXVII, Abhandlung XI (1892), 19, discussing an alternate reading from Kumārila's *Tantravārttika*: "It is for this reason [because Draupadī is an incarnation of Śrī] that Vāsudeva says to Karṇa: 'And on the sixth day [*ahani*] Draupadī will serve thee.' For how else could a person, whose word is authoritive, speak thus?" Although Bühler and Kirste view the variant as the original, it is surely a substitution that reveals some considerable postepic embarrassment at Krishna's behavior.

[63] Krishna's suggestion is of a different order from extratextual stories which speak of a secret attachment of Draupadī for Karṇa—even making the one sin which stops her from reaching heaven (which the traditional text says was a "partiality for Arjuna"; 17:2,6)—that she harbored a desire for Karṇa. I have several times heard such stories, in both Maharashtra and Tamilnadu.

by Kuntī, his mother: "Acquired formerly by Arjuna [*arjunenārjitam*], greedily seized by the wicked—snatching it away from the sons of Dhṛtarāṣṭra, enjoy that prosperity belonging to Yudhiṣṭhira" (*bhuṅkṣva yaudhiṣṭhiraṃ śriyam*; 5:143,8). This *śrī* which Kuntī speaks of must certainly refer, even if not solely, to Draupadī. Moreover, when Draupadī was "acquired by Arjuna" as a bride, it was Kuntī's fateful words that united her with her four other sons as well. In fact, the present words to Karṇa seem unmistakably reminiscent of the earlier words concerning Draupadī. Thinking her sons had returned home with edible alms (*bhikṣā*; 1:182,1), she told them: "May you all enjoy [it (her)] together" (*bhuṅkteti sametya sarve*; 182,2).[64] In each passage, the use of the root *bhuj*, "eat, enjoy," carries a sexual overtone.[65] Do we not honor the poets most if we assume that these coincidences—all concerning words of Kuntī to her sons about Draupadī—are "real" and intended?

As suggested in earlier chapters, the relationship of Draupadī, Śrī incarnate, to Viṣṇu's *avatāra*, Krishna, is full of ambiguities: identical names, a coded language, and, at times, the sense that while she is "in essence" and "in intention" united with him, she is forever provisionally preoccupied with others. Taking this intimate but noncommittal relationship into account, one cannot escape the impression that Krishna—whom we have seen elsewhere in archaic priestly roles[66]—is, at least in the present scene, Draupadī's Gālava. He is implicitly empowered (and we may assume that he anticipates Karṇa's negative response) to facilitate, as a go-between or

[64] Some Southern texts give *bhuṅkṣvadhvamiti pramādāt*.

[65] As insisted to me by Robert Goldman.

[66] Cf. also the matchmaker role of the famous brahmin Vasiṣṭha, *purohita* to the Pāṇḍavas' ancestors at the time of King Saṃvaraṇa, who went to the Sun to obtain permission for the king to marry the Sun's daughter Tapatī (1:162,12–163,9; and see above, Chapter 7, n. 60); similarly, Drupada's *purohita* (presumably the same as will later precede Krishna as prewar envoy for the Pāṇḍavas; see above, Chapter 6, n. 63) serves as messenger and go-between in arranging Draupadī's marriage with the Pāṇḍavas (1:185,14–15).

royal matchmaker, what amounts to a transfer of sovereignty. Moreover, there is a passage which confirms a role for Krishna in maintaining the standards and the mechanisms of kingship. In the first meeting between Krishna and the Pāṇḍavas at the beginning of the forest exile, Draupadī herself, in the mythologically allusive exchange that she and Krishna have, says to him:

Of Rājarṣis who are of meritorious acts, unretreating in battle, and endowed with every virtue, you are the refuge [or way], O best of men.
rājarṣīnāṃ puṇyakṛtāmāhaveṣvanivartinām
sarvadharmopapannānāṃ tvaṃ gatiḥ puruṣottama. [3:13,49]

Krishna is thus the "refuge" of every "omnivirtuous" monarch, or claimant to the sovereignty which Draupadī, as Śrī incarnate, represents "on earth."

CHAPTER 9

Sins of the Sovereign

The last two chapters have provided a framework within which to interpret the virtues that enhance the royal figure of Yudhiṣṭhira. Despite much variation and considerable inflation, a consistent trifunctional theme has been detected. Now for the countertheme. Underlying the discussion will be two assumptions, familiar from the opening chapter. First, it is the nature of epic (treating as it does of human "psychology" and "destiny") to open vistas on the nature of sin and virtue; second, the two—virtue and sin—must be studied and interpreted through their relation to each other.

Probably no facet of the *Mahābhārata* has elicited more varied comment than the Pāṇḍavas' and Krishna's involvement in numerous sins.[1] I will not attempt to discuss every incident, but I will try to place some of them in a new perspective by examining their "motive": the goal of sovereignty. The brief begins with the "legal precedents" set by certain famous moments in the career of the divine sovereign, Indra.

The Sins of Indra

The theme before us is one which Dumézil has explored from different angles: "the three sins of the warrior," that is, a series of sins against the three functions. Dumézil's discussion of this

[1] See, most prominently, Holtzmann (elder), *Indische Sagen*, II, vii, and Holtzmann (younger), *Mahābhārata und seine Theile*, I, 80–84; E. W. Hopkins, "The Social and Military Position of the Ruling Caste in Ancient India, as Represented by the Sanskrit Epic," *JAOS*, XIII (1899), 58–65; Held, *Ethnological Study*, pp. 172–75, 304; Ruben, *Krishna*, pp. 256–59.

mythologem has undergone several refinements. His original comparisons concerned the "cadre," or "frame," of three "sins" and three "losses," culminating in an annihilation of the sinner, which he discovered in the legends of the Scandinavian Starkadr-Starcatherus, the Greek Heracles, and in the mythology of Indra.[2] More recently, however, he retains only the first two figures and adds two more heroes: the *Mahābhārata*'s Śiśupāla, and, possibly in protracted form, the Roman warrior king Tullus Hostilius.[3] The total picture has thus been greatly sharpened, in particular by the discussion of Śiśupāla. But Indra has perhaps been dropped too quickly. According to Dumézil, "It now seems probable that it [the Indra myth] is a question of a secondary application, of an artificial extension into mythology, of the epic theme."[4] Dumézil thus bases his view on a distinction drawn between myth and epic, with the theme of the three sins having originally pertained to the latter: "Indra's sins are matters of mythology, those of Starkadr and of Heracles [and of Śiśupāla] are matters of epic."[5]

It does not seem likely that any evidence will emerge to dispute the historical side of these judgments. No Indo-European figure of myth, no warrior god, other than Indra, has been found to commit a trifunctional assortment of significantly interrelated sins. Thus, as a mythical theme, Indra's three sins may well be an Indian invention. But this does not mean that one must follow Dumézil in regarding Indra's three sins as an "artificial extension" of the epic theme. There is no way to account for Indra borrowing, or copying, the sins of Śiśupāla, or, for that matter, of assuming the sins from an earlier form of the legend. Nonetheless, the one myth which

[2] Dumézil, *Destiny of the Warrior*, pp. 65–104 (from the original French of 1956).

[3] On Śiśupāla, see Dumézil, *ME*, II, 66–68; *Mbh.* 2:42,7–11 (his sins); and above, Chapter 4, n. 2; on Tullus Hostilius, see *ME*, II, 358–59.

[4] Dumézil, *ME*, II, 129–30 (my translation).

[5] *Ibid.*, p. 20 (my translation).

attributes to Indra three successive sins against the three functions does seem to be an "artificial extension" of something. This is the myth of *Mārkaṇḍeya Purāṇa* 5, discussed in Chapter 7,[6] in which Indra's three sins result in the losses of his *tejas*, *balam*, *vīryam*, and *rūpam*, and ultimately in the births of the Pāṇḍavas. It was argued in Chapter 7 that this myth represents an "artificial" attempt to clear Draupadī of the polyandry charge. But here, in speaking of an "artificial extension," I have in mind not a continuation of a heroic tradition like the Śiśupāla legend, but an artificial treatment, in the sense of synthetic and eclectic, of earlier traditions about the sins and punishments of Indra.

On this subject, I am much in debt to Dumézil. He has shown that while "Indra has no criminal record in the *Ṛg Veda*,"[7] the Brāhmaṇas provide extensive lists of Indra's misdeeds, usually mentioning one or more of those which come to be included in more complete renditions. *Aitareya Brāhmaṇa* 7,28, for instance, has Indra commit his first two sins against the same two figures—Viśvarūpa and Vṛtra—as *Mārkaṇḍeya* 5; and *Śatapatha Brāhmaṇa* 1,6,3,1–17 provides a detailed narrative of this same sequence. According to the latter passage, also discussed in Chapter 7,[8] Indra first slew the three-headed Viśvarūpa, son of Tvaṣṭṛ. Furious, Tvaṣṭṛ created Vṛtra, and as the latter developed, he "came to be possessed of Agni and Soma, of all sciences [*vidyās*], all glory [*yaśas*], all nourishment [*annādyam*], all prosperity" (*śrī*; 8). In order for Indra again to become "what Indra now is," it was necessary that all the divinities (*devās*) and each of the above qualities return to him (15), after which Indra slew Vṛtra (16–17). As

[6] See Chapter 7, following n. 68.

[7] Dumézil, *Destiny of the Warrior*, pp. 65–68; he maintains this against the otherwise very valuable study of Hanns Oertel, "Contributions from the Jāiminīya Brāhmaṇa to the History of Brāhmaṇa Literature," 2d ser., pt. 3, "Indrasya kilbiṣāṇī," *JAOS*, XIX (1908), 118–25.

[8] See Chapter 7, following n. 38.

suggested earlier, these losses and recoveries probably have a tripartite structure, like those in *Mārkaṇḍeya* 5. But they are all connected in this passage with just one incident, the slaying of Vṛtra, which the passage does not actually speak of as a sin.

Not until the *Mārkaṇḍeya* 5 account is all this systematized to include not only the trifunctional losses and recoveries, but the concurrence of each loss with a sin against the corresponding function. Moreover, this myth provides the first mention of Indra's violation of the brāhmaṇī Ahalyā (a story long known) in a list of Indra's sins, and thus the first ascription of this episode to the zone of the third function.[9] To recapitulate briefly, first Indra slays the brahmin Viśvarūpa, losing his *tejas*; second, breaking a warrior's agreement to "friendship" (*sakhyam*), he slays Vṛtra and loses his *balam*; and third, violating Ahalyā, he loses his *rūpam*.[10]

As I argued that this myth offers an "artificial" reinterpretation of Draupadī's polyandry, I must now suggest that it has rearranged certain traditional, albeit entirely Indian, material concerning Indra's sins. Once again, there is a more coherent myth within the *Mahābhārata* itself, one dealing not with three sins and the births of the Pāṇḍavas, but, as probably already reflected in *Śatapatha Brāhmaṇa* 1,6,3, two sins, a series of losses, and a final restoration of Indra to sovereignty.[11] In the epic, the version of this myth that is contextually most important occurs in the *Udyogaparvan* (5:9–18), with another complete version told in the *Śāntiparvan* (12:329,17–41) and numerous spinoffs elsewhere.[12] As will be suggested mainly through footnotes, there are reasons to regard the *Udyogaparvan*

[9] On the Ahalyā story, see Dumézil, *Destiny of the Warrior*, p. 70.

[10] See above, Chapter 7, at n. 68, and the note.

[11] See also *JB* 2,134 (cited by Dumézil, *Destiny of the Warrior*, p. 69).

[12] For further discussion, see Dumézil, *Destiny of the Warrior*, pp. 124–27 (possible Indo-Iranian features [not concerning the sins and losses] of the myth); Holtzmann (younger), "Indra nach den Vorstellungen des Mahābhārata," *ZDMG*, XXXII (1878), 305–11; Hopkins, *Epic Mythology*, pp. 129–32.

version as the more ancient treatment of the sequence, which concerns three great threats to Indra's throne.

(1) "From hatred of Indra" (*indradrohāt*), Tvaṣṭṛ, by his great *tapas*, created a son having three heads: Viśvarūpa, who "longed for Indra's seat" (*endraṃ sa prārthayatsthānam*; 5:9,3–4).[13] Viśvarūpa was a brahmin, who read the Vedas with one of his three mouths and was "intent upon a life of religious practices and austerities"; he was also a threat to Indra because of his "unlimited *tejas*" (9,7). In order to deprive Viśvarūpa of this "energy," Indra ordered the Apsarases to try to tempt him; but he would not be distracted. Indra then "decided on a weapon"—his *vajra* (9,20)—to destroy Viśvarūpa.[14] However, after killing him the chief of the celestials found no peace (*śarman*) and felt himself scorched by Viśvarūpa's *tejas* (*dīpitastasya tejasā*; 9,24). Though Indra soon returned to heaven as king, his sin of killing a brahmin—one who threatened him especially by his *tejas*—was yet to be atoned for.

(2) Enraged that Indra had slain his son "who had committed no offense at all," Tvaṣṭṛ, again by *tapas*, created Vṛtra to kill Indra. In their first fight, Indra was swallowed by Vṛtra. But Vṛtra was made to yawn, and Indra escaped, only to retreat from his foe, who was "endowed with strength" (*balasamanvita*; 9,50). In distress, the gods, led by Indra, repaired to Viṣṇu, who told them: "I shall tell you a contrivance [*upāyaṃ vakṣyāmi*] whereby he shall be annihilated. . . . Adopt toward him a conciliatory policy . . . ; remaining

[13] This theme of rivalry for the sovereignty is not found in 12:329, where Indra's opposition turns on Viśvarūpa's change from *purohita* of the gods to that of the Asuras (18–23).

[14] In 12:329, Indra obtains advice from Brahmā (24–25) and help from Viṣṇu, who pervades the *vajra* by which Indra kills Viśvarūpa (27). This version ascribes the origin of the *vajra* to Dadhīca's bones (25) and is thus oriented to show, as it concludes, that Indra was able to overcome a brahmin foe only by having access to another brahmin's (Dadhīca's) "energy" (*brahmatejas*; 41).

invisible, I shall enter Indra's thunderbolt" (5:10,10–13).

The ṛṣis then went to Vṛtra and said: "Let there be eternal friendship [*sakhyaṃ bhavatu . . . nityadā*] between you and Indra" (10,19). Then they delivered a sermon on *sakhyam* and declared what a faithful "friend" Indra would be (10,23–26). Vṛtra agreed on the condition that "Indra himself or the gods do not kill me by what is dry, or wet; by a stone, or by wood; by a weapon [*śastreṇa*] or by a missile [*vajreṇa*]; in the daytime, or at night" (10,29). Thus an accord was reached, but Indra passed his time searching for a "loophole" (*randhram*; 10,32). Then, one evening (neither night nor day), seeing Vṛtra by the seashore (neither land nor sea?), Indra saw his opportunity, and, "bearing Viṣṇu in mind, he beheld at that instant in the sea a mass of froth [*phena*] as large as a hill. And he said, 'this is neither wet, nor dry. . . .' And he threw the mass of froth, blended with his thunderbolt, at Vṛtra. And Viṣṇu, having entered within the froth, put an end to Vṛtra's life" (10,35–39).

Soon, however, after much rejoicing, Indra became "overpowered by falsehood" (*anṛtenābhibhūta*; 10,42), that is, by the sin of not keeping his agreement with Vṛtra; and he was also "overpowered by the brahminicide" (*abhibhūtaśca . . . brahmahatyayā*; 10,42) of killing Viśvarūpa.[15] Departing from his throne, "bereft of his senses and consciousness and overpowered by his own sins" (*abhibhūtaḥ svakalmaṣaiḥ*; 10,43), he could not be recognized. "And he lay concealed in the water, just like a writhing snake" (43).[16]

(3) Without a king for the divine throne, the gods sought out the "handsome" (*śrīmān*; 5:11,1) Nahuṣa, a human being and, by dynastic reckonings, the father of Yayāti. Addressing him, "O lord of earth, be our king" (*rājā no bhava pārthiva*), the gods convinced him to "protect the kingdom in heaven"

[15] This differentiation between the two sins is not made in 12:329; there it is the sin of brahminicide doubled (*tasyāṃ dvaidhībhūtāyāṃ brahmavadhyāyām*; 28) that causes Indra, out of fear, to enter the lotus stalk.

[16] Cf. *JB* 2,234: when Agni succeeds in purifying Indra of his sins by sacrifice, Indra, "as a serpent would get rid of its skin, . . . got rid of all his evil."

(*pāhi rājyaṃ triviṣṭape*; 11,2–4). But having assumed power, Nahuṣa, till then "always of virtuous soul, fell into a sensuous turn of mind" (*dharmātmā satatam bhūtvā kamātmā samapadyata*; 11,8). He surrounded himself with Apsarases and numerous enjoyments (9–12). But his voluptuous existence soon brought him to commit a most critical error, in fact, a sin: he coveted Śacī,[17] Indra's wife.

In fear and distress, Śacī sought protection from Bṛhaspati, the gods' chaplain, who promised to reunite her with Indra. Nahuṣa was outraged at Śacī's refusal, and the gods and ṛṣis attempted to pacify him, urging him to "turn back his inclination from the sin of outraging another's wife" (12,4). Then, most intriguingly in this context, Nahuṣa reminded them that "Ahalyā of spotless fame, the wife of a ṛṣi, was outraged by Indra while her husband was still alive" (12,6). Nahuṣa thus convinced the gods and ṛṣis to bring Śacī to him, but Bṛhaspati refused to abandon one who had come to him for refuge (12,26). After some deliberation, it was agreed that Śacī should go and beseech Nahuṣa for a delay, which Nahuṣa granted, in which to make up her mind and to learn what had become of Indra (13,4–5). Returning to Bṛhaspati, she then went with all the gods to seek the advice of Viṣṇu, who said that Indra would be absolved of his sins and would regain his kingdom when he performed a horse sacrifice (13,13). The gods then found Indra (it is not told how[18]) and performed a horse sacrifice (*aśvamedha*; 13,26) for him. Viṣṇu then "distributed [*vibhajya*] the sin of brahminicide [the foremost sin] among trees, rivers, mountains, earth, and women" (13,27), and Indra became "free of sin" (*pūtapāpmā*; 13,28).[19]

[17] 12:329 condenses the enjoyment theme to the essentials: *sarvaṃ māṃ śakropabhuktam upasthitamṛte śacīm*; "everything enjoyed by Indra is obtained by me except Śacī" (31).

[18] Cf. the smoother, and thus probably later, 12:329,40: they learn Indra's whereabouts from Śacī, who gets Indra to come forth from the lotus stalk.

[19] See Hopkins, *Epic Mythology*, pp. 130–31. 12:329,41 has no parallel role for Viṣṇu.

The account continues at some length, but Nahuṣa's fall is finally occasioned by a device: Indra tells Śacī to inform Nahuṣa that she will yield to him if he will have his vehicle borne by the celestial ṛṣis (15,9–13). While being carried one day, Nahuṣa uttered an untruth and touched one of his bearers, Agastya, on the head with his foot. "At this . . . he became divested of power and good looks" (*niḥśrīkas*; 17, 12).

The connection between this continuous mythical narrative and the *Mārkaṇḍeya Purāṇa*'s division of the three sins of Indra among the three functions should be apparent. Whereas in the *Mārkaṇḍeya* account Indra loses his *tejas* after conquering *Viśvarūpa*, and his *balam* after conquering Vṛtra, in this epic narrative his opponents are characterized by just these attributes. Viśvarūpa has "unlimited *tejas*" (*amitatejas*), and Vṛtra is "endowed with strength" (*balasamanvita*), as well as with honor in the contract that Indra breaks. But the myth of the three sins finds no such parallels in the third episode. Instead, there are inversions. First, rather than being committed by Indra, a sin, or an affront, is committed against him, or more exactly against his wife. And this sin, or at least its intent, is the stated equivalent of the third-function sin committed by Indra, and in the present context even attributed to him: the violation of Ahalyā. In fact, just as in the *Mārkaṇḍeya* account of Indra's third sin, Indra is marked by the loss of his beauty (*rūpam*), so Nahuṣa falls "without his beauty" (*niḥśrīkas*) in consequence of his attempt to seduce Śacī. Furthermore, in both of the third-function episodes—and in contrast to the first two episodes which concern only gods and Asuras—the sin concerns a sexual transgression between gods and humans, but again inverted: in one case, Indra violates the brāhmaṇī Ahalyā; in the other, Nahuṣa, a man, covets the divine Śacī. Nahuṣa's status as a human king will be discussed later. His voluptuous, sensuous turn makes his reign representative of the third function: here not as a level against which Indra sins, but as a level no longer accessible to Indra. The epic gives us, then, an account of two sins of Indra, with a third sin committed against rather than by him, ultimately allowing him to regain his throne.

Yudhiṣṭhira the Sinner

In the epic narrative the first person (aside from Krishna who is involved in nearly every misdeed) who might be expected to continue the sins of Indra would be Indra's son Arjuna. But Arjuna is not helpful when it comes to committing sins. As Dumézil puts it, Arjuna, "the son or partial incarnation of Indra, . . . has all this god's qualities and in addition a certain refinement, and sometimes a self-control, which are sadly lacking in his model."[20] Arjuna may have a guilty hand in the deaths of Bhagadatta, his father's "friend" (7:28,18; 29,1; 168,27), of Bhuriśravas, Jayadratha, Bhīṣma, Karṇa, and Duryodhana; or he may be charged with one sin—too much pride in his heroism (17:2,21)—which makes him temporarily experience Hell at the end of the epic. But next to every other hero (except perhaps the twins), Arjuna stands as the very model of decency and purity, surely the most frequent recipient of the epithet "sinless one" (*anagha*) and of such titles as "he of unstained" or "of pure deeds" (*akliṣṭakarman*; 3:39,1; *viśuddhakarman*; 3:161,29). Nor is it just a matter of epithets and titles, for several episodes portray Arjuna in this shining light.[21]

One might propose several explanations for this discontinuity between myth and epic. Surely one factor is that Arjuna's mystical identity with Krishna, his status as the "warrior yogi" who learns in the *Gītā*—before the battle—that he must fight with detachment, makes actual sins inconceivable. As Walter Ruben has perceived, the *Gītā*'s ethic of desireless action, or of action for another's sake, justifies the "sins," and this would

[20] Dumézil, *Destiny of the Warrior*, p. 163.

[21] See 4:67,2–9 (refusal to marry Uttarā), 7:164,69–70 (refusal to lie to Droṇa), and, interpolated, *Āraṇyakaparvan*, App. I, no. 6 (refusal to be seduced by Urvaśī).

apply not only to Krishna but to Arjuna.[22] But the most important factor is that Indra's sins are committed not as "warrior sins" but as "sins of a sovereign." This means that the Indian myths do not allow one to apply an otherwise most useful distinction set up by Dumézil between the single "sin of the sovereign" (usually a form of lying or pride, as with Yayāti) and the "three sins of the warrior."[23] In the myths concerning Indra, the two categories merge. Though Indra's sins are close to, and in the *Mārkaṇḍeya* account even identical with, the warrior pattern, he is never totally destroyed by them like Śiśupāla and the latter's European legendary counterparts.[24] Rather, Indra commits his sins as a sovereign, with sovereignty as the end ever held in sight. This motive does not apply to Arjuna or for that matter to any of the triple sinners of legend who are in general servants of, and spokesmen for, sovereigns rather than sovereigns themselves.

The setting of Indra's sins is thus the perennial contention between the Devas and the Asuras, one aspect of which was noticed earlier. In the epic transposition of the theme of the "three steps," the one feature that ties in Krishna's maneuvers with the Vāmana myth—the more recent, post-Vedic, rendition of the three steps theme—is that Krishna helps the Pāṇḍavas regain what was formerly theirs.[25] The conflict between the Devas and Asuras over universal sovereignty is marked by a recurring pattern of reversals and triumphs. The same, on the epic level, is true of the conflict between the Kauravas and the Pāṇḍavas. The figure analogous to Indra, the "sovereign sinner" whose sins are part of such a seesaw

[22] Ruben, *Krishna*, p. 256; it would not apply to Yudhiṣṭhira or Duryodhana, whose motive is sovereignty.

[23] See *ME*, II, 356–57.

[24] See *Destiny of the Warrior*, pp. 43 (Tullus), 88 (Starcatherus), and 101 (Heracles); and see p. 69 on the "optimistic" character of the end of the Indra myths.

[25] See above, Chapter 6, from n. 35 to end of chapter.

drama, is not Arjuna but another of the "five Indras among men": Yudhiṣṭhira.

Let us concern ourselves with the questions of Yudhiṣṭhira's complicity and "motivation" and reserve discussion of his particular sins for the next chapter. Nowhere are these matters more in evidence than in a scene after the battle, where Yudhiṣṭhira, in a sort of *mea culpa*, renounces all desire to rule and expresses the wish to perform acts of penance.

First he recalls the fall of Bhīṣma (12:27,4–13): "He on whose limbs I used to roll about in sport, that son of Gaṅgā has been caused by me, covetous of sovereignty [or kingship;[26] *mayā rājyalubdhena*], to fall" (4). The responsibility is not lessened or contradicted by further reference to the parts played in slaying Bhīṣma by Arjuna and Śikhaṇḍin, for over and over Yudhiṣṭhira claims the fault as his own, his words culminating in the lament: "He by whom we were reared as youths, by whom we were protected, has been caused to be slain by me, covetous of sovereignty, sinful, a slayer of gurus, stupefied, all for the sake of short-lived sovereignty" (*sa mayā rājyalubdhena pāpena gurughātinā/alpakālasya rājyasya kṛte muḍhena ghātitaḥ*; 13).

Next he recalls the death of Droṇa (12:27,14–17): "And the *ācārya*, the great bowman revered by all kings—having approached [me] in battle, he was addressed falsely by [my] sinful [self] concerning his son" (*mithyā pāpenoktaḥ sutaṃ prati*; 14). He recounts briefly the details of his own lie, laments that he hypocritically "resorted to the garb of truth" (*satyakañcukamāsthāya*; 17), and asks: "What *lokas* shall I now obtain having performed such a cruel act" (*karma daruṇam*; 16–17)? This lie, indeed, is consistently represented as Yudhiṣṭhira's most explicit sin, the one which, at the end of the epic, makes

[26] I will use the word "sovereignty" to cover Yudhiṣṭhira's aspirations, whether it translates *rājyam* or *aiśvaryam*. Both are used interchangeably in this regard.

him see Hell with his brothers (18:3,14). It will be discussed further.

Then, in just one *śloka*, he recalls the death of Karṇa, fully admitting his personal guilt: "And having caused Karṇa, unretreating in battle, my eldest brother, exceedingly fierce, to be slain, who is there that is more a sinner [*pāpakṛttamaḥ*] than I" (18)?

And finally, Yudhiṣṭhira laments the deaths of the Pāṇḍavas' children. First he takes the blame for the death of Arjuna's son Abhimanyu, accepting the sin of "lineage destruction" (*jñātighātin*; 12:27,3) through the symbolism of a violation of youth, sexuality, and fertility: "And Abhimanyu who was like a lion born in the fields, a youth—covetous [*lubdha*], I caused him to penetrate that array protected by Droṇa. Since then I have not been able to look Arjuna . . . or Krishna in the face, [being] like one who commits the offense of slaying an embryo" (*kilbiṣī brūṇahā yathā*; 27,19–20). In this same connection, mentioning no special fault of his own, he also laments the deaths of the five sons of Draupadī, comparing her loss to that of the earth (*pṛthivī*) deprived of her five mountains (21), a simile seemingly reflected in his words of summary: "This am I, a doer of evil [*āgaskaraḥ*], sinful [*pāpaḥ*], a destroyer of the earth" (*pṛthivīnāśakārakaḥ*; 27,22).

This confession presents much intriguing symbolism that I will discuss later, but there is one more scene—from before rather than after the battle—which sheds considerable light on Yudhiṣṭhira's involvements. It falls into place directly after that other "preparation" (*udyoga*) for battle in which, after Arjuna and Duryodhana have both come to Krishna's bedside, it is determined that the latter will side with the Pāṇḍavas.[27] In one scene we see how Arjuna and Krishna will work together; in the next we see how Yudhiṣṭhira works alone.

[27] See above, Chapter 5, at n. 1.

Hearing that war is likely, Śalya—the king of Madra and brother of Mādrī, Nakula and Sahadeva's mother[28]—sets out with his troops to join forces with the Pāṇḍavas. But when Duryodhana learns of this, he has groups of festive halls or pavilions (*sabhās*) built to welcome him. We thus see Śalya in a circumstance identical with one in which we earlier saw Krishna, for each has his progress to Hāstinapura halted by such *sabhās* which Duryodhana and, in Krishna's case, Dhṛtarāṣṭra have constructed to put them under obligation to the Kurus.[29] We will see contrasts and juxtapositions elsewhere between Krishna and Śalya, but in these present scenes, Krishna is beyond temptation, "not even looking" at the *sabhās*, while Śalya's response reveals a most significant flaw in his character: "There [at the most splendid *sabhā*], preoccupied with sense-enjoyments [*viṣayairyuktaḥ*] that were beautiful and fit for beings superior to men [*atimānuṣaiḥ*], he thought himself to be extraordinary and despised Indra [*avamene puraṃdaram*]. And that bull among kṣatriyas, thrilled [*prahṛṣṭaḥ*], then asked the servants: 'Which of Yudhiṣṭhira's men built these *sabhās*? . . . They deserve to be rewarded'" (5:8,9–10). At this point out of the wings comes Duryodhana and claims the reward for himself: that Śalya be "the leader of my entire army."[30] Śalya is bound by his own sensually motivated generosity. But upon agreeing to Duryodhana's terms, he still insists on visiting the Pāṇḍavas, and when he arrives and tells of his new employ, Yudhiṣṭhira wastes no time in responding:

[28] Probably one key to the proximity of these episodes is that both Krishna and Śalya are related to the Pāṇḍavas through the latter's mothers, the two maternal alliances being thus dealt with consecutively.

[29] For the scene involving Krishna, see above, Chapter 6, following n. 49.

[30] *Sarvasenāpraṇetā*; this is curious, for Śalya is the last marshal, not the first; one might align this with Ruben's notion that the fight with Śalya was perhaps the original single battle of the great war (see *Krishna*, p. 231); but Duryohana probably just anticipates that Śalya will eventually be his *senāpati*.

It is well done. . . . Fortunately, there is only one thing that I wish done by you, O lord of the earth. Here you are the equal of Vāsudeva in battle. When the duel between Karṇa and Arjuna occurs, there is no doubt that Karṇa's driving will be done by you. On that occasion, if you wish me well, Arjuna is to be protected by you and the destruction of Karṇa's energy [*tejovadhas*] is to be achieved, producing our victory. Even though this surely ought not to be done, you should do it [*akartavyamapi hyetatkartumarhasi*],[31] O uncle. [5:8,25–27]

Śalya's alleged parity with Krishna draws no comment. The former simply agrees, point by point, without hesitation, to do Yudhiṣṭhira's bidding. But then his words take a surprising turn. Referring sympathetically to the hardships suffered by the Pāṇḍavas, he predicts that they will "have their end in happiness" (8,35). Then, referring to the "great suffering" (*mahādduḥkham*) once experienced by Indra and his wife, he makes the point that even the gods must sometimes endure misery (36–37). When Yudhiṣṭhira asks how Indra and his wife suffered, Śalya launches into the "history" of Indra's sins that was met in the first part of this chapter: the trilogy of Indra's sin-ridden conflicts with Viśvarūpa, Vṛtra, and Nahuṣa.

The question now is whether there is a significant connection between the myth and its place in the epic. Certainly Śalya's initial reasons for reciting it are unrevealing and would be more suitable if the Pāṇḍavas were still "miserable" in the forest. The Indra cycle, as we have seen, is more than just a tale of "woes"; it is, in its various forms, a tale of increasing defamation through flawed triumphs leading to a temporary loss of heaven's throne and a final restoration. Fortunately, when Śalya has concluded his narrative, he gives another, much more satisfactory reason for its telling:

[31] Some Northern manuscripts insert this concluding admission of immoral intent a second time, just before the actual request; see *Udyogaparvan* 62*, after 5:8,25.

Even so, you will obtain sovereignty [*rājyam*] as did Śakra, having slain Vṛtra. . . . The ill-behaved Nahuṣa, that brahmin hater, was overthrown by Agastya's curse and ruined for endless years. So too your wicked-souled foes—Karṇa and Duryodhana to begin with—will quickly meet with destruction. Then will you enjoy the earth [*medinīm*; "she having fatness or fertility"], bounded by the ocean, together with your brothers and Draupadī. . . . This story of Indra's victory, of status equal to the Veda, should be heard by a king desirous of victory when his armies have been arrayed. Thus do I have you hear of victory, O best of victors. [*upākhyānamidaṃ śakra-vijayaṃ vedasaṃmitam / rājñā vyūdheṣvanikeṣu śrotavyaṃ jayamicchatā / / tasmātsaṃśrāvayāmi tvāṃ vijayaṃ jayatāṃ vara*; 5:18,12–17]

It is most important to stress that, as the "preparations" for the battle begin, it is just after the Dharmarāja has proposed his first "improper" (*akartavya*) act that he hears a recital of the full story of Indra's tainted victories. This can hardly be fortuitous: the poets have seen the rapports between the myth and the epic and have juxtaposed the two of them. Let us also note that it is Śalya who forecasts Yudhiṣṭhira's enjoyment of the earth. Indeed, one is pointed toward a matter of considerable irony. Śalya, the narrator of Indra's conquests, is one of the chief figures Yudhiṣṭhira will have to overcome.

CHAPTER 10

The Deaths of the Four Marshals

The *Mahābhārata* war is the scene of numerous questionable acts which the text does not hesitate to call sins.[1] Nearly all are committed by heroes on the Pāṇḍava side, and the guiding hand seems almost always to be that of Krishna.[2] There is, however, in one set of incidents, a definite and consistent series of involvements by two figures: Krishna and Yudhiṣṭhira. This is the series that provides the very scansion of the epic war: the deaths of the four *senāpatis*, "armylords" or "marshals," of the Kaurava side, the deaths of the four figures who give their names to the four battle *parvans*. Let us now take them up one at a time.

Death of Bhīṣma

Deep in the night after the ninth day on which Bhīṣma has played havoc with the Pāṇḍava troops, the latter take counsel

[1] Against this usage (rather unconvincingly), see Ruben, *Krishna*, pp. 257–58, and above, Chapter 9, n. 22.

[2] Outside of the four episodes discussed below, which have their own interior coherence, the main cluster occurs in the *Droṇaparvan* and includes Krishna's most audacious and miraculous tricks: stepping in front of Bhagadatta's Vaiṣṇava weapon to turn it into a garland of flowers (7:28,18); urging Arjuna to cut off Bhuriśravas' arms from an unseen position to protect Sātyaki (7:117,47–118,2); making it appear that the sun has set so that Arjuna can kill Jayadratha (7:121); and tricking Karṇa into using the weapon he had saved for Arjuna to kill Ghaṭotkaca (7:154). Each episode has an atmosphere of its own and seems to have been developed as an independent narrative.

with their allies. After some deliberation, Yudhiṣṭhira turns to Krishna for advice "not incompatible with our dharma" (*svadharmasyāvirodhena*; 6:103,24). Krishna's answer is the first mention of this episode's dominant theme, and it comes up in connection with the question of *svadharma*. It concerns the intricate matter of fulfilling one's vows. First Krishna offers, in effect, to go against his word, his vow to participate in the battle only as a noncombatant: "Command me, O Pāṇḍava; out of friendship [*sauhārdād*] I will fight with Bhīṣma. . . . I will slay Bhīṣma in battle if Arjuna does not wish to do so" (103,28–29). Second, indicating that this matter of vows is of deepening complexity, he adds: "What was formerly vowed [*pratijñātam*] by Arjuna at Upaplavya in the presence of Ulūka—'I will slay the son of Gaṅgā' [Bhīṣma]—that vow [*vacas*] of the intelligent Pārtha is to be kept [*parirakṣyam*] by me. Permitted by Pārtha, no doubt it will be accomplished by me. Or else, as this burden is but moderate for Arjuna in battle, he will slay Bhīṣma [himself]" (103,35–37).

In answer, Yudhiṣṭhira will not, of course, cause others to break their vows: "I cannot bear out of regard for my own goal to make you untruthful [*tvamanṛtam*]; not fighting, give assistance as you have promised" (103,43). Far better than making others break their vows is getting them to keep them. Says Yudhiṣṭhira: "A certain agreement [*samaya*] was made with Bhīṣma by me. . . : 'For your sake I will advise, but I will not fight in any way. . . .' Surely he is my giver of sovereignty as well as of counsel [*sa hi rājyasya me dātā mantrasyaiva ca*], O Mādhava" (103,44–45). Yudhiṣṭhira thus recalls a scene just before the war. Crossing the lines and "taking leave of his superiors" (*gurūnanumānya*; 6:41,17 and 18), he had asked the latter—Bhīṣma, Droṇa, Kṛpa, and Śalya—for their blessings and, in the case of the first two, the means to conquer them.[3] To this second request, Bhīṣma had replied: "It is not yet time

[3] Hopkins, "Ruling Caste," p. 200, n. 3, and Winternitz, *History of Indian Literature*, I, 317, n. 2, all too easily take this scene as an interpolation.

for my death. Come to me again" (41,43). By keeping Bhīṣma to this invitation, or "agreement," it will be possible to bring about his death. Thus it is no accident that in the remainder of his speech Yudhiṣṭhira places a high value on Bhīṣma's celebrated penchant for keeping vows:[4] "Therefore, O Madhusūdana, together with you we shall all, once again approaching Devavrata ['He whose Vow is Godly'; see n. 4], ask after the means of his own death. . . . He will speak words to our advantage, and do so truly [*tathyam*] . . .; as he will say, O Krishna, so shall I do in battle. Of firm vow[s] [*dhṛtavrata*[5]], he is our giver of victory and counsel" (103,45–48).

Krishna's response—continuing to accent the interplay of personal commitments—has an air of shrewdness: "What you say is always pleasing to me, O long-armed one. Devavrata Bhīṣma, active, would scorche [us] by a mere glance. . . . He will be able to speak the truth [*satyam*], especially if asked by you" (103,50–51). Krishna thus puts Yudhiṣṭhira into a position where an aspect of his own omnivirtuous character becomes the means to an unvirtuous act. But the aspect in question is not as clearly delineated as it will be in later incidents. We have just seen that in talking about vows, truth (*satya*) can serve as the virtue which links Bhīṣma and Yudhiṣṭhira.

[4] Born with the names Gañgādatta or Gāñgeya (as the son of Gañgā) and Devavrata ("Divine Vow"; 1:90,50), his most popular name, Bhīṣma ("The Terrible"), reflects what the name Devavrata had anticipated; for, to satisfy his father Śaṃtanu's desires for more sons and a second wife, "Devavrata" provided assurance that this wife's sons would have no rivals to the throne by undertaking the divinely acclaimed "terrible" (*bhīṣma*) vows of renouncing his own title to the throne and of adopting the celibate *brahmacarya* mode of life (1:94,77–94). In gratitude, Śaṃtanu granted him the boon of "death at his own will" (*svacchandamaraṇam*; 94), that is, indefinite postponement of death.

[5] In the *Ṛg Veda* the epithet *dhṛtavrata* is attached to Varuṇa and to Mitrāvaruṇā; see *ṚV* 1:25,6 and 10; 1:44,14; 8:25,2 and 8, and Gonda, *Vedic God Mitra*, pp. 2 and 29, Schmidt, *Vedisch* vratá, pp. 52–54. Gonda's words (p. 10) that the *vratá* relates to "'rules of conduct,' 'observances,' and 'institutions'" and is not primarily "a verbal affair" are worthy of note; but where the *vrata* is personal and expressed orally, I see no reason to reject the translation "vow."

This does not mean, however, that the vow is to be reduced to a form of truth; rather, the latter virtue is the former's guarantee: one's vows and personal "rules of conduct" (see n. 5) are fulfilled if one is truthful to them. Yudhiṣṭhira, however, is not—like Arjuna—renowned for his vows in a way that might complement Bhīṣma. But they do share a virtue, one being its incarnation and the other, especially after the war, its leading authority: the virtue of dharma. And, as suggested earlier, there are reasons to regard the vow (*vrata*) as a specialization of this more general quality.[6]

With this correlation in mind, the scene upon the Pāṇḍavas' return visit to Bhīṣma's tent gains in depth of meaning. Greeted profusely by Bhīṣma, "Yudhiṣṭhira the son of Dharma, depressed at heart [*dīnātmā*], said: 'O thou conversant with dharma (*dharmajña*), how shall we conquer?'" (103,57–58). And once again, he asks how Bhīṣma might be slain. On the first visit Bhīṣma had responded to this question elliptically: "I do not see him [*tam*], O Kaunteya, who might conquer me while I am fighting in a challenge—not any man [*pumānkaścid*], not even Śatakratu [Indra] himself" (6:41,41).[7] While Yudhiṣṭhira shows no signs of reading between the lines, it is likely that Bhīṣma is tipping him off that no "male being" (*puṃs*) may slay him. On the second visit, Yudhiṣṭhira seems to have picked up this apparent riddle when he says: "A slayer of elephant riders, chariot riders, horsemen, and foot soldiers [*narāśvarathanāgānāṃ hantāram*], O slayer of hostile heroes, what man [*pumān*] is there able to slay you?" (103,62). This might be phrased: "As you are invincible by *men* from each of the four divisions of the army, what *man* can kill you?"[8] It thus seems, from this and a number of other exchanges between Yudhiṣṭhira and

[6] See above, Chapter 8, at n. 45.

[7] See also the variants to 6:41,43: Bhīṣma saying in the CE that he knows no "enemy," *śatrum*, who can slay him, but many manuscripts retaining what is here the more specific *tam*, the masculine pronoun.

[8] Ganguli-Roy (*Mahabharata*, V: *Bhishma Parva*, 290) has "cars, steeds, men, and elephants"; though gramatically correct, it overlooks the absurdity of slaying "cars."

authorities on dharma, that one of his royal functions is to decipher the often riddlelike character of "subtle [*sūkṣma*] dharma." The exchange with Bhīṣma is thus the third in a series of incidents involving what might be called royal dharmic riddles.[9] This would include not only the riddle test of Yudhiṣṭhira by the Yakṣa, Dharma incarnate.[10] When the Pāṇḍavas are on their way to the lacquer house, Vidura, another incarnation of Dharma, tells Yudhiṣṭhira of the trap Duryodhana has set for them, communicating with Yudhiṣṭhira through a series of riddles that only the two of them can understand (1:133,18–29). Moreover, in all of these cases, Yudhiṣṭhira is able to "save" his brothers.

So far, then, the drama of the vows has developed through three phases: first, Krishna's promptings recalling his and Arjuna's vows; second, Yudhiṣṭhira's reflections, recalling the vows of Bhīṣma; and third, Yudhiṣṭhira's confrontation of Bhīṣma, with whom he has a special dharmic rapport, to fulfill an earlier vow or promise. Bhīṣma's answer leads to a fourth phase. The only way to slay the unslayable Bhīṣma will be through one of his own vows. On certain conditions, which he lays down with precision, he would be indisposed to fight:

> With [literally, "in"] one who has abandoned his weapon or fallen down, with one whose standard or armor is loosed, with one who is fleeing or terrified, or who says "I am yours," with women or with one having a woman's name [*striyāṃ strīnāmadheye ca*], with one who is maimed or who has but one son, with one who has not produced offspring [? *aprasūte*] or who is disagreeable to look at—[with these] battle is not pleasing to me [*na yuddhaṃ rocate mama*]. [103,72–73]

There is nothing unusual in this list, echoing other guidelines for fair combat,[11] except for the references to women. On this

[9] On kings and riddles, cf. the riddle exchanges (*brahmodyas*) at the end of the Aśvamedha, mostly between the various priests (*ŚB* 13,5,2,11–22), but the last one asked of the *adhvaryu* by the royal sacrificer (3).

[10] See above, Chapter 7, at n. 106.

[11] See Hopkins, "Ruling Caste," p. 228.

point Bhīṣma has more to say: "Listen, O Pārtha, to this resolution [or vow; *saṃkalpam*] of mine, formerly thought out. Having seen an inauspicious sign [or "banner"; *amaṅgalyadhvajam*; cf. 103,78], I will never fight" (103,74). Bhīṣma makes it explicit that, in particular, his "resolution" concerns the "inauspicious sign" of one who was "formerly a woman, afterwards a man" (*strī pūrvam paścātpuṃs*; 103,76), that is, the Pāñcāla prince Śikhaṇḍin.[12]

From here on, as Bhīṣma maps out his own death, the final phase of this episode is one of deepening irony. First, Bhīṣma hints at the reversals in virtues that his proposed "means of death" will involve for the two principal Pāṇḍavas. As for Indra's son: "Let Arjuna, coated in mail, heroic in battle [*samare śūraḥ*], having placed Śikhaṇḍin before him, attack me quickly with arrows" (103,77). As for Dharma's son (resorting here not to the Critical Edition but to several Devanāgarī manuscripts[13]): "Do this, O Kaunteya, as indicated, O thou of excellent vows [*suvrata*]; then will you conquer the assembled Dhārtaraṣṭras in battle" (103,82). Despite his overall allegiance to dharma, Yudhiṣṭhira uses vows only in a way that he will later judge to be sinful;[14] and Arjuna will not show much heroism having to fight from behind another's back.

The last touch is then applied by Krishna. When the "sinless" Arjuna, "burning with grief and feeling shame" (*duḥkhasaṃtaptaḥ savrīḍam*; 84), rejects the part assigned him, Krishna draws everything full circle: "Having formerly vowed

[12] See 5:170ff; Śikhaṇḍin was in his previous life the princess Ambā of Kāśi, one of three sisters whom Bhīṣma abducted from their Svayaṃvara to be his half-brother Vicitravīrya's wives; but as Ambā had chosen another man, King Śālva (see Chapter 4), she was allowed to leave and go to him. When he would not accept a once-abducted woman, however, she became an ascetic and obtained a boon from Śiva enabling her to be reborn as a man so as to exact her revenge against Bhīṣma.

[13] The CE reads *yathoktaṃ vacanam mama* for *yathoktam mama suvrata*, the latter seemingly an insightful variant or alteration.

[14] This would seem to be the unspecified sin referred to and lamented in his *mea culpa*; see above, Chapter 9, at and following n. 26.

Bhīṣma's death in battle [*pratijñāya vadham . . . pura bhīṣmasya saṃyuge*], O Jiṣṇu, firm in the duty of a kṣatriya [*kṣatradharme sthitaḥ*], how can you not kill him?" (103,90). Not only is the link drawn once again between vows and dharma; we are taken back to the first phase of this drama where Krishna had offered to break his own vow in order to fulfill Arjuna's vow for him.

In summary, Yudhiṣṭhira appears guilty of a misuse of the vow.

Death of Droṇa

On the fifth day of Droṇa's marshalship, the Pāṇḍavas, seeing the great carnage brought on by Droṇa's prowess and Arjuna's reluctance to oppose him, despair of victory. Krishna then confers with Arjuna on how to get Droṇa to lay aside his weapons: "Casting aside virtue [*dharmamutsṛjya*], . . . let a device be adopted for victory" (*āsthīyatāṃ jaye yogo*; 7:164,68). Someone, he says, should tell Droṇa that Aśvatthāman, his son, has fallen; then he will desist. Although Arjuna does not approve of this advice, everyone else does, and Yudhiṣṭhira accepts it "with difficulty" (*kṛcchreṇa*; 164,70). This is reminiscent of the behavior of these two in the slaying of Bhīṣma: Arjuna "grieved and ashamed," Yudhiṣṭhira grieved but calculating. Bhīma then slays a terrible elephant named Aśvatthāman and announces treacherously that someone with that name has fallen. But Droṇa, not believing Bhīma, continues to fight. Then a host of famous Ṛṣis descends toward Droṇa to discourage him from further fighting. Twice urging him to lay down his weapons, their main argument is that he has overstepped the boundaries of caste:[15] "You are fighting unrighteously [*adharmatas*]. This is the time for your death. . . . Henceforth you should not perform this most cruel karman

[15] The argument is repeated by Bhīma (7:165,28–32), and upon hearing it again (along with Yudhiṣṭhira's confirmation of Aśvatthāman's death) Droṇa lays down his arms. It is raised again by Dhṛṣṭadyumna (7:168,23–24) to justify his part in the killing, especially in the words, "fallen off from his *svadharma*, he took up *kṣatradharma*" (24).

again. Knowing the Vedas and Vedāṅgas and having the virtue of truth as your chief object [*satyadharmaparasya*], especially being a brahmin, this [fighting] is not suitable for you" (164,89–92). Hearing these words, which call attention to Droṇa's allegiance to "truth," Droṇa cheerlessly asks Yudhiṣṭhira whether Aśvatthāman has been slain or not, for, according to the narrator Saṃjaya: "Droṇa had firm knowledge [*sthirā buddhir*] that Yudhiṣṭhira would not speak an untruth [*anṛtam*], even for the sake of the sovereignty of the three worlds [*trayāṇāmapi lokānāmaiśvaryārthe*]. Therefore he asked him especially, and no one else, for in this Pāṇḍava, beginning with childhood, Droṇa surely had his hope for truth" (*satyāśā*; 164,95–96).

As we saw in Chapters 7 and 8, this "sovereignty over the three worlds" is often (and sometimes by Krishna) said to require certain virtues. This seems to be Droṇa's assumption here (as it will also be Arjuna's), and he is attentive above all to the virtue of "truth." But in Krishna the opposite assumption now seems to be operative: sovereignty also requires sins. Thus he tells Yudhiṣṭhira that a lie is his only course: "Save us from Droṇa. Untruth may be better than truth [*satyājjyāyo 'nṛtaṃ bhavet*]. By telling an untruth for the saving of life, untruth does not touch one" (*na spṛśyate 'nṛtaḥ*; 98–99). Bhīma also tells Yudhiṣṭhira that he is known "in the world of men as one who is truthful" (*satyavānhi nṛloke*; 104); and, after some deliberation, Yudhiṣṭhira is ready: "Sunk in the fear of untruth [*atathyabhaye magno*] but clinging to victory [*jaye sakto*], Yudhiṣṭhira said to him [Dorṇa] inaudibly [*avyaktam*]: 'An elephant is slain.'[16] Before this his chariot had remained four fingers above the earth, but when he said this his vehicle touched the earth" (*tasya pūrvaṃ rathaḥ pṛthvyāścaturaṅgula uttaraḥ / babhūvaivam tu*

[16] Ganguli-Roy (VI, 448): "Yudhishthira distinctly said that Asvatthaman was dead, adding indistinctly the word elephant"; thus drawing from the later description of the episode by Kṛpa (165,115–16), no doubt fairly, for Yudhiṣṭhira has certainly conveyed to Droṇa the first part of this message even if the text records only the qualification.

tenokte tasya vāhāspṛśanmahīm; 106–7). Soon, after more bloodshed, Droṇa lays down his weapons, seats himself on his chariot where he devotes himself to yoga, and tranquilly ascends to Brahmaloka before the head is cut from his lifeless body by his determined adversary, the Pāñcāla prince Dhṛṣṭadyumna (165,33–47).

This illustrates the main point: that, similar to the way that he caused Bhīṣma's death by a misuse of the vow, Yudhiṣṭhira slays Droṇa by a misuse of the truth—in this case an actual lie. But, most intriguing and equally significant is the amplification of this episode in its retelling and immediate aftermath.

The first to retell it is Kṛpa, Droṇa's brother-in-law and fellow fighting brahmin, who must break the news to Aśvatthāman. On the whole he is quite "accurate," repeating certain of Saṃjaya's phrases almost word for word.[17] However, in one point he adds and in another he subtracts. Yudhiṣṭhira's lie is given a fuller treatment; not only is its inaudible part cited (see note 16), but the "loudly" spoken part is given as well: "He for whose sake you bear weapons and looking upon whom you live, your ever-cherished son Aśvatthāman has been overthrown" (165,16). Thus the lie appears in a much starker and more "disagreeable" form, evoking the leave-taking scene before the war in which Droṇa tells Yudhiṣṭhira how he may be conquered: "I shall abandon my weapon in battle having heard something very disagreeable" (*sumahadapriyam*; 6:41,61). One gets the impression that Droṇa stops fighting in grief not so much for his son but because, as one who is "clear-sighted into the nature of the world" (*lokatattvavicakṣaṇaḥ*; 165,119), he has at last heard these "greatly disagreeable" (*mahadapriyam*; 165,117) words. As to his omission, Kṛpa leaves out the visit of the Ṛṣis and the ascent to Brahmaloka—the latter with significant repercussions.

When Aśvattháman reacts, the focus of blame begins to shift. Having heard not only about Yudhiṣṭhira's lie but about

[17] Cf. 164,68 and 165,110; 164,70 and 165,112; 164,106 and 165,115.

Dhṛṣṭadyumna's dastardly act of seizing Droṇa's hair and cutting off his head, thinking that the latter is not merely an indignity (*paribhava*; 166,24) but the physical cause of Droṇa's death,[18] he wavers between blaming the one and blaming the other. His first words are undoubtedly as scathing a repudiation of Yudhiṣṭhira as one will find: "How my father was slain by wretches [*kṣudrair*] when he had put down his weapons, how a sin [*pāpam*] was perpetrated by one bearing the banner of virtue [*dharmadhvajavatā*],[19] this is known to me; I have heard about the dishonorable act of the very mischievous son of Dharma" (*anāryaṃ sunṛśaṃsasya dharmaputrasya*; 166,19). Nowhere is the ambiguity of his status as Dharmarāja more apparent. But Aśvatthāman's disgust with Yudhiṣṭhira is overshadowed by his rage at Dhṛṣṭadyumna, leading him to utter the fateful vow that will result in the latter's death (106,28–29).

The compass of blame turns back one more time toward Yudhiṣṭhira and then jumps wildly in all directions as a quarrel breaks out among the Pāṇḍavas and their allies over the responsibility for this and other sins. In Arjuna's speech the blame swings toward Yudhiṣṭhira, and here we have the reaction of the most sin-conscious of all the Pāṇḍavas to Yudhiṣṭhira's most glaring sin. His insights do not disappoint us. For one thing, in leveling the brunt of the blame at Yudhiṣṭhira, Arjuna sees his brother's sin against the background of the royal virtues: "The guru was attended upon falsely by you for the sake of sovereignty [*mithyā bhavatā*

[18] The CE clears up a source of confusion here: Drona's ascent, says Saṃjaya, was seen by only five men: "I myself, Arjuna, the brahmin Kṛpa, son of Saradvat, Krishna, and Yudhiṣṭhira" (165,42–43). It was not observed by Aśvatthāman (*bhāradvājasya cātmaja*), whom many Northern manuscripts substitute for Kṛpa. One can only wonder at Kṛpa's silence; he lets Aśvatthāman think that Droṇa has gone (merely) to *vīraloka*, "the world of heroes" (166,22).

[19] See Ganguli-Roy (VI, 400, n. 1): "Dharmadhvajin, literally means a person bearing the standard of virtue; hence, a hypocrite, sanctimoniously talking only virtue and morality but acting differently"; cf. Hopkins, "Ruling Caste," p. 246.

rājyakāraṇāt]; indeed, by being conversant with dharma [*dharmajñena satā*], very great is the adharma you performed. [Thinking:] 'This son of Pāṇḍu is endowed with every virtue [*sarvadharmopapanno*] and is my disciple; he will not speak falsely,' he put his trust in you" (167,33–34). This, in effect, verifies the assumption I attributed to Droṇa earlier: that Droṇa would expect the virtue of "truth" in an omnivirtuous pretender to world sovereignty and that he could rely on him for its exercise. Moreover, Arjuna is adept at detecting oppositions. Not only has Yudhiṣṭhira used dharma to perform adharma; more specifically, Arjuna charges Yudhiṣṭhira with "untruth in the garb of truth" (*satyakañcukam . . . anṛtam*; 35).

Most intriguing, Arjuna is convinced that this sin and these oppositions affect not only Yudhiṣṭhira but all the brothers. He thus accepts the guilt even while protesting his own innocence: "Surely while I was crying out vehemently, eagerly longing for the guru, having discarded his own dharma [*avakīrya svadharmam*] the disciple slew the guru. When the greater part of our life is gone and only the shortest time remains, now this great injustice [*adharmo . . . mahān*] has caused even its [the remainder's] disfigurement" (*vikāra*; 167,41–42). Again: "Harm was done to this old guru, ever our benefactor, by ourselves [*asmābhiḥ*], dishonorable and of trifling insight, for the sake of sovereignty" (167,47).

Such admissions point to a delicate balance: just as "all the virtues" (which, Arjuna says, Droṇa ascribed to Yudhiṣṭhira in this very scene) are to be found not only in Yudhiṣṭhira singly but in the Pāṇḍavas collectively, so too is there a sharing of the royal sins. Both are intertwined with the symbolism of sovereignty, and this symbolism—as we have seen as far back as our discussions of Śrī and Draupadī—is shared by the king with his brothers. All are "Indras among men."

Death of Karṇa

One of the factors leading to the death of the third Kuru marshal, Karṇa, was outlined at the end of Chapter 9:

Yudhiṣṭhira's scheme to have Śalya destroy Karṇa's "energy" (*tejovadhas*; 5:8,27 and 6:41,81) in battle. From this, an important measure of the responsibility for Karṇa's death belongs to Yudhiṣṭhira. In fact, thinking at one point that Karṇa is dead, Yudhiṣṭhira exults at the elimination of this most personally troubling of all his foes:

Thirteen years have passed through which, terrified [*bhīta*], O Dhanaṃjaya, I obtained neither sleep at night nor comfort [*sukham*] by day. Filled with hatred for him, I burn [*tasya dveṣeṇa saṃyuktaḥ paridahye*]. . . . My time has passed reflecting on how I might destroy Karṇa in battle. Waking and sleeping, O son for Kuntī, I always see Karṇa; indeed, this universe has everywhere become Karṇa [*tatra tatraiva karṇabhūtamidaṃ jagat*]. Truly, wherever I go, terrified by Karṇa, O Dhanaṃjaya, there I surely behold Karṇa before me. [8:46,16–20]

But to fix the motive and place the blame does not clarify the nature of the crime. For this we must examine the repercussions of Yudhiṣṭhira's scheme, that is, the favor he exacted from Śalya.

On the morning of the second and last day of Karṇa's marshalship, after a frustrating first day, Duryodhana and Karṇa agree (as Yudhiṣṭhira had foreseen) that the latter's only chance against Arjuna will be to have Śalya as his charioteer (8,22). Finally persuaded, Śalya is thus provided with the occasion to begin the "destruction of Karṇa's energy" as the two set out for the crucial duel. This he does, first by scorning, one might even say "satirizing,"[20] Karṇa's courage and eagerness to fight (8:27,18–27). Karṇa's answer is the first articulation of the theme around which this episode revolves and which stems directly from Yudhiṣṭhira's intrigues: "Relying on my

[20] His rebukes culminate in a series of comparisons: Karṇa is to Arjuna as a jackal to a lion, a mouse to a cat, as falsehood to truth, as poison to *amṛta* (8:27,50–52); see Donald Ward's "On the Poets and Poetry of the Indo-Europeans," *JIES*, I (1973), 127–44, on the archaic character of satire and invective verse (think of the *sūta*, "charioteer," as bard!) in Indo-European societies.

own vigor [*vīryam*], I am seeking Arjuna in battle. But you, an enemy with the face of a friend [*mitramukhaḥ śatruḥ*], seek to terrify me" (27,28). The death of Karṇa will involve a betrayal of friendship.

When Śalya's rebukes become still more stinging, Karṇa says that he is prepared for whatever may happen and begins to trade insults of his own:

> You are evil-natured, foolish, unskilled in great battles. Overcome with fear, out of terror you utter such nonsense. Or you are praising them for some other reason, O you who are born in a bad country [*kudeśaja*]. Having slain them in battle, I will certainly slay you together with all your kinsmen. O you who are born in a sinful country [*pāpadeśaja*], you mean-minded low defiler of the kṣatriya class [*durbuddhe kṣudra kṣatriyapāṃsana*], having become a friend [*suhṛd*], why, like an enemy, do you frighten me with the two Kṛṣṇas? [8:27,66–68]

Two aspects of the theme of friendship have surfaced here, which it will be best to treat separately: the evocation of the two Kṛṣṇas and the references to the wickedness of Śalya's homeland.

First, it is to the credit of Walter Ruben to have noticed that this "insult contest between Śalya as charioteer and Karṇa" is "a caricature-like counterpart to the *Bhagavad Gītā*."[21] Nowhere is this contrast more apparent than when Karṇa sets out with Śalya—supposedly the most skillful of charioteers—at the reins, and the horses tumble to the ground (8:26,36). Throughout the episode are consistent references to parallels and contrasts between the relationship of Arjuna and Krishna and that of Karṇa and Śalya. Indeed, Krishna and Śalya have been observed as a pair before: both maternal relatives of the Pāṇḍavas, and each responding differently to the elaborate *sabhās* constructed by the Kauravas to win them over or impress them.[22] Now it is another comparison, made by Karṇa, that

[21] Ruben, *Krishna*, p. 221, n. 11.

[22] See above, Chapter 9, at and following n. 27.

tells us why Karṇa himself requests Duryodhana to assign Śalya as his driver: "Surely Śalya is superior to Krishna and surely I am superior to Arjuna. As [Krishna] knows horsemanship . . . , even so does Śalya. . . . As there is no bow-bearer equal to myself with weapons, so there is no one equal to Śalya in the guiding of horses" (8:22,53–56). Using these lines of flattery, Duryodhana at last gets Śalya to agree (23,48–50). And finally, as they are about to fight, each warrior asks his driver what he would do should his companion die. While Śalya says he will slay both Krishna and Arjuna (74), Krishna says smilingly that if such a thing should occur it would mean the "overturning of the world" (*lokaparyasanam*), and adds, only as a sort of afterthought, that he would slay both Karṇa and Śalya (77).

If there is a lesson in these contrasts, it would seem to be that Arjuna and Krishna's success will be related to their true friendship, while Karṇa and Śalya's failure will be related to their false friendship. The friendship of Arjuna and Krishna thus merits some attention. Here, it is not solely a matter of their mystical identity as Nara and Nārāyaṇa.[23] Rather, we are concerned with a specific social or dharmic bond. In the beginning of Chapter 6, I sought to differentiate levels of Krishna's self-disclosure in the *Gītā*: first, in the fourth chapter, having to do with dharma and the yuga structure; and second, in the

[23] Since I discuss Arjuna and Krishna's relationship mainly through their identifications as Indra's son and Viṣṇu's *avatāra*, a few words are due on their other identificaiion: whereas the Indra-Viṣṇu transposition can be traced to the *Ṛg Veda*, the Nara-Nārāyaṇa identification seems rooted in more recent themes. Nārāyaṇa appears first in name in *ŚB* 12,3,4 and 13,6,1 and then not again (unmentioned in Upaniṣads) until the epic. Biardeau has offered the most convincing discussion (EMH, 1, pp. 33–37; 2, pp. 68–80; 3, pp. 48–56; *Clefs*, pp. 156, 224), seeing the god Puruṣa-Nārāyaṇa of *ŚB* as the model for the pair Nara-Nārāyaṇa (*puruṣa* = *nara* in the epic); see also van Buitenen, *The Mahābhārata*, I, xxi and 435, n. 1.0. Guesses at Narāyaṇa's origins do not inspire confidence; see R. G. Bhandarkar, *Vaiṣṇavism, Śaivism, and Minor Religious Systems* (1913; repr. Benares: Indological Book House, 1965), pp. 35–38; L. B. Keny, "The Origin of Nārāyaṇa," *ABORI*, XXII (1942), 250–56; Jaiswal, *Origin and Development*, pp. 32–51.

eleventh chapter where Krishna discloses himself as Kāla (Time), with *mokṣa*, *bhakti*, and the kalpa structure. Recalling that at the end of the eleventh chapter, Krishna says he reveals his universal form only to his *bhaktas* (11,54), let us now note why he tells Arjuna of his role concerning the maintenance of dharma from yuga to yuga:

This very same by Me to thee today,
  This ancient discipline, is proclaimed.
Thou art my devotee and friend [*bhakto 'si me sakhā ca*], that is why;
  For this is a supreme secret. [4,3]

Friendship (*sakhyam*) is thus a suitable relationship for understanding Krishna's dharmic role, but, as Arjuna says, it is not adequate to carry the devotional appreciation of Krishna in his universal form. Thus, after the theophany, Arjuna apologizes for his earlier familiarity with Krishna, that is, as he puts it, for:

Whatever I said rashly, thinking thee my boon companion [*sakhe 'ti matvā*],
  Calling Thee "Kṛṣṇa, Yādava, Companion (*sakhe*)!" [11,41]

Arjuna is, of course, forgiven his familiarities, and he stands as the exemplar of both of these relationships to Krishna: those of *sakhi* and *bhakta*, the former implying a variety of social and dharmic relations,[24] the latter a means to salvation. In fact, the *Gītā* seems to reserve the word *sakhi* solely for the "companionship" of Arjuna and Krishna and to use other terms where "friendship" is discussed more generally.[25] The term, however, is one with a "prehistory." As seen in Chapter 9, it describes the relationship between Indra and Vṛtra, or, in variants, between Indra and Namuci.[26] Karṇa uses it, although not

[24] Cf. Ganguli-Roy (*Mahabharata*, XII: *Asvamedha Parva*, 166, n. 1): "Draupadi was always styled by Krisha as his 'sakhi' or 'friend.'"

[25] For *sakhi*, see also 11,44; for other terms (*suhṛd*, *mitra*, *bandhu*), see 5,27; 6,9; 9,18; 14,25.

[26] Although the epic passages discussed in Chapter 9 tell of Indra breaking "friendship" with Vṛtra, the story is first told about Indra and Namuci;

exclusively, to address Śalya. And, with some likely Indo-European parallels, it provides a key term in Dumézil's analysis of the typical sin—the breaking of a "friendship" or warrior pact—committed, as it was by Indra, against the second function. As Dumézil puts it: "The translation 'friendship' is inadequate, but it is difficult to establish with precision the variety of social relationship which the word *sakhi*—probably from the same root as the Latin *socius*—signifies."[27]

It seems, then, that the poets have found in the "insult contest" between Karṇa and Śalya—together on a chariot before their crucial battle—a perfect counterpart to the exemplary communication between Arjuna and Krishna in the *Gītā*. One friend offers encouragement, the other discouragement. Against such a background of contrasts concerning two warriors and their charioteers the *Mahābhārata* amplifies the theme of friendship to its fullest extent.

Turning back to the insult contest, we can afford to be much briefer on the second matter raised by Karṇa's first denunciation—the wickedness of Śalya's homeland—for it will claim our attention later. Karṇa sees this baseness as the very reason why "true" friendship with Śalya is impossible: "Madrakas are always injurers of friends [*mitradhrun*]; whoever hates us, he is a Madraka. There is, in a Madraka of mean speech, the lowest of men, no friendship" (or "alliance," "association": *saṃgatam*; 8:27,73; cf. 83–84). And then friendship (*sauhārdam, saṃgatam*) is discussed (27,79–83) alongside ritual purity (*śaucam*; 80), with the analogy drawn that friendship with a "fickle" or "dirty"[28] Madraka is as much a degradation as the failure to observe caste rules in sacrifices.

---

see Maurice Bloomfield, "The Story of Indra and Namuci: Contributions to the Interpretation of the Veda," pt. 1, *JAOS*, XV (1893), 152–63; Dumézil, *Destiny of the Warrior*, p. 78. It seems that in some respects the "Encloser" (*vṛtra*) and the "Nonreleaser" (*na-muci*) became interchangeable.

[27] Dumézil, *Destiny of the Warrior*, p. 20.

[28] The CE (8:27,80) favors *sacāpalaḥ* ("fickle") over *sadā malaḥ* ("ever dirt"), but the latter is widely used, North and South.

Karṇa, however, continues still further with this surgery of "friendship." Other figures are involved: "I am the dear friend [*priyaḥ sakhā*] of the intelligent son of Dhṛtarāṣṭra [Duryodhana]. Surely my life-breaths [*prāṇāḥ*] and whatever wealth is mine exist for his sake. Evidently you have been consigned by the Pāṇḍavas, you offspring of a sinful land, since you have behaved toward us in every way like a foe" (*amitravat*; 27,94–95). The fabric of "friendships" which holds this episode together is thus further complicated. One might put Karṇa's position into the following formula: for his own true friend, he must fight against a pair of true friends and thus face death by letting a false friend live. As he says himself, concluding his first denunciation of Śalya: "Out of regard for a friend [*mitrapratīkṣya*], for Duryodhana's sake, and so as not to endure blame—for these three reasons [I let] you live" (27,102). But more than this, Karṇa is the tragic model of true, loyal friendship,[29] even though Śalya, claiming to speak as a friend (*suhṛd*; 28,2), holds his loyalty up to ridicule. Through his dedication to Duryodhana, Karṇa can answer Śalya with authoritative words on friendship:

Surely friendship is seven-paced [*saptapadaṃ hi mitram*].[30] . . . Duryodhana has come to battle himself. Desiring success for his sake, I long for him where there is no singleness of purpose [? *tamabhyeṣye yatra naikāntyamasti*]. Friendship [*mitram*] consists of making fat [*mider*], gladdening [*nandater*], or pleasing [*prīyater*], or protecting [*saṃtrāyater*], or rejoicing [*modater*]; . . . and all this, no less, is mine in

[29] Just before the battle, Karṇa tells Krishna: "I will do nothing disagreeable to the son of Dhṛtarāṣṭra; know me surely to have abandoned life desiring Duryodhana's welfare" (6:41,87).

[30] There does not seem to be any numerical correlation with what follows. On the "seven-paced friendship," see also 3:246,35 and 281,22; 13:51,35 and 105,8 (the word for "friend" being consistently *mitra*). According to Ganguli-Roy (*Mahabharata*, XI, 189, n. 1): "The sense . . . is that if the righteous meet and exchange seven words (or walk each other for only seven steps), they become friends." Cf. the seven steps in the Hindu marriage rite.

Duryodhana. Enmity consists of destruction, punishment, putting down, crushing, swelling [? with pride; *śvayater*], or even by weakening the will through repeatedly visiting misfortune. And, in general, all this is in you toward me. [29,21–25]

Karṇa and Duryodhana's friendship dates back to their first encounter (1:126,38). And in several manuscripts, from both North and South, it is "through the condition of friendship" (*sakhibhāvena*) that Duryodhana is finally able to prevail upon Karṇa to stop the insult contest.[31]

This suffices to demonstrate that the theme of friendship is central to the events leading to the death of the third *senāpati*. There also is evidence—of a most baffling nature—that the epic's poets (or at least some of its redactors) saw a definite link between this episode and Indra's triumph over Vṛtra or Namuci. The uncertainty lies in the surprising fact that all but one of the references to such a connection occur only in the Northern recension. I will thus refer to this one instance first, as it provides the Critical Edition's only support for this causeway between myth and epic.

After Karṇa has had some initial success in baffling Arjuna's weapons, Bhīma and Krishna take turns addressing Arjuna (8:65,14–21). Both urge him to recover his "firmness" (*dhṛti*; 18 and 20), and both, in effect, offer him the service of their weapons. Bhīma volunteers to do the job himself with his mace (*gadā*; 15); and then Krishna, observing that Arjuna is not winning the fight with his usual independent flair, proposes: "Cut off the head of this foe, putting forth strength, with this razor-edged Sudarśana [Krishna's *cakra*], entrusted by me [to you], as Śakra with his *vajra* [cut off the head] of the foe Namuci" (*anena . . . kṣuraneminā . . . mayā nisṛṣṭena sudarśanena vajreṇa śakro namucerivāreḥ*; 65,18–19). These invitations to rely on others' weapons are, of course, rejected by Arjuna, who calls upon his own resources (23). But the comparison reminds

[31] *Karṇaparvan*, 401*, line 7, following 8:30,86.

us that Arjuna will rely on Krishna here just as Indra relied on others,[32] and in Śalya's *Udyogaparvan* account specifically upon Viṣṇu (who enters Indra's "weapon," the frothy *vajra*; 5:10,39),[33] in his disloyal dealings with Vṛtra and Namuci.

To be sure, this convergence of themes concerning the reinforcement of Indra and Arjuna's weapons is not enough to go on. The battle scenes abound in descriptions comparing heroic opponents to Indra and his foes, and in this particular duel comparisons are made to Indra's combats with many other enemies besides Namuci and Vṛtra.[34] Yet, as a glance at Sörensen's *Index* will show, the description of Arjuna and Karṇa's duel that appears in the Northern recension "Vulgate" includes five out of the forty-two references to Vṛtra that occur in all the four battle *parvans* and four of the ten references that are made in the same immense span to Namuci. The latter, at least, is a significant statistic, inviting a closer look at the strange, apparently intrusive references that occur only in the Northern recension.[35] They are given here in order and in brief.

First, Krishna warns Arjuna of Karṇa's approach: "Slay Karṇa, O mighty-armed one, as Vṛtrahan [Indra, "Slayer of Vṛtra"] [slew] Namuci. Let good fortune [*śreyas*] be yours, O Pārtha; obtain victory in battle" (Appendix I, no. 36, ll. 31–32 = Calcutta Edition 8:86,4363). Second, when Karṇa's chariot wheel is engulfed by the earth and Arjuna is reluctant to slay him at a disadvantage, Krishna mocks such chivalry: "When he is able, the *sūta*'s son [Karṇa] will encounter you

[32] In *ŚB* 12,7,3,3 (cf. *ṚV* 10,131,4–5), Indra gets his help from the Aśvins and Saravatī; see Bloomfield, "Indra and Namuci," pp. 147,151,153–60, and 162; and Dumézil, *Destiny of the Warrior*, p. 31.

[33] See above, Chapter 9, at n. 14; Gonda's atmospheric interpretation is unconvincing: *Early Viṣṇuism*, p. 38.

[34] Arjuna and Karṇa are compared to Indra and Bali (8:63,5; 65,5), Indra and Śambara (63,19 and 63; 64,8), Indra and Jambha (64,11), and Indra and Bala (66,30).

[35] The only Southern exception, one in Telegu script referred to as T_2, is described by P. L. Vaidya (ed., CE, *Karṇaparvan*, "Introduction," p. xviii) as "showing signs of the influence of the N recension."

as before. Strike this one as Hari [Viṣṇu-Krishna[36]] struck Namuci" (*vidhya tvam enaṃ namuciṃ yathā hariḥ*; App. I, no. 41, ll. 19–20 = Calcutta Edition 8:90,4700). When Arjuna finally slays the disabled Karṇa, the narrator's comparison is still pointed, though this time referring not to Namuci but to Vṛtra: "Then Arjuna removed [Karṇa's] head as Indra [removed] Vṛtra's with the *vajra*" (*tato 'rjunasya śiro jahāra vṛtrasya vajreṇa yathā mahendraḥ*; 8,1159* = Calcutta Edition 8:91,4798). And finally, at the beginning of the last *adhyāya* of the *parvan*, Krishna launches the Pāṇḍavas' victory celebration with an embrace of Arjuna and the most mystifying words of all:[37] "Slain by the destroyer of Bala was Vṛtra, by you Karṇa [*hato balabhidā vṛtrastvayā karṇo*], O Dhanaṃjaya. Men shall talk of just [one] death for Karṇa and Vṛtra [*vadhaṃ vai karṇavṛtrābhyāṃ kathayiṣyanti mānavāḥ*].[38] Vṛtra was slain in battle by the much-splendored [*bhūritejasā*] bearer of the *vajra*; by you, then, was Karṇa slain with bow and sharp arrows" (8:69,2–3).

What is one to make of these consistencies? All of the passages cited except for the first are exclusively Northern, although it might be argued that the last and most crucial passage is ancient and that the Southern recension has replaced it with a different ending (see note 37). But to account for all the passages, perhaps one must suppose that at some comparatively recent date, the Northern redactors seized upon the initial allusion, the only one definitely common to North and South, and extended it in order to make some point. But what point? Considering that in all but one case the speaker is Krishna, we may be encouraged to look for a meaning that is "divinely

[36] One Devanāgarī text, as if seeking to standardize, has *yathendraḥ* rather than *yathā hariḥ*. One wonders whether it is not Viṣṇu concealed in Indra's *vajra* that the poet—or Krishna—has in mind.

[37] The CE includes this Northern ending by default; the Southern recension has a wholly different concluding *adhyāya*.

[38] Cf. Ganguli-Roy (*Mahabharata*, VII: *Karna Parva*, 292): "Men will talk (in the same breath) of the slaughter of Karna and Vritra." Note the use of the compound dual.

known," mythical and secret. Although there is more than one possibility,[39] it is most likely that the true point of Krishna's insistence that "men shall talk of just one death for Karṇa and Vṛtra" is that each was undone by the same device: a violation of friendship encouraged and reinforced by his opponent's closest "friend."

As is well known, in the *Ṛg Veda*, Viṣṇu is Indra's "intimate friend" (*índrasya yújyaḥ sákhā*; *ṚV* 1,22,19), his frequent ally against Vṛtra; and in one celebrated passage, when Indra is about to slay Vṛtra, he says: "Friend Viṣṇu, stride out widely" (*sákhe viṣṇo vitarám̩ ví kramasva*; 4,19,11).[40] Similarly, in the *Mahābhārata*'s *Udyogaparvan* account, Viṣṇu helps Indra by entering the foam of the waters which Indra combines with his *vajra*. No doubt this is the point where the Vṛtra cycle fuses with the Namuci cycle: Indra's friendship with Viṣṇu coming from the former, his broken friendship coming from the latter. In any case, it seems that on the epic plane Indra's role has been divided between the two most prominent of the *Mahābhārata*'s "Indras among men."

On the one hand, just as Indra is helped by his "friend" Viṣṇu to kill Vṛtra, Arjuna is helped by his "friend" Krishna to kill Karṇa. Indeed, the accounts contain a similar pattern concerning the reinforcement of the two warriors' weapons. Arjuna does not use the *cakra* proffered by Krishna, whereas Indra does use the reinforced *vajra*. But it seems that Arjuna's weapons have taken effect only after Krishna has spoken, that is, after they have been reinforced by his words.

[39] Both Karṇa and Namuci have a rapport with Sūrya: Karṇa is Sūrya's son; Namuci's falling out with Indra, according to certain versions, began when, "terrified by Vāsava, Namuci entered a ray of the sun [*sūryaraśmim*]; then Indra made friendship [*sakhyam*] and an agreement [*samayam*] with him" (*Mbh.* 9:42,29; cf. *MS* 4,3,4 and Bloomfield, "Indra and Namuci," p. 147). On sun-storm imagery in the Karṇa-Arjuna duel, see Dumézil, *ME*, I, 131,135–38.

[40] See Arthur A. Macdonell, *Vedic Mythology*, Grundriss der Indo-Arischen Philologie und Altertumskunde, Vol. III, I A (Strassburg, 1897), 39–40.

On the other hand, Indra's sin of a breach of friendship is not Arjuna's; it is Yudhiṣṭhira's. If Bhīṣma has been slain by a misuse of the vow and Droṇa by a misuse of the truth, Karṇa has been slain by a misuse of friendship. The latter theme has had both distant mythical echoes and more recent devotional amplifications. But at bottom it is still Yudhiṣṭhira's fault that has brought it all about, for it is he who urged Śalya to destroy Karṇa's "energy," an act—involving a betrayal of "friendship"—which Yudhiṣṭhira himself admitted "ought not to be done" (*akartavyam*).[41] One might thus draw the following representation of what has occurred on the two planes of myth and epic:

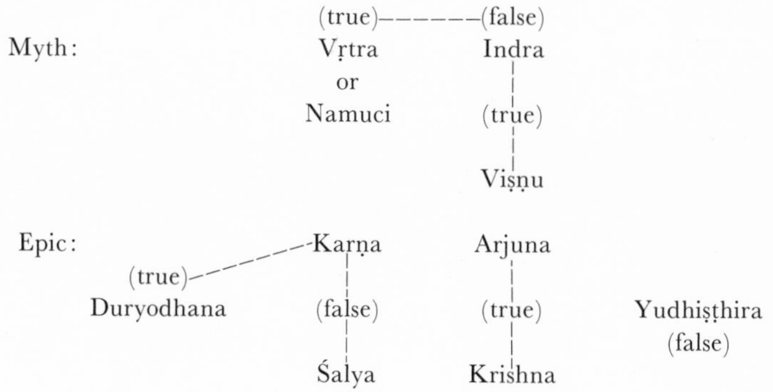

If Duryodhana stands behind the false friends as a true friend, Yudhiṣṭhira stands behind the true friends as a false friend, not only of Karṇa but of Śalya. Once again, Arjuna remains "pure."

When it is Śalya's turn to be named *senāpati*, there is a final touch of irony; as Duryodhana puts it: "The time has come, O you who are devoted to friends, when among friends wise men examine carefully for friendship or enmity" (. . . *mitrāṇāṃ mitravatsala / yatra mitramamitraṃ vā parikṣante budhā janāḥ*; 9:5,23). Śalya is thus put to the test of friendship and fatefully

[41] See above, Chapter 9.

accepts. But this is a reflection of the symbolism of Karṇa's fall; the symbolism of Śalya's lies elsewhere.

Death of Śalya

Śalya is related symbolically to the earth, as shown by the poets' description of the symbols on the banners (*dhvajas*) of the heroes (7:80,2–29): "On the standard-top of Śalya, king of Madra, like the tip of a flame [*agniśikhāmiva*], we beheld a golden furrow [*sītām*], incomparable and splendid" (7:80,18). Although this emblem is mentioned just once, its significance is not to be underestimated.[42] Śalya stands out from the rest not only by his earth-related emblem, but by being the only warrior to bear a feminine device on his banner.[43]

As one might expect, this is likely to be a very rich symbolism, first because it is the Earth's distress—her complaint to the gods that she was being oppressed by an overpopulation of incarnated Asuras (1:58)—that has led to the incarnation of the gods on earth and to the entire war. One underlying fact relates Śalya to her: he has been cast in the part of the one king *outside the central Kuru kingdom* who represents "all the other kings of the earth." This claim finds support in the following three passages, two of which were cited in Chapter 8. First, when Śalya is selected by Aśvatthāman to be the fourth marshal, his royal nature is emphasized in the familiar—but unusual for those outside the Kuru line—formulaic way: "This one, with [his] lineage [*kulam*], heroism [*vīryam*], majesty [*tejas*],

[42] Such passages are not to be treated lightly; cf. Bhīṣma's evaluation of the prowess of each hero in the "tale of the *rathas* and *atirathas*" (5:162,17–169,13) and the description of the colors of the heroes' horses (7:22). One might call them visual aids. On the *dhvaja*, see F. B. J. Kuiper, review of J. Duchesne-Guillemin's *Symbols and Values in Zoroastrianism*, *IIJ*, XI (1968–1969), 153–57.

[43] Sītā, "furrow," is not only a feminine word but a term connoting feminine imagery. The father of the *Rāmāyaṇa's* Sītā, who was born from a furrow, is called the "plough-bannered" (*sīradhvaja*); see Jaiswal, *Origin and Development*, p. 127.

fame [*yaśas*], and prosperity [*śrī*], is endowed with every virtue; let Śalya be our leader" (9:5,18). Second, Śalya's death is linked with Duryodhana's loss of his royal *śrī*. At Śalya's death, the Pāṇḍavas rejoice that "Duryodhana has today been abandoned by his blazing royal prosperity" (*hīno diptayā nṛpatiśriyā*; 9:18,14),[44] and acclaim: "Who other than Yudhiṣṭhira son of Pṛthā, whose protector is Hṛṣikeśa [Krishna]—ever the refuge of dharma and fame [*dharmayaśonidhiḥ*]—ever conquer Bhīṣma, Droṇa, and Karṇa, and even the king of the Madras as also other heroic kings by hundreds and thousands?" (*tathānyānnṛpatīnvīrāñśataśo 'tha sahasraśaḥ*; 18,26–27). Finally, this way of referring to Śalya as the index to the other kings is found when Śiśupāla berates Bhīṣma and the Pāṇḍavas for honoring Krishna as the most worthy person present at Yudhiṣṭhira's Rājasūya: "Why do you not praise the rulers of the earth, Śalya and so forth?" (*śalyādīn api kasmāt tvaṃ stauṣi vasudhādhipān*; 2:41,13). Śalya thus rounds out the four *senāpatis* as the figure heading the countless rājas of the earth. In this light, it is not so strange that with his fall, Duryodhana's *śrī* abandons him even while he is alive; for all the earth's kings are no longer there to sustain Duryodhana as sovereign and yield to him the earth's "prosperity."

One feature differentiates Śalya's death from those of the other marshals, as observed by Walter Ruben. Śalya is slain by Yudhiṣṭhira alone; and the victory is achieved "in righteous combat."[45] According to Ruben, this was evidence that the original war took place without Krishna, but Krishna is not so easily set aside. When Yudhiṣṭhira hears the shouts of acclamation at Śalya's installation, he asks Krishna what to do. Once again, Krishna gives the advice which is to achieve the immediate end, only this time Yudhiṣṭhira is to be the sole agent in carrying it out. There are two key points in Krishna's

[44] For these two passages, see Chapter 8.

[45] Ruben, *Krishna*, p. 284 (my translation); Ruben's "in ehrlichem Kampf" probably translates *dharmye . . . yuddhe* of 9:16,55.

rather long speech (9:6,24–37). First, he stresses twice the continuity between Śalya and the other marshals, but in contrary directions: in one case Śalya is compared favorably with the others (26), in the other unfavorably: "Having crossed the Bhīṣma, Karṇa, and Droṇa ocean, . . . do not, with your troops—having encountered Śalya—sink in a cow-track" (*goṣpadam*; 36). Such contradictions point to an ambiguity in Śalya's character and also dignify him as a worthy opponent for Yudhiṣṭhira, who has never showed himself to be the greatest of fighters. Second, and more important, it is Krishna who puts Yudhiṣṭhira to the task that Ruben would have him do entirely on his own: "I do not find a well-matched opponent [*pratiyoddhāram*] for him [Śalya] in battle except you, O tiger among men, of prowess equal to a tiger's; in the heavenly world and in this entire world, there is no man other than you who would be able to slay the angered king of the Madras" (30–31).

In what sense is Śalya such a "well-matched opponent" (*pratiyoddhṛ*)? One does well to note that in a list where suitable "shares" (*bhāga*) are delegated to the Pāṇḍava warriors, only in Yudhiṣṭhira's case is some qualification expressed: "The share of Pāṇḍu's eldest son will be the mighty king of the Madras, although some tell us that these two are considered uneven" (*viṣamau*; 5:56,13). The matter of their being "well-matched" yet "uneven" is unresolved, but Yudhiṣṭhira seems to have regarded Krishna's words as being very weighty. When Śalya at first gets the best of the fighting, Yudhiṣṭhira asks: "How, verily, can these important words [*vaco mahat*] of Mādhava's become true" (9:12,35)? When he finally decides he must take matters into his own hands as Krishna had prompted, his reflections translate *pratiyoddhṛ* into the very suggestive term *bhāga*, "share," which occurred in the passage concerning the appointments of personal opponents. Speaking to his brothers and Krishna, Yudhiṣṭhira says: "Bhīṣma, Droṇa, Karṇa and the other rulers of the earth who were energetic for the sake of the Kauravas have all gone to their death in battle. Each according to his share, each according to his strength [*yathābhāgaṃ yathotsāham*], you have fought in manly fashion. One share remains. This is mine: the great chariot-warrior Śalya" (*bhāgo 'vaśiṣṭa eko 'yaṃ mama śalyo mahārathaḥ*; 9:15,16–17). We have already anticipated what this "share" consists of in the present context.[46] As the two kings fight, other warriors, watching the progress of their fight, could not tell "whether the son of Pṛthā, having slain the king of Madra, would enjoy the earth [*vasuṃdharām*], or whether Śalya, having slain the son of Pāṇḍu, would give the earth [*dadyāt . . . gām*] to Duryodhana" (15,58–59). Yudhiṣṭhira's "share," in the person of Śalya, will be the earth.

The combat takes place in two stages, the end of the first marked by the fall of Śalya's "furrowed" banner (15,64). Then, after Śalya recovers the initiative for awhile, Yudhiṣṭhira recalls Krishna's words: "And, having reflected that his share was still remaining [*bhāgamathāvaśiṣṭaṃ smṛtvā*], his mind was firmly set on the death of Śalya as had been counseled by the younger brother of Indra [Krishna]" (16,37). At this point, Yudhiṣṭhira takes up the special dart (*śakti*) he had just called to mind[47] and slays Śalya with it. In describing the latter's fall the poets have given their most careful attention to the themes under discussion. The notion of "shares," for instance, is probably bound up with the double insistence that Yudhiṣṭhira is performing a sort of sacrifice in which Śalya is likened to the fire which at first blazes up (16,48) and is then extinguished (55). Most revealing is the resonant description of the end of King Śalya's affair with the earth:

Having spread his arms, he fell from his chariot to the earth [*gām*] with his armor cut away. . . . Having spread his arms, facing toward

[46] For more on this and related terms, see below, Chapters 13 and 14.

[47] It is given a long description (16,38–47): created by Tvaṣṭṛ for Śiva, it had been long worshiped by the Pāṇḍavas (43–44). In connection with Śalya, the only point of interest is that it was "unerringly fatal to haters of brahmins" (45), a theme I will discuss below.

> the Dharmarāja, the king of Madra fell on the earth [*bhūmau*] like a tall Indra-banner. Then, all his mangled limbs bathed in blood, it was as if that bull among men was risen up to be the earth, out of love [*pratyudgata iva premnā bhūmyā*].[48] A lover to his dear beloved, as if fallen on her breast [*priyayā kāntayā kāntaḥ patamāna ivorasi*], that lord, having for a long time enjoyed the earth [*vasumatīm*] like a dear loved one [*priyāṃ kāntāmiva*], clinging to her with all his limbs, was like one who was sleeping [*sarvairaṅgaiḥ samāśliṣya prasupta iva so 'bhavat*]. [16,49–54]

The position, as another passage tells, betokens the fall of a king. In Krishna's words: "The lords of the earth, slain for the earth's sake, having embraced the earth with their limbs like a dear beloved, are sleeping" (*pṛthivyaṃ pṛthivīhetoḥ pṛthivīpatayo hatāḥ / pṛthivīmupaguhyāṅgaiḥ suptaḥ kantāmiva priyām*; *Droṇaparvan*, App. I, No. 17, ll. 14–15).

It is by now evident that this figure who has been tricked by his taste for luxury into taking Duryodhana's side,[49] whose death has deprived Duryodhana of his *śrī*, and whose body finally mingles with the earth, is consistently evoking themes of the third function. The terms used for the earth in her relationship to Śalya seem, to a marked degree, ones which emphasize such symbolism. Earth is the "cow" (*go*; 9:15,59; 16,49–51: "the earth [as the milk-cow of kings]," Monier-Williams)—a term that gives depth to Krishna's counsel not to "sink, having encountered Śalya, in a cow-track" (*goṣpadam*).[50] Earth is Vasuṃdharā, the "bearer of riches" (9:15,58), and Vasumatī, "the possessor of riches" (16,54). Or, when Śalya moves his troops, it is as Medinī, "she having fatness," that the earth "seems to tremble" (5:8,5). These are not exceptional terms for the earth, but they underline the relationship between the earth and the king in the direction of third-function themes. The embrace with the earth at Śalya's death even calls to mind aspects of the mythology of Śrī-Lakṣmī. As he lies clasping

[48] Or "it was as if the earth, out of love, rose up to meet him."
[49] See above, Chapter 9, following n. 29.
[50] On cow similes and sovereignty, cf. Chapter 7, following n. 64.

his beloved earth with outstretched arms,[51] the last words to describe him strike a deep chord: "His heart split by that dart and his standard and weapons scattered, even altogether stilled [*saṃśāntam*], *lakṣmī* did not desert the lord of the Madras" (*madreśaṃ lakṣmirnaiva vyamuñcata*; 16,56). I would prefer not to translate *lakṣmī* here, for, although the meanings "beauty" (Ganguli-Roy)[52] or "fortune" are no doubt involved, the associations of royalty with Śrī-Lakṣmī give the passage a depth that should not be lost.

At this point, one may ask: what has all this to do with sins? In fact, at least on the surface, and as Ruben saw so clearly, Yudhiṣṭhira—fighting "singly" (*eko*; 15,50) and "in righteous combat"—does not sin in slaying Śalya. Though one might certainly raise eyebrows at his behavior (and probably Krishna's complicity) in claiming as his "share" the foe with whom he had laid the secret scheme to slay Karṇa, any suspicions that he is wiping out the evidence are apparently unfounded: the *Mahābhārata*, remarkably, never raises the possibility. Moreover, the poets take great pains to give an official respectability to Yudhiṣṭhira's triumph. In the passage describing Śalya's death embrace, it is said that he lay "slain by Dharma's son of righteous soul in righteous combat" (*dharmye dharmātmanā yuddhe nihato dharmasūnunā*; 16,55). Yet one cannot help but ask, what with all these puns and this highly stylized claim to virtue, whether the poets speak with true praise or heavy irony.

In any case, Yudhiṣṭhira is not the only sovereign to have questionable dealings with his foes. In the last chapter I discussed the *Mahābhārata*'s (indeed, Śalya's) reorientation of the mythology of the sins of Indra. There we saw how the epic accounts are close in basic outline to myths from the Brāhmaṇas in their treatment of Indra's first two sins, against Viśvarūpa and Vṛtra, and how the epic accounts differ from a later, more "artificial," *Mārkaṇḍeya Purāṇa* myth in their handling of the third-function sequel to these sins. First, the *Mahābhārata* has

[51] On "long arms" and royalty, see above, Chapter 8 at n. 11.
[52] *Mahabharata*, VII; *Salya Parva*, 50.

Indra commit no third-function sin like the violation of Ahalyā; rather, he is sinned against in the same fashion, by Nahuṣa who covets his wife. Second, this third episode is the only one in which Indra is challenged by a human king. These differences in the epic's myth, or myths, help to give us an account, not of the annihilation of the warrior god through three sins, but of the restoration of the not-so-perfect divine sovereign to his throne. On the level of heroic action, the epic story is oriented in the same direction, and it seems that the epic poets have worked, or perhaps reworked, mythic and epic material into recognizably complementary patterns.

Śalya, as indicated, is the beloved of the earth, and we have so far seen little indication that he may have violated her, "Yudhiṣṭhira's earth," in any way that might run parallel to Nahuṣa's ill intent toward Śacī. Admittedly, no strict parallel will be found. But when one examines the mythic and epic scenes within the context of the third function, their divergent plots will show their reliance on a common store of themes and symbols. We have already noticed a certain ambiguity in Śalya's character. Not surprisingly, it is bound up with his relationship to the earth. For its most complete expression, we must turn back to the "insult exchange" between Śalya and Karṇa.

In Karṇa's tirade Śalya is frequently the recipient of epithets like *pāpadeśaja*, "born in a sinful country." Karṇa charges the people of Śalya's land not only with the subversion of friendship, but, in two very long speeches (8:27,71–91 and 30,9–82), with a whole host of sins. It would be fruitless to file all the charges, but their central thrust is illuminating.

In the first denunciation, friendship is related to the question of purity and in one phrase (which, though widely found, is not in the Critical Edition), Karṇa depicts the Madraka as "always dirt" (*sadā malaḥ*).[53] But if the first speech does not generalize on the alleged Madraka character to any great

[53] See above, n. 28.

extent, the sins it records are all breaches of the orthopraxy demanded by brahminical society. People of all ages and sexes mingle freely (27,75–76), impure food and incoherent speech are common (77–78), and, most notoriously, Madraka women (76 and 85–90) are wanton, drunk, mercenary, "pass urine like camels and asses" (86), and are "very shameless, hairy, gluttonous, and impure" (*aśaucās*; 89). These, says Karṇa, are *mleccha* (barbaric) traits and practices (91); and especially as they concern women, they are tied in most intimately with Śalya's birth: "Being the son of one of these, how can a Madraka speak of dharma" (85)?

Looking outside the insult exchange, some corroboration for these charges can no doubt be found in Madraka "family practice" (*kuladharma*) which Śalya upholds in marrying his sister Mādrī to Pāṇḍu by selling her. Dumézil, in calling attention to this "matrimonial practice 'unworthy' of kṣatriyas, reserved for vaiśyas," argues that these traits bear further relation to the quasi-vaiśya character of Nakula and Sahadeva, Mādrī's sons.[54] Karṇa's first speech, however, is only a sort of warm-up. There is no clear formulation of what underlies the adharma and *aśauca* ("impurity") of the Madraka. His second speech is more helpful.

At the outset, Karṇa bases his remarks—according to the authority of a brahmin (8:30, 8–9)—upon certain geographical considerations: "Those who are situated away from the Himavat and apart from the Gaṅgā, Sarasvatī, Yamunā, and also Kurukṣetra; who are dwellers in the region of the five rivers with the Sindhu as the sixth—one should avoid these Bāhlīkas who are impure [*aśūcīn*] and beyond the pale of dharma" (*dharmabāhyān*; 8:30,10–11). There have been various efforts to determine who the Bāhlīkas (apparent variant Bāhīkas) are and what their relationship is with the

[54] Dumézil, *ME*, I, 73–76, quote on p. 75; he thinks the CE is unjudicious in rejecting the marriage episode, it bring the *lectio difficilior* and without alternative. He modifies this stance, however, in *ME*, II, 12.

Madrakas,[55] but they are regarded here as Śalya's subjects. This geographical partitioning of the pure and the impure is reinforced several times, but nowhere more forcefully than in the notion that the inhabitants of Bāhlīka country do not descend from the original creation:

Where the five rivers flow, having just issued from the mountain, among those named Āraṭṭas and Bāhlīkas a respectable person [*ārya*] should not dwell for even two days. Two Piśācas named Bahis ["Outsider"] and Hlīka ["Ashamed"?] live on the Vipāśā [one of the five rivers]. The offspring of these two are the Bāhlīkas; this creation is not Prajāpati's [*bahiśca nāma hlīkaśca vipāśāyāṃ piśācakau / tayorapatyaṃ bāhlīkā naiṣā sṛṣṭiḥ prajāpateḥ*]. [30,43–44][56]

Such a notion of impurity as that which stands outside the categories of the divine creation certainly sits well with Mary Douglas' celebrated analysis of the impure in the Old Testament.[57]

If the impure is, in the general sense, that which is outside the ordered *arya* world, Karṇa's further specifications of the

[55] See Vaidya, ed., *Karṇaparvan*, "Critical Notes," p. 686: "Bāhlīka country did not form part of Āryavarta" and probably consisted of Madra and Pañcanada. He cites (p. 85) J. M. Chatterji, "Ahura-Mazda in the *Mahābhārata*," *Iran League Quarterly*, XIX (1948–1949), 50, who takes Madra as Media and Śalya as a Persian king who performed his own sacrifices, Madrakas being called *rājayājakāḥ*, "those whose sacrificers are kings" (8:27,81; 30,70). A. D. Pusalker, *The History and Culture of the Indian People*, I: *The Vedic Age*, A. K. Majumdar, ed. (Bombay: Bharatiya Vidya Bhavan, 1951), 263, doubts that Bāhlīka, "Outsider," implies Iranian. Most implausible, Robert Shafer, *Ethnography of Ancient India* (Weisbaden: Otto Harrassowitz, 1954), p. 141, links Bāhlikās with Harappā. See also M-W, s.v. Bāhīka.

[56] Vaidya, ed., *Karṇaparvan*, p. 687, notes that the names of the two Piśācas form a "very fanciful etymology. . . . So the Bāhlīkas are a Piśāca race, and not an Āryan race, which alone is propagated by Prajāpati, the Creator." Shafer, *Ethnography of Ancient India*, p. 141, says: "I interpret this as meaning that they were the offspring of two devils." Bahis' sex cannot be determined.

[57] Mary Douglas, *Purity and Danger: An Analysis of Concepts of Pollution and Taboo* (New York: Praeger, 1966), pp. 41–57, shows that what is consistently impure about the abominations of Leviticus is that they do not fit the divinely ordered "holy" categories of Genesis.

pure are equally interesting: "Among the Matsyas and those of the Kuru-Pāñcāla countries, among the Naimiṣas, the Cedis, and others who are distinguished [*viśiṣṭāḥ*], the good [*santaḥ*] uphold the ancient dharma; but not the Madras and the crooked people of the five rivers" (30,62–63). These verses would seem to recall the sacred geography, cited above, of the Gaṅgā, Yamunā, Sarasvatī, and Kurukṣetra areas. They also suggest, first, that excepting the "Naimiṣas" who do not form one of the combatant kingdoms in the epic (elsewhere Naimiṣa is a forest), these "distinguished" and "good" peoples—the Matsyas, Cedis, and Pāñcālas—form the very core of the Pāṇḍava army. Second, the region which they broadly represent seems to evoke the idea of a "sacred center," one reminiscent of the central region, *madhyadeśa*, which, near the beginning of the Lunar Dynasty and long before Kuru, Yayāti gave to his youngest son Pūru, leaving the "outlying regions" to his four older sons (1:82,5).[58] Such a geography is in fact confirmed, despite the different interpretation, by Robert Shafer's study of the distribution of the epic's peoples.[59] One thus perceives that the symbolic geography of the battle of Kurukṣetra represents a defense and a regeneration of the Center of the Earth by a reassertion of its purity, and its peoples' relative purity, over and against the periphery. This is not the only instance concerning the Pāṇḍavas where the purity of the Center comes into question. When Yudhiṣṭhira asks Krishna whether to perform a Rājasūya, Krishna, voicing his support of the ordered continuity of the Lunar Dynasty

[58] See above, Chapter 8, following n. 18, and *ME*, II, 258–64; cf. also 1: 189,39, where Vasiṣṭha consecrates Pūru's descendants "the one horn [*viṣāṇabhūtam*] of the entire wide earth" (van Buitenen, *The Mahābārata*: I, 212, with n. 35, p. 455).

[59] See Shafer, *Ethnography of Ancient India*, p. 48: "The Ayran strength was along the Yamunā and upper Ganges. The Pāṇḍavas received very little aid from the Indo-Aryans of the northwest"; supporting this, see Shafer's "map 2" (back of book), which he says makes clear "the concentration of Pāṇḍava forces about the central Ganges-Yamunā doab." Shafer's theory of a "great rebellion" is less reliable than his geographical reconstructions, which themselves must often be viewed cautiously.

(2:13,4–6), says that before Yudhiṣṭhira can assert his sovereignty, he must rid himself of Jarāsaṃdha—a figure also much bound up with symbolisms of impurity and adharma[60]—who has established himself in "middle earth" (*avanīm madhyamām*; 13,7). But the symbolism of a great battle in which the center reasserts itself against the periphery also joins the growing list of *Mahābhārata* themes which find striking parallels in Saxo Grammaticus' account of the Battle of Brávellir.[61] For in that battle too, as Saxo describes it, the ordered array of "firm and stout" Swedish and Norwegian soldiery led by the princes Ringo (in charge of the land forces) and Olo (in charge of the fleet) faces an army of "unmanly peoples," "a mass of fickle offscourings," arrayed in support of their blind old uncle Haraldus Hyldetan and the Danes.[62]

Śalya, then, is the king of a people who, at least for Karṇa, come from the impurest of all the decentralized lands; and as their king, according to a familiar notion, he is "the bearer of a one-sixth share of their merits and misdeeds" (9:30,63; cf. 30,27). Moreover, despite his lifelong love affair with the earth, he is named in one of the "dictionaries of incarnations" (1:61) as one of those Asuras, born into royal lineages, whom the earth had called upon the gods to overthrow.[63] This is the underside of his ambiguous character and of the ambiguities in the symbolism of the outlying kingdoms which he represents. Not only are such lands potential suppliers of wives, troops, and tribute to the rulers of the "central kingdom"; such contacts with the central realm are among the factors that involve the

[60] See Biardeau, *EPHE*, LXXIX, 142 (Jarāsaṃdha intends an adharmic sacrifice of a hundred kings to Śiva), and Dumézil, *ME*, II, 96–107.

[61] See above, Chapter 1, n. 87, and Chapter 5, following n. 16.

[62] See Elton, *Danish History*, pp. 476 and 478; the barbaric character of the Danish forces need not imply "an invasion by non-Scandinavians": see Kemp Malone, "Ubbo Frescius at Brávellir," *Studies in Heroic Legend and Current Speech* (Copenhagen: Rosenkilde and Bagger, 1959), p. 83.

[63] See Dumézil, *ME*, I, 75–76; he is the Asura Saṃhrāda, younger brother of Prahrāda (or Prahlāda), and is referred to, in this context, as *bāhlīkapuṃgavaḥ*, "bull among Bāhlīkas" (1:61,6).

latter, and thus the whole earth, in the greatest menace imaginable: what the *Gītā* calls "a languishing of dharma" (*dharmasya glānir*; 4,7; cf. 1,40–43), as well as what Karṇa is calling the danger of impurity.

In this connection Karṇa evokes the "master symbol" for Śalya and his peoples, that of dirt, *malam*. To appreciate its aptness, however, requires that we recall the source of an earlier observation. As Mary Douglas says, quoting William James, dirt is "matter out of place."[64] Outside *madhyadeśa*, outside even the Creation, ruled by an incarnated Asura, the Madras and Bāhlīkas are "people out of place" and dirt is their "natural" symbol. Not a great number of verses are devoted to this subject, but the key passages pile up toward the end of Karṇa's tirade as if in summation: "Begging is a kṣatriya's dirt, untruth is a brahmin's dirt, Bāhlīkas are the dirt of the earth [*malaṃ pṛthivyā bāhlīkāḥ*], Madra women are the dirt of women" (*strīṇam madrastriyo malam*; 30,68). And again: "*Mlecchas* are the dirt of mankind [*mānuṣāṇāṃ malaṃ mlecchā*]; rogues [*mauṣṭikāḥ*] are the dirt of *mlecchas*; eunuchs [*śaṇḍāḥ*] are the dirt of rogues; those whose sacrificial priests are warriors[65] are the dirt of eunuchs; and whatever dirt there is of Madrakas whose sacrificial priests are warriors, that dirt shall be yours if you do not release me" (30,70–71).[66] Finally, there is a *śloka* found throughout the Northern recension but not in the Southern which the Critical Edition naturally rejects. Nonetheless, it sums things up neatly: "On earth the Madraka is called the dirt of every region; and so too the Madra woman is called the dirt of all women" (*pṛthivyāṃ sarvadeśānāṃ madrako*

[64] Douglas, *Purity and Danger*, pp. 35 and 164; see William James, *The Varieties of Religious Experience* (first published 1902; New York: Mentor Books, 1958), p. 116.

[65] See above, n. 55.

[66] Karṇa quotes a Rākṣasa for these two proverbs (*gāthās*) which are clearer than the story that connects them. The Rākṣasa seems to have plunged into the water to purify himself of Madraka defilement and has warned some unnamed king to unhand him lest he be polluted too. It is added that the Rākṣasas' words can be used as a "curative charm" (*bheṣajam*; 72).

malamucyate / tathā strīṇāṃ ca sarvāsāṃ madrikā mala ucyate; 397* and 398*, after 30,81).

How are we to understand this association, this symbol for the darker side of Śalya's character? The passages themselves give the clue: "the Bāhlīka is the dirt *of the earth*"; "*on earth* the Madraka is called the dirt of every nation." Dirt falls within the context of the symbolism of the earth; it is earth's unregenerate side, her "matter out of place." In the concluding chapter of *Purity and Danger*, Mary Douglas offers a key with which to interpret this correlation within the larger context of the subject of Part Four: eschatology. Against the background of the epic's symbolic geography, which places the Madras, Bāhlīkas, and other Kaurava allies on the "outside" while the Pāṇḍavas' defense of the center becomes a climactic regeneration of *śauca* and dharma, Douglas' hermeneutic of dirt as undifferentiated formlessness is most revealing:

> In this final stage of total disintegration, dirt is utterly undifferentiated. Thus a cycle has been completed. Dirt was created by the differentiating activity of mind, it was a by-product of the creation of order. So it started from a state of non-differentiation; all through the process of differentiating its role was to threaten the distinctions made; finally it returns to its true indiscriminate character. Formlessness is therefore an apt symbol of beginning and growth as it is of decay.[67]

In the *Mahābhārata*, such a cycle has been completed: the cataclysm of battle has dissolved the impure world not into the primeval ocean, as will occur at the end of the kalpa, but, appropriately for the end of a yuga, into the earth.[68] Numerous are the descriptions of the earth, in the midst of battle, covered with rivers of gore bearing the dead to her own infernal

[67] Douglas, *Purity and Danger*, p. 161.

[68] See Mircea Eliade, *Patterns in Comparative Religion*, Rosemary Sheed, trans. (Cleveland: World, 1963), p. 254, distinguishing the eschatological symbolisms of earth and water. As regards Eliade's point, Douglas is to be criticized for making a facile equation; see *Purity and Danger*, p. 161.

regions.[69] Through this battle, the earth is relieved of her burden. When she rises up to clasp Śalya to her, it is the culminating scene not only of a love affair, but of a regeneration. In this moment impurity and purity, dirt and soil, earth's kings and earth herself, are one. Through his victory over Śalya, the earth is now Yudhiṣṭhira's "share," given, even if only for a moment, anew.

Returning now to the *Mahābhārata*'s myth of the sins and restoration of Indra, there are features that comprise its final episode—the conflict with Nahuṣa—that are analogous to this final episode of the Kurukṣetra war.[70] Like Indra, Yudhiṣṭhira does not sin; rather, the adversaries of both commit sins within the area of the third function. More specifically, each has his mind turned by sense enjoyments and wealth, and each, in one way or another, sins by "despising Indra."[71] Their opponents' sins help give both Indra's and Yudhiṣṭhira's triumphs a look of comparative righteousness. For not only does Nahuṣa covet Indra's wife and Śalya "defile" Yudhiṣṭhira's earth; not only is each associated with a third-function sin; but each is charged additionally with a total violation of dharma: Śalya reaping the sins of his subjects, Nahuṣa offending the brahmin Agastya by touching his foot to his head. Finally, both the epic and mythic episodes hinge upon the opponent being a human king. This last point, however, calls for further examination, which I turn to now, of the four episodes discussed above and the underlying themes which link them together.

The Four Marshals and the Symbolism of Sovereignty

Concerning the nature of the sins committed in the slayings of the four marshals, I have shown that the four episodes form a cohesively structured group. Not only do the slain give their

[69] See, for example, 6:66,12; 7:13,9–18; 7,68,47–54; 8:33,45–70; 8:36; sometimes the blood and gore lend the earth an eerie beauty, as in 6:53,21–22.

[70] After this, the Kuru forces, without a marshal, are scattered.

[71] On Śalya, see 5:8,9–10, cited in Chapter 9, following n. 29

names to the four battle *parvans*; not only do Yudhiṣṭhira and Krishna figure prominently at the deepest level of each misdeed; but the episodes refer to, recall, and reinforce each other at a number of levels.

To interpret their coherence, let us first turn to the moral dimension. As was argued earlier, sins and virtues can best be seen as complementary to each other. The shifting assortments of trifunctional royal virtues, such as were discussed in Chapters 7 and 8, show a significant correlation with the sins committed, or engaged in, by Yudhiṣṭhira. On the first level, it will be recalled that *tejas*, an ancient first-function virtue, is often replaced by the pair *satya* and dharma, and, moreover, that *vrata*, the "vow," where it occurs, seems to function as a specialization of dharma.[72] As we have seen, Yudhiṣṭhira's first two sins are violations of the vow and of truth.

On the second level, the traditional virtues were seen to be such qualities as *yaśas*, "fame," *balam*, "strength," and *vīryam*, "courage." But we also observed that some lists focus on the quality of honorable relations with other kṣatriyas.[73] Yudhiṣṭhira, at this level, is at the root of a complicated violation of friendship. Finally, on the third level, the most frequent virtues were *śrī*, "prosperity," and *dānam*, "generosity." As we have seen, on this level the sin, or sins, is not Yudhiṣṭhira's but Śalya's, consisting, in general, of a violation or despoliation of the earth, and, in particular, of an oversensitivity to wealth, gifts, and sense enjoyments.

Thus, through the deaths of the four marshals, the epic illustrates a theme of moral decline and restoration within the framework of the three functions. Still within the moral dimension, however, another connecting link between the four episodes has been mentioned. Śalya, like Nahuṣa, is a human king and, moreover, the only *senāpati* who is a complete and legitimate king. Each of the others is what may be called an

[72] See beginning of this chapter and Chapter 8, above, n. 45.
[73] See above, Chapter 8, following n. 48.

incomplete or illegitimate *rāja*. Bhīṣma, a potential king, would have ruled the Kurus were it not for his vows.[74] After Droṇa's fateful battle with the Pāñcāla king Drupada, he becomes the ruler of half that kingdom even though he is a brahmin (1:128,14–18). And Karṇa, like Bhīṣma a potential king of the Kurus, is also, thanks to his friendship with Duryodhana, made king of Aṅga, despite his status, in everyone's eyes, as the son of a *sūta*, a mixed-caste charioteer (1:126,35–36).[75] In contrast with such flirtations with kingship, Śalya is the only one born and consecrated a king within a "legitimate" line of succession. Like Nahuṣa, the last opponent of Indra, Śalya is a king by descent; but neither is a legitimate challenger for the "stake" or "share" which his opponent seeks: the sovereignty of "middle earth," or the sovereignty of heaven.

Further in this direction, a third factor linking the four marshals is closely related to their royal or quasi-royal identities. Each of them is, in one way or another, of confused caste status. Bhīṣma, though a kṣatriya, is a lifelong *brahmacārin*.[76] Droṇa, though a brahmin, is a foremost weapons expert. Karṇa, though a kṣatriya by birth, is a mixed-caste *sūta* by upbringing and by reputation. And Śalya, though a kṣatriya, is a "vaiśya" (or even a *mleccha*) in his behavior and is said to perform his own sacrifices. Confusion of caste is, of course, one of the great horrors of the epic, of the *Gītā* no less than of its "caricature," the insult exchange between Karṇa and Śalya.[77] These indeterminate identifications appear to be either at, or very near, the root of the circumstances which bring each of

[74] See above, n. 4; Bhīṣma is sometimes called "king," even "best of kings" (*rājasattama*; 12:54,15) by Krishna! In heaven (18:4,17) he is *bhīṣmam . . . nṛpam*, the "kingly Bhīsma."

[75] See Chapter 8, at nn. 14 and 60; on the implausibility of Droṇa and Karṇa as actual kings, van Buitenen, *The Mahābhārata*: I, 12, points up the need to explain the *symbolic* character of these titles.

[76] This does not necessarily imply brahmin caste status, but as a lifelong commitment it does involve the neglect of numerous kṣatriya duties.

[77] Cf. Douglas, *Purity and Danger*, p. 53, on prohibitions against "mixing" and "confusion" (*tebhel*) in Leviticus.

the marshals to his final fall. This is explicit in Droṇa's case, for, when he continues to fight after he has heard the lie, the Ṛṣis tell him that he is "fighting unrighteously, . . . especially being a brahmin" (7:164,89–92). But it is also true that if Bhīṣma falls because of the complicated fabric of his "terrible" vows, it is the *brahmacarya* vow which holds this fabric together. Karṇa's mixed status encourages the Pāṇḍavas' and Draupadī's contempt for him (a contempt nutured by Krishna) and sustains his own tragic resentment which leads inevitably to his death. Śalya, according to Karṇa, is a "mean-minded low defiler of the kṣatriya class" (8:27,68) who dies having made one "kṣatriya" agreement to violate another.

In sum, from the Pāṇḍavas' perspective, there is a kind of moral justification for killing these flawed foes. Each violates the ordered hierarchy of caste. Thus each is guilty, albeit in the first three cases as an unwilling victim of fate, of endangering the fabric of dharma. Logically, their chief antagonist is Yudhiṣṭhira, the Dharmarāja, who emerges as a true champion of dharma, one who, out of necessity, has faced its intricacies and burdens so as to preserve its essence. For it is Yudhiṣṭhira's *royal* dharma that he must seek to rule; and the intricacies result from it being a time for *āpaddharma*, for practices allowable in times of distress. He has, in other words, violated dharma, or at least sustained it in a precarious balance, in order finally to uphold it. The key to this whole matter is the "righteous combat" (9:16,65) in which Yudhiṣṭhira slays Śalya. No doubt the words are two-edged, but on the just side Yudhiṣṭhira is the righteous victor over the most impure and adharmic of all his foes. Indeed, with his triumph, and with the triumph of the Pāṇḍavas in general, despite his violation of first- and second-function virtues, the rehabilitation is one of the structure of the three functions itself, over and against the forces of impurity, adharma, disorder, chaos.[78]

[78] On this point, cf. Biardeau, EMH, 2, Appendice, p. 104: "The unstructured group of the Kauravas symbolizes the society that is disorderly and literally sunk into chaos: their victory would signify the earth's return

The four marshals reflect upon each other in their symbolism on two more levels. And here we begin to move away from the dharmic and societal considerations to cosmological ones. In Chapter 2, we observed at one point that a special color symbolism applies to the four *varṇas* and the four yugas: the sequence white, red, yellow, and black.[79] The same colors seem to have been held consistently in mind regarding the four marshals.

The most obvious color associations are those of Bhīṣma. Just before the Kurukṣetra war, before the *Gītā*, we see him thus: "The aged Bhīṣma was in the van of the entire army, having a white umbrella, white bow and conch, white head-gear, with a white banner, white horses, having the appearance of a white mountain" (6:20,9).[80] Right after this Droṇa is described as having red steeds (*śoṇairhayaiḥ*; 6:20,11), elsewhere "great red steeds" (*śonā bṛhanto 'śvāḥ*; 7:8,15; cf. 7:7,10). Karṇa is usually thought of with his natural-born golden mail and earrings (3:292,5) like those of his father Sūrya (3:290,5), but the epic draws no sharp distinction between gold and yellow: when Kuntī invokes Sūrya to father Karṇa, the god appears before her "yellow as honey" (*madhupiñga*; 3:290,8). Although Śalya draws no color descriptions, his connection is with the "black" earth[81] and with dirt.

If one cannot be certain whether to relate this "descent by color" to the structures of society (the *varṇas*) or to those of time (the yugas), there can be little doubt that the four marshals articulate an elaborate spatial symbolism. First, recalling that

to chaos" (my translation); also Wikander, "Eschatologie," pp. 86–87, making much the same point.

79 See above, Chapter 2, following n. 10.

80 See also 5:179,10–14, mentioning six white articles which Bhīṣma wears in his fight with Paraśurāma; also 6:16,40; however, Droṇa also wears white, as in 1:124,17–18. Several manuscripts, mostly from the North but one from the Southern recension, describe a very long battle between Bhīṣma and a son of Virāṭa named Śveta, "White" (*Bhīṣmaparvan*, Appendix I, No. 4); no doubt the colors are significant in this duel, making "Śveta" one of Bhīṣma's "shares."

81 On the earth and blackness, see Biardeau, cited above, Chapter 2, n. 25.

when Śalya fell, "it was as if the earth, out of love, rose to meet him," it suddenly becomes clear that in each of the other episodes, indeed at their very conclusions, the earth has likewise undergone a dramatic change in position vis-à-vis the heroes. The *Bhīṣmaparvan* ends with Bhīṣma, on his bed of arrows, not touching the earth at all (*dharaṇīṃ nāspṛśat*; 6:114,84)—as if his character had remained "elevated," like that of his foes, especially Arjuna who (recalling Indra?) brings forth fresh pure water from the earth herself with one of his arrows so that Bhīṣma may wash his wounds and slake his thirst (6:116,19–23).[82] The *Droṇaparvan* then provides the point where this elevated position is lost, where the hero comes down to earth: when Yudhiṣṭhira lies, his chariot, until then provided with an air cushion of four fingers, "touched the earth" (*vāhāspṛśanmahīm*; 7:164,107). Next, the *Karṇaparvan* shows the earth taking the initiative, but with the heroes still on the descendent. In a passage in which Dumézil has found an important transposition from the *Ṛg Veda*,[83] the earth "swallows" Karṇa's chariot wheel (*agrasanmahī cakram*; 8:66,59), leading to his defeat. Thus when the earth rises, as it were, to clasp Śalya to her, it is the culmination of a four-act drama.

One may thus find a sympathetic connection between the earth and the fall of the heroes. Yet the meaning of this four-part progression becomes clear only when it is seen against another spatial dimension. Not only are the four marshals a ladder of descent to the earth; they also seem to symbolize an ascent, or an access, to the "three worlds."[84] The final destinies of

[82] Cf. Yayāti, not touching the earth on his fall from heaven; discussed by Dumézil, *ME*, II, 276.

[83] Dumézil, "Karṇa et les Pāṇḍava," pp. 60–66: in the *ṚV*, Indra overcomes Sūrya by somehow disabling one of the wheels of the Sun god's chariot; see especially *ṚV* 4:28,2: he "pressed the wheel downward" (see above, Chapter 1, n. 28).

[84] It may also be significant that the four marshals approximate a four-directional location: Karṇa's Aṅga is east of Hāstinapura, Droṇa's Ahicchatrā is south (or southeast), Śalya's Madra is west (or northwest),

Bhīṣma and Droṇa, after their deaths, are in the heavens: Bhīṣma returning as the Vasu Dyaus ("Heaven")[85] to the invisible heaven of the Vasus (13:153,44; cf. 154,5–7), Droṇa ascending to Brahmaloka (7:165,41). In contrast, Karṇa's destiny is to have his *tejas* re-enter the sun (8:67,27), which in the epic would seem to connote a residence in a lower realm.[86] And, once again, Śalya's fate is to be embraced by the earth.[87] In other words, their essences conform to the three levels of the universe, or perhaps to a fourth if Brahmaloka refers to an absolute realm. This is the universe Yudhiṣṭhira has conquered, the last world of which—the earth—is not only the final stake of battle but an active agent in the victory she had sought. In this respect, it is interesting that in Brāhmaṇa texts, the earth, known as the kṣatriya's *loka* (*ŚB* 11,8,4,5; 12,8,3,5), is said to be the "most essential" (*rasatama*) of the worlds (*ŚB* 9,1,2,36)[88] and the "foundation" (*pratiṣṭhā*; *ŚB* 6,1,1,15; 6,7,3,4) from which to obtain the other worlds.[89] Indeed, as the heroes are drawn closer to the earth through sins (beginning with Yudhiṣṭhira's lie), the earth rises to meet them, finally claiming

---

and Bhīṣma, though resident at Hāstinapura itself, postpones his death until the sun reaches its "northern course" (*uttarāyana*): one might even call him the "northern Kuru." See also 7:10,43 (marshals-yugas-lokas).

[85] See Dumézil, *ME*, I, 178–82.

[86] Traditionally the sun, Sūrya, is connected with heaven; see Jan Gonda, *Loka: World and Heaven in the Veda*, Verhandelingen der Koninklijke Nederlandse Akademie van Wetenschappen, AFD. Letterkunde, Nieuwe Reeks, LXXIII, no. 1 (Amsterdam: Noord-Hollandsche Uitgevers Maatschappij, 1966), 37 and 92. In the epic, however, Sūrya's appearances as Indra's opposite show him to be connected with the atmosphere, or at least with a level of the universe far closer to human affairs than the world of the Vasus and Brahmaloka; see Hopkins, *Epic Mythology*, pp. 84,87–88.

[87] Cf. Dumézil, *Myth to Fiction*, pp. 142–43: in contrast to the Odinic hero who ascends heavenward, "the *Vanic hero* [the third-function hero] goes into a dissolution, *is assimilated into* the substance of the earth, *in its most material form: food, drink*"; see also *ibid.*, p. 145.

[88] For these and other citations, see Gonda, *Loka*, p. 37.

[89] See *ibid.*, p. 62; on the earth as *pratiṣṭhā*, see further F. B. J. Kuiper, "Cosmogony and Conception: A Query," *HRJ*, X (1970), 110.

Śalya, the most "dirt"-ridden of all, as her own. And in the process, with Yudhiṣṭhira as her champion in the "righteous battle" with Śalya, the earth becomes a "firm support" for the "sovereignty of the triple world" which Yudhiṣṭhira had always "deserved"[90] and has now finally obtained.

The aggregate of the four marshals, and the four *parvans* bearing their names, thus present a complex ethical-societal time-space symbol. At the battle of Kurukṣetra, the structures of time and space are condensed. In terms of time, all the epic's events occur at the end of a yuga (*yugānta*), a sort of "liminal" period in which these four figures and their *parvans* (literally "knots, joints"[91]) seem to represent the sum of the yugas, as if all four yugas were potentially present at the point of transition. In terms of space, representatives of all the lands of the known world are present within the land of the "Center," where the deaths of their rulers—in particular that of Śalya—symbolize the attainment by Yudhiṣṭhira of his "share," the earth, as a firm "support" for the establishment of his triple-world sovereignty, and the base for his ultimate attainment of heaven.

[90] See the passages (5:88,21; 5:34,81) cited above, Chapter 8, following n. 9.

[91] The word *parvan* can also be used for "a period of time"; see Monier-Williams, s.v., and *Mbh.* 18:5,35.

CHAPTER 11

Absolutions

The conquest of the three worlds is a perennial Indian symbol. Gonda links the theme most closely with the "soteriological theories" of the period of the Brāhmaṇas.[1] According to *Śatapatha Brāhmaṇa* 12,8,2,32, "one might secure these three worlds by three victims."[2] Although the point will be discussed in Chapter 13, for the moment one may say that even in the Brāhmaṇas, the taking of animal victims (*paśu*) involves impurities and dangers which must be neutralized.[3] It is no different in the epic. The acquisition, or recovery, of the three worlds is achieved by triumphing over human victims, "shares," in a great "sacrifice of battle," where there are mechanisms to neutralize, or absolve, the sins which have been committed to attain sovereignty by means of such an uncompromising "ritual."

On this last point we return to Krishna. We saw in Chapter 6 how, before the war begins, Krishna provides a justification for it—indeed a "just base" for conquest within the Kuru lands—by going to Hāstinapura. Now, within the war, he takes part in a series of episodes that from a certain standpoint are sins.

The first problem is to differentiate between "viewpoints" on this matter, and the best initial guideline is provided by the

[1] Gonda, *Loka*, p. 44.
[2] *Ibid.*, p. 62, citing also *ŚB* 6,7,2,13ff.
[3] So, also, does the slaying of Viśvarūpa, in *ŚB* 1,2,3,1–5; see Dumézil, *Destiny of the Warrior*, pp. 24–26.

insight of Walter Ruben that Krishna's involvements are not sins because, in conformity with his own ethics of the *Gītā*, he acts not for his own ends, but for those of others.[4] This does not mean that Krishna is beyond reproach. When Duryodhana falls, delivered a foul blow by Bhīma's mace which he knows was prompted by Krishna, he blames Krishna for the deaths of Bhīṣma, Droṇa, Karṇa, and Bhuriśravas (9:60,30–34), the latter seemingly a royal stand-in for the "righteously slain" Śalya.[5] And when Gāndhārī sees her hundred sons slain on the battlefield, she charges Krishna with "overlooking" (*upa-īkṣ-*; 11:25,36,38 and 40)[6] the destruction while being able to prevent it. But these insights are drawn from personal passions and attachments. There is no doubt that they capture the surface events and produce charges that any "secular" judge would honor in the courtroom. But they do not capture the essential. Indeed, there is some irony in the charge that Krishna "overlooks" or "is indifferent to" the heroes' fates. One thinks of his advice to Arjuna to cultivate "indifference" (*sāmyam*, *samatvam*; *Gītā* 5,18–19; 2,48; 4,22, etc.).

Ruben, however, takes us only this far, for Krishna's "innocence" does not automatically exculpate those whom he counsels. Yudhiṣṭhira in particular, contrary to Arjuna, falls outside the umbrella of the *Gītā*. As we saw in Chapter 9, his own *mea culpa* stresses over and over that he has sinned out of the desire (*lubdha*) for short-lived sovereignty. Indeed, his sins have such impact that they affect his brothers: when he lies to Droṇa, Arjuna sees this "great injustice" as the "disfigurement" (*vikāra*) of the remainder of their lives.[7]

But although Krishna is undoubtedly involved, the sins do not really affect him, unless it be with what the epic calls "shame" or "embarrassment." In the scene just mentioned

[4] See above, Chapter 9, at n. 22 and the note.
[5] For Bhuriśravas' death, see above, Chapter 10, n. 2.
[6] Ganguli-Roy: "being indifferent to"; *Mahabharata*, VII: *Stree Parva*, 41.
[7] See above, Chapter 10, above n. 15.

in which Duryodhana blames Krishna for the deaths of his major warriors, Duryodhana continues, after Krishna denounces him in turn, with a recitation of his own virtues. It is roughly trifunctional and reminiscent, in structure, of another bit of boastful self-praise by Yayāti.[8] Following each citation with the formulaic question: "Who is there having a better end than myself," Duryodhana marks off three areas of self-fulfillment:

[By] study [*adhītim*], [by] donation according to prescription [*vidhivaddattam*], I have been ruler [*praśāstā*] of the earth with her seas. . . .[9]

What is sought by members of the kṣatriya class reflecting on their *svadharma*, that end [*nidhanam*; death in battle[10]] is obtained. . . .

Human shares [*mānuṣā bhāgāḥ*] worthy of the gods, difficult for kings to obtain, were obtained.[11] [60,47–49]

These three areas of achievement, he says, have won him heaven, and his words are given sanction by a shower of heavenly flowers falling to melodies of the Gandharvas, Apsarases, and Siddhas (60,51–53). Momentarily, victory has turned to defeat, defeat to victory. Seeing this *pūjā* of Duryodhana and "hearing that Bhīṣma, Droṇa, as well as Karṇa and Bhuriśravas were slain unrighteously" (*adharmataḥ*), the Pāṇḍavas, "headed by Vāsudeva" (*vāsudevapurogamāḥ*), became ashamed (*vrīḍāmupāgaman*; 60,54–55).

At this low point, the true end of the battle, Krishna begins to set things right. Before the battle, he had established the conditions for a dharmic victory by Yudhiṣṭhira and a yogic battle performance by Arjuna. Within the battle, while remaining "indifferent," "aloof," he guided these two and

[8] 1:88,21–24; see above, Chapter 8, at n. 28.

[9] The first two achievements have to do with following specifically religious injunctions and the last with sovereignty—all connected with the first function.

[10] This is the interpretation, surely correct, in Ganguli-Roy, *Mahabharata*, VII: *Salya Parva*, 181.

[11] These shares presumably refer to Duryodhana's material position, his wealth, prosperity.

their brothers to a victory which nonetheless left them flawed and ashamed. Now, from two of the "three Kṛṣṇa's"—Vāsudeva and Vyāsa—we learn why these sins were necessary and how they can be absolved. In general, this may be called the "restorative" or "reconstructive" phase, carried out, as Biardeau has enabled us to anticipate, by the two incarnations of Viṣṇu-Nārāyaṇa.

First, with regard to the necessity of the sins, there is the justification by divine precedent, so contemptuously discounted as "late" by the younger Adolf Holtzmann.[12] On the contrary, however, parallels drawn between mythic scenarios and epic events are often invaluable guidelines for cross-interpretation. In the present scene, after Krishna and the Pāṇḍavas' shame at the cosmic approval of Duryodhana, Krishna sets himself the task of restoring the good cheer of victory. First he admits that such formidable foes as Duryodhana has cited could not have been slain "in fair fight" (*ṛjuyuddhena*); "therefore these stratagems were contrived by me" (*upāyā vihitā hyete mayā*; 60,57). Then, in reply to Duryodhana's specific charges, he says: "Surely these four were all high-souled and first-rate chariot warriors on earth; they could not have been slain righteously [*dharmatas*] even by the Lokapālas themselves" (59). So far, in substantiating the superiority of the foe and admitting his own part in three of the four episodes analyzed in the last chapter, Krishna would seem to have provided only further cause for humiliation. But now comes the justification: "Enemies of superior number are to be slain falsely [*mithyāvadhās*], as also by stratagems [*upāyair*]. This path [*mārga*] was formerly followed when the gods were slayers of the Asuras. A path followed by the good [*sadbhis*] may be trodden by all" (60,62).

This speech, concluded with an invitation to take a well-earned rest, fills the victors with delight. In it, Krishna has

[12] Holtzmann, *Mahābhārata und seine Theile*, I, 84.

referred only to a general divine-asuric situation and has specified no particular mythic "stratagems." One cannot, however, help but think of the triumphs of Indra; indeed, in one of these, his triumph over Vṛtra, we have seen Śalya's epic account attribute his success to a "contrivance" (*upāya*) proposed by Viṣṇu.[13] One cannot, of course, insist that it is the *Udyogaparvan*'s three-part sequence that Krishna has in mind. But, as we see from a second speech by Vyāsa, such general references to the gods can hardly be imagined without Indra's involvement.

Addressing Yudhiṣṭhira who has just declared that he and his brothers can only expect to fall into Hell head downward (*narake . . . adhaśirasaḥ*) for their sins (12:33,11), Vyāsa calls to mind the former battle between the younger Devas and the older Asuras (12:34,13) in which the gods, "having made the earth one ocean of blood" (*ekārṇavāṃ mahīṃ kṛtvā rudhireṇa pariplutām*), slew the Asuras and "obtained heaven" (*tridivaṃ . . . lebhire*; 34,14). One recalls here the younger-elder theme which the epic plays out in connection with Arjuna and Duryodhana at Krishna's bedside,[14] but is also reminded of the theme of conquering heaven having made the blood-bathed earth a firm foundation. In the battle which Vyāsa is describing, having won the earth (15), the gods had to slay the Śālāvṛka brahmins who, promoting adharma (18), sided with the Asuras (16–17).[15] Thus the gods committed the transgression of necessary brahminicide in a fashion reminiscent of the slaying of Droṇa. At this point Vyāsa advises Yudhiṣṭhira to realize that "virtue sometimes takes the form of vice" (*adharmarūpo dharmo*;

[13] 5:10,10; see above, Chapter 9, following n. 14.

[14] See above, beginning of Chapter 5.

[15] Certain Sālāvṛka wolves are mentioned as figuring in Indra's sins in the Brāhmaṇas (see *AB* 7,28; *JB* 2,134; *Kauś. Up.* 3,1), but there it is *to them* that he has "given" the Yatis. Perhaps, in a fashion similar to the handling of the Vṛtra myth, the epic poets have "clarified" this ancient sin which probably always involved the murder of holy persons (the Yatis are presumably ascetics) into a direct brahminicide.

20) and that he has merely "followed the path formerly trodden by the gods" (*devaiḥ pūrvagataṃ mārgam*; 21). Moreover, since he has acted "unwillingly, forced by the fault of another" (*para-doṣeṇa kārataḥ anicchamānaḥ*; 25), and is repentant, it will now be possible for him to achieve expiation (*prāyaścittam*; 26) by performing an Aśvamedha. The model Vyāsa cites here is Indra, who presumably after the conquest just cited, performed his hundred sacrifices (thus the name Śatakratu; 27). But one will recall that it is even more specifically after his flawed triumphs over Viśvarūpa and Vṛtra, and the recovery of his throne from Nahuṣa, that Indra is again (?) absolved of his sins by an Aśvamedha which he performs at the advice of Viṣṇu.[16]

At this point a number of themes converge. First, with regard to the Aśvamedha, although traditionally performed as a rite that gives proof to and expression of the highest sovereignty, it comes, in the epic, to be associated almost exclusively with expiation.[17] Once again we meet with the collusion of Vyāsa and Krishna. Having gotten permission from Vyāsa to perform this sin-cleansing rite (14:70,15–16),[18] Yudhiṣṭhira addresses Krishna:

O mighty-armed one, may you now perform what I tell you, O Acyuta. The enjoyments we enjoy are acquired by your might, O delighter of the Yadus. Through prowess and intelligence, by you this earth has been conquered. Let yourself undergo the rites of initiation [*dīkṣayasva tvam ātmānam*]. You are our highest guru. If you perform the sacrifice [*tvayīṣṭavati*], O knower of dharma, I shall be

[16] 5:13,13; see above, Chapter 9, at n. 18.

[17] One wonders whether the Brāhmaṇa authors have left unmentioned one of the inherent aspects of this rite, an expiatory function necessitated by the fact that the attainment of sovereignty would almost inevitably involve martial acts requiring expiation, or whether the epic authors have innovated.

[18] It seems that the smoke from the burnt marrow of the horse (14:91,4) and the bath at the conclusion of the rite (14:90,13–14) are regarded as the features of the Aśvamedha that are the most sin-cleansing.

free from sin [*vipāpmā*], O mighty one. Surely you are sacrifice, you are imperishable, you are all, you are dharma, you are Prajāpati [*tvaṃ hi yajño kṣaraḥ sarvastvaṃ dharmastvaṃ prajāpatiḥ*]. [14:70,19–20]

I have several times referred to this identification of Krishna with the sacrifice and with Prajāpati, and of Viṣṇu with both of these as well.[19] In connection with Krishna, we now see that one of the most forceful expressions of this identification is made where it concerns expiation from sins.

Viṣṇu performs a similar expiatory function in the Aśvamedha that restores Indra to his throne. Not only, like "his" incarnation Vyāsa, does he propose the rite, but, like his other incarnation Krishna, who will make Yudhiṣṭhira "free from sin," he "distributes the sin of brahminicide among trees, rivers, mountains, earth, and women" so as to make Indra "purified of sin" (*pūtapāpmā*; 5:13,27–28). But our most important information comes from the Brāhmaṇas. One best appreciates the implications of the identification of Krishna with the sacrifice (and with Prajāpati) at a point concerning expiation in the well-known formula of the sacrificial texts: "Viṣṇu is the sacrifice" (*yajño vai viṣṇus*; *ŚB* 3,2,1,38, etc).

Gonda, in discussing this formula, says that Viṣṇu "is not only the sacrifice or its life (cf. *ŚB* 4,2,3,10), he is also its guardian and protector: . . . Viṣṇu guards that of the sacrifice which is badly sacrificed."[20] Indeed, in the texts where this formula is used, or where related notions are aired, Viṣṇu is identified with the sacrifice most frequently at points where his restorative power, his power to "atone," is at the very forefront of the authors' interests. Thus, not only does he "guard" or "protect" the rite (see *TS* 3,1,10,3; 6,2,9,2; cf. *ŚB* 4,2,2,4) but "heals" the sacrificer who is ill (*TS* 2,3,11,2), maintains "continuity" (*TS*

[19] On Krishna, Viṣṇu, and Prajāpati, see above, Chapter 5, nn. 4 and 5; for Krishna and other priestly roles, see Chapter 6 and n. 63 and Chapter 8, at n. 68 and following; see also *Gītā* 9,16.

[20] Gonda, *Early Viṣṇuism*, p. 79.

3,5,1,4), and "unites" the "broken" sacrifice (*TS* 3,2,5,3; cf. 6,1,4,4). But most interesting are the passages where Viṣṇu is spoken of as the god who brings about "atonement" (*prāya-ścitti*; cf. *Mbh.* 12:34,26, cited just above[21]) for sacrifices badly performed. For instance, we are told that should the *dīkṣita* (a person undergoing preparation for a religious ceremony) fail to confine his speech during the *dīkṣā* to appropriate mantras, the sacrifice abandons him: "In that case, then, let him mutter a *ṛk*, or *yajus* addressed to Viṣṇu, for Viṣṇu is the sacrifice [*yajño vai viṣṇus*]: thereby he again gains hold of the sacrifice; and this is the atonement [*prāyaścittiḥ*] for that [transgression]" (*ŚB* 3,2,1,38). These words are nearly echoed in *Śatapatha* 1,7,4,20, a passage we shall turn to in Chapter 12. But on the present topic, the most informative passage comes from the *Aitareya Brāhmaṇa*, part of a long discussion of "penances" (*prāyaścitti* again) which can be performed for various ritual mistakes. In particular, if the fire offering is spilled or boils over, after touching water one moves the right hand over what fell out and mutters this mantra:

> "May a third go to heaven to the gods as a sacrifice; might I obtain thence wealth! May a third go to the air, to the Pitaras . . .; may a third go to the earth, to men. . . ." Then he mutters the Viṣṇu-Varuṇa verse, *yayor ojasā sthabitā rajāṃsi* ("by whose force were established the spaces"—*AV* 7,25,1). For Viṣṇu watches over what is performed badly in the sacrifice, and Varuṇa over what is performed well [*viṣṇur vai yajñasya duriṣṭam pāti varuṇa sviṣṭam*]. To appease both of them this penance (is appropriate). [7,5,2–4][22]

[21] See after n. 15; Vyāsa uses the related neuter, *prāyaścittam*.

[22] Martin Haug, trans., *The Aitareya Brahmanam of the Rig Veda*, vol. I (text) and vol. II (trans.) (Bombay: Government Central Book Depot; London: Trübner, 1863), I, 172, and II, 446–47. Unless he has a variant, Arthur Berriedale Keith, trans., *Rigveda Brāhmaṇas: The Aitareya and Kauṣītaki Brāhmaṇas of the Rigveda*, Harvard Oriental Series, XXV (Cambridge: Harvard University Press, 1920), 292, errs in having Viṣṇu guard the well-sacrificed, Varuṇa the ill-sacrificed (and also in having "me" for "men").

The line of thought seems to move from the commission of a ritual mistake, to the re-establishment of a proper relationship with the three worlds, to a verse honoring Viṣṇu and Varuṇa for their parts in stabilizing these "spaces," thus achieving *prāyaścitti*. Varuṇa's role in "establishing" the "spaces" no doubt evokes his relation to the *ṛta* and thus implies the supervision of what is well "ordered" or "performed well." But Viṣṇu's role of overseeing what is "performed badly"—which would, after all, seem to explain the need for *prāyaścitti*—seems to recall something else. As discussed in Chapter 6, from the Brāhmaṇas on through the epics and Purāṇas, Viṣṇu's three steps are taken to help recover for the gods what was once theirs, what, for one reason or another, they have lost. In other words, the steps have a restorative value. Moreover, by marking off the three zones, Viṣṇu recreates an order, "establishes spaces"[23] which the gods, or the sacrificer, may then conquer.

In connection with the *Aitareya* passage, these last points are somewhat speculative. To confirm them, one would have to demonstrate that a connection has been drawn between Viṣṇu's expiatory function and his three steps. As far as I know, the sacrificial texts are silent here. But the epic is not, or so it would seem from the words which Yudhiṣṭhira, after his *Śāntiparvan* laments and confessions, says to Krishna: "We have got back the kingdom and the earth stands under [our] sway. Through your grace, O you whose steps traversed the three worlds [*trilokagativikrama*], victory and foremost fame have been won, and we have not fallen off from dharma" (12:45,18–19). Yudhiṣṭhira's choice of this epithet—certainly unusual for Krishna—thus connects the strides with the establishment of sway over the earth, the attainment of victory and fame, and the maintenance of dharma, all through Krishna's grace.

We have thus moved from ritual faults to personal sins. Whereas in the Brāhmaṇas, Viṣṇu expiates the one, in the epic,

[23] Note that in the *AV* mantra cited in the *AB* passage, *rajas* is plural; according to M-W (s.v.), this usually signifies "three spaces," sometimes six.

Viṣṇu and Krishna expiate the other,[24] that is, Viṣṇu provides atonement for the sins of Indra, Krishna for those of Yudhiṣṭhira. This shift from sacrificial faults to moral faults is as smooth as the shift from sacrificial virtues to moral virtues in the mythology of Śrī, and it is a transition that by no means implies a break in continuity. The moral defects by which Yudhiṣṭhira achieves the deaths of the four Kuru marshals are committed within a great sacrifice of battle, one which he has "performed badly." And the atonement which frees him from sin is achieved by the "king of rites" (*ŚB* 13,2,2,1), the Aśvamedha, supervised by the *avatāra* of the god who himself embodies the expiatory function of the sacrifice.

[24] See *Gītā* 18,66: "Abandoning all dharmas, go to me as your sole refuge; from all sins I shall release you; be not grieved" (*sarvadharmān parityajya mām ekaṃ śaranaṃ vraja / ahaṃ tvā sarvapāpebhyo mokṣayiṣyāmi mā śucaḥ*) (my translation).

PART FOUR

THE END OF AN AGE

CHAPTER 12

Epic Eschatology

A curious fact about the Hindu tradition is that from Vedic through Purāṇic times there is no myth of a once-and-for-all end of the world. The "optimism" of the Vedas and the cyclical time of later Hinduism seem to make such a notion impossible. Yet within the cyclical view, the world does end over and over again. So it is with the great myth of the *pralaya* and, on a lesser scale, with the general myth of the "end of the yuga." And in loose connection with these official time schemes, numerous myths offer descriptions of world-ending destructions, cataclysmic reversals of the world order (such as most *avatāra* myths, the Bāṇāsura myth, *tripuradāhana*, and the destruction of Dakṣa's sacrifice).

In recent years, several scholars have raised suspicions that the *Mahābhārata*, which tells about the end of the yuga previous to ours and involves an *avatāra*, incorporates a variety of rich and perhaps very ancient, eschatological symbolism. Stig Wikander, in his comparisons of the *Mahābhārata* with Iranian and Scandinavian myths and legends, has noticed that in both the Iranian and Indian epics there stands, over and against the differentiated forces of "good" (like the Pāṇḍavas), one dominating "demonic" figure—Afrāsiyāb or Duryodhana—who leads the otherwise undifferentiated forces of "evil."[1] As Wikander says, these epic figures correspond, in their leadership roles, to such mythical "demon"-leaders as the Scandinavian Loki and the Iranian Ahriman. This suggests to him

[1] Wikander, "Eschatologie," p. 87.

that an Indo-European eschatology, known from the mythologies of Scandinavia and Iran, has also survived, transposed into epic, in Iran and India. However, although Scandinavian mythology yields a single leader of the demonic host in the person of Loki, the Scandinavian epic tradition closest to the *Mahābhārata*—the account of the Battle of Brávellir—does not. Nor, as Dumézil points out, does the role of Odinn in the Scandinavian eschatological myth correspond to the same Odinn's role—as the treacherous impersonator of Bruno—at the Battle of Brávellir.[2]

These disjunctions raise questions which are as yet unsolved. If the Indo-Iranian epic parallels do result from mythic transpositions, perhaps the parallels between the *Mahābhārata* and the Battle of Brávellir show us something of the older heroic story, not without eschatological or at least "age-ending" themes,[3] that these myths helped to reshape. But Duryodhana does not provide the only hint that eschatological themes have surfaced in the *Mahābhārata*. Nor must one suppose that, during the story's presumably long history and development, only one eschatology has been "transposed" into it.

To date, besides Wikander, two authors have expressed their views on this subject, one pressing the Indo-European quest further, the other turning back to more recent periods in the traditions of India.

Dumézil and Biardeau

Notwithstanding the contribution of Wikander, Dumézil has gone farthest in examining Indo-European eschatologies for parallels to the *Mahābhārata*. In fact, Wikander seems to accept Dumézil's analysis, as Dumézil does his. But although they do

[2] Dumézil, *ME*, I, 257; on Bruno, see above, Chapter 5, at n. 17 and following.

[3] See above, Chapter 10, at n. 61 and nn. 61–62: the Indo-Scandinavian epic parallels concerning the regeneration of the Center.

not contradict each other, neither has attempted to show how the two sets of results might support each other.[4]

Dumézil's work has proceeded in essentially two steps: first, in the chapter, "Le drame du monde," of his *Les Dieux des Germains*,[5] he has made the initial direct confrontation of the Indian drama with the Scandinavian myth of the Ragnarök, the "Doom of the Gods" (more commonly, but corruptly, Ragnarökr, "Twilight of the Gods"), and second, still loyal to his original conclusions and supposedly reinforcing them, he has, in *Mythe et épopée*, I, examined one additional episode from each tradition—the Scandinavian and the epic—and proposed parallels for these.[6] Dumézil has in mind an ancient eschatological intrigue developing in three phases and found in both the *Mahābhārata* and the myth of the Ragnarök: "It is thus, in outline, a cosmic conflict which takes place in three 'epochs': the rigged game [*jeu truqué*], by which Evil triumphs for a long time, removing from the scene the representatives of Good; the great battle in which the Good takes revenge, eliminating the Evil definitively; the government of the good."[7] Let us follow Dumézil's discussion of these three "époques" in the Scandinavian traditions[8] and then see whether he can justly point to a similar scansion in the *Mahābhārata*.

(1) *Jeu truqué*. The drama of the world's end begins in the past, a precarious balance as the axis of their society having been established by the gods at the end of the war between the two divine groups, the Aesir and the Vanir.[9] The functional posts are manned by several gods: Odinn the magical sovereign

[4] See Wikander, "Eschatologie," p. 87; Dumézil, *ME*, I, 255–57.

[5] Dumézil, *Dieux des Germains*, pp. 78–105.

[6] Thus, from the Ragnarök, parallels between Vidar's role and that of Viṣṇu as the Dwarf (*ME*, I, 230–37); and, from the epic, allusions to intra-Indian parallels to the *Sauptikaparvan* (*ibid.*, pp. 213–18).

[7] *Dieux des Germains*, p. 89, quoted in *ME*, I. 227 (my translation).

[8] In opposition, see Edgar Polomé, "The Indo-European Component in Germanic Religion," in *Myth and Law among the Indo-Europeans*, p. 64.

[9] *Dieux des Germains*, pp. 3–39; I follow Dumézil here.

and patron of war, Thor the sole bearer of the thunderbolt, and Njordr and Freyr the givers of riches, pleasure, and peace. But no god, not even Odinn, offers any kind of high moral example: the world is without a Mitra. The gods "govern the world just as it is, on a moral level that is rather low and with little of the ideal."[10] There are, however, two sons of Odinn—Baldr and Hodr—who seem to make up for this lack. In Hodr and his role as the blind instrument of fate, Dumézil sees a continuation of certain aspects of "Bhaga the blind," the Vedic "minor sovereign god" subordinate to Mitra and Varuṇa, who is responsible for the apportionment of goods. And in Baldr, he sees a continuation of another important "minor sovereign," Aryaman, patron of the *ārya* society.[11] The ideal is especially found in Baldr, and to show this Dumézil cites a passage, which we shall re-examine, from the *Gylfaginning* (The Beguiling of Gylfi) of Snorri Sturluson:[12]

He is the best of them and everyone sings his praises. He is so fair of face and bright that a splendor radiates from him, and there is one flower so white that it is likened to Baldr's brow; it is the whitest of all flowers [Turville-Petre: the Ox-eye daisy, or matricary[13]]. From that you can tell how beautiful his body is, and how bright his hair. He is the wisest of the gods, and the sweetest-spoken, and the most merciful, but it is a characteristic of his that *no judgment of his may be realized.*[14]

[10] *ME,* I, 223 (my translation); see also the discussion of Tyr's "debasement," *Dieux des Germains,* pp. 66–76.

[11] On Hodr and Baldr, see *Dieux des Germains,* pp. 98–99; *ME,* I, 227–28; on Hodr-Bhaga, cf. Polomé's skepticism, "Indo-European Component," p. 76, n. 56.

[12] See *Dieux des Germains,* pp. 93–94; *ME,* I, 224.

[13] Turville-Petre, *Myth and Religion,* p. 106.

[14] For Snorri, I quote from Jean I. Young, trans., *The Prose Edda of Snorri Sturluson* (Cambridge: Bowes and Bowes, 1954), p. 51; for the italicized ending I follow the reading of Dumézil and Turville-Petre (see citations in nn. 12 and 13, and, with the text, Dumézil, *Myth to Fiction,* p. 184); Young mistranslates: "Once he has pronounced a judgment it can never be altered"; the verb in question, *haldast,* means rather "be held," "be made good," "be realized."

As Dumézil says, he represents a high ideal, the highest of all, no doubt, but a thwarted one—not to be realized with the world as it is.

Then tragedy strikes. Baldr has dreams which indicate to him that his life is menaced, and when he tells the other gods, they seek to protect him. Frigg, Odinn's wife and Baldr's mother, obtains an oath from every object—fire and water, metals, stones, trees, sicknesses, beasts, birds, serpents—that it will do Baldr no harm. The gods then take up the pastime of hurling objects at Baldr and delighting in his invulnerability. But they have failed to reckon on the maliciousness of Loki who, under disguise, obtains from Frigg the information that she has omitted to extract an oath from one plant, the mistletoe, which she regarded as too young.[15] Loki secures the plant and comes back with it to the assembly.

> Now Hodr was standing on the outer edge of the circle of men because he was blind. Loki asked him: "Why aren't you throwing darts at Baldr?" He replied: "Because I can't see where Baldr is, and, another thing, I have no weapon." Then Loki said: "You go and do as the others are doing. . . . I will show you where he is standing; throw this twig at him." Hodr took the mistletoe and aimed it at Baldr as directed by Loki. The dart went right through him and he fell dead to the ground. This was the greatest misfortune ever to befall gods and men.[16]

This is the disastrous *jeu truqué*, rigged game, of the Scandinavian eschatological drama, the prelude to the "doom of the gods." There are, however, certain sequels that are of interest. When the gods recover from their shock, Frigg promises that her affection and favor can be won by the god who will ride to Hel to ask the demoness of that name, Loki's own daughter,

[15] On the mistletoe and the discussion provoked by Sir James Frazer, see Jonathan Z. Smith, "When the Bough Breaks," *HRJ* XII (1972) 342–71; see also Polomé, "Indo-European Component," p. 75: "the plant of life that belongs to death, or better, of a life that is not granted to man."

[16] Young, trans., *Prose Edda*, p. 81.

whether Baldr can somehow be ransomed. A son of Odinn, Hermod, does the honors, riding on Odinn's horse; but when he inquires if Baldr may ride back with him, Hel, "to see whether Baldr was loved as much as people said," devised a test:

"If everything in the world, both dead or alive, weeps for him, then he shall go back to the Aesir, but he shall remain with Hel if anyone objects or will not weep." . . . [Upon this good news] the Aesir sent messengers throughout the whole world to ask for Baldr to be wept out of Hel; and everything did that. . . . When the messengers were coming home, having made a good job of their errand, they met with a giantess sitting in a cave; she gave her name as Thokk. They asked her to weep Baldr out of Hel. She answered: "Thokk will weep dry tears . . . let Hel hold what she has." It is thought that the giantess there was Loki.[17]

Though Loki could not be slain at the site of Baldr's death since it was a sanctuary, he is finally caught and chained to a cave by the gods.[18] But the chains will someday break, and he will return at the head of his demonic offspring and various other minions of evil at the time of the Ragnarök.

(2) *The great battle of the Ragnarök.* No detailed discussion of the war is necessary. In a fashion similar to the climactic battle of the Zoroastrian tradition,[19] each god, including those connected with the three functions, faces off against a single formidable adversary; but in a fashion dissimilar to the Zoroastrian battle, most of the gods—even taking their foes with them—meet their doom, the chief exception being Vidar,

[17] *Ibid.*, pp. 83–84.

[18] Disagreeing on the "originality" of Loki's role, see Dumézil, *Myth to Fiction*, pp. 181–82, and Turville-Petre, *Myth and Religion*, p. 46 (ancient) and Polomé, "Indo-European Component," p. 64 (Snorri's fabrication along lines of ethical dualism); on the bound demon theme, see above, Chapter 6, at n. 56.

[19] Dumézil, *Dieux des Germains*, pp. 83–84; *ME*, I, 221, n. 1; see *Bundahishn* 34,27–28 (Behramgore Tehmuras Anklesaria, ed. and trans., *Zand-Ākasīh*: *Iranian or Greater Bundahisn* [Bombay: Rahnumae Mazdayasna Sabha, 1956], pp. 291–92).

who steps forth to avenge Odinn and to save the world from being swallowed, that is, totally annihilated, by the Fenrir wolf.[20]

(3) "*Renaissance.*" The "rebirth" thus made possible is multidimensional—cosmic, "political," individual:

At that time the earth will rise out of the sea and be green and fair. . . . Vidar and Vali [Baldr's avenger against Hodr] will be living, . . . and they will inhabit Idavoll where Asgard used to be. And the sons of Thor, Modi and Magni, will come there and possess Mjollnir [Thor's hammer]. After that Baldr and Hodr will come from Hel. They will sit down together and converse, calling to mind their hidden lore and talking about things that happened in the past.[21]

These two, both personally revived in some inexplicit manner, will head up the government of the renewed world in Odinn's hall (cf. *Vǫluspa*, 62). In this return of the "ideal" ruler, Dumézil sees Baldr's collaboration with Hodr as a continuation of their identities as minor sovereigns—a pattern for which Dumézil then finds parallels in the *Mahābhārata*.

Dumézil finds a similar three-phase drama in the *Mahābhārata*, but not without evoking some questions. His arrangement of the epic drama seems designed mainly to bring into relief the two figures whom he identifies as further continuations of the "minor sovereigns": the blind king Dhṛtarāṣṭra as a continuation of Bhaga and, more particularly, of Fate or Destiny; and Vidura as a transposition of Aryaman, the overseer of the integrity of the Bhārata family, *kula*. Once again, let us take up the "three epochs" in order. Here, for each one, Dumézil gives a convenient summary in *Les Dieux des Germains*:[22]

[20] See above, n. 6. Dumézil compares this step with Viṣṇu's three.

[21] Young, *Prose Edda*, pp. 91–92.

[22] Dumézil, *Dieux des Germains*, pp. 91–92; my translations (bracketed material is Dumézil's; the asterisks refer to the prototype figure for that role, whether a divinity by that name or not).

(1) *Jeu truqué.* "In the first decisive 'temps' of the action, Duryodhana [-demon] induces the blind Dhṛtarāṣṭra [-*Destiny], despite the warnings of Vidura [-*Aryaman], to organize the game of dice in which, normally, Yudhiṣṭhira [-*Mitra] would be invincible but in which, by the supernatural fixing of the dice, he will be defeated and, as a result, obliged to disappear for a long time." First, Dumézil is able to find certain parallels with the missile-throwing game of the Scandinavian gods. Each is a game in which tragedy occurs through some sort of treachery. In each case a blind personage (both, according to Dumézil, continuations of *Bhaga) serves as an instrument of fate, impelled by a character of demonic stature. Both games end with the disappearance of an "ideal" figure who will return to rule only after a long time. Dumézil then discusses certain divergences which he attributes to changing conditions over long stretches of time and space. Some of these, however, seem rather marked. The character of the two games varies widely: Dhṛtarāṣṭra is a blind accomplice, knowing full well what he is doing, whereas Hodr is innocent; Duryodhana rules after the dice game, whereas Loki is chained. But none of these "divergences" is more important than a fact which escapes mention in Dumézil's treatment. Whereas one can truly say of Baldr that he plays "complacently at the game of projectiles"[23] because everyone thinks him invulnerable, one cannot say that Yudhiṣṭhira "should fear nothing from the dice game, since he is the best of players."[24] He cannot be the best, for, as the deceitful gamester Śakuni says to Duryodhana, Yudhiṣṭhira is "fond of dicing, but he doesn't know how to cast" (*dyūtapriyas . . . na ca jānāti devitum*; 2:44,18). Nor does he have nothing to fear. On this point his most forceful statement concerns the invitation to the rematch after the disaster, or near disaster, of the

[23] Dumézil, *ME*, I, 228 (my translation).
[24] *Ibid.* (my translation).

first match: "This challenge to a game of dice comes from the command of the old [king]. Even knowing that it will cause destruction, I cannot get out of it" (2:67,4).

Yudhiṣṭhira and Baldr, then, are different sorts of "losers"; and one begins to suspect that it is not a matter of *divergences* in these games so much as real *differences*. Yudhiṣṭhira has already been a king whereas Baldr has not. Yudhiṣṭhira goes into exile, Baldr dies. These and the variances cited by Dumézil put enough strain on the comparison to make one question whether Baldr and Yudhiṣṭhira, who have so little in common other than their "ideal" character and "ideal" rule, should really be compared. Both represent an "ideal," but are there no other archaic ideals than those associated with Mitra and the "minor sovereigns"?

(2) *The great battle of the Mahābhārata.* "In the second decisive 'temps,' Duryodhana [-Demon] mounts a formidable coalition against Yudhiṣṭhira [-*Mitra] and his brothers and allies, and in the battle which follows, the Pāṇḍavas [-trifunctional gods incarnate] each kill an adversary of their own rank, including Duryodhana." All these points (except for a Scandinavian *Mitra) have reasonably close parallels not only in the Scandinavian drama but in the Iranian, and once again detailed discussion is not needed. Here there truly seem to be divergences and different orientations, and Dumézil is attentive to these. Thus in Scandinavia most of the "good" gods die; in Iran the "good" Amesha Spentas triumph; and in India, though the "good" heroes triumph in the name of the gods, there are also "good" heroes who fight for the "bad" side. I will return to some of these problems.

(3) "*Renaissance.*" "Finally, in the renovation which follows the crisis, the blind Dhṛtarāṣṭra [-*Destiny] and the just Vidura [-*Aryaman], fully reconciled, back up the work which is most fully exemplified in the person of Yudhiṣṭhira [-*Mitra]." This definition of the "renaissance," which, according to Dumézil, allows for direct parallels with the

return of Baldr (-*Aryaman *and* -*Mitra)[25] and Hodr (-*Bhaga, "Blind Destiny"), again creates difficulties with his interpretation. Essentially, it is a matter of determining what constitutes the "reborn" world of the epic, and I doubt that Yudhiṣṭhira's postwar rule can be considered idyllic. Before the battle, the poets can refer to him gracefully as the *dharmarāja*, the ideal ruler;[26] but after the war, in which his sins are the most instrumental in attaining victory, he is the reluctant king of a decimated earth whose chief act is the performance of a sin-cleansing Aśvamedha. To be sure, his postwar assistants include Dhṛtarāṣṭra and Vidura, who may well be prolongations of Bhaga and Aryaman; but it seems extravagant to assign eschatologically significant roles to these two old counselors whose most important moments, after the battle, are their deaths.[27] The traditional Hindu view,[28] which is best followed here, links the beginning of the new age not to the rule of Yudhiṣṭhira, but rather to the rule which he and his counselors set up for Arjuna's grandson Parikṣit. He will be an ideal ruler, but, like Baldr, the ruler of an attenuated age, retaining the ideal and the hope of a fresh beginning but without his glorious yet imperfect grandfathers (the trifunctionally arrayed Pāṇḍavas)—just as Baldr must rule without the former gods (likewise trifunctionally arrayed), worthy of reverence yet "with little of the ideal."

Dumézil, however, has reached other conclusions on the question of Parikṣit's birth which allow him, even while calling attention to it as a key eschatological theme, to set it apart. Beyond the eschatological intrigue in three phases, he sees "the rest of the epic, the episode of the embryo with its antecedents and consequences [the birth of Parikṣit], the

[25] See above, n. 11.

[26] See especially 4:27,12–24, cited in *ME*, I, 152–54.

[27] See *ME*, I, 174–75.

[28] The Kali yuga begins with the accession of Parikṣit; see Pargiter, *Dynasties of the Kali Age*, p. x; it also ends (see *ibid.*) with the death of Krishna.

opposition of Krishna and Aśvatthāman, and through them of Viṣṇu and Śiva, being perhaps a posterior adjunction or at least the considerable rehandling of a non-Śaivite story which it would be vain to pretend to reconstitute."[29] Thus this crucial scene, which Dumézil has so brilliantly brought into the open in *Mythe et épopée*, I, takes a back seat to the "three epochs" he had previously outlined in *Les dieux des Germains*. Of the three, only the battle, the most general of all, seems certain to pass as a common theme. The embryo episode, which is central to Biardeau's treatment of the epic crisis, will bear further scrutiny.

The alignment of the eschatological crisis of the epic with the Hindu myth of the *pralaya*, which has only begun to take shape in the ongoing studies of Madeleine Biardeau, was anticipated by Dumézil with regard to the opposition of Krishna and Aśvatthāman, Viṣṇu and Śiva, over the fate of the embryo.[30] But Dumézil drops the matter here, suggesting that this opposition "corresponds to a state of the mythology that is post-Vedic, late, already nearly Hindu."[31] He finds no way in which these themes might be combined in an overarching model with the three-phase drama he considers older. Here, by introducing the *pralaya* as a possible structuring myth, Biardeau opens up a number of new perspectives.

Although she has yet to address herself directly to the episodes which make up the first and third "epochs" of Dumézil's scheme, she distrusts the Indo-European comparison: "The cosmic crisis which forms the intrigue of the epic does not have an exact analogue in the most ancient literature, whereas one can find its model in the Pūraṇic accounts of the reabsorption and recreation of the world."[32]

[29] *ME*, I, 230 (my translation); see also pp. 219–22.
[30] Dumézil, *ME*, I, 219.
[31] *Ibid.*, p. 220 (my translation).
[32] Biardeau, *EPHE*, LXXVII, 169 (my translation).

Although Purāṇic tradition commonly distinguishes three types of *pralaya*, and even though the three form "a whole"[33] and are often narrated in sequence, it is the *naimittika-pralaya*, "the occasional reabsorption," which claims Biardeau's attention. There is no convincing reason to reject the *pralaya* as a "model" for the epic on the grounds that the myth is Purāṇic and "late." Biardeau speaks of the epic as being concerned more with the cycle of the yugas and the appearance of *avatāras* and less with the kalpa cycle, which it leaves in the background.[34] But if the kalpa system is in the background, allusions to the *naimittika-pralaya* abound throughout—in particular, as she convincingly shows, in the theophany of the *Bhagavad Gītā*.[35] Moreover, the epic gives a *pralaya* account of its own (3:186,56–78).

Biardeau shows that there are essentially three phases to the *pralaya*. First comes a terrible drought and the desiccation of the entire earth. In the second and third phases occurs what she calls the "double *pralaya*": first a "reabsorption" by Kālāgnirudra[36] (Śiva) of the three dead and desiccated worlds through yogic fire; and second, a "reabsorption" of the remains (ashes) and of all beings in the flood waters upon which Nārāyaṇa (Viṣṇu) reposes in his yogic ṣleep, thence to recreate the three worlds through Brahmā. She detects this three-act drama beneath the surface of the *Mahābhārata*.[37] Thus (1) the desiccation of the earth corresponds to the symbols and intrigues that set up the oppositions between the Pāṇḍavas and the Kauravas, between dharma and adharma, in the early books;[38]

[33] Biardeau, EMH, 3, p. 33 (my translation).

[34] *Ibid.*, p. 31.

[35] See above, Chapter 6, at n. 2.

[36] Variant: Kālāgni, Kālarudra, or, in Vaiṣṇava terms, Rudrarūpījanārdanaḥ (*VP* 6,3,30), *sughoramasivaṃ raudram . . . pāvakam*; *Mbh.* 3:186,72].

[37] Unfortunately, these correspondences are not yet set forth in any published work; I base the following summary on a letter from Biardeau of June 4, 1971.

[38] Biardeau regards the role of Bhīma in the house of lac episode as modeled on the Vāyu of the *pralaya* (*EPHE*, LXXVIII, 157–58); the burning of

(2) the burning of the three worlds, presided over by Rudra-Śiva, corresponds to the epic war which culminates in the extinction of the Kuru-Pāṇḍava line when Aśvatthāman (possessed by Śiva) destroys the last hope of its continuity—the embryo in the womb of Uttarā, wife of Arjuna's slain son Abhimanyu; and (3) the deluge and the recreation of the worlds correspond to the womb in which the embryo lies and Krishna's revival of the stillborn baby.

Biardeau is still investigating the parallels, so a hasty judgment on the confrontation of these two dramas should not be formed. But some impressions are worth expressing. Negatively, there are difficulties in accepting any close ties in the first two phases of the schema. As Biardeau notes in her letter (see n. 37), there is little symbolic correspondence between the desiccation of the earth and the signs and situations preceding the battle.[39] And in phase two, the burning of the three worlds presents no "dualistic" battle like that in the epic war or, for that matter, in the Scandinavian and Iranian myths of the end of the world. Nor is it possible to put the whole battle under Śiva-Aśvatthāman's sign, like the destructive phase of the *pralaya*. As Dumézil says, until the *Sauptikaparvan*, "the activity of Aśvatthāman is very subordinate."[40] Keeping the divine

---

Khāṇḍava forest as "a new figure of the war of destruction to come" (see above, Chapter 4, n. 1); more fragmentary, Jarāsaṃdha's imprisoning of the hundred kings as a "new image of the end of the world" (see above, Chapter 10, n. 60); Draupadī's polyandrous marriage, through Śiva's involvement, as an eschatological destruction of rules "necessary to the renewal of the world" (see above, Chapter 3, n. 9); and Draupadī's refusal of Karṇa-Sūrya as a refusal of the solar hero "who symbolizes the conflagration of the world" ("Brāhmaṇes et potiers," p. 42, n. 2) (my translations).

[39] Based on this comparison, Biardeau also proposes an answer to why there are "good" heroes on the "bad" side: Karṇa is the son of Sūrya, the sun which, "at the end of the cosmic cycle is narrowly associated with Śiva in the task of destruction" (*EPHE*, LXXVIII, 152; also EMH, 3, p. 82 and n. 1; my translation). But this does not explain why incarnations of the Rudras and Maruts (Kṛpa and Kṛtavarman), of one of the Vasus (Bhīṣma), or of Bṛhaspati (Droṇa) should side with the Kurus.

[40] Dumézil, *ME*, I, 214 (my translation).

and heroic planes of action distinct, it would be more correct to say that the battle itself, up to the *Sauptikaparvan*, is presided over by Krishna.

On the positive side, however, Biardeau indicates that *pralaya* imagery is frequently employed in descriptions of the epic action. A striking instance occurs in the third phase of her schema, when Subhadrā pleads with her brother Krishna to revive the stillborn child: "Surely, just by wishing it you could revive the three worlds [*lokāṃstrīñjīvayethāḥ*] if they were dead; what then of this cherished one born dead of your sister's son?" (14:66,17). For the most part, however, such *pralaya* imagery occurs in similes and metaphors, where it certainly does not serve to structure the epic drama. It would be more accurate to say that the *pralaya* mythology complements the epic story as a cosmological metaphor than to say that it lends form to the story as a background myth. It is true, as Biardeau points out, that in the *Gītā*, Krishna refers to the *pralaya* as the backdrop against which Arjuna is to understand the cataclysmic battle to come; but this, as Krishna says, is a divine, one might say ultimate secret, delivered only to his dearest *bhakta* (see *Gītā* 11,54). I will try to demonstrate that these sequences in the *Mahābhārata* draw their basic structure not from this "universe of *bhakti*,"[41] but from other, no doubt older, mythic and ritual scenarios—joined together and integrated not under the sign of the *pralaya* but under that of the Brāhmaṇic sacrifice.

The *Sauptikaparvan* and the Destruction of Dakṣa's Sacrifice

One principle, suggested by the *Mahābhārata* text itself, has proved valuable at several points: to examine whether there is some relation between the many myths narrated in the course of the text (usually regarded as interpolations or interruptions)

[41] I use Biardeau's term here, which she uses (EMH, 3, especially p. 84) to describe the cosmology of *pralaya* and *pratisarga*.

and the juncture in the narrative at which they are told.[42] Several fruitful paths have been opened up by comparing such myths with immediately foregoing or forthcoming incidents in the epic plot.[43] It seems likely that the texture of the epic has included a balance of didactic (including mythic) and narrative portions for as long as it has existed in India, and many of the interpretive myths seem to have conserved their place in the narrative for a long time. Nowhere does this seem more likely than at the end of the *Sauptikaparvan*. Asked there how Aśvatthāman could have carried out his night raid, Krishna tells Yudhiṣṭhira that it was through the grace of Śiva. "I know Mahādeva truly" (*tattvena*), he adds, "and also his various former deeds" (*purāṇāni karmāṇi vividhāni*; 10:17,8). The second deed he recites, the one he concludes with and links directly to the preceding events (10:18,24–26),[44] is Śiva's destruction of the sacrifice of the gods (elsewhere of Dakṣa).[45]

[42] This procedural principle was first articulated by Joseph Dahlmann, *Das Mahābhārata als Epos und Rechtsbuch: Problem aus Altindiens Cultur- und Literaturgeschichte* (Berlin: Felix L. Dames, 1899), pp. 119–22.

[43] See especially Chapter 7 (myth of Śrī and the five Indras told after Draupadī's Svayaṃvara) and Chapters 9 and 10 (myth of Indra's sins told to Yudhiṣṭhira before the war).

[44] In a just verdict, H. D. Velankar, ed., *Sauptikaparvan*, CE, "Introduction," p. xxix, refers to the first "former deed"—a myth about the *liṅgam* (10:17)—as "rather extraneous." Critical studies of the *Sauptikaparvan* are few: in addition to Dumézil (see above, n. 6), see the "inversionist" views of Holtzmann (*Mahābhārata und seine Theile*, II, 201–3) and the "solar myth" views of Ludwig ("Mythische grundlage des Mahābhārata," p. 10) in which the night raid, brought on by the "Winter God" Śiva, symbolizes the "last night-frost in spring"!

[45] I will use the term Dakṣayajña, although Dakṣa does not appear in the "early" versions of the myth, by which I refer to those in the Brāhmaṇas (see Bhattacharji, *Indian Theogony*, pp. 121–22) as well, it would seem, as the one at the end of the *Sauptikaparvan*; see also *Mbh.* 7:173,41 where Dakṣa gets only an interpolated line. Where Dakṣa does not appear, I put the term in quotes.

Recent studies of the Dakṣayajña myth include Bhattacharji, *Indian Theogony*, pp. 121–24; Jan Gonda, *Viṣṇuism and Śivaism: A Comparison* (London: Athlone, 1970), pp. 133–35; Joe Bruce Long, "Śiva's Heroic Feats—Destruction of Dakṣa's Sacrifice," thesis chapter, University of

Krishna's cue should not be ignored, but to follow it means to face some new hurdles. Krishna's account of the myth does not present it in its full scope. Yet the events of the *parvan* often seem to reflect the fully developed myth. It would seem then that while the myth told at the end originally served to complement the events of the *parvan*, the *parvan* itself has been elaborated in the light of later versions of the myth. By following the course of the *Sauptika* itself episode by episode (I can unfortunately reduce it to no less than fourteen), let us see whether the myth (or the developing tradition of myths) of the destruction of Dakṣa's sacrifice can be read as its companion tale.

(1) *Absence of Krishna.* In a matter about which the epic tells us surprisingly little, Krishna, his kinsman Sātyaki, and the five Pāṇḍavas have all conveniently absented themselves from the victory camp on the very evening of Aśvatthāman's night raid. After plundering the Kuru camp for goods, servants, and other royal spoils (9:61,33), the victors rest until Krishna interrupts: "'For the sake of acting auspiciously [*mañgalārthāya*], we should stay outside the camp.' Having said, 'So be it,' all the Pāṇḍavas, as also Sātyaki, went outside, together with Vāsudeva, for the sake of acting auspiciously" (*mañgalārtha*; 9:61,35–36). While Krishna's words are mys-

---

Chicago, kindly made available by the author; and Wendy Doniger O'Flaherty, "The Origin of Heresy in Hindu Mythology," *HRJ*, X (1971), 315–23. The texts cited are the following: along with 10:18, the *Mbh.* has four more versions: 7:173,41–51; 12:274; 12:283V–284V (*V* = *Mahābhārata* Vulgate); 12:330; 13:145,10–23 (close to 7:173); *HV* 3,22 (Gorakhpur: Gītāpress, 1967–1968); *Vām. P.* 2–5 (S. M. Mukhopadhyaya et al., trans., A. S. Gupta, ed. [Benares: All India Kashiraj Trust, 1968]); *Bhāg. P.* 4,2–7 (Gorakhpur: Gītāpress, 1964–1965); *Liñga Purāna* 69 (Bareli: Saṃskṛti-Saṃsthana, 1969); *Kūrma Purāna* 15 (R. S. Bhattacharya, ed. [Benares, 1968]); *Vāyu Purāna* (H. H. Wilson, trans., *Vishńu Puráńa*, pp. 53–60); *Śiva Purāṇa* 2,2 (*Satīkhaṇḍa*), 12–43 (P. L. Shastri, ed., trans. by a board of scholars, "Ancient Indian Tradition and Mythology," I [Delhi: Motilal Banarsidass, 1970]). See V. R. R. Dikshitar, *Purāṇic Index* (Madras: University of Madras, 1952), II, 38ff.

terious and refer only to some unexplained "welfare" (*mañgala*), the lack of explanation has been sensed in two Devanāgarī manuscripts, in which Krishna seems to refer to the role of the goddess as Kālarātrī, the "Night of Time": "Where the goddess Victory is [*jayantī yatra devī*], however, do not go about there for long. This is my request, arranged at the beginning of battle" (9,380*; following 9:61,35). This would seem appropriate, since Krishna did have Arjuna (likewise only in the Northern recension) honor Durgā on the eve of battle (*Bhīṣmaparvan*, Appendix I, n. 1), praising her not only as Victory (*vijaye jaye*; line 11) but as Bhadrakālī and Mahākālī (line 9). But within the *Sauptikaparvan*, Krishna makes way more for Śiva than for the goddess.

More interesting than the reference to Devī is the implication that Krishna has arranged this exodus beforehand. Can the *śloka* be trusted here? The only other passage which bears on these events would seem at first to make it doubtful. Just after Krishna has urged that the night be spent outside the camp, the Pāṇḍavas send him off to Hāstinapura to tell Dhṛtarāṣṭra and Gāndhārī, as gently as possible, of their sons' deaths. There, having comforted them, Krishna gets up suddenly and begs their leave, explaining: "Evil has entered the mind of Droṇa's son; . . . he has indicated the thought of slaying the Pāṇḍavas in the night" (9:61,68). Thus it would seem that Krishna does not have any foreknowledge of what will happen. But when he rejoins the Pāṇḍavas that very night, presumably not only to rescue them but to foil Aśvatthāman's plan, he merely sits down and tells them what happened at the Kuru court. Here, where we know that he knows, he is troublingly silent. We are thus left with the impression that the added *śloka* is right, that Krishna has absented himself and the Pāṇḍavas by design.

In the Dakṣayajña myth, we find a variety of attitudes expressed in different versions about the roles of Viṣṇu and Śiva. Some do not mention Viṣṇu at all, some not until the end,[46] and some say that Dakṣa's rite was dedicated to Viṣṇu (*Mbh.* 12:283,21V; *Bhāg. P.* 4,2,34; *Kūrma* P. 15,23,24; *Śiva P.* 2,2,27,37–38). But all agree on one point: Viṣṇu was not present when the sacrifice was destroyed. Some texts are quite explicit, although just as mysterious as the *Mahābhārata* is on the absence of Krishna. According to the *Kūrma*, "all the gods came for the sake of shares, Indra and so forth; but they did not see the god Īśana or Nārāyaṇa Hari" (15,21). Most pointedly, the *Bhāgavata* says: "Having formerly perceived exactly this [destruction], the lotus-born god [Brahmā] and Nārāyaṇa, the soul of all, did not go to the sacrifice" (4,5,3). Or Viṣṇu may be present until the destruction takes place. Thus the *Vāmana* tells us: "Seeing Śaṃkara with eyes reddened with anger, Hari retired from that place and stood concealed [*sthānādapākramya . . . antarhitaḥ sthitaḥ*] in Kubjāmra [a *tīrtha*]" (5,1); and in the *Śiva*, Viṣṇu is warned by a celestial voice to leave the sacrifice (2,2,31,34), which he does—after a standoff fight with Śiva's agent Vīrabhadra—both he and Brahmā going to their respective *lokas* (37,41–44) just before the destruction begins.

It is apparent that in these absences of Krishna and Viṣṇu we are, on the levels of both myth and epic, confronted by a statement about the theological complementarity of Viṣṇu and Śiva.[47] But we must postpone discussion of this (see item 14 below) until we see what is made of it by the epic itself.

(2) *Celebrants and outsiders.* Aśvatthāman and his two allies, Kṛpa and Kṛtavarman, have entered a forest near the camp just absented by Krishna, and there, as night sets in, Aśvatthāman alone remains awake. Taking his cue (*upadeśa*) from a bird of prey which he sees massacre a flock of sleeping crows, he forms the plan which Krishna became aware of at Hāstinapura: he will kill all the Pāṇḍavas and Pāñcālas while they

[46] See Gonda, *Viṣṇuism and Śivaism*, p. 135, where he says the antagonism between Śiva and Viṣṇu is a late concern. Below I discuss a Brāhmaṇic precursor.

[47] See the analogous situation at the dice game, above, Chapter 4.

are sleeping.[48] Awakened and hearing of this scheme, Kṛpa and Kṛtavarman are filled with shame, but in a series of exchanges they are persuaded. Of special interest is Aśvatthāman's first response:

The Pāñcālas are roaring out, shouting, and laughing; filled with joy, they are blowing their conches in a hundred ways, and beating their drums. The tumultuous sound of their musical instruments, mingled with the blare of their conches, is frightful, and, borne by the wind, it fills up, as it were, all the points of the compass [*diśaḥ pūrayatīva*]. Very great is the sound heard from the neighing horses and the grunting elephants, and the lion-roar of the heroes. [10:1,59–61]

Having depicted this festive gathering with what one might call its world-wide repercussions, Aśvatthāman turns, in sharp contrast, to the plight of himself and his fellows: "In this vast carnage, only we three remain. . . . I regard this as a reversal of Time" (*manye kālasya paryayam*; 63–64). This argument for the night raid thus centers on a pattern of reversals, juxtapositions: on one side is festivity, on the other embittered isolation; on one side inclusion, on the other exclusion.

Though the divine emotions may differ from the human anguish and pathos of the three Kuru survivors, the essential pattern holds. Śiva is excluded from a celebration whose universal proportions only grow with the enlargement of the universe from text to text: if it is the gods alone who take part in some apparently early versions (Brāhmaṇas; *Mbh.* 7: 173,50—"the thirty"; 10:18), the Vulgate version in the *Mahābhārata* has the sacrifice shared in by the inhabitants of the three worlds (12:283,5–8V), and the *Vāmana Purāṇa* extends this to the fourteen worlds (4,9). But, most crucial, Aśvatthāman, like Śiva, has heretofore been deprived of a "share." The very core of the Dakṣayajña myth is that Śiva has been allowed no share (*bhāga*) in the sacrifice. For Aśvatthāman the matter is less obvious but no less important.

[48] He does not know the Pāṇḍavas are absent; see also 9:65,33.

To clarify the sense in which Aśvatthāman's share is still unclaimed involves discussing what is probably the fundamental symbolism shaping the *Mahābhārata* war: that of the *raṇayajña* (5:57,12; 154,4; cf. *śastrayajña*, 5:139,29, and description thereof), "the sacrifice of battle." Although a general analogy between war and sacrifice in the epic has been long recognized,[49] few of its implications have been worked out. One of these concerns the attainment of heaven: Yudhiṣṭhira assumes that it is heroes "who poured out their bodies into the [sacrificial] fire of battle" [*juhuvurye sarīraṇi raṇavahnau*; [18:2,2] who should obtain heaven, and Nārada tells him that he sees Duryodhana there because the latter has fulfilled this requirement (18:1,14). A "heaven of heroes" (*vīraloka*) finds a place in other Indo-European afterworlds,[50] but India's thoroughgoing articulation of the warrior's death as a sacrifice is probably unique.[51] A second implication concerns the epic's use of the terms *bhāga* and *aṃśa*, "share, portion."[52] Dumézil has pointed to the importance of these terms in connection with the incarnations of the "portions" of various gods on earth. But they are also used with the combined meaning, pertinent to both the sacrifice and the battlefield, of "victim." It is interesting to note who it is that determines such war-"shares." In one crucial instance Krishna delegates Śalya as Yudhiṣṭhira's share.[53] But more generally the *senāpati*, marshal, performs this task. For the Pāṇḍavas this position was filled throughout the entire war by the Pāñcāla prince Dhṛṣṭa-

[49] See Held, *Ethnological Study*, pp. 109,270–71; Sukthankar, *Meaning of the Mahābhārata*, p. 35.

[50] See Dumézil, *Destiny of the Warrior*, pp. 111–14 So too, in reverse, the sacrificial impliments—placed on portions of the body on the funeral pyre—become the sacrificer's weapons as he conquers heaven (see *ŚB* 12,5,2,8).

[51] For a different articulation among the Celts, see the intriguing interpretation of the chief's self-sacrifice by Jean Markale, *Les Celtes* (Paris: Gallimard, 1969), pp. 50–88.

[52] See above, Chapter 10, following n. 45, and Chapter 11, n. 2.

[53] See above, Chapter 10, following n. 45.

dyumna, born, like his sister Draupadī, from the sacrificial fire and himself "a portion of Agni" (*agnerbhāgam*; var. *agneraṃśam*; 1:61,87), in fact, "an auspicious portion of Agni" (*agnerbhāgaṃ śubham*; 15:39,14). In a key passage (5:161,5–10), as the Pāṇḍava army approaches the battlefield, this indispensable ally,[54] Agni's own "auspicious portion," assigns each of his major warriors an appropriate "victim." "Having apportioned [*vibhajya*] those warriors individually and collectively, that mighty bowman of the hue of fire [*jvālāvarṇa*] fixed Droṇa as his own portion" (*aṃśa*; 10). This fatality, when it is accomplished, will then lead Dhṛtarāṣṭra to remark: "It is Asvatthāman who was created the slayer of Dhṛṣṭadyumna by the high-souled [Droṇa], even as the Pāñcāla prince . . . was [created to be the slayer] of Droṇa" (7:166,14). In this context we understand Aśvatthāman's various vows to avenge his father's death by slaying Dhṛṣṭadyumna: the latter will be his share, and the sacrifice of battle will not be complete until Aśvatthāman has claimed it.

(3 and 4) *Barring of the gate and possession.* Aśvatthāman's entry into the camp is at first barred by images of Krishna-Janārdana, which are dispelled by Aśvatthāman's homage to Śiva who, in turn, possesses Aśvatthāman (10,7,65). These episodes are theological doublets, mythical reinforcements for what occurs elsewhere on the plane of the epic narrative itself. Thus the dispelling of Krishna's images duplicates the absence of Krishna. As Dumézil has pointed out,[55] Śiva's possession of Aśvatthāman doubles the latter's identification with Śiva, as Aśvatthāman was born a mixture "of Mahādeva [Śiva] and Antaka ["Finisher"], of Krodha [Wrath] and Kāma combined into a unity" (*ekatvam upapannānām*; 1:61,66). Dumézil shows

[54] On Dhṛṣṭadyumna as distributor of shares for the Pāṇḍavas, and for the most complete list of the shares appointed to them and their allies, see 5:56,12–25; see also Biardeau's remarks on Dhṛṣṭadyumna-Agni's alliance with the Pāṇḍavas, "Brāhmaṇes et potiers," p. 43, n. 2.

[55] Dumézil, *ME*, I, 213 and 220.

this conception of Aśvatthāman to have its closest analogue in a Brāmaṇic conception of Rudra.[56]

In view of these duplications, the two episodes cannot be expected to have exact counterparts in the Dakṣayajña myth, except where figures appear who similarly duplicate the roles of Viṣṇu (such as Dharma, who is the *dvārapāla*, gate-keeper, who seeks and fails to prevent Vīrabhadra from entering the sacrifice in *Vām. P.* 4,23) or of Śiva (Vīrabhadra himself, like Aśvatthāman a "portion of Rudra," in *Bhag. P.* 4,5,4).

(5) *Entry.* "As with Īśvara entering the camp of his foe, around Aśvatthāman on all sides rushed invisible beings and Rakṣas" (10:7,66), that is, Śiva's *gaṇa*. This could be an allusion to Śiva's entry of Dakṣa's sacrifice itself. Whether it is or is not, Aśvatthāman is aided not only by Śiva's *gaṇa*, but by Kṛpa and Kṛtavarman—incarnations of the Rudras and Maruts respectively. This may reflect an "early" form of the narrative in which, without the *gaṇa*, representatives of Rudra's Vedic hosts, the Rudras and Maruts, would have aided Aśvatthāman in his act of destruction. The *gaṇa* plays no role in what appear to be the earlier versions of the "Dakṣayajña" myth (Brāhmaṇas; *Mbh.* 10:18; 7:173,41–51).

(6) "*Brutal*" *deaths.* These next two episodes form the most crucial sequence of the night raid. Aśvatthāman's activities occur in two neatly demarcated phases: in the first, ignoring the sword that Śiva has given him, he kills his foes "brutally"; in the second, using the sword, he kills by performing symbolic mutilations.

This first phase recalls the telling of his plan to Kṛpa and Kṛtavarman, to whom he predicted: "Among the Pāñcālas I shall move about, slaying them now in battle like the enraged Rudra himself, Pināka [bow] in hand, moving about among animals" (*svayaṃ rudraḥ paśuṣviva*; 10:3,19). As to his chief

[56] *Ibid.*, p. 213; to create Rudra-Bhūtavān in order to avenge Prajāpati's incest against their sister Uṣas, the gods "put their most fearful bodies in one" (*ghoratamāstanva . . . ekadhā*; *AB* 3,33,1).

antagonist: "I will grind off [*pramathiṣyāmi*] Dhṛṣṭadyumna's head like an animal's" (*paśoriva*; 3,33). Having entered the camp, he goes first to Dhṛṣṭadyumna's tent and finds him sleeping in a luxurious bed. He kicks him to wake him, seizes him by the hair (as Dhṛṣṭadyumna had done to Aśvatthāman's father Droṇa), and presses him down to the ground.

> Striking him with his foot on both his throat and chest [*tamākramya padā . . . kaṇṭhe corasi cobhayoḥ*] while he was roaring and writhing [*nadantaṃ visphurantam*], he made him die the death of an animal [*paśumāramamārayat*]. Tearing at him with his nails, Dhṛṣṭadyumna, not very clearly, said, "Slay me with a weapon [*śastreṇa*], do not delay; if you do this, I may go to well-made worlds [*sukṛtāṃllokān*]." Having heard these indistinct sounds of his, Droṇa's son said: "There are no worlds for slayers of their preceptors; therefore you do not deserve to be slain with a weapon." . . . And the wrathful one struck him in the vital parts [*marmasu*] with violent kicks of his heels." [8,18–21]

These blows bring on Dhṛṣṭadyumna's death cries which awaken certain guards, whom Aśvatthāman slays with a Rudra weapon. This first phase of butchery concludes with the deaths of two more Pāñcālas, the shadowy but strangely inseparable Uttamaujas and Yudhamanyu, who also die crying out (*vinardantam*) and writhing like animals (*visphurantaṃ ca paśuvat*; 8,31–35). The text itself indicates that these "brutal" deaths, at least beyond the particular case of Dhṛṣṭadyumna (see also 5,33–34), are not brought about simply as devices to keep the victims from reaching the heaven of heroes: "Having slain them, Aśvatthāman rushed here and there against the mahārathas . . . ; trembling and quivering, they were slain [*śamita*; or: prepared as an oblation] like animals in a sacrifice" (*iva paśūnmakhe*; 8,36).[57]

[57] It is true that animals should be silent in a sacrifice, strangled without a sound; this seems to be one of several indications that the *Sauptikaparvan* tells of a sacrifice gone out of control.

The epic also makes it clear that these slaughters portray Aśvatthāman in Śiva's ancient role of Paśupati, "Lord of Animals": "The wrathful one caused thousands of shrinking, shuddering men to fall, like Paśupati among *paśus*" (8,122). But why are these animalian deaths singled out as so especially significant for Dhṛṣṭadyumna and the Pāñcālas? In the Brāhmaṇas the name Paśupati occurs frequently in connection with the "Dakṣayajña" myth and its "multiform,"[58] the myth of Rudra's vengeance against Prajāpati for the latter's incest with Uṣas. In this second myth, *Śatapatha Brāhmaṇa* 1,7,4,1 tells us that the gods called on Rudra as Paśupati to avenge their sister, and *Aitareya Brāhmaṇa* 3,33 (in which the gods make Rudra of their most terrible forms; see n. 55) says that it was as a reward for his service that Rudra claimed *paśūnāmādhipatyam*, "sovereignty over animals." But more interesting is *Śatapatha* 1,7,3 (see also *TS* 2,6,8,1–3), one of the earliest versions of the "Dakṣayajña" itself. Here, when Rudra has interrupted the gods' sacrifice to demand his share, the gods set up the practice of giving him the last oblation under the euphemistic name of Agni Sviṣṭakṛt, "Agni the Maker of Good Offering." Accordingly: "That [offering] then is certainly made to 'Agni.' His are these names: Śarva as the eastern people call him, Bhava, as the Bāhikās [call him]; Paśūnām Pati, Rudra, and Agni. The name Agni, doubtless, is the most auspicious" (*śānta*; 1,7,3,8). On this passage, Biardeau's comments are helpful concerning "the identification of Agni with Rudra Paśupati: the sacrifice, which involves putting victims—*paśu*—to death, has for this reason an impure and dangerous aspect which must be abolished by an oblation to Rudra. It is in this that Rudra is 'master of *paśu*,' and it is also this which places him in relation to death and impurity."[59] In these early versions of the

[58] The term is used in a related way by O'Flaherty, "Origin of Heresy," p. 319; Prajāpati is "the sacrifice" whom (which) Śiva attacks. Cf. *ŚB* 1,7,3 and 4.

[59] Biardeau, EMH, 3, p. 80 (my translation); Jarāsaṃdha (another of Śiva's epic counterparts) similarly plans a sacrifice by placing the "mark

"Dakṣayajña" myth Rudra's character as "Lord of Animals" involves his identification with Agni as "slayer of animals." Under the "auspicious" name of Agni Sviṣṭakṛt, he takes his "remainder" share and permits the sacrifice to be completed. But as Paśupati, Śarva, Bhava, and Rudra, he holds the threat of destruction.

In the *Sauptikaparvan*, Aśvatthāman-Paśupati has claimed his "share" of the "sacrifice of battle" by slaying Dhṛṣṭadyumna, none other than the incarnation of "the auspicious portion of Agni" himself. In some cases, most clearly in that of Yudhiṣṭhira and Śalya, it is evident that when a combatant slays his "share," some quality which both opponents possess is enhanced in the victor at the expense of the vanquished.[60] Such seems to be the significance here. In slaying the incarnation of Agni, Aśvatthāman, as his very first act of destruction, eliminates the "auspicious Agni" and takes on the character of "the fire at the end of the yuga" (*yugānte . . . pāvakaḥ*; 10:8,137). Also, "desiring to please the son of Droṇa, Kṛpa and Kṛtavarman set fire to the camp in three places" (8,103)—a transparent allusion to the three sacrificial fires (no doubt to be correlated with the three worlds) put to inauspicious use.

If this interpretation is correct so far, a problem remains. The episode does not follow the usual schema of the Dakṣayajña myths, where Śiva obtains his share at the end of his destructive raid rather than at the beginning. Actually, in all the versions of the Dakṣayajña that I have examined, only in one case is there a parallel episode at this point. According to the *Liṅga Purāṇa*, the following is included among the mutilations inflicted by Vīrabhadra: "Having cut off the two hands of Vahni

---

of an animal" (*paśusaṃjñām*) on his royal victims (2:20,11); see also above, chapter 10, n. 60.

60 Śalya as a "share" symbolizes kingship, sovereignty, and the earth, the share which Krishna urges upon Yudhiṣṭhira (9:15,16–17); see above, Chapter 10, following n. 45; see also Chapter 10, n. 80, on Bhīṣma and "Śveta."

[Agni] and having torn out his tongue in sport, the high-powered Vīrabhadra kicked him in the head with his foot" (*jaghāna murdhni pādena*; 69,16). Dhṛṣṭadyumna was kicked in the chest and throat; both cases probably indicate a crude symbolism of "putting out a fire." But there is no sense in the *Liṅga* that in maiming Vahni, Vīrabhadra has obtained his or Śiva's share. Rather, epic and myth seem to diverge here. In the former, Aśvatthāman, by slaying foes like *paśu*, subsumes the "auspicious Agni" as his own share and takes on the aspect of the inauspicious fire at the end of the yuga. In the myth, more optimistic, Rudra becomes the auspicious fire (Sviṣṭakṛt) rather than the inauspicious (Paśupati). This is what we may call the first "inversion" concerning the matter of "shares" (see item 13 below).

(7) *Symbolic mutilations.* Having completed the first phase of the night raid, Aśvatthāman takes up his sword. This instrument, turned against particular foes, is used with precision. First, he attacks the Draupadeyas, Draupadī's five sons by the Pāṇḍavas. Yudhiṣṭhira's son Prativindhya falls when struck "in the region of the abdomen" (*kukṣideśe*; 8,50); Bhīma's son Sutasoma's arm is cut off (*bāhuṃ chittvā*; 8,52) and then he is slain when pierced through the heart presumably from his unprotected side; Śatānīka, Nakula's son, has his head cut off (*apāharacchiraḥ*; 8,54); Śrutakarman, son of Sahadeva, is struck by the sword on his mouth (*āsye*) and falls, his "mouth disfigured" (*vikṛtānanaḥ*; 8,56); and last, having let loose a brief volley of arrows to remind us of his father, Arjuna's son Śrutakīrti is decapitated, whereupon "his radiant head, adorned with earrings, fell from his body" (8,58).

The Draupadeyas present no clear structure of their own,[61] and while symbolic meaning is certainly present in their disfigurations, the symbolism is borrowed from their fathers. In three instances the correlations are striking: the son of

[61] See Dumézil, *ME*, I, 246–49; they incarnate the Viśvedevas.

Bhīma, the mightiest and most "long-armed" of the Pāṇḍavas, loses his arm; the son of Nakula, the most beautiful Pāṇḍava, loses his head; and the son of Sahadeva, noted for his eloquence and "sweet words," has his mouth disfigured.[62] Arjuna's handsomeness is also a subject of frequent praise, so it is fitting that his arrow-shooting son should be decapitated. This leaves us in the dark only about Yudhiṣṭhira's belly.[63] But the real question is why the poets have paused on this occasion to work out a tableau of mutilations for these pale and poorly defined victims.[64]

The question, of course, comes back to the Pāṇḍavas and the continuity of the Kuru line. With Abhimanyu slain and with the pregnancy of his wife still unknown (Krishna has not divulged this information yet), the deaths of the Draupadeyas symbolize not only the apparent extinction of the dynasty but—with the mutilations—the fact that the ideal image of sovereignty which the Pāṇḍavas represent (here in face, mouth, arms, and belly) cannot be revived. As to why the poets have found this a suitable occasion to display their ingenuity at the game of symbolism, one does well to look to the Dakṣayajña. The two sets of mutilations which concern different limbs and apparently unrelated victims involve the same principle in different contexts. If one symbolism concerns the mutilation of those limbs, destroyed by Aśvatthāman, which represent the effective continuity of the Kuru line, the other concerns the mutilation of those limbs and organs, destroyed by Śiva, which represent the effective continuity of the sacrifice. No one has

[62] See, for example, 3:254,5–21, Draupadī boasting about her husbands: Bhīma with "long arms as developed as *śāla* trees" (9); Nakula "whose beauty [*rūpam*] is the utmost on earth" (14); and Sahadeva, "of whom one finds no equal in wisdom and eloquence" (*vaktā*; 17).

[63] But see *GB* 1,2 and *TS* 2,6,8,7 where the sacrifice is placed on the belly (*jaṭhara*) of Indra (*GB*) or Brahman (*TS*), as these two are never harmed.

[64] Only one other figure is multilated, the half-male, half-female Śikhaṇḍin, fittingly shot between the eyes and cut in two with the sword (8,59–60). One suspects several Śiva symbols here too.

appreciated the paradoxical character of the latter symbolism as well as Dumézil: "Bhaga, who distributes 'parts' and who is blind, appears beside Savitṛ, the 'Impeller,' who sets all things in motion and who has lost his two hands; and also beside Pūṣan, protector of the 'meat on foot' which are the herds, and who, having lost his teeth, can eat only pap."[65] From the Brāhmaṇas on to the *Śiva* and *Bhāgavata Purāṇas*, for Dakṣa's sacrifice to continue it has been necessary that these limbs and organs be restored—either directly, through Śiva's grace, to those who have lost them (*Mbh.* 10:18,22; cf. *Śiva P.* 2,2,43,28), or indirectly, under the guidance of Bṛhaspati (*Gopatha Br.* 1, 2; *ŚB* 1,7,4,13–15) or Śiva (*Bhāg. P.* 4,7,3), when these latter stipulate that the rite be handled or continued with the eyes of Sūrya (*GB*) or Mitra (*Bhāg. P.*), the arms of the Aśvins, the hands of Pūṣan, and the mouth of Agni (*ŚB*) or the sacrificer's teeth (*Bhag. P.*).[66]

(8) *Kālarātrī.* The dying warriors now envision Kālarātrī, the black (*kālī*) Goddess Night of All-Destroying Time (8,64–67). In some Dakṣayajña myths, the goddess comes in her terrible Mahākālī or Bhadrakālī form to do her part in the destruction (*Mbh.* 12:283,31V; *Vām. P.* 4,53–57; *Śiva P.* 2,2,33,11–12). Just as the myth can do without the goddess in this role, so it is easy to imagine the *Sauptikaparvan* without this brief intrusion of Kālarātrī.

(9 and 10) *Dawn and vengeance.* As dawn approaches (*pratyūṣakāle*), "having left his foes without a trace, Aśvatthāman

[65] Dumézil, *Dieux des Germains*, p. 81 (my translation); see also *idem*, "Pūṣan édenté," *QII*, *Collection Latomus*, XLIV (*Hommages à L. Hermann*) (1960), 315–19.

[66] See *VS* 11,9 "By impulse of the god Savitṛ I take thee [the sacrifice] with the arms of the Aśvins, with the hands of Pūṣan"; Ralph T. Griffith, trans., *The Texts of the White Yajur Veda* (Benares: E. J. Longmans, 1899), p. 88. Most prolific with added mutilations are *Liñga P.* 69,15–20, where Īśana (!) and Candramas are maimed, Indra loses his head, Vahni his tongue and hands, Yama his staff; and *Kūrma P.* 15,60–63, where, in addition to these, the munis are kicked in the head; also *Bhāg. P.* 5,17–24 deprives Bhṛgu of his beard and Dakṣa of his head.

shone forth in this human habitation like the fire at the end of the yuga, having turned all beings into ash" (*yugānte sarvabhūtāni bhasma kṛtveva pāvakaḥ*; 8,136); this is a free use of *saṃdhyā* ("twilight") and *pralaya* imagery. Draupadī then demands revenge against Aśvatthāman, and Bhīma sets out after him. He is soon followed by his brothers and Krishna when the latter says that Bhīma will be unable to deal with Aśvatthāman's weapons. Possible connections with the *pralaya* come to mind—Bhīma-Vāyu as first to act in the "recreation"; Draupadī-Kṛṣṇā-Śrī as the earth despoiled of "prosperity"[67]—but I doubt that these correlations are any more than coincidental. Draupadī's wrath (she has just lost her sons and brothers) and her reliance on the strong-armed Bhīma (cf. the Kīcaka story; 4:13–23) are easily explained as logical outcomes of the development of the plot.[68]

(11) *Contest of the weapons*. Taking off after Bhīma and Nakula, who is acting as Bhīma's charioteer, Krishna and the rest of the Pāṇḍavas catch up with them just as Bhīma is aiming his weapon. Meanwhile, Aśvatthāman is sitting among a group of ṛṣis surrounding Vyāsa beside the Ganges. Seeing them, Aśvatthāman picks a blade of grass, converts it into a Brahmaśiras ("Head of Brahmā") weapon capable of world destruction, and, "Filled with wrath [*ruṣā*], he uttered the terrible word '*apāṇḍavāya*' ['for the annihilation of the Pāṇḍavas']. He then released that weapon for the sake of the bewilderment of all worlds. Then in that blade of grass, a fire was produced which seemed about to consume the three worlds" (10:13, 18–20). Immediately, Krishna urges Arjuna, who alone can match Aśvatthāman, to counteract this weapon; and Arjuna releases his Brahmaśiras from his bow, wishing only to "neutralize" or "appease" (*śāmyatām*; 14,6) that of his opponent.

[67] On Vāyu, see EMH, 2, p. 60; on Bhīma and Vāyu, see above, n. 38; on Draupadī and the earth, see above, Chapter 2, at n. 25.

[68] The undertow of feeling between Draupadī and Bhīma is nicely appreciated by Irawati Karve, *Yuganta*, pp. 128–32.

Once released, it too "blazed up like the fire at the end of the yuga" (7). At this impasse, "desiring the welfare of all creatures" (*sarvabhūtahitaiṣiṇau*; 13) as well as of the worlds (*lokānām*; 15), the two *munis* Nārada and Vyāsa take position (*sthitau*) between the two weapons to neutralize their energy. From this station they rebuke the heroes for their rash act of releasing the deadly arms, thus setting up an interesting contrast between the two combatants. To Arjuna is dedicated a long passage (15,1–10) praising the extraordinary ability—possible only through *brahmacarya*, truthfulness, and the observation of vows—which allows him to withdraw the weapon. Aśvatthāman, however, having released his weapon out of wrath and fear of Bhīma, tells the two ṛṣis that he is unable to withdraw it (11). After further efforts have failed, Vyāsa can only convince him to relinquish his gem so as to satisfy Draupadī. The curse has been made.

Here the closest parallel is found in an unusual version of the Dakṣayajña, although similar episodes are found in other versions of the myth.[69] Krishna is speaking, this time to Arjuna, telling him that when he, Arjuna, fought in the battle it was Rudra, proceeding in front of him, who actually slew his foes (12:330,69). Most interesting, however, is a description of what occurred after this same Rudra had finished his destruction of Dakṣa's sacrifice. His rage unspent, Rudra attacked the ṛṣis Nara and Nārāyaṇa (= Arjuna and Krishna) in their hermitage at Badari. As they fight, the whole universe darkens, the Vedas are concealed from the ṛṣis, *rajas* and *tamas* pervade the gods, the oceans dry up, the mountains crack, "and indeed Brahmā was shaken from his seat" (*brahmā caivāsanāccyutaḥ*; 54). "When such signs occurred, Brahmā, surrounded by the divine host and the high-souled Ṛṣis, quickly came to the spot where the

[69] Brahmā intercedes often and so, sometimes, do the Ṛṣis (*Mbh.* 7:173,47); many versions also speak of a conflict between Śiva and Viṣṇu after the sacrifice is destroyed, sometimes Viṣṇu prevailing (*HV*), sometimes Śiva (*Liṅga P.*).

battle was raging. Joining his hands in reverence, Brahmā addressed Rudra: 'May it be well [*śivam*] for the worlds; throw down your weapons for the sake of the welfare of the universe' " (55–56). His intercession works: "Thus addressed by Brahmā, Rudra, casting off the fire of his wrath [*krodhāgnimutsṛjan*], then caused the powerful god Nārāyaṇa to be gratified. . . . And then that boon-granting god, whose wrath is conquered and whose senses are conquered [*jitakrodho jitendriyaḥ*], became pleased there and was reconciled with Rudra" (61–62).

The contrast between the two gods is thus homologous to the contrast between Aśvatthāman and Arjuna. As Aśvatthāman must discharge his weapon, Rudra must "cast off" the fire of his wrath;[70] and as Arjuna (one with Krishna) restrains his weapons, so Nārāyaṇa (one with Nara) has his wrath and senses under control. Moreover, there are parallels in the roles of the intercessors. For the sake of the "welfare of the worlds" Brahmā on the one hand and Vyāsa and Nārada on the other are roused from their "seats" to plead for a cessation of hostilities. A variant of the crucial theme of the unleashing of Śiva's wrath (*Mbh.* 12:274,45–46) makes it clear that Brahmā's bargain was no less costly to the world than the one struck by Vyāsa and Nārada. In the one case, the fever (*jvara*) from Śiva's wrath will be dissipated among various minerals, animals, birds, and men, to afflict them, especially the latter, at the times of birth and death. In the other, the detoured Brahmaśiras will wipe out the last hope of the Kuru line.

(12) *Promise of the "renaissance."* Unable to withdraw his weapon, Aśvatthāman can only alter its course through a reinterpretation of his curse's meaning: it will go into the wombs (*garbheṣu*; 15,31) of the Pāṇḍava wives. The Pāṇḍavas

[70] Cf. the Bāṇāsura myth (*HV* 2,123,16–28) where after Śiva's *jvara* ("fever") and Krishna's *jvara* fight to a standstill, it is agreed that Krishna will dissolve his into himself (*mayyevaiṣa pralīyatām*; 18) while Śiva's will be distributed among diseases and deserted things. The connection between the myths is noted by Ruben, *Krishna*, pp. 196–97.

will thus be slain symbolically, with no hope of "rebirth." To console them, Krishna then commits "an imprudent act."[71] He tells them of Uttarā's pregnancy: being the wife of Abhimanyu and not of the Pāṇḍavas, she will escape the curse. But Aśvatthāman overhears and extends the weapon's effect to her. At this point Krishna must promise to intercede. True, he says, the weapon will take effect and the child will be stillborn; but he, Krishna, will give it life. There will be a renaissance after all.

This crucial episode has no true parallel in the "renaissance" of the Dakṣayajña which, as we have seen, concerns only the renewal of Dakṣa's rite through the restoration of the mutilated limbs of the gods. One may accept Biardeau's position that this event is cast in the imagery of the *pralaya*. But my next chapter will present an "older" comparison that will rely not on common images but on similar narratives.

(13) *Aśvatthāman's fate*. In addition to his promise, Krishna curses the "child-slaying" Aśvatthāman to reap the fruit of his acts in a terrible destiny:

For three thousand years you will wander over this earth without a companion and without being able to talk to anyone. Alone and with no one by you, you will wander through deserted places [*nirjanān . . . deśān*]. O wretch [*kṣudra*], there will be no place for you in the midst of men. Stinking of pus and blood, you will have your home in inaccessible wastelands [*durgakāntārasaṃsrayaḥ*]. You will rove about, O sinful soul, infested with all diseases. [16,9–12]

This is the point in the Dakṣayajña myths where Śiva is given his share: certainly more a blessing than a curse. This is the second "inversion" of the share (see above, item 6): where Śiva is blessed, Aśvatthāman is cursed. Both inversions follow an intelligible pattern: positive and optimistic for the divine Śiva, who takes on the character of the auspicious fire and is blessed; negative for the "human" Aśvatthāman, who

[71] Dumézil, *ME*, I, 217 (my translation).

takes on the character of the inauspicious fire and is cursed. Nonetheless, a closer look shows that Śiva's share expresses a similar outsiderhood: it is "the remainder [*vāstu*], that part of the sacrifice which [is left] after the oblations have been made" (*ŚB* 1,7,3,7; cf. *Bhāg. P.* 4,7,4: the *uccheṣaṇam*). Thus Dumézil can point to the outsiderhood of Aśvatthāman as a feature shaped by the character of Śiva: "Such will be the destiny of Aśvatthāman, wandering alone in the bush, as does the god Rudra whom he incorporates and who possesses him."[72]

But if Aśvatthāman receives his "share" elsewhere and is cursed where Śiva obtains his, on another occasion in the Brāhmaṇas Rudra receives a share that brings him even closer to Aśvatthāman. This is at the end of the Śākamedhāḥ, the third of the three seasonal rites which marks the end of the rainy season. The rite concludes with an offering to Rudra Tryambaka, and I include the pertinent passages from *Śatapatha Brāhmaṇa* 2,6,2:

2. When he performs these offerings, he . . . delivers from Rudra's power both the descendents that are born unto him and those that are unborn [re-emphasized, stanzas 3–4].

[5–9. Cakes are made and taken to Rudra's quarter, the north, and offered on a crossroad to Rudra and his sister Ambikā:]

10. Now as to that additional [cake], he buries it in a mole-hill, with the text, "This is thy share, O Rudra! The mole is thy animal [victim (*paśu*)]." He thus assigns to him the mole as the only animal, and he [Rudra] does not therefore injure any other animal. Then as to why he buries [the cake]: concealed, indeed, are embryos [*garbhās*], and concealed also is what is buried. By this [offering] he delivers from the power of Rudra those descendents of his, that are not yet born.

[11–17. The sacrificial party now returns, having propitiated Rudra. Circumambulations are performed, and then the sacrificer takes the remains of the cakes and fastens them to something high in the northerly direction, saying:]

[72] *Ibid.*, p. 218 (my translation).

17. "These, O Rudra, are thy provisions; therewith depart beyond the Mujavats [mountains]!—[supplied] with provisions people indeed set out on a journey: hence he thereby dismisses him supplied with provisions whithersoever he is bound. Now in this case his journey is beyond the Mujavats!"—"with thy bow unstrung and muffled up—," whereby he means to say, "Depart propitious, not injuring us"; "Clad in a skin,"—whereby he lulls him to sleep; for while sleeping he injures no one: hence he says, "Clad in a skin."

This remarkable passage reads like a ritual text to the early "Dakṣayajña" myths, or vice versa. But more, it seems to provide a ground plan for some of the most prominent themes in the *Sauptikaparvan*: not just the "skin-clad" exile beyond the mountains and the "muffling" of the weapon, but the matter of the "concealed embryos." As A. B. Keith points out,[73] the whole family participates symbolically in this rite, including the Pitṛs and the unmarried women. It is but a short step to the destiny of the Kuru line: surely Krishna "delivers from the power of Rudra those descendents of his [and of the Pāṇḍavas], that are not yet born."

(14) *Theological reflections*. In almost every case, the Dakṣayajña draws to a close by offering some sort of theological key to the events that have transpired. And although sectarian interests sometimes prevail, beneath them lies an emphasis on the complementarity of the two gods (see *Mbh*. 12:330,64–66; 12,284,111–13V; *Liñga P*. 69,89; *Śiva P*. 2,2,43,12–20). These reflections go back to the Brāhmaṇas, suggesting that even there the "Dakṣayajña" myth inspired such a view. After its version, *Śatapatha* 1,7,4 continues with directives on how the Brahman priest, representing Bṛhaspati, should handle the dangerous "foreportion" (*praśitra*) which has become Rudra's share. Having followed the careful ritual (9–16) and kept the "power of Rudra" (*rudriyam*) from the sacrificer's cattle (*paśu*),

[73] See Keith's summary, *Religion and Philosophy of the Veda*, Harvard Oriental Series, vols. XXXI and XXXII (Cambridge: Harvard University Press, 1925), XXXII (pt. 2), 322.

he eats the *praśitra* "with Agni's mouth" (15) and then rinses his mouth with water. Then he is brought his own portion (*brahmabhāga*): "Henceforth he watches what remains incomplete of the sacrifice" (*asaṃsthitaṃ yajñasya*; 18), and maintains silence:

19. Now the Brahman, assuredly, is the best physician; hence the Brahman thereby restores the sacrifice; but if he were to sit down there talking, he would not restore it: he must therefore maintain silence.

20. If he should utter any human sound before that time, let him there and then mutter some Ṛc or Yajus-text addressed to Viṣṇu; for Viṣṇu is the sacrifice, so he thereby obtains a hold on the sacrifice: and this is the expiation of that (breach of silence) [*vai viṣṇustadyajñam punarārabhate tasyo haiṣā prāyaścittiḥ*].

This passage, along with analogous ones, appeared in the last chapter's discussion of the expiatory role that is shared by the Brāhmaṇic Viṣṇu and the epic Krishna. It now appears that this is a Brāhmaṇa instance of Viṣṇu's absolving function being available directly after the dangerous portion of the sacrifice, connected with Rudra, has been neutralized by "fire" and water.

Similar theological keys to these are found in the *Sauptikaparvan* where, as we have seen, Krishna concludes the narrative with an account to Yudhiṣṭhira of the former deeds of Śiva (including the "Dakṣayajña"). But this is not the only place where there is a pause for such reflections. Earlier, as they are being slain, the Pāṇḍava warriors reflect: "The son of Droṇa in anger could never perform such acts as these in battle; . . . surely through the nonpresence [*asāṃnidhyād*] of the Pārthas has our slaughter been achieved. There is no one able to defeat the son of Kuntī whose protector [*goptā*] is Janārdana" (10:8,115–17). And when the bereaved Kuru king Dhṛtarāṣṭra asks why Aśvatthāman, so irresistible now, could not have prevented the slaughter of the Kauravas, Saṃjaya (who has been given the "divine eye" by Vyāsa) answers in much the same terms: "Surely the son of Droṇa was able to achieve this feat only through the nonpresence [*asāṃnidhyād*] of Pṛthā's sons, as also of the insightful Krishna and Sātyaki" (8,146–47). We have already discussed the background for this "nonpresence." Let us now appreciate the symmetry in the theological reflections. In reciting the former deeds of Mahādeva, Krishna was responding to the same question from Yudhiṣṭhira (17,2–6) as was asked of Saṃjaya by Dhṛtarāṣṭra. Where the Kuru king learned that Asvatthāman could succeed only by Krishna's absence, the Pāṇḍava king learned that he could succeed only by Śiva's presence. This is the same pattern, but this time much clearer, as in Śiva's potential "involvement" and Krishna's explicit "nonpresence" (*asāṃnidhyam*; 3:14,14) in the dice game[74]—a confirmation also of Held's insight into the complementarity of the dice game and the war.[75]

Thus close correspondences exist between the structure of the Dakṣayajña and the intrigue of the *Sauptikaparvan*. Other themes connected with the sacrifice also suggest that the epic narrative has been fashioned, once again, by poets closely familiar with the ideology of the Brāhmaṇas. One might object, on the grounds that there is no eschatology in the Brāhmaṇas, that this alignment of the *Sauptikaparvan* with the "Dakṣayajña" has undermined the whole notion of the eschatological character of the epic crises. Here Krishna's version of the "Dakṣayajña" meets such an objection: it took place, he says, "when a *devayuga* had passed" (*devayuge 'tite*; 10:18,1). This could refer to the end of a Kṛta yuga,[76] or to the end of a *mahāyuga*, a full cycle of four ages; but the poets have clearly perceived the eschatological potential of the "Dakṣayajña" myth.[77] In

[74] See above, Chapter 4.

[75] See Held, *Ethnological Study*, p. 304.

[76] So Ganguli-Roy, *Mahabharata*, VII: *Sauptika Parva*, 42.

[77] This epic treatment is in fact the only one I have found where the "Dakṣayajña" occurs explicitly at the end of a yuga; cf. *Mbh.* 12:283,1V: "in the period of Manu Vaivasvata." However, at one Sarasvatī *tīrtha*, "a blessing was formerly uttered by Dakṣa while he was sacrificing: 'Whoever

all the post-Brāhmaṇic texts there is a passage which expresses this potential unequivocally, but none more forcefully than the one in the version with which Krishna concludes the *Sauptikaparvan*: "The goddess Earth trembled and the mountains shook. The wind did not blow, nor did the fire, though kindled, blaze forth. And even the constellations in the sky, agitated, wandered about. The sun did not shine, the lunar disc lost its *śrī*. All confounded, space became covered with darkness [*timereṇa*; cf. 7:173,46 and 13:145,15: *tamasā*]. Then, overcome, the gods did not know their domains [*viṣayānna prajajñire*], the *yajña* did not shine forth, and the Vedas abandoned them" (10:18,9cd–12).

Yet if the themes and frame of the Dakṣayajña were found to be appropriate vehicles to carry along the narrative of an eschatological crisis, the deeper question, raised by Dumézil, remains: is there an earlier, perhaps Indo-European, eschatology which has been refashioned here in the matrix of the Brāhmaṇic sacrifice?

---

dies here, these men shall be conquerors of heaven" (3:120,2); to which the Northern recension adds: "There is also a marvelous thing which occurs in this region: whenever a yuga is waning, there is an appearance of Śarva [Śiva], assuming any shape at will, together with his companions and Umā" (3,639*).

CHAPTER 13

"Renaissance"

If an Indo-European interpretation of the epic's eschatological crisis is to be extended beyond the common but general theme of a great battle, one must look elsewhere than at Yudhiṣṭhira's dice play and his less than "idyllic" postwar reign. To put it as cautiously as possible, two figures, Abhimanyu and Parikṣit, are brought into surprisingly sharp relief when their story and characters are compared with the mythology of Baldr.[1]

First, Abhimanyu offers a more satisfactory definition of the "royal ideal" than Yudhiṣṭhira. When Saṃjaya begins his account of how this heir of the Pāṇḍavas died, he describes Abhimanyu as the epitome of the omnivirtuous but essentially trifunctional royal ideal that was outlined in Chapters 7 and 8. In a lengthy but beautiful eulogy (7:33,1–10), the first seven *ślokas* describe, in roughly trifunctional form, the virtues of Krishna,[2] of each of the Pāṇḍavas, and of all six together. Then it continues:

8. Those virtues flourishing in Krishna and those virtues in the Pāṇḍavas—that assemblage of virtues was indeed found in Abhimanyu.

[1] See above, Chapter 12, following n. 5.

[2] Of Krishna it is said (*śl.* 2): "In goodness [*sattvam*], deeds [*karman*], and lineage [*anvaya*]; in intelligence [*buddhi*], character [*prakṛti*], fame [*yaśas*], and prosperity [*śrī*], there never was and never will be a man having such virtues [*guṇas*] as Kṛṣṇa."

ye ca kṛṣṇe guṇāḥ sphītāḥ pāṇḍaveṣu ca ye guṇāḥ
abhimanyau kilaikasthā dṛśyante guṇasaṃcayāḥ.

9. In firmness [*dhairyam*] he was the equal of Yudhiṣṭhira, in conduct [*caritam*] of Krishna, and in deeds [*karman*] of Bhīma of terrible deeds;

10. In beauty, strength, and learning [*rūpeṇa vikrameṇa śrutena ca*] he was the equal of Arjuna, and in modesty [*vinaya*] of Nakula and Sahadeva. [7:33,1–10]

Nowhere in the epic does a more ample treatment of the virtues retain an equally trifunctional outline. Moreover, it is not only trifunctional in general but in particular: Arjuna, Abhimanyu's true father, is the only one to be individually characterized by single virtues for each function: beauty, strength, and learning.

The significance of this endowment should be apparent. Both the core of virtues that he shares with Arjuna and the full "assemblage of virtues" that he shares with the Pāṇḍavas and Krishna have been lost to the Kuru line with Abhimanyu's death. And who, "in reality," is Abhimanyu? In the dictionaries of incarnations he is described variously as "the good Varcas [Splendor], the splendid son of Soma" (1:61,86), and as "Soma, who became Subhadrā's son here having divided himself in two through yoga" (15:39,13). Soma here is certainly the moon, although as I will try to show, certain resonances of the archaic double character of Soma as both sacrificial plant and moon are detectable in Abhimanyu.[3] Dumézil has called attention to the lunar phenomena that attend his birth, and both Hopkins and Dumézil have recognized that the brief sixteen years of his life correspond to the days in the light half of the lunar month (*śuklapakṣa*).[4]

[3] The age of this double character has long been debated, but it is at least as early as the late Vedas; see most recently Jan Gonda, "Soma, Amṛta and the Moon," *Change and Continuity in Indian Religion* (The Hague: Mouton, 1965), pp. 38–70.

[4] Hopkins, *Epic Mythology*, p. 91; Dumézil, *ME*, I, 245–46.

Disappointingly, however, Dumézil refers to Abhimanyu's link with the moon as one of several divine-heroic associations in the epic that "appear artificial and without consequence."[5] This is an oversight. The dynasty whose virtues and continuity Abhimanyu and his son represent is the "Lunar Dynasty" (*candra vaṃśa, soma vaṃśa*). And the Vedic Soma whose Varcas he incarnates is a *rājā*, King Soma, as well.

Dumézil's first-function portrayal of the "ideal" Baldr was not entirely convincing—Baldr does not remind one of Aryaman or Mitra. But let us recall Snorri's description of his virtues: he is "the best of them . . . fair of face and bright . . . you can tell how beautiful his body is, and how bright his hair [from the comparison of his brow to a flower]. . . . He is the wisest of all the gods, and the sweetest spoken, and the most merciful."[6] Compared with Abhimanyu, Baldr shows the highest perfection on two levels—wisdom (first function) and beauty (third)—but no warrior traits. This may suit Snorri's portrayal of Baldr as the innocent, unarmed victim in the missile-throwing game, but it is not the complete picture that Norse traditions give of Baldr. His death in the *Gylfaginning* is brought about by the fact that he is invulnerable to weapons. And, as several scholars have noticed, Saxo Grammaticus' portrayal of Balderus in the *Gesta Danorum*,[7] the use of his name in the formation of warrior kennings, and perhaps also the meaning of his name,[8] all present him with a martial side. Baldr quite plausibly becomes, like Abhimanyu, an embodiment of the highest virtues of all the functions, not just a first-function figure.

[5] Dumézil, *ME*, I, 245 (my translation).

[6] Cited above, Chapter 12, n. 14.

[7] Elton, *Danish History*, I. 177–90 (Book 3); of the two portrayals, Dumézil's "Balderus and Hotherus," *Myth to Fiction*, pp. 171–92, is to me convincing in demonstrating the priority and reliability of Snorri.

[8] See Turville-Petre, *Myth and Religion*, pp. 112–17; Polomé, "Indo-European Component," p. 68.

Such similarities in the physical and moral descriptions of the two "youths"[9]—and others may be cited[10]—are not significant by themselves. But if it can be shown that their biographies coincide on a number of major points, there will be reason to regard these two omnivirtuous figures as representatives of a common and ancient eschatological hope.

Jeu Truqué

First, a major focus of Dumézil's discussion was the comparison between the missile game in which Baldr dies and the dice game which sends Yudhiṣṭhira into exile. Certain differences, among them those varying fates of the two "losers," have cast doubt on whether these two "fixed matches" really have much in common. But if the death of Baldr compares poorly with the exile of Yudhiṣṭhira, it holds surprising parallels with the death of Abhimanyu.

Arjuna's son has fought illustriously in the first eleven days of the war, but on the twelfth Droṇa promises to take his life. He stipulates that Arjuna must be detained elsewhere on the battlefield, and the Saṃśaptakas (those "sworn-together" never to flee from Arjuna) agree to keep him busy. With Arjuna out of the way, Droṇa commands his troops to form a "circular array" (*cakravyūha*, var. *padmavyūha*; 7:32,18, etc.). This singular configuration is described (7:33,12–20) as a sort of mobile circle which can mount an attack, and which, though it includes thousands of warriors, has certain key figures placed on the rim and in the center. When the Pāṇḍavas (minus Arjuna) find themselves unable

[9] Whether plant or moon, Soma is a youth (*yuvan*) or child (*śiśu*; *ṚV* 9,16,17). Also, Frigg did not pick the mistletoe because it was "too young"; see above, Chapter 12, at n. 15.

[10] "A splendor radiates" from Baldr; Abhimanyu "shines surpassingly" (*atirocata*; 6:69,29) while fighting. Baldr's brow is like the ox-eye daisy; Abhimanyu's eyes are like Krishna's, that is, like the lotus (14:60,7–8; 7:50,30), and he has "beautiful brows" (*subhrū*; 7:55,33).

to break this circle, Yudhiṣṭhira calls upon Abhimanyu, who tells him that Arjuna has indeed taught him the technique of penetration. "But," he adds, "I shall not be able to come out again if any distress overtakes me" (34,19). He is thus entering a sort of military maze.[11] Bhīma then gives assurance that he will lead others into the breach to protect Abhimanyu once he has broken through, and the latter sets off. He enters the circular array and for some time gets the best of it; and at one point he performs a noteworthy trick of his father's: "Having encompassed [*koṣṭhakīkṛtya*: "having made a wall around"] him with a host of chariots, collectively [*saṃghaśaḥ*] they released showers of different kinds of arrows at him. These he cut off in mid-air by means of his own sharp shafts and then pierced his foes in return" (7:36,10). But while he is careening about displaying his marvelous talents, Bhīma and the rest of his allies are barred from following him by Jayadratha who uses a boon obtained from Śiva (who else?) allowing him to harm the Pāṇḍavas by being able to check all of them "except Arjuna" (*ṛte 'rjunaḥ*; 3:256,28) once on the field of battle. The pattern that develops is then made clear (7:46,4–5). Jayadratha keeps back Abhimanyu's rescuers from a mobile position outside the circle, closing its gaps wherever necessary. At the same time, Abhimanyu is encircled by six of the foremost Kuru warriors, five of whom incarnate Vedic divinities: Droṇa (Bṛhaspati), Kṛpa (the Rudras), Karṇa (Sūrya), Aśvatthāman (Mahādeva [Rudra]-Antaka-Krodha-Kāma), and Kṛtavarman (the Maruts). The sixth

[11] Both *cakravyūha* and *padmavyūha* can designate a maze. Kinjawadekar, ed., *Shriman Mahābhāratam*, IV: *Droṇaparvan* (Poona: Chitrashala Press, 1931), facing p. 55, so interprets the former term, showing the diagram of a circular maze with a Nandī and Liṅgam in the center, with the Sanskrit caption that it is a "picture of a *cakravyūha* well known in Maharashtra. . . . The right or wrong direction is to be determined by those of good understanding." V. R. Ragam, *Pilgrim's Travel Guide*, pt. II: *North India with Himalayan Regions* (Guntur: Sri Sita Rama Nama Sankirtana Sangham, 1963), p. 175, cites a "Padma-Vyuha" at Porbandar, Gujerat, which "pilgrims enter . . . and after going round in it they finally manage to come out with great difficulty."

and least significant is Bṛhadbala, whom Abhimanyu kills in a last blaze of glory (46,22); but his position is filled by an apparently unnamed son of Duḥśāsana (oldest of Duryodhana's ninety-nine brothers). Droṇa marvels at the prowess of this *kumāra*, boy, "whose opening [flaw, loophole] the furious *mahārathas* do not see" (*antaram . . . na paśyanti*; 47,22), and reveals how he may be taken. By well-placed shots, Abhimanyu can be deprived, piece by piece, of all his equipment. The six warriors then cut away his armor and weapons and, after a brief flourish in which Abhimanyu courses through the air like Garuḍa (47,35) and reminds everyone of Krishna by holding up a chariot wheel (47,39–48,1), he is reduced to his last weapon, the mace. With this he engages in a final duel with Duḥśāsana's son. They knock each other to the ground; and then, "having risen up first, the son of Duḥśāsana, that increaser of the fame of the Kurus, struck Subhadrā's son on the head with his mace" (*gadayā mūrdhnyatāḍayat*; 48,12).

The role of Droṇa-Bṛhaspati in seeing to all the details of this slaying, the participation of *all* the figures on the Kuru side who incarnate Vedic divinities, the use of the mace on the "head" all allow one to interpret Abhimanyu-Soma's death within the context of the ritual pounding of the Soma.[12] The six warriors who surround him may not find exact counterparts in the Soma rite,[13] but on other levels parallels are striking. As Bhīma was to be Abhimanyu's protector, Bhīma's father Vāyu was the Vedic "protector of Soma" (*ṚV* 10,85,5; and see notes 9 and 12). Yet even this may just be an Indian rehandling, perhaps quite early, of a more ancient drama.

[12] On Soma's head (*mūrdhán*) in the *ṚV*, see R. Gordon Wasson, *Soma: Divine Mushroom of Immorality* (The Hague: Mouton, 1968), pp. 45–46, especially *ṚV* 9,27,3: "This bull, heaven's head, Soma, when pressed is escorted by masterly men [*nṛ́bhir*] into the vessels."

[13] But see Keith, *Philosophy of the Veda*, I, 326: In the Soma sacrifice, "the earth thrown up from the pit (of the four sounding holes) serves to make six fire hearths or Dhiṣṇyas, which extend from north to south, and are appropriated to" various priests.

Baldr is also slain when encircled. Like Abhimanyu he is surrounded by gods (whom Snorri refers to euhemeristically as men).[14] Strangely, too, the figures who make the two slayings possible, and against whom vengeance is taken—Hodr and Jayadratha—both stand outside the circle.[15] In one case, the figure who represents the plant of immortality (Soma) is slain, while in the other his counterpart is slain with the plant of immortality (mistletoe).

These analogies, and this one striking inversion, seem stable enough that certain differences can be seen as divergences. Clearly the most apparent is that Abhimanyu is slain while the great battle is in progress, whereas Baldr's death is an important foreshadowing of the Ragnarök. Here Saxo's version is of interest, for he places Balderus' (Baldr's) conflict with Hotherus (Hodr) in the context of a strange battle—probably, as Dumézil says, a transposition of the Ragnarök itself—in which Hotherus defeats the euhemerized gods, who side with Balderus, by cutting off the tip of Thor's club (that is, his hammer).[16] Here too a parallel emerges, for just as Thor, Balderus' second-function protector, is rendered inoperative, so is Bhīma kept from helping Abhimanyu by Jayadratha. The upshot of these remarks is that the tradition which Snorri represents, which, as we have seen, "pacified" its ideal figure by recording only his first- and third-function virtues, may have idealized him further, dreams and all,[17]

[14] See above, cited Chapter 12, at n. 16.

[15] There is no encirclement in Saxo's version, although Dumézil, *Myth to Fiction*, pp. 180–83, shows that Baldr's invulnerability and the theme of "inoffensive bombardment" are probably transferred to Hotherus (Hodr). However, both Hotherus and Jayadratha must endure penances in the wilds to receive the divine favor that will enable them to slay their foes: Hotherus from certain forest virgins (Dumézil, *Myth to Fiction*, p. 190: "a cross between the Norns and the Valkyries"; see Elton, *Danish History*, I, 188), Jayadratha from Śiva (see above).

[16] See Elton, *Danish History*, I, 184, and Dumézil, *Myth to Fiction*, pp. 165–66 (on Thor's club as his hammer) and 191 (on Saxo's *theomachia* and the Ragnarök).

[17] On the "night phantoms" which Balderus has within the context of his conflict with Hotherus in Saxo's account, see Elton, *Danish History*, I, 186.

out of the scene of battle. One might think of Baldr's death as having taken place originally within the framework of the battle of the Ragnarök, toward its beginning, like the death of Abhimanyu in the *Mahābhārata*. In each case, a youth is the first to die of the divine company,[18] and to die, moreover, at the latter's hands.

A second difficulty with these comparisons is that unlike Baldr, Abhimanyu does not appear to die in a rigged game, a *jeu truqué*. The parallels that Dumézil cites elsewhere for Baldr's death make it unlikely that Snorri's tradition has innovated here.[19] Yet the encirclement of Abhimanyu has a certain gamelike quality. He knows the way into the "maze," but not the way out. As cited above,[20] when he is in the "circle-array" he is able effortlessly to turn aside weapons in mid-air. And on two additional occasions leading up to his last fight, he is encircled in arrays which clearly foreshadow Droṇa's *cakravyūha*: each time, fighting fearlessly and with ease—and aided by Arjuna—he emerges unscathed.[21] Thus, like Baldr, he is involved in a sort of game,[22] each one to a certain extent invulnerable in his circle, each able to make weapons turn aside in mid-air. He has far more invulnerability than Yudhiṣṭhira does when the latter enters the game of dice.

[18] Abhimanyu does die on the twelfth day of the eighteen-day war, but up to then, of the major heroes, only Bhīṣma has been "slain," and he is not really slain.

[19] Dumézil, *Loki* (Paris: Maisonneuve, 1948), pp. 239–46; *idem.*, "Balderiana minora," *Indo-Iranica. Mélanges présentés à Georg Morgenstierne* (Weisbaden: Harrassowitz, 1964), pt. 3, "Les pleurs de toutes choses et la resurrection manquée de Baldr," pp. 70–72.

[20] See above, after n. 11, citing 7:36,10.

[21] See 6:57,1–5: five warriors "surrounded him on all sides" (*samantāt-paryavārayan*); and 6:97,29–33: Bhīṣma has him surrounded (*paryavārayat*), having made a wall or ring around him (*koṣṭhakīkṛtya*) as in the passage (7:36,10) cited above. Both times Arjuna comes to his aid.

[22] In fact, according to an interpolation (*Ādiparvan*, App. I, no. 42), Abhimanyu's game has been fixed all along; his "father" Soma would only allow him to join the celestials on earth for sixteen years, at which point he would be slain in a *cakravyūha* in Nara and Nārāyaṇa's absence (line 12).

Lamentation

If Baldr's death brings weeping from all and everything but Thokk, Abhimanyu is incontestably the most wept-for figure in the *Mahābhārata*. Arjuna's long lament (7:50,19–60) mentions over and over, as if in a refrain, how Abhimanyu was loved by others: by Subhadrā, by Krishna, by Draupadī, by Kuntī, and by Pradyumna (25–29 and notes). He says: "If I do not see my son, I will go to the abode of Yama" (27 and 32). This parallels Baldr's brother Hermod's descent to Hel to see if Baldr can be brought back. Abhimanyu is also deeply mourned by Vasudeva, father of Krishna and Subhadrā (14:59,4–8). And two descriptions are given of Subhadrā's touching lament. In the first (7:55), she, too, says she will go to Yama's abode (10), and then in a sequence that begins with a reinforcement of Abhimanyu's trifunctional character, she prays that her son may obtain the end of all those who have led good lives in the three functional zones[23] and other widely varying capacities as well (*munis*, good kings, good hosts, good wives, good husbands; 23bc–31). In the second account (14:60,24–29), Krishna tells how she ran wailing like a female osprey from Kuntī to Uttarā, asking where Abhimanyu had gone and imploring Uttarā to tell her when he returned. She leads the weeping, then, as did Frigg.

It is my impression that such lamentations over death, and the ritualized themes they might imply, are unusual in Hindu India.[24] The analogues with Baldr, and with the slain or

[23] 7:55,20–23ab: (1) "May you obtain the way of those who are liberally disposed sacrificers, of brahmins of accomplished soul, of those who have practiced *brahmacarya*, of bathers at sacred *tīrthas*, of those who are grateful, liberal, and attend their gurus; of those who have given thousands of *dakṣiṇās*; (2) may you go the way of those heroes who never turn back while fighting, of those who have fallen in battle after having slain their foes; (3) of those who give away thousands of cattle, who give in sacrifices."

[24] See Fred Clothey, "Skanda-Ṣaṣṭi: A Festival in Tamil India," *HRJ*, VIII (1969), 249–50: comparing the enthronement festival of the Tamil Murukaṉ with ancient Near Eastern patterns, he notes the absence in the

"martyred" youths of other Indo-European traditions,[25] are thus all the more striking, even considering the typically Indian handling of the events.

"Nonresurrection"

Several scholars have spoken of the "nonresurrection" of Baldr and the fact that the true lesson of his death is that, as Thokk says, Hel will "hold what she has." Edgar Polomé in particular has given an attractive reading of this episode. Arguing that Snorri merely guesses that Thokk is Loki and that she is actually Hel herself, he says: "Her very words give us a better idea of the real meaning of the Baldr myth: through his death, Baldr has entered the land of no return. There is no question of resurrection. The core of the theme of Hermodr's descent to Hel is accordingly the same as that of the Babylonian epic of Gilgamesh or the Greek myth of Orpheus: no one can escape death."[26] I cannot agree with Polomé's interpretation of Baldr's death,[27] as he ignores the question of Baldr's return, but I am interested in his idea that Baldr's disappearance holds a profound lesson about the finality of death. Both Baldr and Abhimanyu hold a close rapport with a plant of immortality: Baldr is slain by the mistletoe,

---

former of a death-lamentation scenario. On Indian *śāstric* injunctions against tears (with their polluting effects), especially those for the dead and those wept in death rites, see Johann Jakob Meyer, *Sexual Life in Ancient India* (New York: Dutton, 1930), pp. 420–22, n. 1.

[25] For example, Siyāvosh in the *Shāh-nāma*; see Davoud Monchi-Zadeh, *Ta'ziya: Das persische Passionspiel*, Skriften Utgivina av K. Humanistiska Vetenskapssfundet i Uppsala, 44, 4 (Stockholm: Almqvist & Wiksell, 1967), pp. 8–9; see also Dumézil's comparison of Baldr with Sosruko, the Nart hero of Caucasus legends (see n. 19): Sosruko is "slain" after a *jeu truqué* and must weep for himself every spring, wishing he could enjoy the earth again; and all the streams which run down from the mountain are in fact his tears. But he will not return (at least not in the present state of his legend). See "Balderiana minora," pt. 3, p. 72.

[26] Polomé, "Indo-European Component," pp. 73–74.

[27] *Ibid.*, pp. 73–78.

Abhimanyu is slain *like* the Soma. In each case their connections with the plants of immortality hold a lesson about death that can be read on either the human or the divine plane: both die prematurely, and both are the first to die of their illustrious company—that of the gods, or that of the gods in human form (see n. 18). Their deaths foreshadow doom and destruction.

But these are just the general lessons to be drawn from the two youthful deaths. Just as the Scandinavian tradition seems to have lent gravity to the scene by deepening it with Thokk's riddles on the themes of immortality, death, and non-resurrection, so the Indian tradition has paused to reflect on the very same matters. In a lengthy passage which the Critical Edition, on questionable grounds,[28] relegates to an appendix, Vyāsa makes one of his sudden appearances. Before Arjuna returns to camp to learn of Abhimanyu's death, Vyāsa seeks to console Yudhiṣṭhira. Once again the epic presents a significant juxtaposition of the main heroic narrative with traditional myths and legends. Here, basically two stories are involved. First, Vyāsa tells Yudhiṣṭhira about a king who, having lost his son, learned from the ṛṣi Nārada about the origin of death (Mṛtyu), the reluctant Dark Red Lady

[28] These stories appear in all but the Śāradā and Kaśmīrī manuscripts, which have conceivably rejected them on the same grounds as the CE editor, S. K. De: that they interrupt the flow of the narrative. I am also not convinced by V. S. Sukthankar's implication, "Epic Studies, VI, The Bhrgus and the Bharata: A Text-Historical Study," in P. A. Gode, ed., *V. S. Sukthankar Memorial Edition*, I: *Critical Studies in the Mahābhārata* (Bombay: Karnatak, 1944), 309–10, that because the brahmin Bhārgava Rāma is included among the sixteen kings in the *Droṇaparvan* but not in the *Śāntiparvan* version (which the CE retains at 12:29–31; 248–50), that the whole *Droṇaparvan* passage is a Bhārgava interpolation. There is no reason why the Mṛtyu story should be part of a Bhārgava insert; if the Bhārgava redactors have tampered with the text, it can only be on the matter of making Bhārgava Rāma the sixteenth "king." Moreover, there are details in the Suvarṇasthivin story that point to the *Droṇaparvan*'s as the more basic (or at least coherent) account: see the clumsy role given Indra in the *Śāntiparvan* (12:31,17), and the slaying of the boy by a *vajra*-turned-tiger rather than by robbers (31,27–34).

(*Droṇaparvan*, Appendix I, No. 8, lines 118–19) whose tears, shed at the thought of killing creatures, ultimately became their diseases at Brahmā's will (ll. 208–25). This feminine personification of Death, who appears where one might expect Yama, thus brings to mind Polomé's remarks about Thokk and Hel: in the Hindu account, even Death's tears cannot prevent death; in the Norse, "Thokk will weep dry tears for Baldr." This could point back to a common tradition, or it could be no more than a fantastic coincidence, each episode provoking similar meditations on weeping and death. If it is a coincidence, however, it is not the only one. The Indian meditation also takes up the theme of nonresurrection.

Vyāsa's second story concerns a king named Sṛñjaya who obtains a boon from the ṛṣis Parvata and Nārada and asks for a son of the following description: "Endowed with virtues [*guṇānvitam*], a possessor of *yaśas* and *kīrti* [fame and glory: two second-function virtues], of *tejas* ["spiritual majesty"], a tamer of foes whose urine, excrement, phlegm, and sweat shall all become gold" (ll. 305–7). There is good reason, as we shall see, to regard this story as a parable concerning a trifunctional endowment of virtues, with the third function filled by this Midaslike capacity to produce excessive and dangerous wealth (*dhanam*; l. 309). The boy is given the name Suvarṇasthivin, "Gold-Spitter," and soon his father has everything around him fashioned from gold. But one day the boy is abducted by greedy robbers who chop him up and, finding no gold, then hack each other to bits (ll. 315–26). When Sṛñjaya sees his son slain, his lament brings consolation from Nārada in the form of the longer of the two versions of the *Ṣoḍaśarājakīya*, "The Story of the Sixteen Kings" (ll. 327–872), biographical sketches of famous figures of legend. Each vignette yields the moral that grief is unsuitable for such a child when greater men by far have died. When Nārada has finished, he asks Sṛñjaya whether his grief is gone, and, when he learns that it has, he favors the king with the resurrection of his son: "I give you back your son, wantonly slain by robbers like an unconsecrated sacrificial animal [*paśumaprokṣitam*], raising him up from a noxious hell" (ll. 877–78). And the child appears. Now comes the Indian meditation on the matter at hand: why could this fantastic lad be resurrected while Abhimanyu cannot? Vyāsa shows that this has been the central question all along (functional traits numbered in parentheses):

> (2) Unpracticed at arms, timid, slain without having donned his armor, (1) not having sacrificed, and (3) childless, this one [Suvarṇasthivin] has thus returned to life. (2) Heroic, brave, and practiced at arms, having churned up foes by the thousands, Abhimanyu has gone to heaven, slain while facing into battle. Your son has gone to those imperishable regions that are obtained by (1) *brahmacarya*, wisdom, learning, and desirable sacrifices.... Therefore, not reaching out to possess anything [any new virtues], surely it is not possible to bring back the son of Arjuna, slain in battle and gone to heaven. [ll. 893–902]

Abhimanyu's place in heaven is thus, like Yayāti's and Duryodhana's,[29] secured by a full trifunctional complement of virtues. It can, of course, be no accident that all three are Lunar Dynasty kings. Moreover, this is the third time that we have noticed a trifunctional endowment in Abhimanyu.[30] In contrast, Suvarṇasthivin has fulfilled none of the virtues his father bargained for and can thus return to earth, resurrected. The explanation for the nonresurrection of Abhimanyu is thus typically Indian, although "early" in the sense that its concern for heaven (*svarga*) contradicts the law of karman. But one important, indeed prophetic matter stands out in Vyāsa's comparison of the two youths. Abhimanyu has clearly fulfilled himself in the second- and first-function virtues

[29] See above, Chapter 8, at n. 28 (Yayāti) and Chapter 11, especially at nn. 9–11 (Duryodhana).

[30] See above, citing 7:33,1–10 (beginning of chapter) and 7:55,20–23 (n. 23).

which are juxtaposed so neatly in the passage just cited. But a third-function quality, perhaps rare but clear,[31] stands out in its solitude: Suvarṇasthivin left the world unarmed, unfulfilled as a sacrificer, and childless; Abhimanyu left the world armed and fulfilled at sacrifices. What about the child?

The Matter of the Embryo: "Renaissance"

Baldr's reappearance as ruler of the renewed world is a miracle. And although the secret which Odinn murmurs in his ear before he is placed on the funeral pyre (*Vafthrudnismal*, stanzas 54–55) is a mystery, it seems to presage his rebirth in this "other world."[32] Only slightly less a mystery than the All-Father's words are the machinations of Krishna in reviving the stillborn child of Abhimanyu. The miracle is achieved by the Indian "All-God" by a method totally consonant with the prophetic hints of Kṛṣṇa Dvaipāyana. In the passage cited earlier, in which Subhadrā implores her brother to keep his word and revive the baby like the three worlds,[33] she prefaces her plea with a eulogy: "Surely, O Keśava, you have a soul of dharma [*dharmātmā*], are truthful [*satyavān*], and have true valor [*satyavikramaḥ*]. It behooves you to make this

[31] See Chapter 9, at n. 26, where Yudhiṣṭhira, after claiming responsibility for the deaths of Bhīṣma and Droṇa (first-function sins) and Karṇa (second-function), admits to the third-function sin of "lineage destruction" for causing the "youthful" Abhimanyu's death, a sin like that of "slaying an embryo" (12:27,3 and 19–20). As we saw in Chapter 8 the notion of continuity of the family (*kulam*) sometimes falls into place in lists of royal virtues as a virtue of the third function: see 8:5,27 (Yayāti) and 9:5,18 (Śalya); also a similar usage of the "virtue" *ārya* at 5:39,50; cf. also 1:103,11: Gāndhārī permitted to marry Dhṛtarāṣṭra because of his "lineage, fame, and conduct" (*kulaṃ khyātiṃ ca vṛttam*)—perhaps also trifunctional.

[32] See Dumézil, "Balderiana minora," pt. 1, p. 67, saying that Odinn's whispered words probably concern the impossibility of present efforts to bring him back and his eventual destiny as Odinn's own successor. See also Polomé, "Indo-European Component," p. 81, n. 72, citing pertinent bibliography: one must, however, appreciate the multivalence of this theme: "initiation" and eschatology are not mutually exclusive.

[33] See above, Chapter 12, above n. 41.

word conform to truth" (*tāṃ vācamṛtām*; 14:66,16). As we saw in Chapter 8, she thereby calls attention to a definite set of qualities: two from the first function (dharma, *satya*) and one from the second (*vikrama*); and it is this very set which Krishna puts into effect—by attesting to it three times in succession—when he chants the dead baby back to life. Here the passage, which appears in full in Chapter 8,[34] is condensed to the essentials:

18 I do not speak falsely, it shall be true . . .
19 I have never turned back in battle . . .

20 Dharma and brahmins are dear to me . . .
21 I have never brought about hostility with Vijaya [Arjuna] . . .

22 *Satya* and dharma are ever established in me . . .
23 Kaṃsa and Keśin were righteously slain by me . . . [14:68]

The cadence is heightened by the repetition in each *śloka* of one of the following phrases, or their equivalents: "accordingly, let this child live"; and "by that truth [*tena satyena*] may this child live." The latter, as we saw in Chapter 8, is an "act of truth" formula,[35] and I can now answer the question raised there. Though this formula concerns only Krishna's second-function traits directly (it is used only in *ślokas* 21 and 23), it activates an "act of truth" that concerns—as seemingly it must to alter a royal destiny[36]—virtues or achievements from each of the three functions. For this is the final effect of Krishna's words: "When these words were uttered by Vāsudeva, the child, O bull among men, softly, softly, O great king, quivered, now having sentience" (*śanaiḥ śanair-mahārāja praspandata sacetanaḥ*; 24).

[34] See above, Chapter 8, above n. 38.

[35] See above, Chapter 8, following n. 30, and nn. 16, 32–34 on W. Norman Brown's studies of the "act of truth."

[36] See not only above, n. 29 (Yayāti and Duryodhana), but now the "truth" or bargain of the ṛṣis Parvata and Nārada which makes it possible for Suvarṇasthivin to be resurrected.

Abhimanyu has thus entered heaven not only with his first- and second-function achievements, but, thanks to Krishna, with a child now living on earth. But can the miracle of the Indian "renaissance" be paired with the return of Baldr? Parikṣit is not, after all, Abhimanyu. Here, in my opinion, is where myth and epic diverge in easily intelligible patterns. Baldr is a god living and dying in the divine time of myth; the ideal which he personifies can thus move from the not-so-golden age of the past to the eschatological hope of the future. Abhimanyu dies and Parikṣit lives in the heroic time of dynastic legend: the ideal they personify is thus restricted to human time, to a single turning of the ages, here of the relatively recent (in Indian terms) past. But because of that event which closes the "heroic age," our age, the dismal Kali yuga, is still, thanks to Krishna, begun with a line of kings descended from Parikṣit—the so-called Lunar Dynasty—in which the ideal represented by Abhimanyu is still intact. As an embryo, Parikṣit "began to grow in the womb [of Uttarā] like the moon in the light half of the month" (*śuklapakṣe yathā śaśī*; 14:61,17). And: "Very handsome, he was unto all creatures like a second Soma; . . . Prosperous, truth-speaking, of firm fortitude [*śrīmansatyavāg-dṛḍhavikrama*[37]], . . . beloved of Govinda; . . . born in Uttarā's womb when the Kuru family was almost extinct [*parikṣīṇa*]; . . . [*Parikṣit*] was skilled in *rājadharma* and *artha*, a king endowed with every virtue" (*yuktaḥ sarvaguṇairnṛpaḥ*; 1:45,10–14). This is the "renaissance" of the Lunar Dynasty, the Soma Vaṃśa, from the last yuga into our present one.

Finally, the parallel between Baldr and Abhimanyu is more than a matter of two youths whose affiliation with plants of immortality holds a lesson about death, or even about death and rebirth. Surely it is the greatest tragedy that the youngest should die first. This youth represents a

[37] See above, Chapter 8, above n. 40, interpreted trifunctionally.

"thwarted ideal" in a most specific sense—an unused potential, a trifunctional potential placed on reserve in an eschatological hope for the return of *the completely endowed king*. In this respect, these unfulfilled youths are the male counterparts of the various virgins who, as Dumézil has so convincingly shown, service the king in numerous Indo-European traditions (myths, legends, rituals) by holding in reserve the essences of the three functions.[38] One indication of a common store of ideas is that a term which the *Mahābhārata* uses for its two virgin rescuers of royal lines—Mādhavī and Draupadī—finds a close analogue in a description of Abhimanyu. Whereas Mādhavī and Draupadī are each described as *sarvadharmopacayinī*, "a promptress of every virtue,"[39] Abhimanyu, as stated in Saṃjaya's eulogy of him at his death, has *guṇasamcayāḥ*, "assemblages" or "accumulations of virtues" which he shares with, or rather by which he surpasses, the trifunctionally described Arjuna, the Pāṇḍavas, and the omnivirtuous Krishna. Moreover, it is Krishna who makes the transfer of virtues possible. As I suggested in Chapter 8, Krishna, at one point, is Draupadī's Gālava: each of these two male figures can facilitate the transfer of a feminine personification of sovereignty and, in the process, of sovereignty's virtues.[40] This is also, in effect, true in the present episode. It is through Krishna that the miracle of the rebirth of the Kuru line, with "all the virtues" intact, takes place. Indeed, the text seems to build a symbolic identity between Krishna and Abhimanyu that makes Krishna's intermediary role, as "reactivator" of the virtues, intelligible. As we have seen, Krishna and Abhimanyu have identical eyes (see n. 10) and identical virtues (7:32,2 and 8; see also 1:213,70); and Abhimanyu's last weapon, with which he goes down fighting, is a *cakra*. The significance of Krishna's constant solicitations

[38] *ME*, II, 362–74.
[39] See above, Chapter 8, at n. 52.
[40] See *ibid.*

of his cherished nephew during the latter's birth, marriage, and training in weapons becomes clear.[41]

These completely endowed youths, Abhimanyu and Baldr, thus act as repositories of royal virtues which, through the agency of Krishna in one case and of Odinn in the other, are carried into a future age. Here, however, there is a disjunction: the hope for their returns hinges on different "unfulfilled" virtues. In the Norse myths we are carried into the future by a first-function virtue, Baldr's unrealized judgments, while in India this is achieved by a third-function virtue, a child to continue the lineage. Presumably it is more—although this is fundamental—than just a case of theology (or myth) on the one hand and epic (with mortal heroes) on the other. In Scandinavia, as Dumézil has pointed out, the ideal of an empowered judge, righteous and impartial, is a theme that runs through several myths and symbols;[42] and in India, especially in the India of the *Mahābhārata*, what theme could be more far-reaching than the duty to have a son?

[41] See above, Chapter 4 (beginning) and Chapter 5 (beginning).

[42] Dumézil, *Dieux des Germains*, pp. 67–76.

CHAPTER 14

Conclusions

If doubts have been aired about some of Dumézil's comparisons of Norse mythology and the *Mahābhārata*, and if more reliable connections have been observed between the epic's crisis and the ideology of the Brāhmaṇas, the Norse myth of the Ragnarök has still proved a suggestive counterpart to a central *Mahābhārata* sequence. Beneath the modeling of the *Sauptikaparvan* on the Brāhmaṇic sacrifice lies that of the death and rebirth of the Soma Vaṃśa's ideal ruler on the Soma sacrifice. And beneath or beyond both of these, the full structure of an Indo-European eschatological myth emerges, once again involving a *jeu truqué*, a great battle, and a renaissance. Accordingly, one can still quote Dumézil about the possibility of such a myth: "That this conception appears neither in the *Ṛg Veda* nor in all that depends directly upon it does not prove that it did not exist. The thought of the Vedic singers is concentrated on the present, on the regular attendance of the gods, for which the exploits of the mythic past serve as the guarantees: the horizons of the future did not interest them."[1] Moreover, Dumézil's more recent work changes the picture on the roles of Krishna and Śiva in such a myth. His study of the *Mahābhārata*'s Śiśupāla legend throws light on an archaic, perhaps para-Vedic, opposition of complementarity between Viṣṇu and Rudra.[2] He thus no longer

[1] Dumézil, *ME*, I, 221.

[2] See above, Chapter 4, n. 2; from the parallel roles of Viṣṇu-Krishna and Thor, Śiva and Odinn, Dumézil coins the terms "*dieux clairs*" for the former pair, "*dieux sombres*" for the latter. However, three affinities occur

seems so ready to reduce Viṣṇu and Śiva's double epic appearances—which we have noticed on a number of occasions[3]—to recent adaptations.

These reflections, by way of conclusion, lead to a point concerning Indian theology—the age of this relationship between Viṣṇu and Rudra is uncertain,[4] but it is most likely at least Brāhmaṇic.[5] Thus interpretations which introduce the notion of sectarianism into the early relations between these gods are inadequate. It is probably erroneous to think of the Dakṣayajña as a sectarian myth,[6] or even (in a historical sense) as a myth that "represents [Śiva's] assimilation into the orthodox pantheon."[7] Likewise, one must discard the traditional view of the *Mahābhārata* as a Vaiṣṇavite or Krishnaite sectarian poem with Śaivite sectarian interpolations. To be sure, interpolations abound, some of them sectarian, but the prevailing mood of the epic has nothing to do with sects.[8] The *Mahābhārata* is a poem where "all the gods" are active

---

between Krishna and Odinn, all involving great battles: see Chapters 5 and 12. One wonders whether, through these comparisons with Krishna, we have begun to integrate disparate elements in the mythology of Odinn.

[3] See above, Chapters 3, 4, 7 (following n. 53), and 12.

[4] See Gonda, *Viṣṇuism and Śivaism*, p. 87: though the two gods "maintained no direct relationship with each other" in the *Veda*, he points to two *ṚV* verses (7,40,5 and 4,3,7) which may, depending on uncertain readings, point to some relation and even opposition. See Karl Friedrich Geldner, trans., *Der Rig-Veda*, Harvard Oriental Series, vols. XXXIII-XXXV (3 vols.; Cambridge: Harvard University Press, 1951), I, 420, speaking, in his note to 4,3,7, of "the opposition between Viṣṇu and Rudra as the procreator (Erzeuger) and the destroyer" (my translation), the former apparently connected with Pūṣan and the seed (*rétas*), the latter with Agni and a firm missile weapon.

[5] See above, Chapter 12, item 14.

[6] Bhattacharji, *Indian Theogony*, p. 124.

[7] O'Flaherty, "Origin of Heresy," p. 322.

[8] See EMH, 2, p. 28, n. 1: "One hesitates to speak of sectarian purāṇas. The tendency is only too strong to think of Śiva and Viṣṇu as being mutually exclusive, something which is not even true in the interior of the sects" (my translation).

in human form, with Viṣṇu—incarnate in Krishna—at their head, or at their "center," while Śiva remains typically remote until the moment when he must, after all, get his share and do his work. The relationship between Viṣṇu and Śiva is thus situated within, or "above," the structure(s) of polytheism.[9] Moreover, their relations to the polytheistic gods are central in the epic crisis, just as they are in the Dakṣayajña myth. In one case, Krishna presides over the "sacrifice of battle," then absents himself for Aśvatthāman. In the other, Viṣṇu "is the sacrifice," yet he is never there when Śiva gets his remainder share. No doubt many formulas could express the multivalent polarity of the two gods,[10] but the lesson here seems well expressed by the opposition: "Pervader" (Viṣṇu—*viś*-?) and "Outsider" (Rudra—*rudis*, Latin, "rough, raw, rude, unwrought, uncultivated").[11] Whatever one may think of these far-flung etymologies, they refer to an intriguing paradox: what possible relation, what underlying unity, can exist between the Outsider and the Pervader?

As to the matter of Indian polytheism, the epic must be appreciated in its correlation with a whole mythology, a mythology, moreover, with an Indo-European past. Yet there is a point where I would disagree with Dumézil over the nature of the relation between myth and epic in the *Mahābhārata*. First, with regard to the question of individual transpositions, Dumézil speaks of a "veritable pantheon" which has been transposed into "human personages by an operation as meticulous as it was ingenious."[12] These transpositions

[9] See Dumézil's remarks, *ME*, II, 107–8 (cf. p. 82), on the relations of the two gods to the three functions: Viṣṇu overflowing them (as from within?), Rudra avoiding them (as from without?).

[10] See Gonda, *Viṣṇuism and Śivaism*, pp. 102–4.

[11] Dumézil, *ME*, II, 86; also discussed in *idem.*, *Archaic Roman Religion*, p. 418, n. 21.

[12] Dumézil, *ME*, I, 21 (my translation).

attest to "an 'author's' will,"[13] and the poets themselves emerge as "erudite, skillful, loyal to a design,"[14] perhaps an academy of priests or several generations of a single school who would have composed the work "before writing, at the time of the four Vedas and of the fifth."[15] All this makes it possible for Dumézil to speak of the heroes as inflexible "copies" of their mythical prototypes.[16] To me, this seems too mechanical and too short-term a process. It says nothing about certain "difficult" transpositions in which the heroes' and heroines' characters and actions differ markedly from what one knows of their mythic counterparts, and it does not account for actions and themes that lack mythic prototypes.

Second, as we saw in Chapter 12, Dumézil regards certain basic moments in the unfolding of the epic crisis as transpositions of an ancient Indo-European eschatological myth, presumably still known at the time of the poem's composition. Thus the epic story, in these essential features, is a "myth learnedly humanized if not historicized."[17] However, in favorably discussing Wikander's treatment of the battles of Brávellir and Kurukṣetra, Dumézil is forced to make an unconvincing distinction. It is not necessary, he says, to interpret the Battle of Brávellir, "like the *Mahābhārata*," by a historicized eschatological myth; for whereas the crisis in the *Mahābhārata* bears a striking resemblance to that in the myth of the Ragnarök, the Battle of Brávellir—particularly in the role of Odinn—does not.[18] Thus, despite the affinities (which Dumézil recognizes) between the *Mahābhārata* and the Battle

[13] Dumézil, *Du mythe au roman: La Saga de Hadingus* (Paris: Presses Universitaires de France, 1970), p. 8 (my translation).

[14] Dumézil, *ME*, I, 21 (my translation).

[15] *La Saga de Hadingus*, p. 8 (my translation).

[16] *ME*, I, 633; see above, Chapter 1, above n. 36.

[17] *ME*, I, 21.

[18] See above, Chapter 12, n. 2.

of Brávellir, affinities which concern *epic material*, he sees the most basic features of the Indian epic story in terms of *transpositions from myth*.

The question thus is: can one speak of the basic outline of the *Mahābhārata* as presenting a distinct epic crisis? Or must one explain the crisis solely in terms of some prior myth? In my view, the evidence presented by Wikander and others[19] is strong enough to suggest that the Indo-Europeans knew a story, in certain basic details like the *Mahābhārata*, about a dynastic struggle which brought to an end their "heroic age." This story itself would seem to have told of an epic crisis of what could justly be called "eschatological proportions": a break in the continuity of the dynastic line, an end to the "age of heroes," a rupture or transition marked by the "moral and physical monstrosities" of the heroes. Should this be so, it would hardly be surprising were some connections to have been perceived, some correlations to have been made, between the crises of the two orders: an epic crisis concerning the end of the heroic age and a mythic crisis concerning the end of the world.

This process of correlating epic with myth would most likely have gone on for a long time, in some cases involving rearrangements of the epic story by the introduction of mythic themes in a "humanized" form. Thus one can certainly speak of transpositions, including eschatological ones. But transposition cannot be regarded as the only key to the "mythic exegesis."[20] More fundamental is what I call a method of correlation or correspondence.

If the main skeleton of the *Mahābhārata* story is old, and if, as Dumézil and others like Biardeau have shown, ancient as well as comparatively recent mythical material is reflected in

[19] I hope to take up this problem in another work; for other scholars, see above, Chapter 1, nn. 86–88.

[20] *ME*, I, 21.

it,[21] can one imagine Indian poets of one period—even assuming it could have all been known at one time—transposing *all* of this mythical material, from vastly remote periods, into one "humanized" or "historicized" form? The "meticulous operation" of the exacting epic bards, carefully transposing all of this at once, is unrealistic. Rather, a long process seems likely in which an epic story of ancient contours, probably at no point completely free of mythic elements, was continually compared and integrated with mythic themes—in fact, with myths and structures of different periods. The process would have to have been conservative to explain certain long-standing para-Vedic, Indo-Iranian, and even Indo-European myths whose influences, as Dumézil has demonstrated, show through. But the way in which they took their footing in the *Mahābhārata* would seem to have been not so much through a process of "transposition" as through a process of correlation between two levels of continually changing and growing tradition: myth and epic. The epic poets would thus emerge not so much as programmers, transposing one set of information into another form,[22] but as ṛṣis, in this case the ṛṣis of the "Fifth Veda" whose "school" is covered by the name of the elusive but ever-available ṛṣi Vyāsa. By calling attention to this term for visionaries and poets, I refer in particular to the ṛṣis' faculty of "seeing connections," "equivalences," "homologies," and "correspondences" discussed by Jan Gonda.[23] This faculty of "seeing connections" would have involved the epic poets not only with correlations between myth and epic,

[21] This process has not stopped. In South India, for instance, Śākta mythology has been transposed onto Draupadī.

[22] Taking Dumézil's view to its conclusion, the form of a story fully "transposed" from a prior level of meaning would be allegory, not epic. Although it is popular in India to view it as such (for instance, Sukthankar, *Mahābhārata*, p. 102), I do not see the *epic* as an allegory.

[23] Gonda, *The Vision of the Vedic Poets* (The Hague: Mouton, 1963), especially his definition of the Vedic term *dhīḥ*, pp. 68–69; see also Louis Renou, *Religions of Ancient India* (New York: Schocken, 1968), p. 18.

but also between epic and ritual—especially that of the Brāhmaṇic sacrifice. Thus the "mythic exegesis" must coexist with a "ritual exegesis." Moreover, if this was the procedure and orientation of the poets, it helps to explain why they have told certain myths at key points in the epic narrative. In some cases, they seem to have perceived correlations between myths and adjacent portions of the epic plot, correspondences which were meant to deepen one's awareness of the meanings on both the mythic and the epic planes, and ultimately, perhaps, to afford a glimpse of broader unities.

APPENDIX I

Genealogical Table

Lunar Dynasty

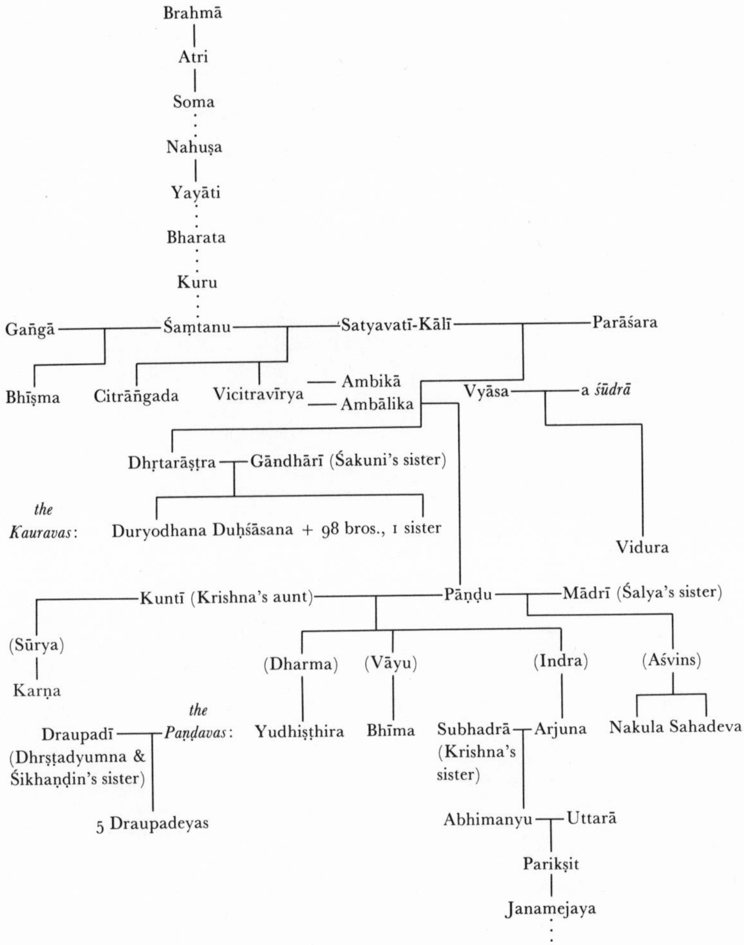

Brahmā
Atri
Soma
Nahuṣa
Yayāti
Bharata
Kuru
Gaṅgā
Śaṃtanu
Satyavatī-Kālī
Parāśara
Bhīṣma
Citrāṅgada
Vicitravīrya
Ambikā
Ambālika
Vyāsa
a *śūdrā*
Dhṛtarāṣṭra
Gāndhārī (Śakuni's sister)
the Kauravas:
Duryodhana Duḥśāsana + 98 bros., 1 sister
Vidura
Kuntī (Krishna's aunt)
Pāṇḍu
Mādrī (Śalya's sister)
(Sūrya)
Karṇa
(Dharma)
(Vāyu)
(Indra)
(Aśvins)
Draupadī
(Dhṛṣṭadyumna & Śikhaṇḍin's sister)
the Paṇḍavas:
Yudhiṣṭhira
Bhīma
Subhadrā (Krishna's sister)
Arjuna
Nakula Sahadeva
5 Draupadeyas
Abhimanyu
Uttarā
Parikṣit
Janamejaya

Index